W9-CTY-851

Rav SHLOMO ROTENBERG

AM OLAM

AM OLAM

The History
of the Eternal Nation

by Rav SHLOMO ROTENBERG

VOLUME ONE

Published by Keren Eliezer
Brooklyn, N.Y.

לעילוי נשמת

בננו האהוב והנחמד

אליעזר נ"ע

שהלך לעולמו בימי עלומיו

ד' אלול תשי"ד

Published and Copyrighted © 1988
by Rabbi Shlomo Rotenberg & Keren Eliezer
221 Rutledge Street
Brooklyn, N.Y.

Second Printing 1989–5749

ISBN 087306-483-6

Distributed by
Feldheim Publishers Ltd.
P.O.B. 6525, Jerusalem, Israel

Philipp Feldheim Inc.
200 Airport Executive Park
Spring Valley, N.Y. 10977

Printed in Israel 1988–5748
by Zur-Ot Press, Jerusalem

This first edition of *Am Olam*
has been sponsored in gratitude by
Mr. & Mrs. DAVID TANNEN שיחיו
London, England
in loving memory of
his parents
MORDECHAI ZEV & SOPHIE TANNENBAUM ז״ל
and her mother
Mrs. SARAH LANDAU ז״ל

לעילוי נשמות
אביו
ר׳ מרדכי זאב בן ר׳ עזריאל יצחק טננבוים ז״ל
שנפטר לעולמו י״ז אדר תש״ם

ואמו
מרת סלאווה ע״ה
בת ר׳ דוד הכהן ז״ל
שנפטרה לעולמה י״ב אלול תשמ״ח

ולעילוי נשמת אמה
מרת שרה לנדאו ע״ה
בת ר׳ אליעזר ז״ל
שנפטרה לעולמה ז׳ אדר תשמ״ו

ת.נ.צ.ב.ה.

CONTENTS

PART FOUR / THE KINGDOM OF MEDIA

RABBI MOSES FEINSTEIN
455 F. D. R. DRIVE
New York 2, N. Y.
—
ORegon 7-1222

משה פיינשטיין
ר"ם תפארת ירושלים
בנוא יארק

בע"ה

הנה ידידי הרה"ג הנכבד מוה"ר שלמה רוטענבערג שליט"א נתן לבו לעשות
ספר דברי הימים ספור הדורות ע"פ דברי חז"ל, באשר שראה בעוה"ר שאנשים האחרונים עוסקים
בעניינים אלו כמעט רק מני הנכרים, וכל ספרי ההיסטוריא כמעט לא נקיים משום מינות אף
אלו שנתחברו משומרי תורה משום שלא עיינו היטב בדברי חז"ל אשר עניינים אלו מפוזרים
וצריך לחפש אחריהם ומשום זה נתחברו כמה ספרים שאין נכונים שהם נגד הקבלה ודברי
חז"ל, לכן לתקן פרצה זו חבר ספר זה אשר הוא כולו ע"פ דברי חז"ל וספרים הקדושים
אחרי עיונו בעמקות שמלאו דברי חז"ל וכמה שמביא מספרים הקדושים ועוד ציין המראה
מקומות לכל דבר דבר הוא נאמן. ועוד בכל מקום כתב דברי מוסר ויראת ה' כדי
שילמדו מה עלינו לעשות ואיך להתנהג, ורואה אני שהוא תקון גדול ויישר כחו להללו
ויתברך לראות ספרו מאושר בגדול המוסף ועל זה באתי עה"ח בז' מרחשון תשכ"ג
נאום משה פיינשטיין

בע"ה

FOREWORD

SINCE the original Hebrew publication of *Toldos Am Olam* approximately twenty years ago, there has been a continual clamor for a translation.

This volume, the first of the series rendered into English, is in response to that demand. The unique character and style of the original, however, made this translation an extremely exacting and time-consuming exercise; and to preserve that very character and style, we often gave preference to exactness and substance over some of the finer points demanded by the English language.

During the past century, Jewish history, more than any other subject, has been misrepresented and falsified, sometimes intentionally and wantonly and sometimes because of sheer ignorance of the subject matter. R' Yitzchak Eizik Halevy ztl., in his monumental history-series "Doros Harishonim" was the first to thoroughly expose their willful falsification of Jewish history. The Gedolei Yisrael, particularly Reb Chaim Ozer Grodzinsky, ztl., of Vilna, pre-war leader of World-Jewry, called upon us to resist the falsification of history, "for it caused many to fall along the wayside." *Toldos Am Olam,* therefore, filled a crying need. It counters the efforts of assimilationists and "Reformers," those self-proclaimed "Jewish historians" who revised and rewrote Jewish history according to their own "non-traditional" concepts. For lack of an authentic History as counter-balance, their books were accepted at face value and eventually caused an unprecedented loss of Emunas Chachamim, the drift toward modern Haskala, and finally a desertion en-masse from traditional Yiddishkeit.

The task of providing an authentic and detailed Jewish history was overwhelming. Contrary to the popular trend of presenting a 'viewpoint' or 'interpretation,' *Toldos Am Olam* presents *the facts* of our real history. Being a teaching of the Past, there is plainly no place in our

10

history for retroactive "change" or "innovation." It is simply a matter of presenting the facts and events of our world-embracing past AS WAS.

Our facts, therefore, are based exclusively on the authentic Sefarim of the Chachamim. A circumstantial presentation of our illustrious past furthermore demanded a tedious, nearly endless search for bits of historical facts and detail casually recorded in Shas, Midrash, Tossefta, Rishonim, Acharonim etc., etc. Substantiated by these authentic sources (quoted on every page), the resulting series of *Toldos Am Olam* provides an inspiring, lively and moving full History. — As if indeed the withered bones of our past suddenly put on sinews, flesh and skin, and, with a Heavenly spirit, came back to life before our very eyes.

By removing the language barrier, this first volume of a *Torah-view* Jewish History is now made available to the masses of English speaking Jewry (and will hopefully cause many to eventually turn to the undiluted warmth and richness of the original Hebrew volumes of Toldos Am Olam).

All thanks and gratefulness, therefore, are due primarily to the translator who by pure zeal and dedication labored for endless days and nights on the seemingly impossible task of this translation; avoiding the painful choice of an "adaptation," and producing a readable truthful translation.

Special appreciation and thanks are further extended to Sheindel Weinbach, Esther Van Handl and Chava Roth for their insight in style and general editorial comments, and to Faygie Bienenfeld for giving of her artistic skills in designing the appropriate jacket for this volume.

Special appreciation is extended to our son R' Chaim Dovid for his pertinent comments, advice and unfaltering dedication in carrying the load and responsibility for the printing of this Sefer; and to all our children for bearing with us and for their helpful advice, criticism, encouragement and assistance; to the printer who gave much of his skill to this venture; very special thanks to Mr. Leonard A. Kestenbaum for his understanding and gracious financial support; to Avrohom Chaim Nussbaum for contributing in memory of his grandparents Z.L. to whom the author was especially close; to Boruch Greisman; to Yossi

11

Shapiro; and to other friends for lending a helping hand. And finally, very special gratefulness to our dear cousins Mr. and Mrs. David Tannen who sponsored this publication.

May they all be blessed and rightly rewarded for their contribution in helping to make our people aware of their eternal historical heritage.

Elul 5748   S. R.

INTRODUCTION

KNOWLEDGE of the events of "the days of the world" ("Yemos Olam") undoubtedly is of crucial importance. Were the study of Jewish History motivated by nostalgia only (or by an instinctive curiosity that stirs the heart into searching and delving into all that happened since the beginning of time) we would stand reprimanded by the Chachamim's long-standing attestation (Yoma 5b): "Whatever was, was." What does it all matter to us? — Bnei Yisrael however, were *commanded* to engage in the study of the events "of the days of the world." The Torah itself teaches us to do so.

At the very last — on the very day of his death — Moshe, "Father of the Prophets," conveyed to Bnei Yisrael the heartbreaking prophecy: "For I know that after my death you will become corrupt, and you will stray from the way that I commanded you; and calamity will strike you at the End of Days for the evil you do in Hashem's eyes, provoking His anger through the deeds of your hands" (Devarim 31:29). Hence Moshe once more admonished each and every one, trying to prevent them from straying from the Way of Life. And *then* he spoke these historical words: "Remember the days of the world, understand the years of generation upon generation!" (ibid 32:7) — For this remembrance will stand you by, so that you will not stray from the right path.

However, Moshe was concerned not only with knowledge and remembrance, but rather with *understanding* History. Understanding, of course, presumes also remembrance of all that happened ever since Hashem created earth and heaven. Hence, "*Remember* the days of the world." and "*understand* the years of each generation!", are in fact two that are truly one.

* *

Why, however, should History in particular be the remedy destined to prevent our nation's going astray? — There are many aspects to it.

In contrast to the Past, the Present, by itself, invites error. Hence, Moshe Rabbeinu warned us (Sefer Devarim 4:25): "When you bear children and grandchildren, and *you will become stale* in the Land, you will do evil and make idols and images of all, and you will do the evil in the eyes of Hashem, your God, to provoke His anger." But when will all this evil happen? Only *after* "you will become stale in the Land." Indeed at the time of Yetziyas Mitzrayim and afterwards, as they were poised at Har Sinai to become the *"Am Segula"* ("a treasured nation"), "a Kingdom of Kohanim and a Holy Nation," there was not the slightest doubt about the unique historical identity of the Jewish nation. All through these 40 years in the Midbar, having journeyed and encamped by Hashem's Command — led by the Heavenly Cloud and the Pillar of Fire — and afterwards, upon entering the Chosen Land, our unique national Torah-identity was as clear as on the very day we received it at Sinai.

With time however, forgetfulness entered the heart; the "chance to err" increased steadily. After centuries of having been settled and living "in our Land," things became stale. There were those who got up and proclaimed: "The House of Yisrael is like all the nations, like all the families of the earth!" And by confusing our unique historical identity with that of the other nations in *their* lands, they fast moved away from the path Hashem had commanded them.

The remembrance of "Yemos Olam" might have prevented this. For it is specifically in the *Past* and the days of yore that the true national character and identity of our People stands out so clearly — to prove that indeed, "who is like Your People, Yisrael, a unique nation on earth."

For as soon as Yisrael looks back at "the rock" whence it "was hewn" — and at the pit from which it was "dug out," retracing the unique supernatural march of our people (ever since Avraham Avinu and Sara our Mother, throughout all these centuries of world-shaking miracles performed before our ancestors' very eyes), then by itself, all hearts and lips *must* testify to what the Torah stated (Devarim 4:32–

34) concerning both, Yisrael, His "Chosen People," and the great miracles Hashem has performed for us: that indeed there is none like us, the one and unique nation on earth!

For indeed, "Ask, I beg you, about the earlier days which were before you since the very day when Hashem created man upon the earth; (ask) from one end of the sky to the other end of the sky: Has there ever been such a great thing or has anything like it ever been heard of? Did ever a nation hear the Voice of Hashem speaking from the midst of the fire, as you did — and live? Or has ever a deity tried to take itself a nation from the midst of another nation, by trials, by signs and wonders; by war and a mighty hand; by an outstretched arm and frightening feats as did Hashem, your God, for you in Mitzrayim, before your very eyes?" — If so, how can Yisrael ever deceive and falsify itself to pretend: "Why, the House of Yisrael is just like all the nations?"

*　*

Moreover, precisely through the remembrance of "Yemos Olam" with their constant march of mighty feats and Divine Providence, man learns to know his Creator. For this very History whose shocks and crises are like a raging sea, whose mass of happenings and upheavals emerge — as if out of "the blood, the fire and pillars of smoke," this march of History is but one long chain whose links match and fit one into the other, leading towards the one and ultimate destiny: *the Historical Plan* from Creation until "the End of Days."

Not so the nations of the earth. Each of them, theirs is a *national* History only, starting somewhere as if in the middle of a chapter — from the time they actually became a nation or somewhat before that. Only Jewish "*national* History" is at once *World*-History, starting from the very "In the Beginning God created."

Because the events of the "Yemos *Olam*" are simultaneously the events of the "Days of *our People*." They all are wrought by the One leading Hand: a World-History laid out by the King, Creator, — the Supreme Guidance.

*　*

For "to do good to His creatures" Hashem created all; like Adam who was placed in the Garden of Eden. But he sinned, and did not live up to Hashem's Command. Hence he was driven out, failing even to dwell overnight in all that splendor. Henceforth, Man walked his path on earth with the sweat of his brow, seeking restoration from the Cheyt Hakadmon (the First Sin). However, the further generations steadily increased Hashem's anger. Out of the bounty which He bestowed upon them, all flesh further perverted its ways on earth, so that Hashem eventually obliterated them from the surface of the earth. From No'ach's descendants the first king on earth then appeared, inciting the creatures to revolt against their Creator — "to make a name" for themselves. Until Hashem eventually scattered them over the surface of the whole earth.

Like the rays from the East Avram the Ivri appeared. Unlike the others, he acknowledged the Master of the Universe. Undauntedly he, all alone, stood on one side confronting the whole world on the other side, becoming the first man on earth to call his Creator "Master" and to serve Him completely with soul and body. Starting to spread Hashem's Name in the world, after "2000 Years of Darkness," Avraham initiated "The 2000 Years of Light."

From all mankind, only his descendants, Yisrael, then became "the Holy Nation" that accepted Hashem's yoke of His Torah which Moshe had brought down from Heaven. That is why the historical world-march from Breishis towards Acharis HaYamim reveals itself only through Bnei Yisrael, "the dwelling-place of God's Glory." So that through them and their light *all the nations* ultimately will stream back to Hashem Be'Acharis HaYamim, proclaiming: "Let us go up to the Mountain of Hashem, to the House of the God of Yaakov; that He may teach us His ways; that we may walk in His paths!"

*   *

For like the heart in the body, so is Yisrael among the mighty nations. This one lone sheep upon which all the hatred of the whole world was poured out throughout all generations and in all the countries; this tiny nation, persecuted, burned and slaughtered, while all through-

16

out, her persecutors triumphantly rejoiced, shouting: "We have swallowed them!" — somehow these Bnei Yisrael killed the ones who killed them, swallowed those who swallowed them, destroyed those empires that destroyed them. From their very midst sprang all the spiritual greatness of the Kohanim, Prophets and Sages, from whom all the world together inherited whatever noble and good they somehow acquired.

Today, as always, the scheming and plotting of the nations is still aimed against Bnei Yisrael "the smallest of the nations." Yet, the existence of these very nations — with their respective lands and borders — is still being decreed and set up only "in reference to the numbers of the Bnei Yisrael" (Devarim 32:8); the Am Olam, *for whom the world was created.*

They, their kings and ministers may not see it that way, and in their hearts they do not think it to be so. — Yet they all are but like pieces on the majestic chess-board of History. Their king really is no king, their queen is no queen, and their knights are not knights. There is but a Divine Hand which moves the pieces to their required positions. — For they and their hearts are but in *His* Hand, — to be led to victory or defeat.

Not only kings and ministers, but all the millennia, and all that has occurred in "the years of generation upon generation" — whether individually or on a national and international scale — *it all leads ultimately to the Acharis HaYamim of world-purpose and destination.* Even the deeds of the wicked who destroy the world, and all the people's evil and sins committed through "freedom of choice" — *through all these* does the Will of Hashem eventually come to pass, *notwithstanding their evil intentions.* — The story of Yosef and his brothers is a classical example to that effect.

Indeed, innocent when sold and free of guilt, he was thrown into prison. Whatever was done to him apparently was only sin and injustice. But Yosef lived with his Emunah, and did not question the Ways of Hashem. — Until eventually (in the most wondrous of ways) all the world came to realize that from all these offenses together, *only the* Will of Hashem prevailed. So far, that Yosef endeavored to

17

speak to his brothers, saying: "And now be not grieved, and let it not anger you that you sold me hither, for *Hashem* sent me before you to sustain life." (Bereishis 45:5). Even though you exerted free will and choice, yet, "*it was not you who sent me here, but Hashem*" (Passuk 8). And as for your bad intentions, "you intended evil against me," but these very evil intentions "Hashem contrived for the good, to bring it to pass as of this day, to sustain life to a great many people" (ibid 45:7). — As if indeed willful evil turned into merit! . . .

However, until the moment when he stated to them (ibid 45:4): "I am Yosef, your brother, whom you sold to Mitzrayim," this whole event was like a strange closed book; indeed as if there was neither Judge nor Justice in this world.

Or, had the brothers come at the outset to seek a ruling on the permissibility to sell Yosef so that Yaakov would eventually descend to Mitzrayim etc., surely they would have been admonished with reference to the Law of the Torah concerning "the one who steals a person and sells him," — even though "Hashem meant it for the good." — For the human judge must consider only that which is before his human eyes (Sanhedrin 6b), . . .while Heaven may do whatever it wishes in whatever way it wishes.

*   *

"For My thoughts are not your thoughts, neither are My ways your ways." (Yeshaya 55:18). Hence all that goes forth and happens "shall not go void, but it will accomplish that which I please." (ibid 11).

The very deed a person does by "Free Choice" guided by his own personal intentions, while someone else does a similar deed with completely different intentions, yet out of all this Hashem's Will is eventually carried out.

Like Yosef, whom his father sent to Shechem to see whether there was peace with his brothers (Bereishis 37:14); yet each had completely different intentions. — Yaakov acted out of concern for the well-being of his sons who were in Shechem — the place destined for visitations; the brothers had gone there to tend the sheep of their father, etc.; Yosef went, out of respect for his father; — whereas Hakadosh Baruch

Hu was implementing "the profound counsel emanating from this Tzaddik (Avraham) who lies buried in Chevron" (Midrash Rabba).

In a similar vein the Chachamim interpret the event of Yehuda and Tammar (Bereishis Rabba 85b)): "For I know the thoughts" (Yirmiyahu 29:11). — The Tribes (Yaakov's sons) were engaged in the selling of Yosef; Yosef (being sold) was busy with his sackcloth and fasting; Yaakov and Reuven were busy with sackcloth and fasting; Yehuda was engaged in taking himself a wife. — And *Hakadosh Baruch Hu was busy creating "the Light of Mashiach."* (From Peretz, the son of Yehuda and Tammar.) — For He knows the thoughts of them all, and out of these and through all of these Hashem executes His Heavenly thoughts and ways.

*   *

As complicated as it may be for human comprehension, the paths of *Hashgacha Pratis* (Individual Providence) and *Hashgacha Klallis* (Collective Providence) furthermore completely go hand in hand, Hence, from all acts, motivated by *individual* Freedom of Choice and personal intentions, only that which Hashem intends will ultimately come through in the course of world-history. Furthermore, "He, the Rock, His work is perfect, for all His Ways are justice." Notwithstanding "Freedom of Choice," He does not bring even upon the indirectly affected ones more than what they deserve. For "He is a trustworthy God, and no injustice (is caused even *indirectly*); Just and Right is He." (Devarim 32:4).

Like the brothers who by their own free will *slaughtered* a kid-goat and dipped the shirt in its blood" (Bereishis 37:30), *because* Yosef deserved the punishment for having accused them of eating parts of a living animal. Similarly, he was sold as a slave, for having suspected them of shaming the sons of Bilha and Zilpa by calling them slaves etc. — For despite each one's individual Freedom of Choice, only Hashem's Will and intentions prevailed.

Not only the acts of the individual, but of nations as well, depend on the Judgment of the "King of the nations" (Yirmiya 10:7). In their domain too, there is a Judge and Judgment! "For I, Hashem, am in the midst of the land," (Shemos 8:18) — not only in Heaven! The rise and fall of nations and kingdoms depend on "the Judge of all the world;" decreed, by imposing on them, in the course of the generations, *reward and punishment*. Like the three generations of kingship which Nevuchadnezar *merited* for having run three steps for the honor of Hashem; or kingship that was eventually snatched away from a nation *when its Measure became full*, for having tortured Yisrael, the Holy People, ever more and more. — "For I, Hashem, raged only a little, but they assisted by increasing the affliction." (Zecharya 1:15).

However, while it happened, Heavenly Intent was altogether hidden from them. No one can grasp the doings of Hashem and His intentions. Even Yaakov, "the perfect one," uttered a vain expression (Bereishis 33:6) when he said to his sons: "Why did you bring harm unto me," as if all that had happened was indeed for the bad. In his mourning, he furthermore complained, saying: "My way is hidden from Hashem, etc." (Bereishis Rabba 91). — For *only in the ultimate end* will man merit to grasp and understand the march and events of all History.

Like the story of the aged R' Akiva (Berachos 60b) whom the townspeople turned away, forcing him to lodge in the field overnight. Came a wind and blew out the candle (Bad indeed); came a wild cat and ate up the rooster. Came a lion and devoured his donkey. (All of it really bad). Said R' Akiva: "Whatever Hashem does, is for the good," even though outwardly everything seemed really bad. Only in the morning, after the robbers had captured the people and set the town on fire, was R' Akiva finally able to say: Did I not say that whatever the Blessed One does, is for the good? (For had the candle burned, the donkey brayed, or the rooster cried, the robbers would surely have noticed him and taken him captive too.) — And, likewise, everything has its Tomorrow (when one will at last understand). There is a tomorrow that comes the very next day, and there is a morrow that comes only after a long time! ...

So that from all that happened in the "Yemos Olam" of the Past, *man should learn to live with his Emunah also in the Present*. (Like Yosef Hatzaddik who did not lose faith or rebel against his Creator when everything that happened to him appeared as plain injustice, sin and transgression. And like R' Akiva who lived with his Emunah that all that comes from Hashem is only for the good, even though, at the time, it all seemed but evil). So that through "understanding the years of generation upon generation," we, too, in every generation and at all times will learn to live with the Emunah of those who set these great examples. That even though before our human eyes all we see is only acts of injustice and years of devastation, as if indeed there were only evil, exile, hatred, bloodshed of the innocent etc., we still may realize that we are now but standing *in the middle of a frightening chapter,* completely unable to grasp the significance and implications of the event, which comes only at its ultimate conclusion. How then could we even expect to understand that which is still hidden, obscured and concealed from us (while it is still evolving and ongoing), and which, only at the end, Be'Acharis Hayamim, we shall be able to perceive?

For at that time, only at the End and in our own "morrow" will we merit to grasp and appreciate it all, and eventually rise to give praise and say retroactively concerning *all* these afflictions that have passed over us: "I thank You, Hashem, that You were angry with me" (Yeshaya 12:1). — For because You were angry with us, *therefore* we returned to you. "Hashem, when in distress, they sought you" (Yeshaya 26:16): Whenever Yisrael fell into afflictions, they suddenly realized and started searching for You — especially out of distress. And *then,* Be'Acharis HaYamim, we will sing before Him, saying: "As Hashem lives, He brought up the Bnei Yisrael from the land of the North and from all the lands into which He had cast them" (Yirmiyahu 16:15). *Then* our eyes will light up, our hearts will rejoice and we shall say Blessings over our Redemption and the freedom of our souls, saying: Indeed, whatever the Merciful One does is for the best, even the terrible and horrible which appeared as pure evil. Even all these nations, with their hostile intentions to bring evil upon us, Hashem contrives it for *our* benefit — to keep us alive for the Final Redemption.

* *

Only out of remembering the "Yemos Olam" can we furthermore become convinced of *the constant decline of the generations.* (On this

21

concept of declining greatness per se depend both our Emunas Chachamim and our acceptance of the transmission of the Messora to all generations). This applies not only to the Avos (Patriarchs), the Tribes and the Prophets, but throughout all generations as well. Said Reb Yochanan (Eiruvin 53a): The heart (i.e. spiritual capacity) of the Rishonim (among the Tannaim) was like the entrance of the Ullam (of the Bais HaMikdash), that of the Acharonim (of them) like the entrance of the Heichal (which was half the size), and *ours* is like the eye of a very fine needle. — Hence, what can we today pretend, we, who are altogether bereft of heart and knowledge?

Yet, by studying the very deeds and words of these Rishonim we came to realize all this; also by probing into their Torah-heritage which indeed was handed down the way it was given at Sinai! For the closer to Maamad Har Sinai, the clearer, more concise and complete was the Torah preserved and handed down to the next generation. Hence, *from their mouth* we live, for *they* transmitted to us this Torah in all its minute details, insight and reasonings. — And if so, how can one haughtily dare to question or disagree with all that they handed down to us throughout the generations?

One may ask: "Why not? Are we not superior to all the generations that preceded us, we who live in this fabulous modern era of continuous progress and 'miraculous' inventions which did not even enter the minds of these very Rishonim as being possible at all?"

However, all this so-called superiority is only a matter of *technological progress*; not a sign of our *intellectual* greatness. (And the continuous moral degeneration of humanity serves as proof.) Furthermore, even this very technological progress and superiority is not really ours (as if it all were indeed the result only of our own knowledge and accomplishment), but merely a rich legacy *inherited* from our ancestors. Only because our present-day generation came to have inherited all the accumulated knowledge, sciences and inventions for which all the past generations toiled and labored, do we now possess all that. And this should be called *our* superiority?

Hence, despite the great legacy which we inherited, each and every one of us still will testify about the Masters who preceded us saying:

"If the Ancients were like angels, then we are but ordinary humans; if the Ancients were like humans, then we are like donkeys — and not even like the donkey of R' Pinchas Ben Ya'ir" (Shabbos 112b).

*　　*

Knowledge of the events of "Yemos Olam" confronts us with a unique basic problem. All other fields of knowledge and sciences depend mainly on a person's capabilities, grasp and understanding of the particular subject. Blessed with a sharp and quick-grasping mind, one may be able to think, reason and invent works of magnitude, grace and beauty. — History, however, is the knowledge of what *has happened* since the days of old. Hence it outrightly becomes a matter of finding ancient sources. Neither capabilities nor a wealth of discourses will help, nor will imagination and the drive for innovating facts of History. By its very nature, History covers solely *old facts,* and there is no room for innovation! It is merely the knowledge and understanding of *facts* that happened before. Hence one can justly search, gather, record and write down *only* that which has been authentically recorded and transmitted to us from generation to generation since those very ancient days when the events actually occurred. As Moshe Rabbeinu commanded: "Ask your father (who was before you) and he will tell you; your elders, and they will recount it to you." — Outrightly, a matter of searching for the sources!

The sources of History, however, have in recent times been gravely tampered with and even falsified, more than in any other field of knowledge. This was due not merely to lack of knowledge or sheer ignorance, but more often to evil intentions. There were many who falsely crowned themselves "historians," and willfully manipulated and misinterpreted the facts of our history. Their main concern was to try to do away with the historical uniqueness of the Jewish nation, and present our history merely as part and parcel of a secular World-History. Hence, theirs was a History, based not on facts and authentic sources, but on the personal opinion of "a prophet with hindsight," who interprets events retroactively (not objectively, but subjectively), ac-

23

cording to his own current modern, distorted and assimilated beliefs and viewpoints.

Furthermore, they even detested the words of the Living God and the wealth of historical facts that our Chachamim so painstakingly preserved and transmitted to us from generation to generation. They but followed hollowness, and became utterly confused. For "sources" they turned only to the broken wells of general-history containing no water, drawing on the poor and questionable sources of so called "Jewish" history that they found in the nations' General History.

We reject all this outrightly not merely as a matter of belief, but from a purely scientific viewpoint. For how dare historians reject or even disregard the wealth of ancient historical sources transmitted in the Written Torah, the Oral Torah, and throughout this magnificent multitude of Holy Sefarim which we possess? — Or shall we perhaps accord unquestionable reliability to the script carved out into ancient stone-tablets which some glory-hungry king may have commanded inscribed as a flattering historical monument for that which he neither did nor even intended to do? Or shall we (just because of its antiquity), grant full credibility to every ancient scroll — the work of some unknown individual to whose name, origin or credibility none is even able to testify? But the words of the Living God, revealed to us by Prophets and Ru'ach Hakodesh, all of it safeguarded over the ages by our Masters, transmitted from one Sage to the other in the very words of his Master, without omissions or additions, — to all these shall we not listen nor even accept them as historical sources — merely *because they are part of the Biblical and Talmudical heritage of Jewish Life?*

Hence we will not dignify these false prophets of history by even debating with them. (By taking on the Jewish Apikores he only becomes worse!) There is also no need for it. The structure of Jewish History stands firm, and the Truth proves its way. There surely is no need to come out and defend the truthfulness of our Chachamim throughout the generations! — We shall only thank Hashem that He set us apart from all those who went astray, and gave us the Torah of Truth.

Therefore, specifically on the words and the sources of our Chachamim (by whose words we live) do we base our foundations. All these are *our* facts of History. Only *they* transmitted to us the details of the facts, as well as the minute facets of the details themselves. For theirs are the words of the Living God, conveying the absolute, objective and factual truth of 'Yemos Olam." Yet before Bnei Yisrael entered the Land, our "ancient History" was written down for us by dictation — Hashem speaking, and Moshe writing (Babba Bassra 15a). After they entered the Land, History was further recorded in the Neviyim and the Kessuvim. Afterwards our Chachamim — the Sages of the Mishna — continued to transmit further details of all these events, exactly the way they received it one from another, back until Moshe at Sinai. Then followed our Masters, the Geonim, the Rishonim and the Acharonim in the various lands of their dispersion, all of them continuing to transmit the chain of the Messorah which has never been interrupted, neither by persecution, Churban or by Exile, until this very day. — For how could we ever exchange all these for the so called "facts" of some obscure and unproven secular sources, which world-history so gladly accepted (because they are *not* part of the authentic Jewish Heritage) from those for whom deviation from the truth is by far not considered a sin? (Do modern Jewish historians not boast and pride themselves that they rightfully can "interpret," "add" and "adapt" facts according to their own concepts and understanding, even without the slightest historical proof?) And because of the "general acceptance" of all this should we turn away from the words of the Living God which were safeguarded and handed down over the generations with a truthfulness and exactness altogether alien to world-history?

*   *

Unlike General-History, the greatness of Jewish History furthermore expresses itself through a unique additional dimension, altogether foreign to World-History. Ours is not merely a human recording strictly of that which happened down here on earth, but rather of that which has emerged from Him "Who calls and designates the generations, yet beforehand." Hence, how can we differentiate between all that came

25

to pass on the historical scene, and the *"What"* and *"Why"* it has been decreed upon us by Heavenly Providence? "Cause and effect," but can one indeed dissociate effect (the event) from the One Who causes it? — Or does general National History, for instance, refrain from adding or explaining the course of their own national history, in the way it was affected, influenced and changed by the outside forces of developing world-events? — Do nations not study the impact on their own history caused by revolutions and political, social or cultural changes which took place in distant parts of the world? Do they not also consider all these "outside events" by way of cause and effect on their own History? And, were they to be aware of other additional "causes", would they not seize and insert them, too, into their own National History?

However, Hashem did not enlighten them on the Higher or Deeper Causes of World-events, and why He has wrought it all. They were left ignorant even as to why they merited kingship, or why kingship was eventually taken away from them. But should all this affect Jewish History too? Because General History does not take into account "Higher Causes" of the March of History, should this be reason for us, too, not to make use of the facts of metaphysical causes and effects of Jewish History which indeed, throughout, have been revealed to us from on High? ... Or just because in conventional General History there is no place for all this, therefore we, too, must deny all that which only we have merited to learn, and wantonly reject all the historical revelations, insights and understanding of the Acts of Hashem, the Ways of His Hanhaga, and the judgments of individuals and nations that were meted out by "the Judge of all the Universe?" — Or, for example, "the pain of the Shechina" and the lament of the Malachim and celestial bodies at the time of the Churban Beis HaMikdash. Just because World-History does not possess historical sources of this sort (and these are anyhow simply not credenced by them), should we, too, therefore have to refrain from transmitting and publicizing and printing a History enriched by all that was indeed transmitted to us and so scrupulously safeguarded from generation to generation? ...

Should we, in fact, detach all the ongoing here on earth below, from

26

the corresponding reality of that which is happening and decreed upon from on High?

*   *

Hence even *Halacha* becomes an inseparable part of Jewish History! Indeed, the Halacha is our life; the specific *national pattern* of the daily life of our people. From its very beginning the whole House of Yisrael was founded upon it. The Beis HaMikdash, the Avodah, the Korbanos, Aliyah LeRegel — is all this not essentially our unique national history? How, for instance, shall we then not mention the event of the Para Aduma made by Ezra the Scribe, upon which depended the Taharah (Purity) of our nation and the continuous national Avodah in the Beis HaMikdash? Or shall we not talk about the Korbanos offered by the impoverished returning exiles, in the days of Zerubavel; or the account of the "Anshei Knesses Hagdola" and their edicts, which are literally the breath of our lives and the mainstay of our days, etc., etc.? ... As if, indeed, all this were not the very national life and real History of the Jewish People, as well as the basis of its eternal existence?

Or is it perhaps that the Halacha is somehow only part of "religion," but not a "national" component? — As if the religious life of a nation were not part and parcel of the very national life of that nation?

But when our whole History is a religious one per sé, how else could we then record Jewish History which from its conception and all throughout has been only a religious one? Do the nations of the world not write in their national history about the various laws they enacted in their law-chambers, the many basic discussions which their founders and ancestors conducted, and the various patterns of national life and religious customs they had introduced at different periods, etc., etc.? — And *they* may have theirs, but Jewish History may not include our Prophets, the act of the Sanhedrin, as well as the phenomenal discussions and deeds of the Tannaim, Ammoraim, etc.? ...

*   *

Very often we lack details and even main points of recorded his-

27

torical events, depriving us of the means to present a comprehensive clear picture. For instance: the slaying of Gedalyahu ben Achikam. One may ask: Where was Yirmiyahu (who was staying with Gedalyahu in Mitzpah) at the time when Yishmael and his men murdered Gedalyahu? Why do we not possess this detail of the Messorah? — Or, who were those sainted 80 Talmidim of Hillel Hazaken (30 of whom were worthy that the Shechina rest upon them like on Moshe, and 30 that the sun should halt in orbit for them, as it did for Yehoshu'a bin Nun, etc.), of whom only Yonassan ben Uziel and R' Yochanan ben Zakkai are known by name? (Babba Bassra 134a).

Ours is not a mere secular human presentation of History, but Torah: *an integral part of our tradition.* Even many Halachos were forgotten with time. Many mainstays of Torah were plainly taken away from us because we no longer merited all of it. Much was, furthermore, caused by Exile, and much more by the afflictions along the endless roads of suffering. So that one cannot even fathom the breadth and wealth of all that was forgotten in the course of all these generations. — And how much more so with the details of history.

Furthermore, much of our history was not even transmitted to us by our Chachamim. It all might have been very interesting as a matter of curiosity, but there was really no compelling need to preserve it all forever. Even prophecies and Ru'ach Hakodesh were recorded in Tanach only when they were needed and relevant to all future generations (Megillah 14a). In a similar vein, our Chachamim also recorded and transmitted to us in the details of the "Yemos Olam" only what was needed for *all* generations. About the rest it may be said: "Whatever was, was" — Why should it concern you?

Even the names of all the Chachamim themselves have not been preserved and recorded for us! We had twice the number of prophets as the men who left Mitzrayim (Megillah 14a), yet only 48 prophets and 7 prophetesses are mentioned by name. Even though we had "600,000 Morey Massnissin" (Chachamim of our Mishna) (Zohar Chadash 103b), less than 300 of them are known by name to this very day. In fact, there were so many Chachamim throughout these Millennia, that were we to erect in Eretz-Yisrael even the smallest monument in memory of each of the Prophets, Tannaim, Ammoraim, Savoraim, Rishonim and Acharonim, there simply would not have been an open spot left for one's foot. Yet they were not even recorded by name for future generations, as there was no compelling need for it.

However, the words of the Torah are brief but indicative, and from a "No" one should deduct the "Yes"; implying that all that was after all recorded and handed down for future generations, indeed must have been considered *needed*, and *for all generations*, and needed for each and every one of every generation. — And may each and everyone come and learn to remember ("Z'chor") and understand ("Binu") the eternal lessons and admonishment of our spectacular History.

*   *

Often we are confronted by differences of opinion in factual details of History transmitted to us by our Chachamim. Each of these Sages, of course, conveyed "words of the Living God," yet it is not always possible to include conflicting versions as part of the story. On the other hand, who dares to judge and decide between these giants, our Chachamim? It would not enter one's mind to decide between two Rishonim in matters of Halacha; likewise, how could we, the smallest of the smallest among the smallest, possibly decide between them in matters of events of Yemos Olam, — all of which were handed down in the Shas, Midrashim, etc.?

Hence, whenever possible, we have not refrained from bringing in this Sefer the various opinions. When not possible, we mentioned either in the "Mar'eh Mekomos" or in the "Tosefes Davar" (in the appendix to the Sefer) that there are other opinions too. — Sometimes, however, we did bring only one particular opinion. This was not done out of personal preference, but by following the judgment of Rishonim or Acharonim. For example, in the story of the withered bones we mention only that these were the bones of the Bnei Ephraim who prematurely left Mitzrayim. In the Gemara (Sanhedrin 92b) other opinions are mentioned, but Rashi in his Peirush to Sefer Yechezkel (37:1) quotes this opinion. — Hence *Rashi decided for us* how to present the event of the withered bones.

* *

Remembrance of Yemos Olam acquires yet another importance in our days. Indeed, we live today in times of absolute scientific freedom. The greater the daring and scientific permissiveness, the more one's fame grows. Science today uses the haughtiest phrases, limitless and without restraint. Powered by an exploding technology, scientists dig and delve ever deeper and farther into Hashem's universe and the wonders of His creation — wildly daring to speculate even on "what was before and what will be after, what is above and what below." Restricted by the physical limitations of human grasp and understanding, they created for themselves a sort of escape — as if indeed, with a fictional astronomical dimension of time, one could explain the secrets of this Universe and even the process of its Creation. Lacking facts and explanation, they just keep increasing the factor of time to their theoretical age of the universe, practically running out of numbers already. — As if indeed, what brains cannot do, time itself may somehow have "evolved" all by itself.

This current purely speculative theory of universal confusion is being cloaked, however, in the respected mantle of Science and Progress. Hence, it sowed degrees of confusion even among those who remain loyal to the words of Torah. How many of our youths can sincerely pretend to have effectively closed ears and heart from being affected by all this? How many today would be baffled when asked outrightly: How do we know that the year we are counting today is really the year 5748 from Creation? Even their eventual stuttering answer, "Why, is it not printed on our calendars," may bring them only little reassurance. For what are a mere 5748 years compared to the constantly growing astronomical numbers of years which one hears and reads about all the time?

Of utmost importance, therefore, is not only to know the year we are counting, but also to have the critical self reassuring answer ready: "Indeed, science may wildly and blindly *speculate,* but *we do know*! We can calculate exactly how we arrive at our count of 5748 from Creation."

Hence it was necessary to preface "Toldos Am Olam" with an exact detailed Chronology starting from Briyas-Haolam; not only to enumerate the basic historical events in their chronological sequence of occurrence, but also to specify the authentic reliable source for every event and for each date. So, that from it all many will find strength and encouragement: to know what to answer to the Apikores.

This Chronology, however, is presented in utmost brevity. (Otherwise it would amount to a full-size History). Yet, notwithstanding its brevity, it contains a wealth of details. It was compiled and arranged with utmost care and exactness, and it should command the reader's full attention. It scrupulously follows the outline and order of our authentic holy Sefarim. — True to the admonishing of Moshe: "Ask your father," — these are the Prophets. "Your elders," — these are the Chachamim. "And *they* shall tell you." (Rashi, Devarim 32:7).

*   *

For only through all these can one fully appreciate the real character and nature of the eternal "Am Hasefer" (the People of the Book"). To realize that in all history there is no nation like Yisrael, "the unique people on earth," whose God is close to them, as is Hashem, our God, whenever we call Him"; the "great nation that has Statutes and just Laws, as is this whole Torah" (Devarim 4:7).

So that — in their spectacular March-of-History — "whoever sees them will (at once) recognize them: 'indeed, these are the Seed blessed by Hashem.' "

Chronology

From Creation until the Destruction
of the Second Beis HaMikdash

CONTENTS

THE TEN GENERATIONS FROM ADAM
UNTIL NO'ACH

"*THIS* is the count of the births of man" (Bereishis 5:1 and Rashi ibid.). In these paragraphs (dictated to him by Hashem) Moshe Rabbeinu wrote down and recorded for all times the births and dates of the generations from Adam till No'ach.

The count of the years of these generations is the beginning and basis of our continuous calendar count of years which starts with Creation, and we cannot do without it.

generation	year born	name	begot son at age	lived	died
1	1 (created)	Adam	130	930	930
2	130	Sheis	105	912	1042
3	235	Enosh	90	905	1140
4	325	Keinon	70	910	1235
5	395	Mahallalel	65	895	1290
6	460	Yered	162	962	1422
7	622	Chanoch	65	365	987
8	687	Mesushelach	187	969 (Mabul)	1656
9	874	Lemech	182	777	1651
			1056		
10	1056	No'ach	502	950	2006

Adam, "the one shaped by the Almighty's Hand," was created in the year one, on the sixth day, "in absolute perfection of beauty, strength and stature" (Ramban, Bereishis 5:5). Adam was 130 years old when he fathered a son in his own form and likeness, "and he named him Sheis" (Bereishis 5:3). Thus Sheis was born in the year 130 from Creation. "Sheis was 105 years old and he fathered Enosh" (verse 6),

— thus Enosh was born 235 years after Creation (105 of his father, plus 130 years of Adam, his grandfather). In the same manner we count all the ten generations — the years lived by the father until the birth of his son. (Enosh 90, Keinon 70, Mahallalel 65, Yered 162, Chanoch 65, Mesushelach 187, Lemech 182), up to No'ach, who was born 1056 after Creation — the first to be born in the second millennia.

Lemech, No'ach's father, is not the Lemech who was one of the grandchildren of Cain, but a descendant of Sheis "from whom the world was set" (Ramban Bereishis 5:3). The Torah enumerates only the descendants of Sheis until No'ach and those of No'ach's son Shem, until Avraham the Ivri, who brought light to all mankind. It does not mention all the other "sons and daughters" who were born in all those generations. They all died and were wiped out by the Mabbul (Flood).

Mesushelach was a total Tzaddik, and he lived longer than any man on earth (969 years [verse 27]). Chanoch, his father, lived less than all of them (verse 24), having died after a third of the average life-span of his contemporaries (365 years). People wondered when he disappeared (Sheis, the grandfather of his great grandfather was still alive then) "as Hashem took him away." (Rashi ibid).

Of all these generations Adam was the first to die (930) and Chanoch, the second (987). Mesushelach was born in 687 and lived 969 years, exactly up until the time of the Mabbul ("Seder Olam" 1).[1]

---

1   Concerning the great length of the life-span of these first ten generations many comments and explanations have been presented. There are those who mistakenly claim that the length of those years was not the same as ours. (For instance, in the Book of Yosephus and in the Sefer Hakabbala of Rayved Halevi we find that the Greek year consisted of 8 months only). However, from the literal meaning of the verses of the Torah we see clearly the fallacy of their assumptions. For the reckoning of the months of the first generations is identical with that of our months today, and their years identical to our years, — all of which is proven by the detailed account of the Mabbul.

"In the year 600 of No'ach's life, on the 17th day of the second month (Cheshvan)" (Bereishis 7:11), the Mabbul began. "On the 15th day of the 10th month, (from the start of the Mabbul, which is Av) the tops of the mountains became visible." (8:5) "It was at the end of 40 days and No'ach opened the Ark's window." (Passuk 6) He sent out the raven,

Since it is recorded in the Torah: "the number of all his years was ..."
etc., we know the year in which each of the ten generations died.

and then the 3 doves, in intervals of 7 days each (60 days of the 2 months
of Av and Elul, completing the 12 months of this 600th year of No'ach.)
Until "in *the 601st year* on the 1st month (which is Tishrei), on the 1st
day of the month, the waters dried up" (verse 13) and in the second
month, on the 27th day of the month, the earth was dry (Passuk 14).
Hence, all those months and days of No'ach's count amounted to one full
year only.

Furthermore, the length of the month of these first generations is identical with the length of our months. For in the 5 months (from the 17th
of the *second* month till the 17th of the *seventh* month) the waters kept
rising — "*for 150 days*" (Ramban ibid 8:1), making it 30 days to the
month (Sefer "Tzemach David" page 1). Also, from the 1st day of the
10th month (that is Av — the 10th month from the start of the rains)
until the time when No'ach opened the Ark's window there were "40 days"
(ibid 8:6). Add to these the 3 intervals of 7 days each for the dispatch of
the 3 doves — altogether 60 days, after which on the 1st day of Tishri he
removed the cover from the Ark (Passuk 14). — Hence 60 days for the
2 months of Av and Elul — exactly like our present months.

THE TEN GENERATIONS FROM NO'ACH
UNTIL AVRAHAM

"*THESE* are the births of Sheim" (Bereishis 11:10). In these paragraphs are further recorded the ten generations from No'ach until Avraham. The first one was the generation of Sheim. (No'ach, his father, was counted in with the ten generations from Adam till No'ach. Yet the 10 following generations too, are named after him, as "he was a totally righteous man.") The year in which Noach fathered Sheim, is not mentioned however.

"No'ach was 500 years old, and he fathered Sheim and Chom and Yefes" (Bereishis 5:32). — He had passed more than half of his life span without having borne any offspring, unlike the previous generations who had children around their hundredth year (Rashi ibid). Although the Torah mentions Sheim — the Tzaddik — first, his brother Yefes was the older (Bereishis Rabba 37:7). No'ach begot him when he was 500 years old. But it is not written at what age he had Sheim. This we learn from another verse.

"Sheim was 100 years old and he begot Arpachshad, 2 years after the Mabbul" (ibid 11:10). 2 years after the Mabbul Sheim was 100 years old, hence he was born 98 years before the Mabbul. "No'ach was 600 years old and the Mabbul of waters was upon the earth" (ibid 7:6). Thus the Mabbul took place 1656 years after Creation. Hence Sheim was born 1558 (98 years earlier) when No'ach was 502 years old.

The Mabbul lasted one full year, (from the "17th day of the second month in the 600th year of No'ach's life," (Bereishis 7:11) until the 27th of the second month — in his 601st year (ibid 8:1) — which equals the 12 months of the Lunar year (Idiyos, end of Perek 2), plus the 11 days by which the Solar year exceeds it.) — Upon leaving the

Ark, No'ach was enjoined not to eat limbs severed from a living animal. This command, added to the six commandments that Hashem had given to Adam, comprise the Seven Mitzvos of Bnei No'ach (Sanhedrin 56b) (obligatory upon all mankind).

From these 3 sons of No'ach came the 70 nations of the earth — 14 from Yefes, 30 from Chom, 26 from Sheim (Breishis Perek 10).

generation	born year	name	begot son at age	lived	died
11	1558	Sheim	100	600	2158
	1656	Mabbul			
12	1658	Arpachshad	35	438	2096
13	1693	Shelach	30	433	2126
14	1723	Eyver	34	464	2187
15	1757	Peleg	30	239	*1996
16	1787	Re'u	32	239	2026
17	1819	Se'rug	30	230	2049
18	1849	Nachor	29	148	1997
19	1878	Terach	70	205	2083
20	1948	Avraham	100	175	2123

* Generation of Haflaga.

In the foregoing table of the generations we also tally the years of the fathers prior to the birth of their sons (Sheim 100, Arpachshad 35, Shelach 30, Eyver 34, Peleg 30, Re'u 32, Se'rug 30, Nachor 29, Terach 70) up to Avraham — who is the 20th generation from Adam — born in the year 1948 after Creation.

Sheim, son of No'ach was a Tzaddik and prophet (Breishis Rabba 63:7), (as it says: [Bereishis 9:26] "Blessed be the Elokim of Sheim.") He was also identified as "Malki Tzedek," the King of Shalem, that is, Yerushalayim. He was also "the Kohen to the Most High" (Bereishis 14:18). In Sheim's House of Study (Bereishis Rabba 63:10) people came to study and search for Hashem (Bereishis 25:22). Sheim's Court dispensed judgments (Bereishis Rabba 67:8) and issued decrees

(Avoda Zara 36b). And the Ru'ach Hakodesh (The Spirit of Holiness) appeared there (Makkos 23b).

Sheim beheld 15 generations. He personally knew No'ach, Lemech and Mesushelach of the first Ten Generations, and he outlived the next ten generations — his sons and grandsons and their descendants. He also lived through the days of Avraham (who died in 2123, while he died 2158), up to Yaakov who was 50 years old when Sheim departed life. Even after he died, his court bore his name, "The Court of Sheim."

Eyver too was a great prophet, as by virtue of the Ru'ach Hakodesh resting on him he named his son "Peleg" ("Seder Olam" 1). For in his (Peleg's) days the earth was divided (Bereishis 10:25). Peleg was born in 1757 and lived 239 years — placing his death at 1996. Upon his birth his father Eyver — by prophecy — named him Peleg for the Haflaga (split) — an event to come 239 years later ("Seder Olam" 1). When it happened people realized that Eyver must be a prophet, and they came to study under him too. ("The House of Study of Sheim and the House of Study of Fyver" [Bereishis Rabba 63:10] — *two* seperate ones). Upon Sheim's death, the House of Study of Eyver still remained.

During the era of the 10 generations from No'ach till Avraham a great change took place in people's life-span. During the first 10 generations men lived a very long life, some of them even longer than Adam. Upon sinning, when "all flesh perverted its ways upon the earth" (Bereishis 6:2) Hashem brought upon them the waters of the Mabbul, and obliterated all existence from the surface of the earth (ibid 7:4); the quality of the air and climate deteriorated (Ramban, Breishis 5:4), their strength and stature diminished, and the number of their years continuously decreased. Thus Sheim, who was born yet *before* the Mabbul was still endowed with the innate strength of the time of his birth. Even though he was later exposed to the harm caused by the poorer quality of the post-Mabbul air and climate, he still lived to be six hundred years (Breishis 11:11). Even his children (who were all born already after the Mabbul) benefited from their father's strong constitution, and they reached about half the life-span of the first generations. (Arpachshad 438, Shelach 433, Eyver 464). When they later sinned again the people of the earth were divided and dispersed and were simultaneously subjected to a further deterioration of the quality of air and climate in the various places of their dispersion (Ramban ibid); their lives were shortened even more, having reached only about half of their fathers' years (Peleg lived only 239 years and so did his son Re'u). Hence these generations began also to beget children at an earlier age (Shelach was 30 at the birth of his son; Peleg 30; Nachor 29, etc.), as did the generations following them, until this very day.

Apparently already in the days of Avraham, Yitzchak and Yaakov, the lifespan of man was seventy years, "and with strength — eighty," as Moshe Rabbeinu mentioned in his prayers (Tehillim 90:10). For Pharaoh wondered at the 130 year old Yaakov, asking (Bereishis 47:8), "How many are the days of the years of your life?" (Ramban, Bereishis 5:4) For Avraham too the joy over the miracle was overwhelming as he said (Bereishis 17:17), "Can a man of 100 beget a child? Or Sara, who is 90 years old, can she give birth?" Moreover, Sara said: "Hashem made me a rejoicing, whoever will hear (of it), will laugh with me" (ibid 21:6). The nations of the world scoffed and said: Have you ever seen an old man and an old woman bring a foundling from the street, claiming: this is our son? (Babba Metzia). Even though Avraham lived 175 years and Sara 127 (making him at the age of 100 like a man in middle age, capable of having children), the many years of his life were not a natural phenomena in those days, only a fruition of the verse (Mishlei 10:27): "Fear of Hashem adds years." (Ramban ibid) (Hence we can see why Sara said: "My master is old," when he was yet in the middle of his years).

In the year 1656 Hashem brought the Mabbul (Flood) upon the earth; another 340 years (numerically Sheim) passed till the generation of the Haflaga (Division, Split) (1996). Avraham (born in 1948) was 48 years old when the people of the earth were divided. (In the Scriptures the account of the Haflaga preceeds the account of Avraham's birth, as the Torah is not bound by chronological sequence of

41

events only (Pesachim 6b). Hence we can understand our Sages Z'l who say (Bereishis Rabba 64:4): "At age 48 Avraham knew his Creator," and Reish Lakish saying: "At age 3 he knew his Creator." Both are correct, as at age 3 he acquired his basic belief in Hashem. However, his deeper *Hakara* (full recognition) of the Creator was reached by the age of 48 as he saw Hashem's Hand and Rule (Bereishis 11:9) — when instantly, in one moment, He mixed up the languages of all the peoples and scattered them over the surface of the earth (Sefer Yuchsin).

Only 5 Tzaddikim lived at the time: Avraham and Sara (who was then 38 years old, having been born when Avraham was 10 years old), No'ach, Sheim and Eyver. (Neither did Ashur, son of Sheim, sin with the Haflaga generation, since "Ashur left that land." Having seen his children follow Nimrod and revolt against their Creator by building the Tower, he left their midst (Bereishis 10:11; Rashi ibid).

No'ach was 940 years old when his children revolted against Hashem. He was the first to die in the third millennium of Creation, 10 years after Haflaga (2006). He beheld 17 generations — his own and all the 10 generations following him; [2] also the earlier generations from Enosh on (except for Chanoch). — Hence 17 generations.

Avraham the Ivri knew No'ach personally, for Avraham was born 1948 and No'ach died in 2006 ("Seder Olam"). They all lived in the plain which they had selected (for themselves) in the land of Shin'ar

---

2   Numerically the names of Sheim, Chom and Yefes are indicative respect-
     ively: "Sheim" — from the Mabbul till Haflaga is 340 years (the gemat-
     riya of Sheim). "Chom" — 48 years old was Avraham at the time of
     Haflaga. "Yefes" — 490 years passed from when our Mother Sara was
     born until the Exodus from Mitzrayim, in the year 2448 (Beur Vehagahos
     HaGra to "Seder Olam").
     "As the days of the Heavens over the earth" (a distance of 500 walking
     years), so were the years of the Patriarchs. Avraham lived 175 years, but
     he recognized his Creator only in his third year, hence it is counted only
     173; Yitzchak was 180, Yaakov 147 — altogether 500. — Also, from the
     birth of Avraham till the Exodus from Egypt is 500 years: 100 till the
     birth of Yitzchak, and 400 years after he was born (ibid; also see Yeru-
     shalmi beg. of Berachos).

(Bereishis 11:2). Avraham saw No'ach for 58 years (the numerical value of No'ach [Ibn Ezra]). He saw 13 generations: No'ach and the 10 generations following him, and Yitzchak and Yaakov.

The foregoing facts and the knowledge of the count of the lives of the earliest generations further proves conclusively the correct facts relating to Creation (Rambam in Moreh Nevuchim). For Avraham enjoined his children and household after him (to obey the Mitzvos) — testifying to them about No'ach and his sons who were eyewitnesses to the Mabbul as well as the Teyva (Ark). Through them he too became a witness to the whole event of the Mabbul. (Also Yitzchak and Yaakov saw Sheim, who testified to them about the Mabbul). Furthermore, Avraham was the fourth successive *witness* to the very fact of Creation. For he knew No'ach, who knew his father Lemech, who saw Adam ("the First man"). All others (except Chanoch, who died yet before No'ach was born) of the first 10 generations too, knew Adam and relayed to No'ach his doings in the Gan, in Eiden from the East; and about Cain and Hevel, etc., etc. Yaakov later knew our Patriarch Avraham (he was 15 years old when Avraham died) who testified to him about all the foregoing — a witness to the earlier witness. Yaakov in turn relayed all this to his children who descended to Egypt, as well as to Pharaoh and his contemporaries. Thus we see that until Yaakov's death in the year 2255 of Creation four successive witnesses have testified for all times to all that took place from the very day when Hashem created earth and heaven: *Adam, Lemech, No'ach and Avraham*. Indeed as in every generation there were old people who heard from their fathers about the events and happenings of the past 4-5 generations and exactly related all these further to their own children. Furthermore, Yocheved, daughter of Levy and Serach daughter of Asher, were among those making their exit out of Mitzrayim (2448). They too had heard and learned all this still from Yaakov (Seder Olam 9). So did Ya'ir, son of Menashe, and Machir, son of Menashe (ibid), who were still among those that entered Eretz Yisrael at the time of Yehoshu'a (Sanhedrin 44a and "Seder Olam", end of Perek 9). Furthermore, *Yaakov* attended *Sheim* for 50 years, Sheim attended *Mesushelach* for 98 years and Mesushelach learned personally from *Adam* for 243 years. These 4 knew one another and spanned the full 22 generations until the descent to Mitzrayim. They thus testified to all that happened from Creation until that time ("Seder Olam", end of perek 1). Furthermore, *seven* men spanned *all* of the world's history: Adam, Mesushelach, Sheim, Yaakov, Achiya the Shiloni and Eliyahu —— "who still exists" (ibid).

All of these — simple historical facts.

FROM AVRAHAM UNTIL MOSHE

1948	**Birth of Avraham**	175	2123

1958 **Birth of Sara** — who was 90 years old when Avraham was 100, and she died at 127   127   2085

1996 **Haflaga** — Toward the end of Peleg's (son of Eyver) life.

THE THIRD MILLENNIUM

2018 **Bris beyn Hab'sarim** (the Covenant) — (On the 15th of Nissan) Avraham being 70 years old (Seder Olam 1). Even though it is written *after* the chapter of the War of the Kings — Torah is not bound by the chronological sequence of events, (Bereishis Rabba 44:5, Beyur VeHagahos Yaavetz Seder Olam 1). After Hashem had spoken to him, Avraham went to the city of Charan where he stayed for 5 years. He was 75 at the time of his exit from Charan (ibid). The Gra (in Seder Olam 1) leans towards the words of the Midrash (Bereishis Rabba 44) that the Covenant took place after he defeated the four kings.

2023 Avraham left his land, his birthplace, and his father's house (Bereishis 12:4).

Famine in Ke'naan. Avraham goes down to Egypt, and returns 3 months later.

The War of the Kings — The Four battling the Five (Bereishis 14:9), — as the evildoers, for the first time, initiated war in the world (Tanchumma Lech Lecha 7). Avraham, the Ivri, defeats them (ibid pasuk 15).

2034 **Birth of Yishma'el** — Avraham is 86 years old   137   2171
(Bereishis 16:17).

2047 **Bris Milah** — Avraham is 99 years old (ibid 17:24).

2048 **Birth of Yitzchak** — Avraham is 100 years old   180   2228
(ibid 25:5). Yishmael is 14 years older than Yitzchak.

2085 **Akeydas Yitzchak** — At age 37. — Upon hearing
the news of the Akeyda Sara dies at age 127. (She
had given birth at 90) (Bereishis Rabba 58:5).

2108 **Birth of Yaakov and Esav** — Yitzchak is 60 years   147   2255
old (Bereishis 25: 26).

2123 **Selling of B'chora** (Birth-right) — Avraham died
and Yaakov cooked lentils (25:29). Yaakov is 15
years old.

2171 **The Brachos** — Yaakov was 63. As Yishmael died
at that time. — When Eysav saw that Yitzchak
had sent Yaakov to Padan to take himself a wife
from there, he too went and betrothed Mochlas the
daughter of Yishmael, son of Avraham. Following
their betrothal Yishma'el died, and her brother Ne-
voyos married her off to Eysav (28:9 and ibid
Rashi).

2185 **In Lavan's House** — Yaakov is 77, having been
hidden in the House of Eyver for 14 years (Bereishis
rabba 68:11). (Sheim, No'ach's son had already
died in 2158, having known 12 generations after the
Mabbul and 3 before).

2192 **Rachel and Lea** — Yaakov worked 7 years for
Rachel. Having completed the 7 days of festivity
for Lea, he also married Rachel (Bereishis 29:27;
ibid Rashi). They were then 21-year-old twin
sisters (Seder Olam 2). Rachel died in childbirth
at age 36 (ibid). (Add 7 years till the birth of
Yosef, 6 years during which Yaakov tended Lavan's

sheep, and 2 years spent on the road en route to his father's house.)

2195 **Birth of Levy** — In the first year Re'uvein was born; Shimon in the second, and Levy in the third. Also, when Yaakov came to the city of Sh'chem (2207), Levy had just turned 13 (Bereishis Rabba 80:10). Hence he was born in 2195. He lived 137 years (Shemos 6:16).   137 2332

2199 **Birth of Yosef** — With Rachel's birth of Yosef, the 14 years of Yaakov's labor for the Matriarchs were completed, and Yaakov said to Lavan, "Let me leave, and I shall go to my place and my country." Also, when at age 130 Yaakov descended to Mitzrayim, Yosef was 39 years old. (30 upon becoming Viceroy, 7 years of bounty, and 2 years of famine.) Hence, Yaakov was 91 years old when he had begotten Yosef (Bereishis 30:5).   110 2309

2216 **Yosef is Sold** — At age 17 (ibid 37:2). Yitzchak still lived an additional 12 years after Yosef was sold.

2229 **Yosef, the Viceroy** — He was 30 years when he stood before Pharaoh (ibid 41:46). (One year was spent in Potifar's house, 10 years in prison, 2 years added on to his imprisonment — thus 13 years from when he was sold at 17.) (The preceding year Yitzchak died [ibid 35:58]).

2238 **Descent to Mitzrayim** — On the 15th day of Nissan (Shemos Rabba 18:11), Yaakov is 130 years old (ibid 47:9).

2332 **Beginning of Enslavement** — In 3 stages: **Galus** ("Your descendants will be foreigners") to last 400 years from the birth of Yitzchak (430 from the "Bris bein Habe'sarim" (Shemos 14:41); **"She'ibud"** ("They will make them labor"), following the death of Levy, the last of the Tribes ("Seder Olam" 3), after 94 years of Yisrael's sojourn in Egypt. Hence

47

they were enslaved for 116 years (delete from these the last 6 months in which our forefathers were already free from all labor) (Rosh Hashana 11) as the period of Mitzrayim's punishment lasted 12 months (Idiyos 4b); **Hardship of labor** ("They will torture them") — for 86 years, from the birth of Miriam (2362). (She was 5 years old when Moshe was born (Shemos Rabba 1:13.) Until before they left Mitzrayim in 2448.

K'hos — Was still among those who descended to Mitzrayim (ibid). 133

Amram — Father of Moshe; the leading sage of his time (Shemos Rabba). He is one of the 4 people who died merely because of the punishment of death decreed upon Adam (Babba Basra 17a). He lived 137 years (Shemos 6:2). 137

2368 **Birth of Moshe** — Son of Amram (7th day of Adar) ("Seder Olam"). Was 80 years old when he appeared before Pharaoh (in Nissan) (Shemos 7:7). The following Nissan they left Mitzrayim (in his 81st year). Yocheved who was born between the walls was 130 years old when she gave birth to Moshe — the 26th generation from Creation (26 is the numerical value of Hashem's Name).

2448 **Exodus from Mitzrayim** — 400 years from the birth of Yitzchak. For with his birth began the exile pronounced by Hashem to Avraham at the "Bris bein Habesarim," as He said, "For your descendants will be strangers in a land which is not theirs; and they will enslave them and oppress them for 400 years" (Bereishis 15:13). The decree covered not only their stay in Mitzrayim, but all the years in which "your children will be in a land not theirs." Neither was the land of K'naan theirs. — In Egypt they stayed only 210 years (numerically R'du = descend). They left Mitzrayim on the 15th day of Nissan (Shemos 12).

Kriyas Yam Suf — On the 21st of Nissan, the seventh day from the Exodus from Mitzrayim.

Descent of the "Mann" — On the 16th of Iyar, "mann" fell from Heaven for the Bnei Yisrael (Shemos 15; Seder Olam 5). The first 30 days they ate from the unleavened dough they had taken with them from Egypt ("Seder Olam" 5). It too had all the qualities of "Mann" (Kiddushin 35a).

2448 **Mattan Torah** — On Shabbos, the 6th day of Sivan.

The Golden Calf — Made 16 days in Tammuz. On the 17th the Luchos (Tablets) were broken.

2449 **Second Luchos** — Brought down by Moshe on Yom Kippur, the 10th of Tishrei of the next calendar year.

2449 **Setting up of Mishkan** — Rosh Chodesh Nissan (Shemos 40:17). Services of the Kohanim (Zevachim 112b).

2449 **Dispatch of the Me'raglim** — On the 29th of Sivan, and their return on Tish'a Be'av ("Seder Olam" 8). After the Me'raglim came the rift of Korach and his being swallowed up by the earth (ibid).[1]

---

1   In the 40th year of the Exodus from Mitzrayim the following events occurred: the demise of Miriam, the Waters of Strife, the demise of Aharon, the war with Sichon and Og, the event of Bil'am and Balak, the story with Pinchas, the war with the Midyanim, and all the events described in the Fifth Sefer — the Mishna Torah — along with the demise of Moshe Rabbeinu. Everything else described in the other Chumashim, beginning with Yetziyas Mitzrayim and onward, happened in the first and second year of their exit from Mitzrayim. About "the years in which we travelled from Kadesh Barne'a until we passed the River Zered — 38 years" (Devarim 2:14) — of these nothing was written except that they made 20 journeys (Rashi Massay 1:1; Sefer "Tzemach David" 449 and 484).

2488 **Demise of Moshe** — The "Father of (all) prophets" [2] (Vayikra Rabba 1:15), in the Plains of
Mo'av by the (river) Yarden, facing Yericho (Devarim 34:1), on the 7th of Adar (Kidushin 38.). at the
age of 120. His death was preceded by Miriam's,
at the age of 125, on the 10th of Nissan and Aharon's at the age of 123, on Rosh Chodesh Av ("Seder Olam" 10). On the 7th of Adar the "mann"
came down for the last time (ibid).

We have reached almost half the span of the world's existence, all
of which is written and recorded in the Five Sefarim of the Torah [3]
by the Almighty Himself — since Hashem spoke, and Moshe wrote
it down (Menachos 30a).

From then and onward the historical events and matters (bearing
on the future generations) were written down in the Sefarim of the
Prophets and the Kesuvim, as well as in the teachings of our Sages
who handed them down from generation to generation.

2 For 3 years only, Hashem spoke to Moshe lovingly, "Face to face." (The
year of Egypt's Judgment in Egypt, the first year in the Midbar (wilderness), and the 40th year). He did not speak to him that way throughout
the 38 years following the sin of the Meraglim in which the Bnei Yisrael
were considered estranged from Hashem (Rashi Devarim 2:17). — To
prove what sin causes.

3 Sefer B'reishis: From Creation until the death of Yosef — spans 2309
years.
Sefer Sh'mos: From Yosef's death until the setting up of the Mishkan —
140 years.
Sefer Vayikra: from the erection of the Mishkan on the first day of Nissan,
until the Second Month — covers 1 month.
Sefer Bamidbar: From the first day of the Second Month (Iyar) of the
second year until the 40th year — 38 years and 9 months.
Sefer Dévarim: From the first day of the eleventh month until Moshe's
P'tira on the 7th of Adar — 37 days.

AFTER YISRAEL ENTERED THE LAND

2488 **Yehoshu'a bin Nun** — leads Bnei Yisrael into the Land. Start of the Mesora, as Moshe transmitted to him all the Torah which he had received at Sinai (Avos 1:1). He lived 110 years.

Entering the Land — On the 10th of Nissan (Yehoshua 4:19). Upon entering, the fulfillment of the Laws of Chala, Orla, and Chadash (not partaking of the new harvest before the Omer) become obligatory (Kesuvos 25b).

Mishkan of Gilgal — Having come up from the Yarden, Yehoshua circumcised the Bnei Yisrael (Yehoshua 5). They erected the Mishkan in Gilgal, "all the way east of Yericho" (Yehoshua 4:19). Offerings on Bamos (private altars) were permitted (Zevachim Perek 14:1).

On the 16th of Nissan they brought the first offering of the Omer, and started to eat from the new harvest of the land (Yehoshua 5:11). (From the Mann they had gathered on the 7th of Adar, they ate for 39 days.)

Conquest of the Land — For 7 years they engaged in the conquest of the Land, as Kalev had said to Yehoshua (14:7), "I was 40 years old when Moshe, Hashem's Servant, sent me out of Kodesh Barne'a to spy out the Land, and behold . . . He has kept me alive . . . forty five years since . . . etc." Following the event of the Meraglim Bnei Yisrael wandered in the Midbar for 38 years. Hence it took 7 years to conquer. (Zevachim 118b).

2495 **Partitioning of the Land** — For seven years El'azar the Kohen, Yehoshu'a ben Nun and the heads of the Tribes were engaged in dividing the Land among the Tribes (even those parts which were not conquered yet) by lots, drawn as instructed by Hashem. (The number of years it took to partition the Land we learn from the writings of Yechezkel [Zevachim 118b].) Upon completion of the Land's partitioning they became subject to the fulfillment of **all** Mitzvos pertaining to the soil (of Eretz Yisrael). During these 14 years the Mishkan stood in Gilgal.

2503 **The Mishkan of Shiloh** — At that time they set up the Mishkan in Shiloh in the Portion of Yosef (Yehoshua 18:1), and the Bamos were forbidden (Zevachim Perek 14 Mishna 1). Mishkan Shiloh was a building of stone, with the Yeriyos (curtains) of the Ohel covering the top (ibid). It stood 369 years (Zevachim 118b). It was here that the Korbanos and Ma'aser-Sheyni were brought.

The Sh'mitos and Yovalos — The counting of the years for the observance of the respective Mitzvos of Ma'aser, Shemita and Yovel began when the conquest and partitioning of the Land were completed ("Seder Olam" 11, Rambam Hilchos Shemita VeYovel 10:2). Yehoshua was with them at the first Shemita (2510). He led Bnei Yisrael for 28 years ("Seder Olam" 12), and died in 2516 (Sefer Yuchsin). El'azar, son of Aharon the Kohen, also died at that time (ibid).

2516 **The Elders** (17 years) — They received the Torah from Yehoshu'a (Avos 1:3). There were many of them (Rambam Hakdama Leyad Hachazaka). The most prominent was Kalev ben Yefune (Nazzir 56b) 'who was their head (Sefer Yuchsin)' (106 years old — as he was 40 years old when sent out by Moshe with the Meraglim [Yehoshu'a 14:7]) and Pinchas ben El'azar. Also the sons of the Tribe of Levy and Eldad and Meydad are mentioned among the Elders (Bamidbar Rabba 3:7).

The era of the Elders did not last very long. Although they outlived Yehoshu'a (Yehoshu'a 25:31), they judged the Bnei Yisrael for only 17 years ("Seder Olam" and "Sefer Yuchsin").

THE JUDGES

2533 The Judges received the Torah from the Elders (Avos de R' Nassan 1:3). 15 Judges ruled over Yisrael. (The author of

"Tzemach David" lists 16, with Osniel ben K'naz as the second Judge). They ruled successively for 350 years. There was not one Tribe that failed to bring forth a Judge (Sukka 27b; for details see ibid Rashi).

Osniel ben K'naz — Brother of Kalev ben Yefune on his mother's side, judged from 2533. His Beis-Din was called "The Court of Yaavetz" (Temura 17a). He judged Yisrael for 40 years (Shoftim 3:11). His years include the 8 years of serfdom to Kushan Rish'asayim, king of Aram Naharayim ("Seder Olam" 12). The Statement (Shoftim 3:11) "And the land was at peace for 40 years," does not mean peace for all the 40 years, but 40 years from the time the serfdom of Kushan began. However, after 8 years of serfdom peace returned. (The same goes for the years of all the Judges (Beur HaGra LeSeder Olam).

The events of the statue of Micha and of the concubine in Giv'a took place in his days, according to the Seder Olam.[1]

1   According to Abarbanel these two events took place in the days of Shimshon; and the verse (Shoftim 18:1 etc.) : "In those days there was no king in Yisrael etc." alludes to the time when Shimshon was exiled among the Plishtim, "and the King was not in the midst of Yisrael" (Abarbanel ibid). As to the opinion of Seder Olam the verse pertains to the whole era of the Judges (Bepeirush Rif Le'Abarbanel Shoftim 17) being there was no king in Yisrael, only a Judge. Furthermore, the people judged their judges (Rus Rabba 1:1) — therefore "every man did what was right in his eyes." The author of "Tzemach David" writes (164) : "If I were not trepidated of my Rabbis I would say, that the Statue of Micha and the concubine in Giv'a took place in the days of the serfdom of Ammon when they had no Judge, from 2764 till 2786." (In Tana De'bei Eliyahu [Perek 11] we read that it happened in the times of Kushan Rishataim [Shoftim 3:8]). (Three times it is written: "In those times there was no king in Yisrael." [18:1; 19:1; 21:25]) Consult the Sefer "Tzemach David," (year 811).

It is also possible that both events took place during the few short intervals between one Judge and the next. As is seen in the Gemara (Chulin 57b; ibid Rashi), Hashem did not grant them a new Judge who would deliver them, on the very same day in which the former Judge died. Even though a new Judge would take over the same year, there was a lapse of time between one Judge and the next, and about this it is written, "In those days there was no king in Yisrael."

2573 **Eyhud son of Geyra** — He judged for 80 years (Shoftim 3:30). Included are the 18 years of serfdom to Eglon, king of Mo'av ("Seder Olam" ibid). He received the Mesora from Osniel (Rashi beg. Avos).
Shamgar — Judged in the final years of Eyhud's life. He died the same year as Eyhud.

2654 **D'vora and Barak ben Avino'am** — For 40 years (5:31. Included are the 20 years of serfdom to Yavin and Sisra ("Seder Olam" 12). Barak is Lapidus, husband of D'vora. Bnei Yisrael accepted her as the Judge, as she judged them by Heavenly Command. Another opinion holds that she did not judge them, only taught them the laws (Tosafos "Kol HaKasher" Nidah 50a).

2694 **Gid'on ben Yoash** (Yerubaal) — 40 years (8:28). Included are the 7 years under Midyan (Ralbag).

2734 **Avimelech ben Gid'on** — 3 years (9:22).

2736 **Toula ben Pu'a** — 23 years (10:2). Upon his death during his twenty-third year of reign, Ya'ir assumes rule.

2758 **Ya'ir the Gil'adi** — 22 years (10:3). First year of his rule included in Tou'la's last year.

2779 **Yiftach the Gil'adi** — 6 years (12:7). He is called "the least" of the Judges. Yet his words too were spoken with Ru'ach Hakodesh (Vayikra Rabba end of 37; see ibid).

2785 **Ivtzan from Beis Lechem** — This is Bo'az (Babba Basra 91a). He married Rus in his old age. Judged 7 years (12.9).

2792 **Eilon the Zevuloni** — 10 years (12:11).

2802 **Avdon, the Pirasoni** — 8 years (12:14).

2810 **Shimshon, son of Mano'ach** — 20 years (16:31). Was the head of his generation's Sages (Rosh Hashana 25b). His Court was considered equal to the Court of Aharon (Yerushalmi end of Perek 2 of Rosh Hashana). "He judged Yisrael like their Father in Heaven" (Sotta 10a). The Shechina rang before him like a bell (Yalkut Shimoni Shoftim 69). He was lame in both legs (ibid).

2830 **Eli, the Kohen Gadol** — ruled 40 years (Shmuel Alef 4:18). He received the Torah from the Elders (of the Court of Shimshon) and from Pinchas (Rambam, Yad Hachazaka). On the very day of his appointment as Kohen Gadol, Chana came to Shiloh where she prayed ("Seder Olam" 13). Within that year Shmuel was born. On the day that Eli died (2870) Mishkan Shilo came to an end (Zevachim 118b).

2871 **The Prophet Shmuel** — The last of the Judges. The prophets received the Mesora from the Judges (Avos De R' Nassan 1:3). His father Elkana was also a prophet. (Seder Olam 2). "There was none like him in Elkana's generation." (Bamidbar Rabba 10:5) His mother Chana was one of the 7 prophetesses mentioned in T'nach (Megilla 14a).

The Mishkan in Nov — At this time they brought the Mishkan to Nov. The Holy Aron (Ark) still remained in Kiryas Ye'arim for 20 years, yet the Bnei Yisrael kept bringing their offerings to Nov ("Seder Olam" 13). In Nov it stood 13 years ("Seder Olam"). Bamos were again permitted (Zevachim 14 Mishna 1). The prophet Shmuel received the Mesora from "Eli and his Court" (Rambam, Hakdama LeYad Hachazaka), and he ruled Yisrael all his life (Shmuel Alef 7:15) (even during Eli Hakohen's lifetime (Radak Shoftim 17). He was called "the master of all prophets." (Midrash Shocher Tov 4:4). It was he who anointed Shaul to be King, and afterwards David, his successor. He died in 2883, at age 52 (Taanis 5b).[1]

THE KINGS

2881 **Sha'ul is anointed** — In the 10th year of Shmuel's Rule (Temura 14b), when Bnei Yisrael demanded a king (Shmuel Alef 10:24). — "For there is none like him in the whole nation"

---

1 Shmuel was 39 years old when Eli died; for 10 years he then ruled alone, one year he shared the rule with Sha'ul (who even though King continued following his advice) and 2 more years while Shaul ruled (Zevachim 118b). Hence 52 years.

(ibid). He was from the Tribe of Binyamin (see commentary of Ramban Bereishis 49:10, on why his kingdom preceded that of the House of David). However, his kingdom was not established firmly in that 1st year. The people did not respect Shaul, and did not bring him their tribute (Shmuel Alef 7:15).

2882 **Beginning of Kingship** — When they reinstituted the Monarchy in Gilgal they made Sha'ul King before Hashem (Shmuel Alef 11:15). Concerning that time the verse says (ibid 13:1): "Sha'ul was one year into his kingship, and he ruled 2 more years over Yisrael," a firmly established kingship from then and onward (Beur HaGra LeSeder Olam 13).[1] When Sha'ul remissed in the war with Amalek, Shmuel departed from him, and David was anointed King (2883).

King Sha'ul died in 2884, bringing about the end of the Mishkan in Nov.

King David — David ben Yishay from Beis Lechem was 30 years old upon becoming King. (He was born in the days of Eli). He received the Mesora from "Shmuel and his Court" (Rambam, Hakdama leYad Hachazaka). He was head of the Sanhedrin, referred to as "The Court of David" (Moed Kattan 16b; Avoda Zara 36b).

The beginning of his kingship was in Chevron for 7½ years while **Ish Boshes, son of Sha'ul,** ruled for 2 years over all of Yisrael except for the Tribe of Yehuda, who followed David (Shmuel Beis 2:10). Thus the Kingdom of Yisrael was without a king for 5½ years ("Seder Olam 13), until David was anointed King over all of Yisrael (Shmuel Beis 5:3) in Yerushalayim.

The Mishkan of Giv'on — When Nov was destroyed they brought the Mishkan to Giv'on ("a metropolis of the whole

---

1   Although so many things happened during those three years of Shaul's reign (hence there were those who wanted to interpret the above verse differently), nevertheless, the general account of years from the Exodus of Mitzrayim until the Construction of the Beis HaMikdash corresponds with the tally in the verses (Melachim Alef 6:1), which is 480 years. Hence, plain interpretation of the verse confirms the count of 3 years.

land" — Yehoshua 12 and Sefer "Tzemach David" 889; "Seder Olam" 13). The Holy Ark was still missing and the Bamos were still permitted. The Mishkan stood in Giv'on (Zevachim 112) for 44 years (40 of David, and 4 of Shlomo) until the start of the Beis HaMikdash (Zevachim 118b).

2892   **In Yerushalayim** — David ruled over all of Yisrael (Shmuel Beis 5:3) for 33 years (Melachim Alef 2:11). He vested Yerushalayim with perpetual holiness, as required by the Law pertaining to Yerushalayim, the Holy City. He bought the granary from Aravna the Yevussi, and built there a Mizbe'ach for Hashem, etc. (Shmuel Beis 24). In his last year, David set up, consecrated and prepared Hashem's Dwelling in Yerushalayim (Divrei Hayamim 2:25).[2] He reigned 40 years (ibid).

Achiyah the Shiloni received the Mesora from David and his Court. Eliyahu received it from Achiyah. Elisha from Eliyahu, Zecharya from Elisha. Zecharya transmitted it to Hoshe'a, Amos received it from Hoshea, Yeshayahu from Amos, Micha from Yeshayahu, Yo'el from Micha, Nachum received it from Yo'el. Then came Nachum, Chabakuk, Tzefanya, Yirmiyahu, Baruch ben Neriya (all of them prophets), each receiving the Mesora directly from the one who preceded him, down to Ezra who received it from Baruch. Ezra and his Court were called "Anshei Kneses Hagdola" ("the Men of the Great Assembly"); from them the Tannai'm received the Mesora (Rambam, Hakdama Leyad Hachazaka). All these men are part of the *Shalsheles Hakabala* (Chain of Mesora), who received the Oral Tora directly, one man from the other, from Moshe until Rav Ashi.

2   There is a generally known Mesora that the spot on which David and Shlomo built the Mizbe'ach in Goren Aravna is the very spot on which Avraham had built his Mizbe'ach and bound Yitzchak for the Akeyda. It is the same spot upon which No'ach (coming out of the Teyva) brought his offerings, as well as Kayin and Hevel each bringing his offering. Adam too, brought there his Korban, upon being created and from this very spot he was created. Said the Sages: "Adam was created from the very spot of his atonement" (Rambam Hilchos Beis Habechira 2:2).

2924 **King Shlomo** — Ascended the throne of his father David (Melachim Alef 2:12) at the age of 12. [For since Shlomo was born (Shmuel Beis 12:24), "It was after 2 years (ibid 13:23) — and Avshalom fled for 3 years" (13:38) — makes it 5. "Avshalom lived in Yerushalayim 2 years" (14:28) — makes it 7. "There was a famine in the days of David for 3 years" (ibid 21:1) — makes it 10. "They wandered throughout the Land, and came at the end of 9 months and 20 days to Yerushalayim" (ibid 24:8) — makes it 11. In his last year (Shlomo's 12th), David set up the Mishmaros (the Shifts for the weeks' Service) and prepared everything for the construction of the Beis HaMikdash (Divrei Hayamim Alef 26:31). Hence, Shlomo was 12 years old when David died ("Seder Olam" 14)].

2928 **Construction of the Beis Hamikdash** — "In the 480th year after the Bnei Yisrael left the land of Mitzrayim" (Melachim Alef 6:1), in the fourth year of his reign (ibid), King Shlomo started to build Hashem's House on the Mount of Moriya (Rambam Hilchos Beis Habechira 1:2). He built it for $7\frac{1}{2}$ years (Passuk 35). As soon as they came "to the possession" (i.e. the Beis HaMikdash), Hashem said: "This is My resting place forever; here I shall dwell, for I have desired this place" (Tehillim 132:14). Henceforth the Bamos, as well as any other places upon which offerings were brought, were forbidden; the Mishkan of Giv'on was stored away. "And there can no longer be a House of Hashem only in Yerushalayim — forever" (Zevachim 112b; Rambam, Beis Habechira 1:3). Shlomo was the head of the Sanhedrin. ("The court of Shlomo" [Makkos 23b and others). He reigned 40 years over all of Yisrael and died in 2964.

2964 **Rechav'am, son of Shlomo** — Discarded the advice of the Elders, and followed the counsel of the young (Melachim 12:8). Bnei Yisrael rebelled against the Davidic Dynasty (Passuk 19), and crowned Yerov'am ben Nevat, from the Tribe of Ephraim, over all of Yisrael. Only the House of Yehuda and the Tribe of Binyamin followed Rechav'am in Yerushalayim. At the time the Kingdom was split, with Yerov'am ruling in the city of Sh'chem.[3]

3   Concerning the years of both the kings of Yehuda and the kings of Yisrael there is much confusion and questioning. The Tzemach David (a disciple of the Maharal) endeavored to explain the rules of the calculations upon which the counting of their years is based. We follow his rules, namely:

1)   Generally, only the full years of the kings of Yehuda are counted, whereas by the kings of Yisrael even the incomplete years are also counted ("Tzemach David" 91 Fourth Millennia).

2)   In general, the years of the kings of Yisrael are counted according to the years of the kings of Yehuda. Thus, if a king of Yisrael began his reign near the end of Yehuda's king's first year, Yehuda's king's second year was counted as his second year as well.

3)   Sometimes even fragmentary years are counted. For instance, the last year of the reigning king who died is also counted as the first year of the king who succeeded him in that very same year (see "Tzemach David" 964 Fourth Millennia 167).

4)   Furthermore, one day of the year may be counted as a full year.

KINGDOM OF YEHUDA

KINGDOM OF YISRAEL

Reigned

2964 Rechav'am   17
Reigned 17 years in Yerushalayim
(Melachim Alef 14:21).

2981 Aviyam (Aviya), his son   3
Reigned 3 incomplete years (ibid
15.2).

2983 Assa, his son   41
Reigned 41 years (ibid 15:10).
He did what was right in Hashem's eyes, like David, his ancestor (Passuk 10).

22 **2964 Yerov'am**
Son of Nevat, of the Tribe of
Ephraim. Reigned 22 years (Melachim Alef 11:23) in Sh'chem.
Placed golden calves in Beis El
and Dan (ibid 12:29). Sinned,
and made the people sin. His
reign began a little earlier than
Rechavam's (Sefer "Tzemach David 981).

2 **2985 Nadav,** his son
Reigned 2 incomplete years (ibid
15:25).

24 **2986 Ba'sha**
Son of Achiya, of the Tribe of
Yisaschar. Reigned 24 years. (ibid
15:33).

THE FOURTH MILLENNIUM

2 **3009 Eyla,** his son
Reigned 2 incomplete years (ibid
16:8).

3010 Zimri, his slave
Murdered all of Eyla's household and reigned in Tirza 7 days
only (16:15).

12 **3010 Omri**
The chief of staff, of the Tribe
of Ephraim. For 5 years, half of
the nation followed Tivni ben
Ginas, while the other half followed Omri (ibid Passuk 21).
In 3014 Omri ruled over the
whole Kingdom. He built the city
of Shomron, on the mountain
(16:24). He reigned 12 years
(16:23).

Reigned

22 3021 **Ach'av,** his son

Reigned in Shomron. Was more wicked than all his predecessors (16:30). He reigned for 22 years (16:29). The prophet Eliyahu prophesied in his time, and during the second year of his successor, King Achazyahu, he went up in a storm to Shamayim (the heavens) ("Seder Olam" 17; Melachim Beis 2).

3024 **Yehoshafat,** his son 25

Reigned 25 years in Yerushalayim (Melachim Beis 22:42). Followed completely in the ways of his father, Asa.

2 3041 **Achazyahu,** his son

Ruled for 2 incomplete years (12:52).

12 3043 **Yehoram**

His brother, in Shomron. Ruled 12 years (Melachim Beis 3:1). Elisha, son of Shafat prophesied in his time.

3047 **Yehoram,** his son 8

Reigned 2 years during his father's lifetime ("Seder Olam" 17). Altogether he reigned 8 years in Yerushalayim (Melachim Beis 8:7).

3055 **Achazyahu,** his son 1

Ruled 1 year (8:26).

28 3055 **Yehu**

Son of Nimshi, of the Tribe of Menashe. Murdered Yehoram, son of Ach'av, without leaving a survivor from the whole family. He ruled 28 years (Melachim Beis 10:36).

3056 **Asalya** 6

Daughter of Ach'av, mother of Achazya, reigned 6 years after the death of her son.

3061 **Yo'ash** 40

Son of Achazyahu. Ruled 40 years. He proclaimed himself a deity (Divrei Hayamim Beis 24:17). He made repairs of the Mikdash (the first since King Shlomo built it 155 years earlier).

61

Reigned

3100 **Amatzya,** his son 29
Ruled 1 year during his father's lifetime (Beur HaGra "Seder Olam" 19). Altogether he ruled 29 years (see Rashi Melachim Beis 14:17).

3115 **Uziyahu,** (Azarya) his son 52
Reigned 52 years, 15 of these during his father's lifetime (Rashi Melachim Beis 15:8). During his reign Yeshayahu ben Amotz began to prophesy (Yeshaya 1:1). He ruled, confined by Tzoraas, from 3142 until the day of his death (Seder Olam 19; Rashi Melachim Beis 15:18).

3167 **Yo'sam,** his son 16
Ruled 16 years (Passuk 33).

3183 **Achaz** 16
Son of Yo'sam. Ruled 16 years (16:2).

17 3083 **Yeho'achaz,** his son
Reigned 17 incomplete years (Melachim Beis 13:1).

16 3098 **Yeho'ash,** his son
Reigned 16 years (Melachim Beis 13:10).

41 3113 **Yerov'am,** his son
Reigned 3 years during his father's lifetime (Rashi 15:8). Altogether he ruled 41 years (Melachim Beis 14:23).

½ 3153 **Zecharyahu,** his son
Reigned 6 months (Melachim Beis 15:8).

3154 **Shalum**
Son of Yavesh. Ruled 1 month (ibid Passuk 13).

10 3154 **Menachem**
Son of Gadi. Ruled 10 years (Passuk 17).

2 3164 **P'kachya,** his son
Ruled 2 years (Passuk 23).

20 3166 **Pekach**
Son of Remalyahu. Reigned 20 years (Passuk 27). Towards the end of his rule (3187) Tiglas Pil'eser, King of Ashur came and took Iyon and Avel ... all the Portion of Naftali, and exiled the residents to Ashur (Melachim

Reigned

Beis 15:29). This was the first exile of Yisrael, comprising the Tribes of Zevulun, Naftali and Dan (Beur HaGra "Seder Olam" 22).

18 3187 **Hoshe'a**

Son of Eyla, of the Tribe of Re'uven, the last of Yisrael's kings. He killed Pe'kach and ruled in his place (Passuk 30) for 18 years. In the year 3195 Shalmanaser, King of Ashur, came and exiled the Tribes of Gad, Re'uven and half the Tribe of Menashe, — this being the second exile ("Seder Olam" 22 and Rashi Melachim Beis 17:1).

3199 **Chizkiyahu,** his son 29

Reigned 29 years (Melachim Beis 40:2). "There was none like him among all the kings of Yehuda" (18:5).

3205 **Exile of the Ten Tribes**

In the 9th year of Hoshea's revolt, the king of Ashur captured Shomron, and the Bnei Yisrael were exiled a third time. This marked the completion of the exile for all the Ten Tribes. — Yisrael being banished from its land into Ashur, "until this very day" (Melachim Beis 17:27).

3228 **Menashe,** his son 55

Reigned 55 years (21:1). Since he humbled himself before the Almighty (Divrei Hayamim Beis 33:12), Hashem added years to his life. Thus he reigned longer than any king, either in Yehuda or in Yisrael.

The sum of the reigning years of all the Kings of Yisrael, including those of Shaul, David and Shlomo, who ruled before the split of the Kingdom, amounts to 333. However, by subtracting from these the fragmentary years of reign, or those in which a son ruled during his father's lifetime, we find that from the beginning of the Kingship (2882) until the final exile of the Ten Tribes (3205) only about 323 years passed.

Reigned

3283 **Ammon,** his son   2
Ruled 2 years (29:19).

3285 **Yoshiyahu,** his son   31
Ruled 31 years (22:1). During
his reign, Yirmiyahu, son of Chilkiyahu, began prophesying.

3316 **Yehoyachaz,** his son
Reigned 3 months.

3316 **Yehoyakim**   11
Son of Yoshiyahu reigned 11
years (23:36). In the fourth year
of his reign (3320) Nevuchadnezar, King of Bavel came up, took
part of the vessels of the Beis Ha-
Mikdash and youths of the Royal
Family and brought them to Bavel (Daniel 1), making this the
first Exile of Yehuda. Nevuchadnezar returned in 3327, and banished Yehoyakim to Bavel. He
died however during the journey.

3327 **Yehoyachin,** (Yechon-
       ya), his son
Ruled 3 months. Nevuchadnezar
then exiled him to Bavel — the
second Exile of Yehuda. There
were ten thousand men with him,
among them the Chorosh and the
Masger, etc. (24:16).

3327 **Tzidkiyahu**   11
Son of Yoshiyahu. Ruled 11 years
(24:18), marking the end of the
era of the Kings.

3338 **Churban of the First Beis
Hamikdash,** which stood for 410

years (Yomma 9; Erechin 12b; Rashi ibid; "Seder Olam" 11 Zevachim 118 b and ibid Rashi). — The numerical value of the word "**Shalach**" from the verse "Send them away from before Me" (Yirmiyahu 15:1) indicates the year 338 of the 4th millennium.

(Adding up the years of all the kings of Yehuda, beginning with the fourth year of Shlomo's reign until the 11th year of Tzidkiyahu — omitting the fragmentary years in which sons ruled during their father's reign — we come to the year 3338).

On the 10th day of Teves, in the 9th year of Tzidkiyahu, Yerushalayim came under siege (Melachim Beis 24:1 and 2). In Nissan (less than 3 months later) starts the 10th year of Tzidkiyahu (as Yisrael's kings count their reign from the month of Nissan [Rosh Hashana 1:1]), adding 12 more months. The following Nissan marked the beginning of the 11th year of the King's reign. Until the 9th of Av (the fifth month) we have 4 more months. Thus from the day when the siege was laid (in the 10th month) until the Churban (the 5th month) it is only 19 months, a little over a year and a half; yet in the count of the calendar years it is figured as 3.[4]

20 kings reigned over Yehuda and 19 in Yisrael, in addition to Sha'ul, David and Shlomo who reigned over both Yehuda and Yisrael at the same time. Altogether, the Kings ruled for 456 years (2882—3338).

---

4   See in "Tzemach David" (year 100 of the fourth millennia) that even Ra'ved Halevi, Re'dak, Ral'bag and R' Yitzhak Abbarbanel never intended to dispute the count of years from Creation as accepted till this very day. "For we do not find even one of them ever to have expressed himself even with the slightest remark as trying to add or subtract from the prevailing Count of the years since Creation."

In the 11th year of Tzidkiyahu [5] the Beis Hamikdash was destroyed and Yehuda went into its third and last exile — to Bavel. Then the Land rested its Sabbaticals through all the years of desolation — "while you were in the land of your enemy" (Vayikra 26:34).

5   This is the 338th year ("Sh'lach") of the fourth millennia. Many more events occurred in years ending with the number 8. As one of the French Chachamim stated: 38 (2238) they descended to Mitzrayim, 48 for the Exodus (2448). 88 they entered the Land (2488), 338 was the Churban (3338) (Sefer Yuchsin 18). Furthermore, we have the birth of Avraham 1948, of Sara in 1958, Yitzchak 2048, Yaakov 2108, Bris bein Habe'sarim 2018, birth of Moshe 2408. Also, 28 for the construction of the First Beis Hamikdash (2928). 08 on the construction of the Second Beis Hamikdash (3408). And 28, the second Churban (3828). — All ending with 8.

THE BABYLONIAN EXILE

The beginning of the Exile of Bavel has 2 counts:

1. The *Exile of Yehuda* — 3320, when Judeans were exiled to Bavel for the first time, in the days of King Yehoyakim.

2. The *Ruins of Yerushalayim* — 3338, when the Beis Ha-Mikdash in Yerushalayim was destroyed.

Completion of 70 years (Daniel 9:2) for both "the Exile of Yehuda to Bavel" (Yirmiyahu 29:10) and "the Ruins of Yeru-shalayim," had been decreed upon them to atone for the 70 Shemita and Yovel-years [1] during which the Land did not rest "while you lived there."

3364 **Death of Nevuchadnezar** — the destroyer. Ruled 45 years.

Evvil Merodach — his son, rules after him 23 years.

3387 **Belshatzar** — his son, rules after him for 3 incomplete years ("Seder Olam" 29).

---

1 The years they had not fully rested are counted as follows: during the 8 years of serfdom to Kushan Rish'asayim — 1 Shemita. During 18 of Eglon, King of Mo'av — 3 Shemitos. 20 of Sisra — 3 Shemitos and 1 Yovel. During 7 years of serfdom to Midyan — 1 Shemita. 47 years of the Judges Avimelech, Tola and Ya'ir — 6 Shemitos. Serfdom of Ammon — 3 Shemitos. 40 of the Plishtim (in the days of Iftzan, Eylon, Avdon and Shim-shon) — 6 Shemitos, 1 Yovel. 22 years of Yerovam ben Nevat — 3 Shemitos. 26 of Nadav and Ba'asha — 4 Shemitos, 1 Yovel. 12 of Omri — 1 Shemito. 22 of Ach'av — 3 Shemitos. 14 of Achazyahu and Yehoram — 2 Shemitos, 1 Yovel. 28 of Yehu — 4 Shemitos. 17 of Yehoyachaz — 2 Shemitos. 16 years of Yeho'ash — 2 Shemitos, 1 Yovel. 41 of Yerov'am — 6 Shemitos, 1 Yovel. 10 years of Menachem ben Gadi — 1 Shemita. 20 of Pekach ben Remalyahu — 3 Shemitos. 18 of Hoshe'a ben Eyla — 3 She-mitos, 1 Yovel. During the years of Menashe they sinned only for 22 years, hence 3 Shemitos. 11 of Yehoyakim — 1 Shemita. 11 of Tzidkiyahu — 2 Shemitos. Thus we have 63 Shemitos and 7 Yovlos in which the Land did not rest its Sabbaticals (Rashi Yechezkel 4:5; also based on the count of the Gra of Vilna).

3389   **Belshatzar is killed** — on the night of Bavel's downfall, upon completion of 70 years of the Empire (Nevuchadnezar 45, Evil Merodach 23, Belshatzar 2 (Megilla 11b).

      Daryavesh the Mede — captures the kingdom.

THE RETURN TO ZION

The Empire of Persia — ruled Judea for 52 years.

3390 **King Koresh** — His Royal Decree allows the ascent of the exiles with Zerubavel ben Shaltiel to Yerushalayim — after 70 years from the first exile of Judea in the days of Yehoyakim (3320).

Foundations laid for Second Beis HaMikdash — but "the foes of Yehuda and Binyamin" disrupted the work. (As 18 years were still missing from the completion of 70 years from the Churban of Yerushalayim).

Artachshasto — his son, rules after him for half a year. He is Darius the Second, also called Kambisi (Rashi Daniel 11:2).

3393 **King Achashverosh** — ruled 14 years.

Purim — The story of Mordechai and Esther takes place in that period, between the Return to Zion and Construction of the Second Beis Hamikdash.

"In the 3d year of his reign Achashverosh made a drinking feast etc."

In the 7th year of his reign "Esther was taken to King Achashverosh etc."

In the 12th year, on the 13th of Nissan, Haman issued the edict "to wipe out and slay etc."

On the 13th, 14th and 15th of Nissan they fasted in Shushan.

On the 16th day of Nissan Haman is hanged.

On the 23d of Sivan the edicts of Mordechai were issued.

13 days in Adar — "It was turned around etc. and the Yehudim slew all their enemies, etc."

In the 13th year Esther wrote the order "to fulfill this Letter of Purim," etc.

In the 14th year "Achashverosh levied a tax etc.", and that same year he died.

3407 **Daryavesh, the Second** ("The Great") — In the second year of his reign (3408), (it being 70 years since the Churban) he reinstates Koresh's decree allowing the Beis HaMikdash to be built in Yerushalayim (Ezra 6).

THE SECOND BEIS HAMIKDASH

3408 **Construction of the Second Beis Hamikdash** — in the 18th year of the Persian Empire (3 years of Koresh and Artachshasta, 14 of Achashverosh and 1 of Daryavesh) upon completion of the 70 years from the Churban Yerushalayim (3338).

3412 **End of the Construction.**

3413 **The Aliyah of Ezra, the Scribe.**
Anshei Kneses Hagdola (Men of the Great Assembly).

3442 **"Exile of Greece"** — (180 years) under Greek rule.
Alexander of Macedonia vanquishes many kingdoms including Eylom, the capital of Persia, thereby putting an end to the Persian Empire which lasted 52 years (3390—3442) 18 years before the Second Beis HaMikdash, and 34 years during its existence (Avoda Zarra 9a). However, the King of Persia did not fall into the hands of Greece until the year 3448.

3448 **Death of Ezra and Nechemya** — With their demise prophecy in Yisrael comes to an end (Hakuzari, Maamar 3, 39a). That same year marks the beginning of the Greek Empire.
"Minyan Shtaros," a new yearly count (starting from 1) for legal documents, started then (Tzemach David, Fourth Millennia 448).

3448 **Era of the Tannaim** — Shimon the Righteous, Kohen Gadol, is the first Tanna (Avos 1:2).

3454 **Alexander Slain** — His empire splits up into four parts (Daniel 11:3).
Under Ptolomeus (The Southern Kings) — Bnei Yisrael come under the rule of the Egyptian kings Talmai (Ptolomeus).
Antignos — from the city of Socho, received the Mesora from Shimon Hatzaddik (Avos 1:3).

The Tzaddokim and Beysusim — (Peirush HaRambam ibid) start in his time.

Yosi ben Yo'ezer and Yosi ben Yochanan — received the Mesora from Antignos (Avos 1:3). Beginning of the Zugos (pairs) — the first being the Nassi; the second, the Av Beis Din (Head of the Court).

3515   **Targum Hashiv'im** ("Septuaginta") — King Talmai forces the Sages to translate the Torah into Greek (Megilla 9a).
Rule of the Northern Kings — Antiochus, the Syrian.
Yehoshu'a ben Prachya and Nitay the Arbeyli (Avos 1:6) — The second Zug (pair), — they received the Torah from Yossi ben Yo'ezer and Yossi ben Yochanan.

3616   **The Decree of Conversion** — Greeks and Jewish Hellenists decreed forced conversions.

3622   **Kingdom of the Chashmonaim** (lasted 103 years) — They seized the reign from Greece.
The Miracle of Chanuka — In the same year. (Approximately the middle of the era of the Second Mikdash). The rulers were successively: Yehuda, Jonasan and Shimon, all sons of Matisyahu. (Of the 420 years of the Second Mikdash we lived only 103 years in complete independence, under the Dynasty of the Chashmonaim).

3642   **Yochanan Hurkinus** — Son of Shimon, becomes king. Served 80 years as Kohen Gadol (Avos 2:5; see Ramban Bereishis 49:10).

3648   **Empire of Rome** — Starts expanding towards Eretz Yisrael (Avoda Zarra 9b).
Aristoblus, son of Hurkinus — takes the reign.
Alexander Yanai, his brother — succeeds him.
Yehuda ben Tabai and Shimon ben Shatach — the Third Zug, received the Torah from the Second Zug.

3688   **Queen Alexandra Shelomis** — wife of Yanai (also called the Queen of Zion [Shabbos 16b]). During her time the Perushim held the rule.

Hurkinus and Aristoblus — her sons, wage war against each other.

3700 **The Romans in the Land** — Hurkinus and Aristoblus bring Pompeus, the Roman army commander, into Yerushalayim.

Hurkinus — is king.

Antignos — son of Aristoblus, rules after him.

Shemayah and Avtallion — The Fourth Zug, received the Mesora from the Third Zug (Avos 1:10). Their leadership did not last long.

3724 **Kingdom of the House of Herodes** (103 years)

Herodes — son of Antipator the Edomite, slave of the Royal House of the Chashmonaim, becomes king (Babba Basra 3b). He kills the Sages.

3728 **Hillel** (from the seed of the House of David) **and Shammai** — the last Zug, received the Mesora from the Fourth Zug. The Nessi'us returns to the House of David.

3742 **Herodus Rebuilds** the Beis Hamikdash in Yerushalayim with greater splendor than the one built by King Shlomo (Sukka 51b).

3758 **Arkilus** — son of Herodus becomes king.

3768 **Rabban Shimmon ben Hillel** — Nassi (near the end of Arkilus' reign). Received the Mesora from his father; is first to be titled "Rabban."

Herodus Antipator — Son of Herodus rules partly.

Rabban Gamliel ben Shimmon — is Nassi. Called Rabban Gamliel "Hazakeyn" ("the old").

The First Roman Procurators.

3788 **Exile of the Sanhedrin** (Avoda Zarra 9b). Rabban Yochanan ben Zakkay, Head of the Yeshiva ("Tzemach David" 810). He received the Mesora from Hillel Hazakein (Babba Basra 134a).

Agrippas, son of Aristoblus — becomes King by assignment of Rome, until 3804.

3804 **The Last Roman Procurators** — while Agrippas son of Agrippas still ruled part of the land.

Rabban Shimmon ben Gamliel — the Nassi. Was slain before the Churban.

3828 **Churban of the Second Beis Hamikdash** — which stood 420 years (Erechin 12b). Under Persia 34, Greece 180, Chashmonaim 103, House of Herodus 103 — together 420 years (Avoda Zarra 9a).

Exile of Edom — Until this very day.

---

1 Hence from the construction of the First Beis HaMikdash (2928) until the Churban of the Second Beis HaMikdash (3829) we have exactly 900 years, as follows: 410 of the First Mikdash, 70 years Exile of Bavel, and 420 of the Second Beis HaMikdash.

THE COUNT FROM CREATION

THE current year 5748 from Creation, Being 1920 years from the Churban of the Second Beis HaMikdash (3828), (even though for quite a long time one has been hearing the customary remark: "We are already 2000 years in Galus") is the date all Bnei Yisrael are counting. It is the accepted traditional count (Mesora) from which one simply cannot budge. The present year is 5748 from Creation, because the year before it was 5747. How do we know that last year was 5747? Because the year before that was 5746 etc, etc. No Mesora (tradition) is stronger than this; no proof more solid. For ever since Mitzrayim (recorded in the Torah as the year 2448) Bnei Yisrael all over were ordered and uninterruptedly counted their months and years. They blew the Shofar on the first of the seventh month (Rosh Hashana), and they would bring the Offerings of the Day as prescribed. It just is absolutely unthinkable to even try to imagine that all of Yisrael together (at one time or another) would have willfully or by mistake forgotten to add one year to the calendar, from the day of Rosh Hashana and onward.

Considering even the "Common Era Count" of the years, we also come to about 5748, although it is impossible to exactly match the 2 counts. Ancient world history sets the time of the Churban at the year 70 after the beginning of their calendar count. (Some general historians say 69, and today many accept the year 68). Hence even according to this count, 1918 years have passed since the Destruction. And since the year of the Churban itself is not included in the 420 year count of the Second Beis HaMikdash (Rashi Erechin 12b; Dibur Hamatchil 420, and Tossafos Avoda Zarra 9b) it follows that it really was destroyed in its 421st year, and the year 3829 after Creation is the 70th of the Common Count. Adding 1918 years to 3829 we come to 5747, a difference of one year only, surely to be considered as confirming the traditional Jewish Count.

The count of the years of the Shemitos and Yovelos further proves our Count of the years to be correct. For ever since entering the Land (in 2488) followed by 7 years of conquest and the subsequent 7 years in which they divided it, the counting of the 7 year Shemita-cycle and the the 50th year (Yovel) *was never* interrupted. (See all in Rambam Laws of Shemita and Yovel Perek 10). It simply could not have been interrupted because the Beis-Din Hagadol (Supreme Court) in Yerushalayim was enjoined by a Mitzvas Asey (positive command) in the Torah to make that count (Vayikra 25:8 and Rambam ibid 10). They thus counted uninterruptedly the 7 successive years of Shemita 7 times to sanctify afterwards the 50th year as commanded. — In Bavel too they counted and voluntarily observed the Shemitos. Even after the destruction of the Second Beis HaMikdash the count of Shmita-years (which had began again with the Aliya (ascent) of Ezra in the "Second Entry" into the Land) continued (Rambam ibid 10:3). For by injunction of our Sages — the laws of Shemita of the land and Shemitas K'safim (waving of money-debts) remained obligatory in Eretz Yisrael, while Shemitas K'safim is obligatory also in exile. All of which depends entirely on the exact, continuous count of the 7-year Shemitos cycle. (Now however without counting the Yovel year).

And who in the whole world and among all the nations can even try to compare their countings and their continuity with those of Bnei Yisrael, the one nation unique on earth?

THE "COMMON ERA" COUNT

TODAY the gentiles too count their years uninterruptedly — but this has not always been so. Contrary to general belief, their count is altogether based on extremely precarious foundations. The Common Era count of years was neither instituted nor preserved with the same strictness and uncompromising preciseness as was our count which has been handed down from one generation to the next one with absolute truthfulness and honesty without compromise or deviation whatsoever. For all the counts and dates of the Catholics (before the so-called Common Era and afterwards) were invented, made and set up only at a *much later date*. While things happened they had yet no common count altogether, and the dates of their events were eventually established *retroactively,* at a much later period. They now just follow the customary count of their ancestors which started in a most questionable manner. Their own encyclopaedias attest to the fact that their count is based on no truthful, concrete factual, basis whatsoever.

"Know what to answer the agnostic," still is our Sages' adage. Prevalent among the masses, however, is the naivete with which they accept the supposedly unquestionable prevailing count (of years) adopted by "the whole world," as if indeed it did not beg inquiry. To ward off the confusion, it is necessary to clarify here the problem — albeit in great brevity. We specifically cite from their own sources in order to prove the unreability of their so called "historical" dates . . .

In ancient times each nation counted its years differently, according to the reign of its respective king or Caesars. However, no continuous count existed, and therefore they even had no definite set date for their birth as a nation. What's more, for hundreds of years the Roman empire only chronicled "the books of the year," but they had no continuous count of years at all. Only at a much later date did they try to establish retroactively the date of the beginning of the Roman Kingdom.

Even concerning the cycle and length of the seasons they had different theories and various calculations at different times. Moreover, in the beginning the Romans also accepted a Lunar Year of 355 days, figured after the months of the moon. The Solar Year of 365¼ days was instituted only shortly before the destruction of the Second Beis HaMikdash (Encyclopaedia Britannica 1965, Vol. 3 page 615). They therefore were forced from time to time to add, change and correct the calendar of their years. Thus the Roman Emperor Julian established a year at 445 days (ibid), and the Emperor August followed him with further change in the yearly cycle (ibid). As late as in the 16th century Gregory the Emperor followed with his calendar reform of the C.E. count.

The matter of the *beginning* of the yearly cycle itself was also a subject of constant confusion. And this custom of correcting and changing dates continued up to the modern era. There were some who first established the New Year from December 25, others from January 1st, others from March 25. Some had set it on the day of their Easter (Britannica 1965, Vol. 5). Their Easter itself was celebrated according to Pesach as counted by the Bnei Yisrael. However, at the Council of Necea, Turkey (in the year they later called 325 ACE), the clergy finally decided on a different way. They established a fixed date for Easter, to demonstrate their complete independence from the Torah of Bnei Yisrael. But even from that Council itself no written account or record whatsoever exists (ibid, Vol. 6 page 633).

The gentiles presently count 1988 years of the C.E. without even realizing that the beginnings of the count remain clouded in a shroud of enigma and uncertainty. For contrary to common belief it was not by decree of a king, nor at a gathering of their heads — the bishops — that a statute was officially established to retroactively begin counting the years from the birth of the Notzri. Apparently it was merely the initiative of *one individual only,* and in later centuries the idea spread and eventually became generally accepted. During the rule of the Roman Empire all conquered European countries began counting their years according to the reign of the Roman Emperors only, not having any other count whatsoever. When the last Western Roman emperor died (523 C.E.) they no longer had one ruler by whom to commonly count their years. This period (corresponding to the middle of the Rabbanon Savarai era, in Bavel) was later publicized by the gentiles as having been the time during which a certain Roman priest by the name of Dionysius Exiguus lived, and being an expert mathematician and astronomer, he eventually filled the void. He is to have advocated that all Catholics in all lands commonly start to count their years specifically from the birth of the Notzri. *It was he* who is said to have somehow (all by himself) *discovered and established for them retroactively the exact day of the Notzri's birth.* And today the gentiles the world over simply follow his version.

However, Dionysius himself, the man who founded the Catholic Count and chronology (called the "Dionisian Era" or "Vulgar Era"), is also shrouded in obscurity and questionable evidence. There are those who say (Collier's Encyclopaedia) that he lived from 475—550 of the C.E. Even in the Encyclopaedia Britannica there are contradictory statements. In chapter 5, page 278 it states that he lived from 496—540, and in the same edition chapter 7, page 465 that he lived from 500—560. Even the plain fact of his introducing the count of years of the gentiles is also based on shaky and confusing sources. Some say (Encyclopaedia of Religion and Ethics, Edinburgh 1910, vol 3, page 91) that he started the count in the year (retroactively numbered) 525. Others (without proof) claim (ibid) that it was in 532. — Furthermore, the whole story of Dionysius himself was hidden in a shroud of obscurity for at least 225 years. The only source mentioning his existence is a document dated 748 (E. B. Edition II, vol. 8, page 285) (already halfway into the period of the Gaonim) discovered centuries later in British archives. On this single questionable source they all depend, even with regard to the mere acknowledgment of the existence of such a person.

The date which Dionysius had retroactively established for the Notzri drew much criticism. For its calculations were (by pure necessity) based on the vague unreliable counts of the Roman Emperors' reign.

It is argued by these critics that he erred by 4—7 years (E.B. Vol. 5, page 728). Nevertheless his calculation has been increasingly accepted universally, but only in the course of centuries. The pope in Rome accepted the date during his years, 955—972 of the C.E. In most European countries the Common Era counting was accepted by the 11th century. In most of Spain's provinces the Catholic calendar was not accepted until the 14th century and in the East European Greek Synod only in the 15th century (ibid E.B.).

The whole story of the Notzri himself (including the date of his birth and the lives of his disciples) was furthermore fixed and dated by the same Dionysius, even though he possessed *no historical source whatsoever* to verify his claim. For hundreds of years the Catholics had not even had one memo or record to attest to his birth or actions, or to the doings of his disciples and assistants (E.B. 1966, Vol. 12, page 1016). (The encyclopaedia goes on at great length to explain how the account of these events spread all over the world, even though they lack any reliable source for the whole story). Only hundreds of years afterwards did the clergy suddenly awaken to disclose writings containing "a new wealth of stories" concerning his life and deeds.

(How sharp is furthermore the pointed mockery of this idol-worship! For to this very day Catholics have not been able to offer even one factual ancient historical source of world history concerning the time of the Notzri's birth or some account of his life, except for what was recorded by our great Sages (Sanhedrin 43b; Sotta 47a, etc.). But of course, they disdained the reliable words of our Rabbis (transmitted directly from one Sage to another), rather placing their trust in a single individual who retroactively made up a story of his own, also shifting the event backwards by about 90 years).

Even though they later "revealed" and presented the events as if the dates and all these details had indeed been preserved and reliably transmitted to them (strangely, claiming even to know the supposed features and the image of the founder of their new faith whom they worship), no amount of publicity will ever be capable to deny the fact that all these dates and account are just pure human fabrications, purposely made up later. Even according to their claims, they had not started counting at the very beginning of the so called Common Era, as their religion was not yet established nor spread out in the world until a very long time after his death. Never ever did they count "the year one," "the year two," "the year hundred," or "the year two hundred," etc. The world never even counted the year 500, 523 or even 524, as there was no one yet in the world who counted that way — neither a people, nor a religion. And just as they did not count before his birth, so did they not count after him, — for no one had yet come up with such a count. They just had no constant, established calendar-count yet.

And on this retroactively structured story of a single individual (whose existence is hardly proven) rests the whole structure and credibility of the C.E. count.

MISCELLANEOUS

For the sake of simplification some additional brief charts follow.

THE YEARS OF THE MISHKAN

Before the Mishkan was set up, Bamos (private altars) were permitted anywhere, and the Avoda (Services) was performed by the firstborn males. With the erection of the Mishkan, Bamos were forbidden and the Avoda transferred to the Kohanim (Zevachim Perek 14 Mishna 1).

These were the places where Hashem's Mishkan stood in the midst of the Bnei Yisrael.

		stood
2449	**Bamidbar** The Mishkan ("Ohel Mo'ed") was first set up in the Midbar (wilderness) on the 1st day of Nissan. It stood in 32 different places, while Bnei Yisrael travelled 42 journeys in the desert. (Deduct the first 10 journeys, as only during the 11th was the Mishkan set up (Bamidbar 33). The Mishkan was erected on a high spot left for this purpose by the Annan (the Divine Cloud which leveled the terrain before them, lowering the elevations and elevating the low places). The same happened during all the Midbar-journeys of the Bnei Yisrael (Bamidbar Rabba 19:9).	39 years
2488	**Gilgal**	14 "
2503	**Shilo**	369 "

82

2871	**Nov**	13	"
2884	**Giv'on** (In Nov and Giv'on together 57 years)	44	" (40 during reign of David and 4 of Shlomo)
		479	"

2928 King Shlomo builds the Beis HaMikdash.

The **Mishkan** which had been set up yet by Moshe was then dimantled and hidden (its boards, clasps, bars, pillars and bases) in the deep caverns under the Heichal (Sotta 9a), never to be desecrated by human hands. It had stood 479 years. Adding to those the first year in the Midbar before it was set up, we arrive at the figure of 480 years from the time of the Exodus of Mitzrayim until the Mikdash was built (Melachim Alef 6:1).

THE SIX THOUSAND YEARS OF
THE WORLD'S EXISTENCE

"*TANNA* d'bei Eliyahu taught us (Avoda Zarra 9a): Six thousand years is the world's existence." The six millennia correspond to the six days of Creation. The seventh millennium will be the Shabbos of the world (Rashi ibid).

These 6000 years are furthermore divided into 3 periods of 2000 years each (Avoda Zarra 9a).

2 millennia of Tohu (confusion): comprising the twenty generations from Adam until Avraham.

2 millennia of Torah: from the time of "the souls which they made in Charan," when Avraham started to make Geyrim (he — the men, and Sara — the women) (year 2000 — Avoda Zarra 9a), until after the demise of Rabbeinu Hakadosh who wrote down the Mishnayos (3979).

2 millennia of Moshi'ach's Times: the present Exile of Edom during which Moshi'ach will come. (And because of our sins all these many centuries have meanwhile passed without his coming).

1	Adam — to observe the Mitzvos of the Bnei No'ach (gentiles)	
1948	Avraham	
2448	Mattan Torah (Torah is given) on the 6th of Sivan	
2449	The Mishkan	stood 479 years
2928	First Beis HaMikdash	410 years
3338	Exile into Bavel	70 years
3408	Second Beis HaMikdash	420 years (Erechin 12b)
3828	Exile of Edom	until this very day

1948	The Patriarchs	
2238	In Mitzrayim	210 years
2448	In the Desert	40 years
2488	Entering the Land	850 years
2516	The Z'keynim (Elders)	17 years
2533	Shoftim (Judges)	350 years
2882	Kings	456 years
2928	First Beis HaMikdash	410 years
3338	Exile to Bavel	70 years
3408	Second Beis HaMikdash	420 years
3828	Exile of Edom	until this very day

May the Redemption come speedily in our days.

THE CHAIN OF MESSORAH THROUGHOUT
THE AGES

Moshe — received the Torah from Hashem (2448).

Yehoshua — to whom Moshe transmitted the Torah (2488).

The Elders — in Eretz Yisrael.
They received the Torah from Yehoshua Bin Nun. Ruled for 17 years, 2516—2533.

Neviim (prophets) — in Eretz Yisrael. (After they entered the Land), except for Yechezkel and the last of Yirmiyahu's prophecies.
The prophets received the Torah from the Elders. Even though through the ages the Bnei Yisrael had "twice as many prophets as the men who left Mitzrayim," (Megilla 14a)[1] only 48 prophets and 7 prophetesses are mentioned by name in the T'nach (ibid) with Chagai, Zecharya and Malachi (he is Ezra) being the last of them (Yomma 9b). For only the prophecies applying to all generations

---

1   The verses of Torah themselves prove that there was an unacountable multitude of prophets among the Bnei Yisrael. As Moshe Rabbeinu so lovingly cried out: "Would that all of Hashem's People were prophets; that Hashem imbued them all with His Ru'ach HaKodesh." Like the 70 Elders who prophesied in the times of Moshe (ibid Passuk 25). — And whenever we find a prophet named after his father (Yeshayahu son of Amotz; Yirmiyahu, son of Chilkiyahu, and likewise), we know that he is a prophet, the son of a prophet (Megilla 15a). Yet his father is not counted among the 48. In Eliyahu's days prophecy embraced thousands and tens of thousands (Russ Rabba 1:2). We find the Bnei Nevi'yim (young prophets) from Yericho, 50 of whom approached Elisha (Melachim Beis 2:5), — "Who were all as great as Eliyahu, and equal to Elisha (Seder Olam Perek 21)." In the same vein we see Ovadya who said to Eliyahu (Melachim Alef 18:13): "Surely it was told to my Master what I did when Izebbel slew the prophets of Hashem and I hid 100 of Hashem's prophets — 50 in one cave

were recorded (Megilla 14a). — Any prophet whose place of origin is not mentioned by name, came from Yerushalayim — the "Gey Chizayon" (Valley of Vision) (Pessichta DeEicha Rabbasi 24).

In 3448 (one thousand years after the exodus from Mitzrayim) prophecy was conclusively withheld from Bnei Yisrael. They still enjoyed Divine Revelation through the Bas Kol (A voice from Heaven) (Megilla 14b). The prophets taught and transmitted the whole Torah to the Anshei Knesses Hagdola (Men of the Great Assembly).

Anshei Kneses Hagdola — Its inception was in Bavel but the Assembly continued mainly in Eretz Yisrael. The Chain of Mesora was in the hands of the Anshei Knesses Hagdola, the assembly of 120 men, some of whom were prophets (Rambam Hakdama LeYad Hachazaka). It is also called "Ezra and his Court." Upon Ezra's ascent from Bavel, the Assembly moved its functions to Eretz Yisrael.

The Anshei Knesses Hagdola "restored the crown (of Hashem) to its former glory" (Yomma 69b). They made "Syog" — a protective fence — to the Torah, and decreed ordinances for all generations to come. They edited and sealed the 24 Sefarim of the

and 50 in another etc." — We find Bnei Neviyim in their respective cities (Melachim Beis 2), even in Yericho, the most corrupt of all cities (ibid and Shir HaShirim Rabba 4:11). In the same way we find King Sha'ul who prophesied along with a whole chain of prophets descending from the Bama (Shmuel Alef 10).

There is further proof of countless prophets and prophetesses coming from all the Tribes of Bnei Yisrael (Sukka 27b).

However, the names of all these were not even mentioned, as only prophecies needed and pertaining to all generations were recorded; otherwise they were not written down (Megilla 14a).

Torah,[2] and formulated for us the prayers and blessings, benedictions of Kiddush (of Shabbos and Festivals), and the Havdalos etc. They transmitted the Torah to the Tannaim. Their leadership ended with the demise of Ezra in 3448.

The Tannaim — In Eretz Yisrael ("Tanna" in the Gemara means one who studies. "Tannu Rabbanon" means the same as "Shanu Rabbanon").

Shimon Hatzaddik (the Righteous), one of the last remaining members of the Anshei Knesses Hagdola (Avos 1:2), was the first Tanna. The era of the Tannaim began with the fortieth year of the Second Beis HaMikdash 3448, (1000 years after the Exodus from Mitzrayim) and lasted until the demise of Rabbeinu Hakadosh (R. Yehuda Hanassi) and Rabbi Nassan, who were the last to conclude the Mishna (Babba Metzia 86a).

Contemplating the length of the Galus, the ever diminishing understanding of the people, the decreasing number of Talmidim (students), the prevailing forgetfulness, and the constant dispersion of our Sages to the far-away corners of the globe (Sefer Yochsin Maamar 5), R. Yehuda Hanassi acted to preserve, compile and record the basic teachings and Halachos of the Oral Torah (handed down from Sinai) in a clear, concise language, dividing them into the 6 Orders (Shas) of the Mishna: Zerayim, Mo'ed, Nashim, Nezikin, Kodoshim, Taharos. — The word "Mishna" is derived

2   Following are the 24 Sefarim of the T'nach (Babba Basra 14b):

Torah: 5 Sefarim	Prophets: 8 Sefarim	Kesuvim: 11 Sefarim
1. B'reishis	*First Prophets*	1. Rus
2. Sh'mos	1. Yehoshu'a	2. Tehillim
3. Vayikra	2. Shoftim	3. Iyov
4. Bamidbar	3. Shmuel	4. Mishlei
5. D'varim	4. Melachim	5. Koheles
	Last Prophets	6. Shir Hashirim
	5. Yirmiyahu	7. Eicha
	6. Yechezkel	8. Daniel
	7. Yeshaya	9. Esther
	8. 12 Prophets	10. Ezra (Nechemya)
		11. Divrei Hayamim

from the expression "Mishne lamelech," meaning, it is secondary to the Written Torah, which is "the King" — (Sefer He'aruch os Mem). Even though one is not permitted to write down the teachings which were to be taught orally, but because of the injunction of "Eys laasos laShem, heyfeiru Torasecha," to preserve Hashem's Torah it was then permitted. The era of the Tannaim lasted 531 years, 3448—3979.

Amoraim — In Eretz Yisrael and in Bavel; known respectively as "the Amoraim of Eretz Yisrael" and "the Amoraim of Bavel." ("Amora," the interpreter who elaborates and explains the details of the teachings of the Tannaim).

The Amoraim further contemplated the increasing length of the Galus, the ever decreasing spiritual qualities of the generations (so that that which was simple and clear in earlier generations somehow was becoming more complicated in the later ones) and acted to preserve Torah in its entirety. First Amoraim of Eretz Yisrael; later Rav Ashi and Ravina of Bavel (who were "the end of the period of Horaah" (the Gemara) (Babba Metzia 86a) compiled, classified and sealed the Hora'ah (Gemara) as it had been transmitted to them from generation to generation presenting the details, reasonings and argumentations of the Mishnayos: the Talmud Yerushalmi and Talmud Bavli (Gemara). — The era of the Amoraim lasted 257 years, 3979—4236.

Savora'im — in Bavel.

The Rabbannan Savoraim did not add nor delete from the Talmud but handed down only the reasons and elucidations of the teachings of the Tannaim and Amoraim.

The era of the Savoraim lasted 113 years, 4236—4349.

Ge'onim — in Bavel.

Only the Rosh Hamesivta (the Head of the Academy, the most famous of which were in Sura and Pumpadissa) was granted the title of Ga'on. The Ge'onim initiated the writing of Responsa, along with S'farim dealing with various topics. The last of the Ge'onim was Rav Hai Ga'on in Pumpadissa. The era lasted 451 years, from 4349—4800. Toward the end of the period of the Ge'onim, the "Rishonim" period had already started in countries of Western Europe and North Africa.

Rishonim — in all countries.

At the time they were called "Rabbanim" (see Rayved Halevi), to distinguish them from the Ge'onim. The Acharonim eventually called them Rishonim (the earlier ones).

Rabbeinu Channanel, Rav Nissim and Rav Shmuel Halevi Hanaggid were the first generation of the Rishonim, followed by Rabbeinu Gershom, Rif, Rashi, Rambam and many others. They wrote a wealth of Sefarim — as the need arose — Commentaries, Halachos, Responsa, Torah discussions, etc.

No fixed date marks the end of the era of the Rishonim. For it was only when their disciples — the Acharonim — saw the further decline of the generations that they retroactively bestowed upon their Rabbis — their Masters — the title "Rishonim" to say: "If the Rishonim are like angels, then we are mere humans. If the Rishonim are like humans, then we are like donkeys" (Shekalim 5a).

It is customary to set the end of the period of the Rishonim at the middle of the second half of the 3d century of the 6th millennia (about 5275).

Acharonim — in all countries.

The Acharonim also continued to teach the House of Yisrael, and to the degree that the generations were declining so grew the need for additional Sefarim.* Moshe Rabbeinu wrote down only the

---

*   The end of the period of the Acharonim has not been established. But even though we have had great sages in the last generations, — Masters of Torah, leading us, — no one would even dare to crown them too with the title of Acharonim. For to the end of time we remain guided by the basic evaluation of the Gemara (Erechin 53a): "The hearts of the Rishonim are like the entrance to the Ulam (Vestibule of the Beis HaMikdash) whereas those of the Acharonim are like the entrance to the Heichal (the Chamber, being half the size) — and *we* are but like the size of the eye of a very fine needle." Hence these Chachamim have not been bestowed any specific title.

5 Chummashim, while the entirety of the Torah and all of its detailed teachings were preserved and transmitted orally. In Ezra's time the T'nach too was sealed and written down. In the days of Rabbeinu HaKadosh the Mishnayos (Oral Torah) were compiled, codified and edited and later, the Gemara in the days of Ravina and Rav Ashi, etc. In the era of the Acharonim thousands of Torah-works had already been written and published. All these then served as the basis for the Shulchan Aruch which was codified for all generations (R. Yosef Karo and R. Moshe Iserles). Successive additional explanations and commentaries to these were eventually written by the later sages. And it is on their rulings and decisions that our lives are grounded. For all of the House of Yisrael is guided by their light, until the end of all generations.

Chapter One

THE GATHERING CLOUDS

TIMES were hard for the tiny yet complacent Kingdom of Yehuda. Some one hundred and thirty years earlier Hashem had already poured His wrath on its brethren, the Ten Tribes of Yisrael, whose kings ruled from the city of Shomron. The kings of Yisrael had done evil in the eyes of Hashem, continuing in the ways of Yerovam son of Nevat, who sinned himself and also led the nation into sin. Hashem therefore incited Ashur, "the rod of His anger," who rose up and swept through the land. He came up to Shomron and besieged the city for three years.[1] Hashem finally rejected the Kingdom of Yisrael, and denied it His Divine Protection (as He had warned them through His prophets). And Yisrael was exiled to the land of Ashur, — "until this very day." [2]

The Verdict is Sealed

It happened in the days of *Hoshea son of Eila,* the last king of Yisrael. He too did evil in the eyes of Hashem, although not as much as the kings who preceded him.[3] Why, then, were the Ten Tribes exiled during his reign? Because until then Yisrael's transgressions had been brought about by its kings, who, since the days of Yerovam, had placed guards on the roads to prevent the Tribes from fulfilling the mitzva of going up thrice yearly for the Festivals to Yerushalayim, the capital of Yehuda. The blame for not going up to Yerushalayim was placed, therefore, on the kings, and Hashem would not exile the many because of the guilt of an individual. But Hoshea removed the guards and proclaimed: "Whoever wants to go up to Yerushalayim may go." Thereby he lifted the guilt from his shoulders, and placed it squarely on the people. When they still did not go up to Yerushalayim, their verdict was sealed.[4]

1 מלכים ב יז, ה.   2 שם יז, כג.   3 שם פסוק ב.   4 תנא דבי אליהו זוטא ט.

Hoshea was then punished together with the people, for he should have *commanded* the whole nation to go up to Yerushalayim. But he had not yet purified himself from idolatry and did not fully accept the yoke of Hashem.[5] He left the Commandments to the discretion of the individual and said: "Whoever *wants* to go up, may go," as if indeed there were no yoke and no Sovereign Who commands. He thereby became Yisrael's seventh royal house of idolatry. (The others are Yerovam, son of N'vot; Ba'asha, son of Achiah; Achav, son of Omri; Yehu, son of Nimshi; Pekach, son of Remalyahu and Menachem, son of Gadi.[6]) Through him was thus fulfilled Yirmiyahu's prophecy: "Miserable is she who gave birth to the seven; sorrowful is her heart! Her sun has set still in daytime. Shame and humiliation upon her!" [7] — and Hashem unsheathed the sword of Shalmaneser, King of Ashur, against Yisrael.

With Fatherly Compassion

Even then, Hashem inflicted the hurt on His people with great mercy, like a father chastening his son. Unceasingly He had warned Yisrael and Yehuda through His prophets: "Desist from your evil ways! Observe My commandments as inscribed in the Torah which I have given to your Fathers and handed down through the prophets!" [8] Day in, day out, morning and afternoon, He sent His prophets to the people, but they did not heed His word. They remained stiff-necked like their fathers before them.[9] Until G-d angrily banished them from His Presence.[10]

Nevertheless, Hashem still treated Yisrael with fatherly compassion. He did not strike them at once with one final, devastating blow: Only gradually did Hashem deliver the Ten Tribes into Ashur's hand, with intervals of many years between one exile and the next. — — Perhaps they would still repent...

---

5 שמות רבה ל, ה.   6 גיטין פח.   7 ירמיהו טו, ט.   8 מלכים ב יז, יג.
9 שם פסוק יד.   10 שם פסוק יח.

Exiles of the Ten Tribes

The Ten Tribes were exiled in three stages.[11] "In the twentieth year of
the reign of Yisrael's King Pekach, son of Remalyahu, the king of
Ashur, Tiglas Pileser, came and captured Iyon, Avel Beis Maacha,
Yanoach, Kedesh, Chatzor, Gilad and the Galil — the entire portion
of Naftali — and he exiled their residents to Ashur.[12] He then took the
golden calf from Dan (placed there by Yerovam to wean the people
away from Yerushalayim) and departed.[13]

Still, the people of Yisrael did not repent. They continued to stray
after the idols of the nations.[14] For eight years Hashem waited, like a
father yearning for his son's return. Then "the G-d of Yisrael aroused
Pul, King of Ashur, and Tiglas Pileser, King of Ashur (his successor),
and he exiled the Tribes of Reuven and Gad and half of the Tribe of
Menasheh and brought them to Chalach, Chavor, Hora and the River
of Gozan, until this very day." He then took the other golden calf from
the city of Beth-El and went back to Ashur, fulfilling the prophecy: [15]
"This one (the calf), too, will be taken to Ashur." [16]

Seeing that both golden calves had been taken away, Hoshea removed
the sentries from the roads — allowing the remaining Tribes to resume
their Aliya Le'regel (going up for the Festivals) to Yerushalayim. That
day was the fifteenth of Av, which together with Yom-Kippur, the Day
of Atonement, was the most joyous holiday in Yisrael.[17]

Still, Hoshea did not perceive Hashem's acts. He did not grasp the
meaning of G-d's reprimand, nor did he bow before His threatening
arm. When he saw the King of Ashur preparing to attack Yisrael for
the third time, Hoshea disobeyed the prophet's warning not to rely on
"Egypt, the splintered reed." He sent messengers to King Soh of Egypt
asking for aid. He then rebelled against the King of Ashur, refusing to
send him the annual tribute.[18] Hashem in His mercy waited another
eight years, after which the King of Ashur overran the land and besieged
Shomron for three years. — Hashem still waited three more years,
hoping His children would repent.

11 רש"י מ"ב פרק יז, א.   12 מלכים ב, טו, כט.   13 סדר עולם פרק כב.
14 ד"ה א, ב, כ"ה.   15 הושע פרק י, ו.   16 ילקוט שמעוני, מלכים ב, יח.
17 תענית כו: 18 מ"ב יז, ד.

End of Yisrael's Kingdom

But "the nation did not return to the One who hit it, nor did they seek the G-d of H-sts." [19] Then (in the sixth year of Chizkiyahu, King of Judea[20]), Hashem removed them all from His Presence.

"And this last one was the hardest." [21] In the two preceding exiles only *some* of the Tribes had been banished. This time, however, Ashur overran the entire land and destroyed everything, like one sweeping the house clean.[22] Only the Kingdom of Yehuda remained [23] (in the year 3205).

Even then, Hashem did not completely withhold His compassion from His people. For, "like a shepherd salvaging from the lion's jaws the two knees or the lobe of the (sheep's) ear, so will the Children of Yisrael dwelling in Shomron [24] be saved." Hashem still salvaged one out of eight from between the teeth of Ashur.[25]

Beginning of Yehuda's End

The Kingdom of Yehuda also failed to fulfill Hashem's commands. Even when the Judeans witnessed the exiles of their brethren (the Ten Tribes) and all the misfortunes that befell them, Yehuda did not take heed but followed in the ways of neighboring Yisrael.[1] Then Hashem despised even Yehuda, last remnant of the whole "Kingdom of Kohanim and a holy nation," and "exposed it to the plunderers."[2] — Still, Yehuda was not as full of sin as Yisrael. Besides, the righteousness of Chizkiyahu, son of Achaz, King of Yehuda, stood them by. For "he was righteous in Hashem's eyes," like his forefather David.[3] Chizkiyahu put his trust in Hashem, and he had no peer among the Kings of Yehuda, neither before nor after him. He clung steadfastly to Hashem, and kept the *Mitzvos*. Hashem therefore was always with him, helping him to succeed in all that he undertook. — And now Chizkiyahu rebelled against the King of Ashur, refusing to serve him.[4]

19 ישעי' ט, יב.   20 סדר עולם כ"ב.   21 ישעי' ח, כג.   22 רש"י שם.

23 מלכים ב, פרק יז, יח.   24 עמוס פרק ג, יב.   25 סדר עולם פרק כ"ב.

1 מ"ב יז, יט.   2 שם פסוק כ.   3 שם יח, ג.   4 שם פסוק ה.

Glory Before Downfall

After the fall of Shomron, Hashem waited another eight years. Then, in the fourteenth year of Chizkiyahu's reign, Sancheriv, King of Ashur, stormed all the fortified cities of Yehuda and captured them.[5] However, he miscalculated;[6] Chizkiyahu's subjects were different from those of Shomron. Being true to his name "Yechizkiyahu," (from "Yechazek," to strengthen), he indeed strengthened the ties of his people to their Father in Heaven.[7] He restored the *Avoda* in the Bais-Hamikdash, and led the people back to the most intense study of the Torah. Refusing to partake of the royal cuisine, he sufficed with a mere litre of vegetables a day, in order to devote all his time to Torah.[8] — And the Jews of Yehuda followed suit.

Chizkiyahu did great things throughout the land of Yehuda, for he was good and just and truthful before Hashem. Whatever he undertook concerning the *Avoda* of the *Mikdash* and Torah and *Mitzvos*, seeking wholeheartedly to fulfill Hashem's wish, he succeeded.[9] — — Then, after all this, Sancheriv, King of Ashur, came upon Yehuda and encamped by the fortified cities ready to conquer them.[10] Haughtily he dispatched his generals who shouted in Hebrew at the Jerusalemites posted on the city wall, intending to scare and confuse them:[11] "On whom do you depend, that you sit quietly under siege in Jerusalem? If it's Chizkiyahu, he is deceiving you, letting you die of thirst and hunger, while calming you by saying: 'God our Lord will save us from the King of Ashur.'[12] Your G-d will *not* save you from my hands, just as He did not save your brethren in Shomron."

Chizkiyahu's Generation

Sancheriv's generals continued to hurl insults at the Creator and His servant Chizkiyahu. They issued scripts containing blasphemy upon blasphemy against the G-d of Yisrael. — Upon hearing this, King Chizkiyahu rent his garments, donned sack-cloth, and rushed to the

---

5 שם יח, יג.   6 סדר עולם כג.   7 סנהדרין סד.   8 סנהדרין צד:

9 ד"ה ב, לא, כא.   10 שם לב, א.   11 שם לב, יח.   12 שם לב, יא.

House of God.[13] He dispatched messengers to summon the prophet Yeshayahu, son of Amotz, as "it was a day of calamity, reproach and affliction" for the Jews.[14] They all prayed and raised their voices high to Heaven, beseeching Hashem for help. The king gathered all the people to the plaza, near the gates of the city. He appealed to their hearts, saying, "Be strong and courageous. Do not fear the king of Ashur and his armies. For we have more going for us than he; he has physical might, but we have Hashem Elokeinu to help us and fight our battles." [15]

Indeed, the wisdom of Chizkiyahu was mightier than all the weapons of Sancheriv and his mighty troops with which he had vanquished all the world's rulers. For Chizkiyahu armed the Jews spiritually, while he fitted their bodies with clean garb. He then prepared himself for battle through prayer, gifts and warfare.[16] Not the kind of warfare Achaz his father had waged. Achaz had fought to make the House of Yisrael "like all the nations." Nature will take its course, Achaz had reckoned. "If there are no kids, there will be no goats. If there are no goats, there will be no flock. If there is no flock, there is no need for a Shepherd. If there is no Shepherd, there is no world!" — He thus figured: "If there are no youngsters, there will be no Talmidim. If there are no Talmidim, there will be no scholars; if there are no scholars, there will be no wise men. If there are no wise men, there will be no prophets. If there are no prophets, Hashem will not let His Shechina dwell on them." [17] — He then locked the synagogues and the Houses of Learning [18] and thus withheld the Torah from the Jews.

Now his son Chizkiyahu came and "made an abundance of weapons and shields." [19] — He planted a sword at the entrance of the House of Learning and proclaimed: "Whoever does not study Torah will be pierced with the sword!" (Referring to this sword it is written: "He made an abundance of weapons." As for the words of Torah, these are "the shields.") — They then searched all over the land, from Dan (in the North) to Beersheva (in the South), and did not find an unlearned person; from Gyvas to Antifras they searched and did not find man

13 מלכים ב, יט, א.   14 שם יט, ג.   15 ד"ה ב, לב, ז—ח.   16 קהלת רבה ט.
17 בראשית רבה מב, ג.   18 ויקרא יא, ז. גם פירוש מהרזו שם.   19 ד"ה ב, לב, ה.

or woman, lad or maiden who was not versed in the intricate laws of *Tumah* and *Taharah* (purity).[20]

Downfall of Ashur

Sancheriv had captured country after country, dragging their populations from one place to another to degrade them [21] and to deprive them of their hold on their land. He made them intermingle to such a degree that he mixed up the entire world.[22]

When he now marched on the cities of Yehuda, Sancheriv said: "Would I have come to destroy this place without Hashem? It was *He* who said to me: Go up to this land and destroy it!" [23] But Sancheriv was wrong. For Hashem's command did not refer to those of Yehuda who had repented. As Hashem had said to the Prophet Yeshayahu:[24] "These times are different from the previous ones, when Shomron was exiled. Before, the Ten Tribes, having thrown off the yoke of Torah, deserved to be banished; but now these who willingly assume the burden of Torah, who weary themselves toiling in Torah, they are worthy of miracles exactly like those who crossed Yam Suf and the Yarden River.[25] If Sancheriv pulls back, fine. If not, I shall make of him a disgrace, a shambles in the eyes of all nations."

But Ashur, the rod of Hashem's wrath, did not regard himself thus. He haughtily boasted: "With the strength of *my* hands I did it; through my wisdom, for I am shrewd! [26] Just as I conquered the idol-worshiping countries (including Shomron with her idols), so shall I conquer Jerusalem and *her* idols!" To wipe out and destroy this nation and its G-d was his intention. — But his vanity was his undoing. For "glory preceeds downfall." [27]

Sancheriv came to Judea in golden coaches,[28] boasting: "All my generals are kings!" [29] With his powerful armies he came up to Ayos, then passed on to Migron to leave his equipment in Michmash, the in-

22 ברכות כח. יומא נד.	ילקוט שמעוני מלכים ב, יח.	21	20 סנהדרין צד:
24 ישעי' ח, כג.	23 מלכים ב, יח, כה.		ורמב"ם הל' איסורי ביאה פרק יב, כה.
28 סנהדרין צה:	27 משלי טז, יח.	26 ישעי' י, יג.	25 סנהדרין צד:
			29 ישעי' י, ח.

101

habitants of the cities fleeing before him. Ten one-day[30] marches were covered in that one day.[31] Without respite he rushed forward in order to reach Nov on the very same day, for his stargazers had told him: "If you arrive there still on this day, you can overpower them (for this was the last day in the guilt-account of iniquities committed against the city Nov in the days of King Shaul); otherwise you will fail."[32] When he finally reached Nov, he looked toward Yerushalayim,[33] and from afar it appeared to him like a small town. Waving his hand arrogantly in the direction of Zion, he said: "For such a little hamlet I mustered all these armies?! Let's lodge here tonight, and tomorrow each of us will throw one stone at this place!"[34] Thus "the hatchet glorified itself against Him who was his Master." And he did not retreat.

However, Hashem had already proclaimed: "I swear that that which I had envisioned happened; and whatever I advised came true: to break Ashur in My land, and trample him on My mountains. His yoke will then be removed from My people and his burden off their shoulders."[35] "And the yoke shall be ruined by the oil."[36] The yoke of Sancheriv would be ruined by the oil that Chizkiyahu burned in the synagogues and in the Houses of Study.[37] All of Yisrael was then engaged in the study of Torah.

"We will lodge here tonight!" — That night happened to be the Seder-night of Pesach.* While Chizkiyahu and his companions were still eating their Pesach offerings in Yerushalayim and praising the Almighty with the Hallel,[38] Hashem had already brought their deliverance.[39] — For that night His angel smote Sancheriv's camp, killing all the one hundred eighty-five thousand of his men. By early morning they were all corpses.[40] Sancheriv returned in shame to his land. There, while he was kneeling before his idols in the temple of Ninveh, his own sons murdered him.

30 מהרש"א סנהדרין שם.   31 סנהדרין צד: 32 שם צה.   33 ישעי' י, לב.
34 סנהדרין שם.   35 ישעי' פרק יד, כד—כה.   36 ישעי' פרק י, כז.
37 ילקוט שמעוני מלכים ב, יח.   * תוספת דבר.   38 שמות רבה יח, ה.
39 שה"ש רבה א.   40 מ"ב יט, לה.

Misleading Pride

While Ashur's prestige sank in shame, Chizkiyahu's honor now grew tremendously in the eyes of all the nations.[41] Even during Chizkiyahu's illness Hashem had given him a miraculous sign, by causing the sun's shadow to turn back a full ten degrees.[42]* Until pride found its way into his heart. — When the emissaries of Merodach Baladan, King of Bavel, came (Hashem indeed had inspired them to come in order to test Chizkiyahu[43]) to inquire about this world-wide miracle, Chizkiyahu was happy to receive them. He feted them at his table, and revealed to them the splendor of the Bais Hamikdash as well as his own greatness. He showed them all his treasures, silver and gold, spices and precious oils, the house of his vessels, as well as the treasures of the Kodesh Hakodashim.[44] He even opened Hashem's Ark and unveiled to them the Luchos written by His Hands. There was nothing in his house and in his domain [45] that Chizkiyahu did not proudly display to these foreign emissaries. Thereby causing Hashem's anger to descend upon him and upon Yehuda and Yerushalayim.

Immediately, Hashem readied another "rod of wrath" (instead of Ashur), in the palace of the King of Bavel. — But Chizkiyahu, even at the height of his pride, and the people of Yerushalayim with him, still humbled themselves before Hashem. Therefore Hashem's anger did not strike them in Chizkiyahu's days,[46] but only later in the days of his children.

The Sins of Menashe

At the age of twelve, Chizkiyahu's son Menashe became king. For fifty-five years he ruled in Yerushalayim, and did evil in the eyes of Hashem. By right he was therefore named Menashe (from Nasho, to forget), because *he forgot* his Master, and also caused our Father in Heaven to forget His people.[47] He rebuilt the altars which his father Chizkiyahu

41 ד"ה ב, פרק לב, כג.   42 מ"ב פרק כ, יא.   * ראה "תוספת דבר".

43 בראשית רבה י"ט, ארבעה הם שהקיש הקב"ה על קנקנם לנסותם ולבודקם וחזקיהו אחד מהם.   44 ילקוט שמעוני מ"ב, כ.   45 מ"ב כ, יג.   46 ד"ה לב, כו.

47 סנהדרין קב:

had destroyed, built places of worship for the idols of Baal, and planted the Ashera (trees originally planted for idol-worship), just as King Achav of Israel had done in his days. He even bowed down in worship to the host of celestial bodies, not omitting even one of all the idols in the world.[48] For extremely great was the passion for pagan-worship in his days.[49]* He therefore even held the ancient idol of Micha with him.[50] He furthermore shed innocent blood, flooding with it the holy city throughout. "Menashe thus led Yehuda and the populace of Yerushalayim astray, causing them to do more evil than even the pagans whom Hashem had destroyed for the sake of the Children of Yisrael." [51]

Suffering and Repentance

Could it be that Chizkiyahu had taught Torah to everyone except his own son? Actually, Menashe was learned and so well versed in the Torah that he was able to interpret the Book of the Kohanim in fifty-five different ways.[52] But all the endeavors and efforts of his father did not cause him to turn back.[53] Hashem even spoke to him and his people through the prophets Nachum and Chabbakuk, but their rebukes went unheeded. What caused Menashe to eventually repent was the suffering that Hashem brought upon him when He aroused the generals of Ashur against him. They took him among the thorns, bound him in copper chains, and carried him to Bavel. — Then, in his misery, he prayed to the L-rd, his G-d.[54]

Since Menashe had sinned even more than the heathens, G-d's Angels kept blocking the windows of Heaven so that his prayers would not come before the Almighty. — "Master of the World," they argued, "is there still repentance for him who placed a pagan statue in the Bais Hamikdash?" Replied Hashem: "If I do not accept *his Tshuvah* (repentance), the door will be closed before *all* who may seek to repent!" Hashem then carved out a small opening beneath His Throne and let Menashe's prayers come through.[55] At that moment Menashe

48 תנא דבי אליהו זוטא פרק ט.   49 סנהדרין דף קב ע"א.   * "תוספת דבר".

50 סדר עולם כד.   51 ד"ה ב, לג ט.   52 סנהדרין קג: 53 ילקוט שמעוני,

מלכים ב, רמ"ו.   54 ד"ה ב, לג, יא.   55 ילקוט שמעוני שם.

humbled himself greatly before Hashem. Hashem caused Ashur to return Menashe to Yerushalayim and his kingdom. Then Menashe knew that Hashem is G-d and proclaimed: "Indeed, there is a Judge. Indeed, there is Judgment!" [56] — And he repented.

Menashe then removed all the idols and images from the Bais-Hamikdash and destroyed all the altars he had erected in Yerushalayim; and Hashem even granted him years of reign, more than to any of the kings of Yehuda and Yisrael.[57] — He ruled for thirty-three years following his repentance.[58] However, Menashe did not destroy all the idols in the land, nor did he remove them from public view. They therefore later became the stumbling block to his son Ammon, who succeeded him.[59]

Abominations of Ammon

Ammon even compounded the guilt.

He did evil in the eyes of G-d, like his father. He paid homage to all the idols made by Menashe, and even went further. For the idol which King Achaz had placed in the upper-chamber of the Mikdash [60] and which Menashe later put into the Heichal,[61] Ammon now placed in the Kodesh Hakodashim.[62] He did it *to spite* his Creator,[63] and never humbled himself whatsoever before Hashem, unlike his father Menashe.[64] Furthermore, he even engaged in incest, and burned the Sefer Torah. [65] Until his servants eventually rebelled, and murdered him in his palace. — The people then crowned his son Yoshiyahu in his place.[66]

Yoshiyahu: The Last Days of Reawakening

For thirty-one years Yoshiyahu reigned in Yerushalayim, and "he was just and pious in the eyes of Hashem." Upon becoming king at the age of eight, "he started seeking the G-d of his ancestor David." [67] At

56 ילקוט שם.   57 תדב"א יט.   58 סד"ע כד.   59 מלכים ב, כא, ח.

60 סנהדרין ק"ג: ורש"י ד"ה ב לג, טו.   61 סנהדרין שם.   62 סנהדרין שם.

63 ילקוט שמעוני   64 ד"ה ב, פרק לג, כג.   65 ילקוט שמעוני שם.

66 ד"ה ב, לג, כד—כה.   67 ד"ה ב, לד, ג.

the age of twelve he moved to cleanse Yehuda of its idols and statues, reduced the statues to dust, felled all sun-pillars, and then returned to Yerushalayim. — In the eighteenth year of his reign he resolved to completely purify the country and the Bais-Hamikdash. He sent Shafan, son of Atzalyahu, and Ma'aseiyahu, the commander of the city, and Yo'ach, son of Yo'achaz the secretary, to repair the House of Hashem [68] (as no repairs had been made since the days of King Yehoash). While removing the silver which had been brought to the Bais-Hamikdash, Chilkiyah the Kohen stumbled upon the Torah-scroll of the Azara, the very one written by Moshe Rabbeinu. (The Scroll had been hidden by the Kohanim under a layer of stones, to save it from King Achaz who burned the Torah-scrolls [69]). Upon being told about the discovery of the Scroll and what they had read in it, Yoshiyahu at once rent his garments. This particular Torah-scroll from the Azara [70] was always rolled back to the beginning of Breishis.[71] Now, however, it was found rolled up near its end, to the place of rebuke [72] spoken by Moshe to the Children of Yisrael. Furthermore, at the head of the column they read the verse, "God will lead you and the king you had taken to rule you to a nation whom neither you nor your forefathers ever knew," [73] indicating how great Hashem's anger was because of the sins of their fathers, and further hinting that Yehuda too would be exiled, like their brethren from Shomron.

This warning, however, was but a sign of Hashem's mercy towards His children. Even more so, for in Yoshiyahu's time three prophets were sent to transmit Hashem's messages to them: Yirmiyahu prophesied in the open market-places (to the plain folk); Tzefanya, his teacher, in the synagogues; and Chulda, the prophetess, among the women-folk.[74] Each one in a manner best suited to the listeners; — if they would only listen with their ears, their hearts would understand, so that they might be cured!

Deeply shaken by the discovery of the Torah-scroll, Yoshiyahu wanted to hear Hashem's Word regarding "this Scroll that was found."

68 ד"ה ב, לד. מ"ב כב ורש"י ורד"ק שם.   69 מ"ב כ"ב ח. ורש"י ורד"ק שם.
70 ס' העיקרים מאמר ג, פרק כב.   71 בבא בתרא יד: 72 שקלים פרק ששי טז.
73 דברים כח, לו.   74 פסיקתא רבתי.

He sent for Chulda the prophetess, since a woman is more merciful than a man.[75] Then Chulda, the wife of Shalom, relayed G-d's Word to them. "Behold, I shall bring evil upon this city and its inhabitants, like all the words of the Scroll read by the King — because they (the people) deserted Me and burned incense to the idols of others. Only you, Yoshiyahu, because your heart was tender and you humbled yourself before the Almighty when you heard what I spoke concerning this place and its inhabitants, and you rent your garments and wept before Me,[76] therefore *not* in your days will I do it so that your eyes shall not see this evil catastrophe."

Said Yoshiyahu: [77] "It is *my* duty to uphold the words of this Torah, to fulfill them." [78] — He assembled all the elders of Yehuda and Yerushalayim. He then went up to the House of G-d, and the people with him: Kohanim and prophets, adults and children. And he read to them all that is written in the Book of the Covenant, found in the Bais-Hamikdash. He then renewed the covenant with Hashem, to walk in His path and to keep His Commandments with heart and soul. — And the whole nation entered the Covenant with him.[79]

The King furthermore burned all the accessories of the idols, banned their priests, destroyed their houses of worship, smashed the statues, and chopped down their sacred Asherot-trees. He even removed all the altars which the Kings of Yisrael had spitefully erected in the cities of Shomron.[80] For he now also ruled over some of the Ten Tribes whom Yirmiyahu had been commanded to admonish: "Repent ye, the strayed ones of Yisrael," [81] and whom he indeed succeeded in bringing back from exile [82] (3302). They too then returned to the ways of Hashem.[83]*

That year Bnei Yisrael celebrated the Pesach-offering (in masses), a manner not seen since the last days of the Judges. Hence Hashem stated concerning Yoshiyahu: "There was no king before him who so returned to God with all his heart, soul and strength, (to protect and

75 ילק"ש מ"ב, כב.   76 מ"ב כב, יט.   77 ירושלמי סוטה ז, ד.   78 דברים כז, כו.

79 מ"ב פרק כג.   80 מ"ב כג, יט.   81 ירמי' פרק ג, יב, ורש"י שם.

82 רש"י במשנה סנהדרין דף קי: 83 מגילה דף י"ד: * "תוספת דבר".

mend[84]), according to all the Torah of Moshe; nor afterwards did anyone stand up like him."[85]

Yoshiyahu Entrapped

Yoshiyahu also performed a frightening act. On the advice of Yirmiyahu the prophet, Yoshiyahu removed the *Aron Hakodesh* from the *Kodesh Hakodashim* and hid it.[86] For, long before, Yehuda had been told[87] "God will lead you and the King you selected to a people unknown to you and your fathers." The Torah scroll found under the layer of stones had hinted that this would occur soon. Yoshiyahu therefore was worried that the Ark containing Hashem's Luchos might also be dragged into exile. He said to the Levites: If the Ark is exiled with you to Bavel, you will never bring it back to its place, as you may not carry it on your shoulders any more since by taking it to Bavel its holiness will be defiled.[88] When he therefore removed the *Aron Hakodesh* he also hid the flask of "Mann," the bottle of anointing oil, Aharon's staff, and the chest sent by Pelishtim as "a gift to the God of Yisrael."[89]

"Serve Hashem now, while the House still stands in its Holiness!" Yoshiyahu commanded his people. He also exhorted the Levites to put their hearts to teaching and enlightening His holy nation.[90] — Until his great merits broke through, reaching up to the Heavenly Throne...[91]

Still, G-d's anger remained against Yehuda, for all of Menashe's wrongdoings, which many (still under his influence) even now secretly followed.[92] Said Hashem: "I will remove Yehuda from My presence just as I have done with Yisrael! I detest this city Yerushalayim which I had chosen, as well as the Dwelling I had said would bear My name!" — But because of Yoshiyahu's merits, his eyes would not see the Destruction.

In his days Pharoh Necho, King of Egypt, set out to battle Ashur on the banks of the Euphrates River, crossing the borders of Yehuda.

84 קינה "איכה אלי קוננו מאליו" לט' באב.   85 מ"ב כג, כה.   86 הוריות יב.

87 דברים כח, לו.   88 שקלים ו, א ובקרבן העדה שם.   89 שקלים שם.

90 ד"ה ב, לה, ג.   91 יל"ש מ"א, יג.   92 מ"ב כג, כו.

Yoshiyahu said: "It is written: 'A sword shall not pass through your land',[93] meaning not even a peaceful sword." [94] He therefore felt secure in resisting Pharoh's armies. Even though his interpretation was the right one, he still failed to ask Yirmiyahu for guidance.[95] Hence, he was unaware that Hashem had ordered Necho (through the prophet Yirmiyahu) [96] to rush into this battle. And he went out to wage war against Pharoh Necho.

Yoshiyahu, however, was oblivious to the fact that his contemporaries still worshipped the idols in secret, only pretending to be fully faithful to Hashem. They placed their idols behind their doors and the door-posts.[97] They drew their images inside on the two panels of the doors, one half on each side. When the king's idol-exterminators entered to search the house, they opened one panel of the door (hiding half of the image behind it), thus disfiguring the idols' shape. Remaining un-noticed, those idols were thus left and further worshipped in secret.[98]

Yoshiyahu therefore was caught in the sins of his generation. And when he made his way to the Valley of Megiddo to battle Pharoh Necho, the Egyptian archers immediately aimed at the King. Their arrows pierced his body, until it became like a sieve. In agony Yoshiyahu humbly accepted G-d's judgment,[99] confessing: "Hashem is righteous, for I disobeyed His word!" And he died. His servants carried him to Yerushalayim for burial, and buried him in his royal grave. — And Yirmiyahu wailed over Yoshiyahu and said: "The breath of our nostrils, the anointed of God, was trapped in their pits" — yes, in *their* corruptions! [1]

The loss of their righteous king was a bitter blow to Yehuda, for Yoshiyahu had treated his people justly and had furthermore returned to Hashem with all his heart and soul. Some three hundred years earlier (still in the days of Rechavam, son of Shlomo) it was foretold: "A son will be born into the House of David; his name will be Yoshiya-hu." [2] "Yaai-Shai-Hu," to say: he will be fine and pleasant like an offering on the *Mizbe'ach*.[3] — Yoshiyahu's piety was all the more

96 ד"ה ב, לה, כא.   95 שם.   94 מסכת תענית כב: 93 ויקרא כו, ו.

99 תענית דף כב: 98 רש"י ירמי' ג, י.   97 ישעי' פרק נז, ח.

1 איכה ד, כ.   2 מ"א, יג, ב.   3 יל"ש מ"א, יג.

precious, coming after the abominations of his father Ammon (when Hashem brought forth this righteous son from such a wicked father [4]). In his days, light returned to Yehuda. His reign grew and spread even over the cities of Yisrael and Shomron.[5] — And then, when he was but thirty-nine years old, suddenly "the sun set at midday," and darkness descended upon the earth. Festivals turned into mourning, and all the songs into wailing.[6] — For it was Hashem's Hand which did this, because He now detested His city and His Mikdash.

The death of Yoshiyahu therefore became part of the writings [7] lamenting all the great calamities that have befallen our nation. To bewail forever this day of Yoshiyahu's death, for it was then that Hashem started to bring the calamity upon Yerushalayim and its inhabitants.

Wickedness of Yo'achaz and Yehoyakim

Following the death of Yoshiyahu, the people crowned his son Yeho'-achaz, who was more capable of fulfilling his ancestors' place than his older brother Yehoyakim.[8] — However, he failed to follow in his father's steps and did evil in the eyes of Hashem. Hence his kingdom did not last. He ruled only three months,[9] after which Hashem delivered Yehuda into the hands of the plunderers. Pharoh Necho came up and had Yo'achaz imprisoned and carried away to Egypt where he died. He furthermore penalized Yehuda with fines: one hundred talents of silver and one hundred talents of gold. He then installed Elyakim, son of Yoshiyahu, in his father's place and changed his name to Yehoyakim,[10] to demonstrate that it was *he* who bestowed upon him kingship, so that Yehoyakim become his vassal.

Yehoyakim was twenty-five years old when he ascended the throne. He too did evil in the eyes of Hashem, like Menashe and Ammon.[11] He did not humble himself before Hashem's threatening Hand, even at the time when Yehuda was about to be put under the yoke of the nations surrounding her. "From the *North* will the evil start out upon

4 במדבר רבה כט, א.   5 מגילה יד: 7 ד"ה ב, לה, כה.
8 הוריות יא: 9 מ"ב כג, לא   6 הוריות יא: 11 שם פסוק לו—לז.   10 שם פסוק לד.

all the inhabitants of the land," [12] Hashem had warned yet through the prophet Yeshayahu.[13] However, having taken them out of Mitzrayim and commanding them not to go back on that road again, it was not Pharoh, but Bavel's kingdom that Hashem had chosen as "the rod of His wrath." "Behold, days are approaching when he (the king) will carry off to faraway Bavel everything that is in your house and all that your fathers had amassed until this very day. Not a thing will remain, says Hashem! — And your sons shall they take away, and they will become officers in the palace of the King of Bavel." And now these days were fast approaching.

Hashem therefore wanted to turn the whole world back into chaos because of Yehoyakim, but when He considered the people of that generation, He was pacified.[14] Were they not like lost sheep led astray by their shepherds (the kings) into the rough mountains, from the mountains onto the hills, until they forgot that Hashem is their real resting place? [15] Furthermore, it was not due to their own sins, but through the sins of Menashe that evil was about to descend upon them. Therefore, Hashem's mercy was not yet cut off from His children, and He kept admonishing them. Perhaps they would still listen and repent, so that He might avert the calamity.

Defying the Prophets

At the beginning of Yehoyakim's reign, Hashem's Word came to Yirmiyahu saying: Thus says Hashem, "Stand in the Court of Hashem's Dwelling and speak to all the people of the cities of Yehuda who come to bow down in God's House! Tell them all I command you; do not hold back a thing! Perhaps they will hearken, and each will repent his evil ways, so that I may withhold the misfortunes I intended to bring upon them because of the wickedness of their deeds." [16]

From the thirteenth year of Yoshiyahu's reign Yirmiyahu reproved the people repeatedly, for a period of twenty-three years (nineteen in Yoshiyahu's reign, and four in Yehoyakim's). But they did not listen.[17]

12 ירמי' א, יד.   13 מ"ב כ, יג.   14 סנהדרין קג: 15 ירמי' נ, ו.

16 ירמי' כו, ב—ג.   17 שם כה, ד.

Hashem sent many more prophets to arouse them, but they did not even lend an ear.[18] Furthermore, when Yirmiyahu finished relaying Hashem's message to the people, the Kohanim and false prophets and the plain folk seized him, shouting: "Death unto thee!"[19] For they refused to believe that Hashem intended to bring disaster upon them. They furthermore bent their ears only to the numerous false prophets who just appeased them, saying: "Peace! There *will* be peace!" They suspected Yirmiyahu of not relaying a prophecy heard from the Almighty, but saying things on his own. Hence, they said, he is subject to[20] what is written:[21] "But the prophet daring to (falsely) speak things in My Name shall be put to death." They said to him: "Why did you prophesy in the name of God saying: This House will be like Shilo, (in destruction, after the Philishtim had carried away the Ark of Hashem[22]) and this city will be a waste, without people?" Hence the Kohanim and the false prophets urged upon the nobles and the common people, saying: Death unto this man! He prophesied falsehood upon this city, as you heard with your own ears![23]

But all their threats failed to move Yirmiyahu. Steadfast as a pillar of iron,[24] Hashem's prophet stood before them, and said:[25] "If it is my life you are after, here I am in your hands — do with me as you wish! But be aware of one thing: by killing me you are taking upon yourselves and this city the guilt of shedding innocent blood. For God truly sent me to tell you all that I have said! — So perhaps instead of judging me whether I prophesied truthfully concerning the coming disaster, would it not be better for you to improve your doings and your way of life, and hearken to the Voice of Hashem? Then you could be assured that Hashem would retreat from the evil He spoke about bringing upon you!"[26]

The nobles and the common folk, however, were more righteous than the Kohanim and the false prophets. "This man does not deserve a death sentence, they reasoned, for indeed he spoke in the name of God. Is it not true that long before him (yet in the days of Chizkiyahu

18 שם. 19 שם כו, ח. 20 סנהדרין פט. 21 שופטים יח, כ.

22 שמואל א, ד, יא. 23 ירמי' כו, יא. 24 ירמי' א, יח. 25 שם כו, יד—טו.

26 שם פסוק יג—טו

112

King of Yehuda), the prophet Micha came and foretold: 'Zion will be plowed into a field; Yerushalayim will be heaps, and Har Habayis will become a wooded hill'? Since *then* God's Arm has been outstretched against us. We will be doing great harm to ourselves if we slay this man and do not turn back from our evil ways as our fathers did in the days of Micha." — — — And Hashem was with Yirmiyahu the prophet, and He saved him from their hands.

Although the people did not kill Yirmiyahu, they did not repent either. Hashem showered still more mercy upon His nation and sent them Uriyah, son of Shemayah the Kohen, from the town of Kiryas Yearim, and he, too, prophesied exactly as had Yirmiyahu.[27] But they did not listen to him either. They even hurled insults at him (he descended from a lowly family), and spread slander about him.[28] Uriyah fled to Egypt, but King Yehoyakim had him tracked down and brought back to Yerushalayim. Yehoyakim slew him by sword and threw his body into the grave of the common people.[29]

Then Yehoyakim continued to sin. He defiled himself through bodily abominations and dared to fling insults at Hashem.[30] "The kings before us did not even know how to spite Hashem, like I do!" he exclaimed. Haughtily he even threw slander and reviled His Name. "All we need of Him is the light He gives us from the sun. Let him come and fetch His light, and we shall make use of Parvim gold which shines even better!" His contemporaries (who were better than he was) answered him: "But silver and gold also belong to Him, as it is written, 'Mine is the silver, Mine is the gold, says Hashem'." [31] But He gave it to us, he retorted, as it is written, "The heavens belong to Hashem, and the earth He turned over to man." [32]

Immediately Hashem wanted to turn the whole world back into chaos, but contemplating Yehoyakim's generation, He found them more deserving than the king and was pacified. He merely sent another prophecy regarding "Nevuchadnezar, My servant": that *he* will reign, and *he* will come and take revenge from the enemies of Hashem.[33]

27 שם פסוק כ. 28 ילק״ש. 29 ירמי׳ שם פסוק כג. 30 סנהדרין קג:

31 חגי ב, ח. 32 סנהדרין קג: 33 ירמי׳ כז, ו.

Babylon's Hour

Hashem waited three more years. In the fourth year of Yehoyakim's reign G-d repeated His message to all of Yehuda through Yirmiyahu, saying: "Repent each of you from his evil ways and from the wickedness of his actions!" [34] — Since they still did not repent, the decree was sealed that they be exiled. (At the same time, however, judgment was also pronounced upon the heathen nations that they too will ultimately drink *their* goblet of G-d's wrath.[35]) Thus the era of Nevuchadnezar King of Bavel was ushered in.

Bavel was a minor kingdom, founded and ruled by Ashur (as it is written: [36] "And the King of Ashur came up from Bavel"). But Nevuchadnezar, the King of Bavel, rebelled against him. He conquered Ashur's capital, the huge city of Ninveh, and destroyed it.[37] Thus he wiped out completely the glory of Ashur, "the rod of Hashem's wrath." (3319) In addition to Ninveh, Hashem also delivered the kings of Edom, Mo'av, Ammon, Tzor and Tzidon, and all the other kingdoms of the earth into Nevuchadnezar's hands.[38] As G-d had said through his prophet Yirmiyahu: "It is I who have created the earth, as well as man and the animals swarming over the surface of the earth. With My great might and outstretched arm I gave it to whomever I saw fit. And now I have given all the countries into the hands of Nevuchadnezar, My servant, King of Bavel, in order that he do as I wish him to do!" — Thus Bavel became the head of all the kingdoms.

Why did Bavel deserve all this greatness? In his younger years, Nevuchadnezar had been the scribe of Merodach Baladan, King of Bavel. After King Chizkiyahu recuperated from his critical illness, Merodach Baladan sent him letters and gifts, inquiring about the miracle (of the sun) which had been seen world wide.[39] Nevuchadnezar, the scribe, was not in the palace when the letters were written, so the King's aides wrote as follows: "Peace unto you King Chizkiyahu! Peace unto the city of Jerusalem! Peace unto the great God!" When Nevuchadnezar

---

34 ‏ירמי' כה, ה.‏   35 ‏ירמי' כה, טו.‏   36 ‏מ"ב יז—כד.‏   37 ‏ערכין יב, ו.‏

38 ‏ירמי' כה, כא, כו.‏   39 ‏מ"ב כ, יב.‏

returned he asked them: "How did you address it?" and they told him. Said Nevuchadnezar: You call Him "the great God" and you greet Him last? You should have written: "Peace be unto the great God! Peace unto the city of Jerusalem! Peace unto King Chizkiyahu!" [40]

At once Nevuchadnezar started to run after the messenger (who had already left with the letters) to call him back, in order to rewrite the letter and give due honor to Hashem. Nevuchadnezar ran three steps before he was stopped from on High. Said Hashem: "Nevuchadnezar ran three steps in My honor, — he is worthy of three generations of kingship! Through *him* will I bring retribution to My children, and bring the evil upon this city and its residents. All the nations will be vassals to him, his son and his grandson. However, upon the nation or the kingdom which refuses to serve Nevuchadnezar the King of Bavel, I shall bring the sword and hunger and the plague — thus says Hashem." [41]

Hashem gave Nevuchadnezar all this power since he merited reward, but also for the sake of Israel's honor.[42] For every nation that enslaved the Jews enjoyed world-rulership at the time (like Egypt, Ashur, Persia, Greece, and Rome at their peaks). For Hashem would not exile His sons into a lowly country or subjugate them to a lowly ruler. Only in the palace of a mighty ruler does the King-of-all-Kings mete out His retribution to His people.

In the second year of Nevuchadnezar's reign (the fifth of Yehoyakim's), the King of Bavel rose up and took Yehoyakim into captivity.[43] — And thus the calamity started (3320).

But Hashem does not seek the death of the wicked. He rather wishes that they repent and stay alive. — Hence, even then Hashem prepared a cure for His people, through the words of the prophet Yirmiyahu.

40 סנהדרין צו.   41 ירמי' כז, ח.   42 יל"ש ירמי' כז.   43 סדר עולם כד.

Chapter Two

TWILIGHT

Chapter Two

TWILIGHT

IN THE fourth year of Yehoyakim, King of Yehuda, (the very year when Nevuchadnezar ascended the throne and conquered Ninveh, and when Israel's sentence to be exiled was sealed), Hashem's Word came to Yirmiyahu saying: "Take a scroll of papyrus and write down all that I speak to you concerning Yisrael and Yehuda. Perhaps the House of Yehuda will hear of all the retribution I intend to bring upon them, and they will retreat from their evil ways, so that I may yet forgive them their sins and wrongdoings."

The Scroll of Lamentations

Yirmiyahu summoned his disciple, Baruch son of Neriyah, and had him inscribe in the Scroll [1] all that Hashem spoke to him about the destruction of the Bais Hamikdash and the impending exile of Yehuda. Yirmiyahu then ordered Baruch to read the Scroll of Lamentation to the people. It was not customary for Baruch to speak before his master, but now the urgency of the hour demanded it. "I am imprisoned," Yirmiyahu told Baruch [2] (for Yehoyakim had meanwhile put him in jail); "I cannot come to the House of God. Therefore, you go in my stead. Read the message of Hashem from this scroll which you have written upon my command before the people in the Bais Hamikdash when they assemble on the day of the Fast to contemplate aloud their afflictions. — Perhaps their pleas will be accepted by Hashem when they retreat from their evil ways."

In the fifth year, Nevuchadnezar came and vanquished Yehoyakim. When the Jews saw the calamity G-d sent upon them, they called a day of fast [3] for the residents of Yerushalayim and all those who had come from the other cities of Yehuda. Baruch then read to them from the

1 ירמי׳ לו, ד.   2 יל״ש ירמי׳ לו.   3 הגהות יעב״ץ לסדר עולם פרק כד, ה.

119

Scroll all the prophecies of Hashem.[4] When the nobles heard about it they sent for Baruch, and he read the Scroll to them as well. They listened with awe.[5] Trembling with fear, they turned to Baruch: "Let us tell all this to the King! Perhaps he will listen, and he, too, will turn back from his evil ways."

Yehoyakim, however, was less righteous than his nobles. As soon as they read to him the first verse of the Scroll, "How is it that she sat lonely and barren," he just replied: "So I shall reign over the remnants!" They read before him the second verse: "She weeps and weeps in the night," and again he said: "Very well, I will be king over the remaining ones." And so on with the third verse, and the fourth. When they read to him the fifth verse, "Her oppressors are now on top, her enemies rest peacefully," (implying that *his* kingdom has come to an end), he shouted, "Who said that? . . ." When they answered, "But Hashem has spoken, because of the enormousness of her transgressions," he exclaimed, "Then I will no longer be King?!" Immediately, he cut out every single one of Hashem's Names written in the Scroll.[6] He furthermore cut up the Scroll with a scribe's blade, and tossed it into the flames of the hearth. Neither the king nor his aides were intimidated. Nor did they rend their garments upon hearing the frightening words of G-d. — They acted as if, by tearing up the Scroll, all its forebodings had indeed been put to naught.

Then, at Hashem's command to Yirmiyahu, Baruch wrote down again all the words of the original scroll that Yehoyakim had burned, adding to it from the second chapter: "How was it that Hashem has clouded . . .,"[7] and further, lamentations without end.[8]

At this time, however, Yehoyakim did not yet dare to revolt against "Nevuchadnezar, *My* servant." He placed his shoulders under the Babylonian's yoke, and served him for three more years. Then in Yehoyakim's ninth year (the sixth of Nevuchadnezar's), Yehoyakim finally rebelled. In the third year of his rebellion (the eleventh year of his reign), Nevuchadnezar went up towards Yerushalayim. Before he went

4 ירמי' לו, ח.   5 אסתר רבה א.   6 מועד קטן כו: 7 איכה פרק ב.
8 סנהדרין צו:

up, however, Nevuchadnezar was resting in the gardens of Antuchia [9] (on the north-western border of Eretz Yisrael [10]). When the Great Sanhedrin came to greet him,[11] they asked, "Has the time indeed come for the Bais Hamikdash to be destroyed?" "No," he replied, "but Yehoyakim revolted against me. Hand him over to me, and I will depart."

Nevuchadnezar then went up to Yerushalayim and had Yehoyakim bound in copper chains to have him taken to Bavel.[12] However, being of a very delicate nature, Yehoyakim soon died in his chains.[13] The Babylonians dragged his body around and did not allow him burial, thus fulfilling Yirmiyahu's prophecy,[14] "A donkey's grave will be his burial, dragged and thrown around behind the gates of Yerushalayim."

Exile of the Youngsters

Although the time for the Destruction had not yet arrived, Hashem's anger already started to come down upon the Bais Hamikdash and the residents of Yehuda and Yerushalayim. Hence, not only Yehoyakim but also some of the holy vessels of the Bais Hamikdash were now carted off by Nevuchadnezar and placed in his palace.[15] Some of the dearest of the sons of Zion ("more precious than pure gold") were also carried off in captivity. For the king had instructed Ashpanaz, the head of his guards, to take "from the Royal Family and the nobles, and bring down to Bavel boys who are flawless, good-looking, perceptive in wisdom, who grasp knowledge, and understand sciences, — and are able to stand and serve in the royal palace. — Then to teach them the Babylonian tongue and its books," [16] so that they might become the King's ministers when they grow up. (Among them were Daniel, Chananya, Mishael and Azarya). — Thus Zion began for the first time to equip herself for the Galus, through this first exile of the youngsters.

For like a father disciplining his son, did Hashem strike at His

9 ספר הערוך.   10 יחזקאל פרק יא, ורש״י שם.   11 ויקרא רבה יט, ו.
12 דה״ב לו, ו.   13 יל״ש מ״ב, כד.   14 ירמיהו כב, יט.   15 דה״ב לו, ז.
16 דניאל א, ג ו־ד.

children with one light stroke, then immediately withdrawing His Hand.
—Perhaps after the initial slap, the son would understand and open his
heart and repent.

Exile of Yehoyachin

After Yehoyakim had emptied his goblet of punishment, Nevuchadnezar crowned his son Yehoyachin (also called Yechonyah) in his
father's place.[17] From the age of eight Yechonyah was already designated as heir to the crown, at his father's wish. Now at eighteen,
he ascended the throne. Like his father, he too did evil in the eyes of
Hashem, and thereby incurred the curse placed on his father: "None
of your sons will ever sit firmly on David's throne." [18]

When Nevuchadnezar returned to Bavel, all the people came out to
greet him. "What have you accomplished?" they asked him. He answered proudly: "Yehoyakim King of Yehuda rebelled against me,
so I killed him, and I put his son Yechonyah in his place." — They
then said to him, "The parable teaches us: don't raise in your home
a good puppy born of a bad dog. — How much more so a bad puppy
born of a bad dog, for this one surely will rebel against you!" Nevuchadnezar listened and went back to Yehuda, to depose Yechonyah.
When Bavel's king was again relaxing in the orchards of Antuchia,
the Bnei Yehuda realized that "the rod of God's wrath" was coming
up towards Yerushalayim for the third time. The Great Sanhedrin came
out to greet him. They asked: "Has indeed the time come for the Bais
Hamikdash to be destroyed?" "No," he replied. "Give me Yehoyachin
King of Yehuda, and I shall leave." [19]

Nevuchadnezar went up and laid siege to Yerushalayim. Immediately
Yehoyachin came out to greet him, — he, his mother, his servants, and
his aides.[20] He came to make peace and to accept the yoke of Bavel, as
Yirmiyahu had commanded in the name of Hashem. — Alas! His
verdict had been sealed already! After a reign of only three months
and ten days,[21] Nevuchadnezar mercilessly deported him to Bavel and

17 מלכים ב כד, ו.   18 ירמי' לו, ל.   19 יל"ש מלכים ב' כב.   20 מ"ב כד, יב.
21 סדר עולם.

imprisoned him there. Exiled with him to Babylon were also the Queen-Mother, his wives, his personal attendants, and the powerful nobles.[22]

Turmoil and confusion ensued,[23] as Hashem kept striking His children with increasingly powerful blows. For He had begun to detest His House, as well as the people of Yehuda and Yerushalayim.

The King of Bavel then removed all the treasures of Hashem's House and of the royal palace. He also brought down all the golden artifacts made yet by King Shlomo, — as had been prophesied through Yeshayahu.[24] Furthermore, all this happened one year to the day after Yehoyakim's banishment, with all of Yehuda witnessing the looting of the holy vessels. "For the Man (Hashem) is not in His house, He went on a long faraway journey." [25] As Hashem had stated already, saying: "I shall detest Yerushalayim, the city which I had chosen, and the House which I desired to bear My name." [26]

The "Chorosh" and the "Masger"

Nevuchadnezar exiled from Yerushalayim all her nobles and army officers — 3023 from Yehuda and 7000 from Binyamin and the other Tribes.[27] Of these, 1000 [28] were the Chorosh and the Masger. "All of them mighty ones, waging war." [29] — These indeed were the most righteous and most learned among them! Why then were they called "Chorosh" (literally, craftsmen)? — Because when they opened their mouths in Torah-discourse, all present respectfully turned "Cheresh" — i.e. mute. And why were they called "Masger" (literally, locksmith)? Because when they closed the Torah debate, nobody dared to open it.

In all, one thousand of them went into exile now, "mighty ones, waging war." — But what kind of might do people driven into exile exhibit? Or, what kind of war can be waged by people captured and shackled in chains? They indeed were the mighty ones, all of them: constantly waging the wars of Torah.[30] — And now that they and the

22 מלכים שם פסוק טו.   23 ישעי' כב, ה.   24 מ"ב כד, יג.   25 משלי ז, יט.

26 מלכים ב' פרק כג, כז.   27 סדר עולם פרק כה.   28 מ"ב פרק כד, טז.

29 סנהדרין לח.   30 סדר עולם כה.

rest of the great ones were driven out of Yehuda amongst "the Exile of Yehoyachin," only the impoverished common folk remained in the land.[31]

The Last of Yehuda's Kings

Still, Hashem's mercy upon His nation had not yet ceased. — And when Nevuchadnezar now ordered "the exile of Yechonya" into banishment, he suddenly felt pity on them. He turned to them, saying: "If there is among you a descendant of Yoshiyahu, I will crown him King over Yehuda."[32]

Among the exiles[33] there was one, Masanya, son of Yoshiyahu. "What is your name?" Nevuchadnezar asked him. Masanya thought to himself, "I will say that my name is Tzidkiyahu (from *Zeddek*, righteousness), so that righteous men will descend from me." (Little did he know that from on High this name had been put in his mouth, for in his days justice (also from the word *zeddek*) would be carried out against them).

Thus at the age of 21,[34] by order of Nevuchadnezar, he became King of Yehuda. Nevuchadnezar also granted him power over the kings of Edom, Mo'av, Ammon, Tzor and Tziddon, all of whom were vassals to Babylon.[35] Thus, through Nevuchadnezar's permission, Tzidkiyahu was able to return to Yerushalayim.[36] However, the king of Babylon was bent on turning Yehuda into a lowly kingdom unable to rise up again.

"Give me your oath that you will not rebel against me," said Nevuchadnezar. Tzidkiyahu replied, "I swear by my soul." Said Nevuchadnezar, "That is not sufficient. You must swear by the Torah given at Sinai." — He brought out a Torah-Scroll, placed it besides Tzidkiyahu, and made a covenant with him.[37] He then confirmed his name to be Tzidkiyahu, saying: "God will carry out justice against you, should you rebel against me."[38] (3327)

31 שם ומ"ב כד, יד.   32 יל"ש ירמי' לו.   33 סדר הדורות.   34 מ"ב כד, יח.
35 ירמי' כז, ג.   36 יחזקאל יז, יד.   37 יל"ש ירמי' לו.   38 כריתות ה:

124

Tzidkiyahu's contemporaries, however, were corrupt and wicked.[39] They had learned no lesson from the banishment of Yehoyachin and his powerful officers, nor from the looting of the holy vessels from the House of G-d. Disgusted with them, Hashem wanted to turn the whole world back into chaos, but when He looked at Tzidkiyahu He was pacified,[40] for Tzidkiyahu was a totally righteous man. In fact, he was also called Shalom (from Shalem, perfect), for he was perfect in his deeds.[41]

As soon as Tzidkiyahu was crowned, he immediately released Yirmiyahu from jail where he had been thrown by Yehoyakim.[42] Yirmiyahu now was able again to mix freely with all the people.[43]

But even of the righteous Tzidkiyahu it is written that he did wrong in the eyes of Hashem. For as a descendant of the House of David he did not humble himself before Yirmiyahu, the prophet of Hashem. He rebelled against King Nevuchadnezar, who had made him swear by the Eternal One.[44] — Hardly was Nevuchadnezar on his way from Yerushalayim to return to his country, when Tzidkiyahu was already intent on rebellion.[45] Other than this, Tzidkiyahu did not sin personally. However, because he was able to hold back his subjects from their wrongdoings and failed to do so, the sins of his contemporaries too are ascribed to him.[46]

Tzidkiyahu's Generation

The nation did not learn a lesson from the punishments that Hashem was inflicting on them. Although Hashem had already struck them once and again (both exiles, Yehoyakim and Yehoyachin), they stiffened their necks and hardened their hearts, and did not return to Hashem. "Why don't you engage in the Study of Torah?" Yirmiyahu asked them. They answered: "If we engage in Torah-Study, how will we provide for our families?" In response, Yirmiyahu brought out the

---

39 שמות רבה כד, א. 40 סנהדרין קג. 41 יל״ש מ״ב כד. 42 רש״י ירמי׳ לו, ד.
43 ירמי׳ שם. 44 דה״ב לו, יג. 45 יל״ש ירמי׳ לו. 46 סנהדרין קג.

flask of Mann that Aharon had placed in the Bais Hamikdash as a keepsake for all future generations, and he said to them, "Your ancestors were involved in the Study of Torah, — look how they found their livelihood! You too, immerse yourselves in the Torah, and Hashem will similarly provide for you."[47] — But they did not listen. Moreover, ever since the day that the mighty ones of Torah were exiled with Yehoyachin, the impoverished plain folk sank lower and lower. Their abominations, learned from the nations around them, kept growing. — Thus defiling the holiness of Hashem's House.[48]

The governors of Yehuda and Yerushalayim too took part in the abominations. They grew haughty and over-demanding, like wolves tearing their prey apart — to gather dishonest profit.[49] They did not judge the orphans, and the dispute of the widow did not even reach them.[50] All of this took place in the midst of "The Faithful City,"[51] which had once been full of righteousness, wherein only justice dwelt — and now they had turned into murderers!

The Kohanim (whose duty it was to study and teach the nation[52]) kept silent and did not expose the people's sins, nor did they restrain them from wrongdoing.[53] (Although they were high-ranking Kohanim, able to do so.) Hence the nation became like lost sheep, without a shepherd. They continued to sin like their forefathers before them, and they strayed after foreign cults and idols. In the beginning they had worshiped only secretly, behind doors. But since nobody protested, they now worshiped openly, on the roofs of the houses. When no one tried to stop them, they brought the idols out into the gardens. Still no one stopped them, so they carried them onto the tops of the mountains. Eventually, "Your idols, Yehuda, equalled the number of your cities."[54][55] They furthermore stumbled and defiled themselves by engaging in incest, and shedding innocent blood,[56] thereby causing the Elders of the Kohanim to be held responsible for the sins of the people.

47 יל״ש שמות רסא.   48 דה״ב לו, יד.   49 יחזקאל כב, כז.   50 ישעי׳ א, כג.

51 שם א, כא.   52 דברים לג, י.   53 יחזקאל כב, כו.   54 ירמי׳ יא, יג.

55 פתיחתא דאיכה רבתי כב.   56 יומא ט:

False Prophets

The false prophets were also a stumbling block to the people, whom they misled with false promises. Chananya, son of Ozer, a false prophet from Giv'on, came to G-d's House. In the presence of Yirmiyahu he spoke to the people, saying: [57] "Thus spoke the Lord of Hosts, the God of Yisrael, saying: 'I have broken the yoke of the king of Bavel. In two more years I shall bring back to this place all the vessels from the House of God which Nevuchadnezar had taken. I shall bring Yechonya, son of Yehoyakim, King of Yehuda, and all the exiles of Yehuda taken to Bavel, back to this place,' said Hashem." "For I will crush the yoke of Bavel's king!" [58]

Yirmiyahu was not one to rejoice over misfortune; all he yearned for was the welfare of his people. Upon hearing the false prophecy, he said, "May Hashem do so! May He make the words you prophesy come true, to return the vessels of the Mikdash and all the exiles of Bavel to this place.[59] May it be His Will that your words come true and mine are nullified, for then I will have gained, and you will have lost. I am a Kohen, and when the Mikdash is rebuilt, I will be able again to eat the Heavenly offerings; and you, a Givonite, will be our slave, a wood-chopper and water drawer." [60]

Yirmiyahu however erred by dwelling too much on Chananya's words. He gave the impression of taking them seriously, when they were merely fabrication. It sounded as if he were flattering the wicked man. And he who flatters the villain eventually falls into his hands, the hands of his son, or of his grandson. Eventually Yiraya, son of Shelimya, son of Chananya, captured Yirmiyahu and had him thrown into prison.[61]

But Yirmiyahu also told Chananya the truth to his face, "In vain," said Yirmiyahu, "are you prophesying falsely in God's Name; in the end you will be exposed! For like myself, all of Hashem's prophets who were before us prophesied 'war, and affliction and hunger.' And even though the punishment did not arrive, these prophets were *not*

57 ירמי' פרק כח, פסוקים ב ו־ג.   58 שם פסוק ד.   59 ירמי' שם פסוק ו.
60 יל"ש ירמי' כח ותוס' יום טוב תענית ד, ד.   61 סוטה מא:

proven to be false. God but reconsidered the evil He wanted to bring about, and chose not to bring it. But *you* prophesied bliss and peace, and when these do not come about, it will be obvious that you have prophesied falsehood. It is only bringing the evil that Hashem reconsiders, but not the good. And so your falsehoods will come to light, to your own disgrace!"

In response, Chananya daringly snatched the yoke-bar (which Hashem had ordered the prophet to wear in order to demonstrate that they were about to be brought under the yoke of Bavel's king [62]) from Yirmiyahu's neck, and burned it. Chananya then said to the people: "Thus spoke God. 'So will I smash the yoke of Nevuchadnezar King of Bavel from the neck of the nations, in two years'." [63]

Chananya was not such a fool that he fabricated messages which anyhow would be proven to be falsehoods. In the beginning he indeed had been a true prophet; only later did he become a false one. [64] And now he erred in the prophecy of Yirmiyahu. [65] For Yirmiyahu had stood in the uptown market place announcing: [66] "Thus speaks the Lord of Hosts: 'I shall shatter the bow of Eilam, the neighbor of Bavel'." Chananya reasoned, "Concerning Eilam, who only came to help Bavel, God said: 'I will smash her yoke;' how much more so will He punish Bavel herself?" He thereupon turned his steps to the downtown market place and said: "Thus spoke God, 'I have broken the yoke of the King of Bavel'." [67]

But in vain did Chananya speak, for the Word of Hashem came to Yirmiyahu: "Go to Chananya, and tell him: 'Thus spoke Hashem, "You broke bars of wood, but you replaced them with bars of iron. For I now have put iron bars on the neck of all these nations to serve Nevuchadnezar King of Bavel. — And they shall serve him." [68]

Yirmiyahu continued to prophesy: "Listen Chananya! Hashem did *not* send you, and you have reassured the people with lies. Therefore God says: 'I shall remove you from the earth.' This year you will die, for you spoke out against Hashem." [69]

62 ירמי' כז, ב.   63 ירמי' כח, יא.   64 סנהדרין צ.   65 סנהדרין פט.

66 ירמי' מט, לה.   67 שם כח, ב.   68 שם כח, יג־ויד.   69 שם פסוק טז.

That same year Chananyah died, on the eve of Rosh Hashana. But even on his deathbed he continued to fool and mislead the common people away from Hashem. — Thus, before he died, he instructed his children and family to carry him out for burial *after* Rosh Hashana, (which would already be the next year) in order to prove Yirmiyahu's prophecy a falsehood.

Chananyah, however, was not alone. There were many more false prophets and prophetesses [70] who led the people astray bringing ill fortune upon them. Even amongst the "exile of Yechonyah" in Bavel (with its multitude of scholars) there were false prophets. Shmayahu the Nechelmi, for example, dreamed up visions [71] and wrote pamphlets filled with lies, in the name of Hashem. He even sent these to the common people and the Kohanim in Yerushalayim.[72] — Not all of these false prophets were plainly rash. Some of them were even imbued with "Ru'ach Hakodesh" (Spirit of Holiness). They were called "prophets" in the Scriptures,[73] as was the case with the false prophet to whom Hashem spoke when he was accompanying the prophet Edo.[74] But the words they spoke, "they prophesied falsely in My Name that which I had *not* commanded them." Not even once had I asked them to relay a prophecy! They came with things on their own, or deduced them by way of their studies. But all of them erred, some way or another. Sometimes one had a dream,[75] or noticed a symbol, or an omen appeared before him,[76] and he then preached what he imagined to have seen, in the Name of Hashem. — They misled the people, and falsely inspired them to come to the prophets of deceit to seek G-d's Word!*

With fatherly compassion Hashem therefore alerted His people through His prophets Yirmiyahu [77] and Yechezkel, son of Buzi,[78] to warn them not to err after those who would lead them astray. The prophet brought Hashem's message to Tzidkiyahu, the King of Yehuda, to the Kohanim, and to the whole nation, to each at his own level of

---

70 יחזקאל יג, יז.   71 רד"ק ירמי' כט, כג.   72 ירמי' כט, כה.   73 ירמי' כז, ט.

74 מלכים א' יג, כ.   75 ירמי' כג, כח.   76 יחזקאל יג.   * "תוספת דבר".

77 ירמי' כו.   78 יחזקאל יג.

understanding: "Do not listen to the words of the false prophets who say to you: do not serve the King of Bavel. It is lies they prophesy, for I did not send them, says Hashem." They just want to mislead you by predicting: "Peace! Peace!" — But there is no Peace.[79]

Before Dark

The closer it came to Yerushalayim's downfall, the more numerous and frequent were Yirmiyahu's prophecies to the people. — "Listen and hearken," he said. "Be not defiant, for Hashem has spoken.[80] Give glory to Hashem, Your God, before dark sets in, before your feet stumble on the mountains of darkness." That is, — before He obscures from you the words of the Torah, and before He cuts off His prophecy from you.[81]

Tirelessly, Yirmiyahu kept increasing his warnings to alert them of the afflictions which Hashem was bringing upon this place. For thus spoke the L-rd of H-sts, the G-d of Israel: "Behold, in *your* days and before your own eyes I shall still the voice of joy and the voice of exultation, the voice of the groom and the voice of the bride.[82] To the house of festivities you shall not come to sit down and eat or drink, nor will you go to the house of the mourners, for I will have taken away My peace from this nation — says Hashem — kindliness as well as compassion. Adults and children alike will die in this land, but they will not be buried (as indeed happened at the time of the Churban), nor eulogized. Nobody will lament them, nor gash themselves, nor make themselves bald in mourning over them. No one will break bread with the mourners to console them upon death, nor will they pour them the cup of consolation, even for a deceased father or mother."[83]

"However, should they yet pay attention and bend their ears to listen! — Then, when you tell all these words to this people, and they ask you, 'Why did Hashem decree upon us such retributions? What are our sins and wrongdoings?' Then, like a father chastening his son,

79 שם פסוק טז.   80 ירמי' יג, טו ו־טז.   81 יל״ש ירמי' יג.   82 ירמי' טז, ט.
83 שם פסוק ז.

Hashem commanded His prophets to enlighten the people: "Tell them, it is because your fathers forsook Me, — says Hashem, and they strayed after the idols, worshiped and bowed to them. But Me they abandoned, and my Torah they did not keep.[84] Would that they had left Me, but kept My Torah, then the light within her would have drawn them back to do good.[85] But they have not acted in this manner. And now you came and did even worse than your fathers, following but the obstinacy of the heart, not to listen to Me. By right, then, am I banishing you from this land."

"Only because of their father Avraham, who commanded them to practice justice and righteousness in this land, have I kept up My kindliness toward them, and granted them mercy. But here they come, turning justice into wormwood, and casting righteousness to the ground.[86] In return, I took back My mercy and my compassion.[87] And as soon as I remove from Yisrael ("My vineyard") its hedge, it shall be consumed; and when I remove its fence, it will be trodden down. — Until I shall banish them completely from before Me!"

An Abundance of Prophecies

In addition to Yirmiyahu, three more great prophets assisted Yehuda at that time.[88]* And through all of them Hashem kept urging Yehuda and Yisrael: "Repent from your wicked ways!" [89] In fact, ninety years already lasted this constant sending of prophets,[90] with Yoel, Nachum and Chabakuk (in the times of King Menashe) the most famous among them.[91] Then came Tzefanya, followed by the prophetess Chulda. — But the more the people sinned, the more Hashem in His mercy sent His prophets. For despite His anger, He still loved them.[92] From early morning Hashem sent His messengers, out of concern for Yehuda and His abode.[93] Daily they came, — one prophet in the morning and another at dusk.[94] But the people did not hearken.

84 שם פסוק י ו־יא. 85 פתיחתא איכה רבתי פר' א. 86 עמוס פרק ה, ז.
87 רש"י ירמי' טז, ה. 88 פסיקתא רבתי. * "תוספת דבר". 89 מ"ב יז, יג.
90 יל"ש יז. 91 סד"ע. 92 במדבר ב, טו. 93 דה"ב לו, טו.
94 יל"ש מ"ב, יז.

False Confidence

At this crucial time Yehuda acted out of arrogance, and with over-confidence in "Hashem's mercy which will never end." Even though they sinned, they still placed their trust in the Almighty.[95] "God is among us," they said. "No harm will befall us!"[96] For ninety years He had been sending His prophets to warn them. Twice already G-d's Hand had struck them (first with the exile of Yehoyakim, and then the exile of Yechonya), but it always appeared as if He were just threatening but would never carry out His threats. One hundred and thirty years had gone by since He had exiled Shomron, the sister-nation, but He had not yet discarded the children of Yehuda. "To us is this land given, an inheritance,"[97] they claimed, "and we shall not be banished from it." — They continued to build themselves houses,[98] and said: "The vision that the prophet sees (now) is a prophecy for a distant future,[99] but not close at hand! — And Hashem will still reconsider." Thus they rested assured that only to warn and to threaten them did He send His prophets, "They did not believe that an enemy or oppressor would ever enter Yerushalayim." And even if he came he still would not enter the Holy House which Hashem had chosen as His dwelling. — They therefore felt assured that Hashem would shield this city to save it, for His sake, and for the sake of David His servant.[1] For the sons of Yehuda were not like the kings of Shomron, who had traded Hashem's glory for hopeless worthlessness, and who did not have the *Mikdash* in Yerushalayim to depend upon.

They further relied on the inexhaustible merits of the Patriarchs, and on the "everlasting love that I love you" which Hashem had proclaimed long ago.[2] "Love covers up all sins," they said. Besides, He has sworn never to exchange Yisrael's glory for any other nation. Therefore they paid no heed to the repeated warnings of Yirmiyahu about the impending punishment, and just continued in their wrongdoings, — thus causing the prophet Amos to complain:[3] "Woe to you, the complacent ones of Zion!"

95 יומא ט: 96 מיכה ג, יא.   97 יחזקאל יא, טו.   98 יחזקאל שם, פסוק ג.
99 שם יב, כז.   1 ישעי' לז, לה.   2 ירמי' לא, ב.   3 עמוס ו, א.

132

Yehuda thus acted like the queen who was most precious to the king. Assured of his strong love for her, she treated him with disdain and disregarded his demands.[4] Until, one day in his anger (notwithstanding all previous love), the king gave the command and his servants dragged her outside by the hair of her head.[5] — Thus Yehuda was not aware that Hashem no longer loved His nation.[6] In fact, He now detested Yehuda, and even Yerushalayim.[7] "Because you have forsaken Me, says Hashem. You regressed. Therefore I shall stretch out My Hand against you to destroy you. I am weary of relenting." [8]

But complacently, Yehuda still reasoned: "Nevuchadnezar amassed all the world's money; does he also need ours?" [8a]

The Shechina Departs

In the sixth year of Yehoyachin's exile, Hashem appeared to Yechezkiel son of Buzi (who was among those exiled to Bavel together with Yehoyachin), and showed him the abominations which the sons of Yehuda had performed in His House.[9]

The prophet thus watched as Hashem's glory started moving up from its place on the *Kruvim*, toward the threshhold of the Mikdash.[10] For He now despised His Dwelling, and His Shechina Started to depart.

This departure was very painful. It took ten separate stages for the Shechina to retreat.[11] (With lapses of time between one stage and the next.) From the *Kapores* it went to the first *Kruv*, then to the second *Kruv*. From there Yechezkiel watched the Shechina move to the threshhold of the House. From the threshhold, into the *Azara* (courtyard), to the *Mizbe'ach*, to the roof of the Sanctuary, to the Wall of the *Azara*, into the city, to the Mount of Olives, into the desert. — For three and a half years the Shechina dwelled in the desert — perhaps Yehuda would still repent.[12] But when they did not repent, the Shechina

---

4 ילקוט שמעוני ירמי' פרק יד.   5 ילק"ש ירמי' יב.   6 ירמי' פרק טו, א.

7 שם יד ,יט.   8 שם טו, ו.   8a פתיחתא דאיכה רבתי ה.   9 יחזקאל ח.

10 שם ט, ג.   11 ראש השנה לא.   12 שם.

left the wilderness and ascended to Its original abode of above. As it is written, "I shall go, and return to My place." [13]

Pact of Rebellion

Israel kept sinning; yet in the merit of the righteous King Tzidkiyahu, the gates of repentance were not closed to them. In the eighth year of his reign,[14] Tzidkiyahu gathered all the people in Yerushalayim and urged them to enter a treaty with him proclaiming freedom for all Jewish servants. The people, nobles and commoners alike, willingly entered into a covenant with Hashem, each to free his slave or maidservant, in accordance with the Torah-limited bondage of six years.[15] However, they very soon had a change of heart. They retracted their promise, and held on to their servants, by force. Moreover, they closed ranks in a stubborn pact of rebellion against the Almighty; the chieftains of Yehuda and Yerushalayim, the nobles and the Kohanim, and the common people.

They all passed ritually between the parts of the calf to symbolize their rebellion against Hashem.[16] Said Hashem: "You did not harken to Me to proclaim freedom each to his brother and to his neighbor, hence *I* shall proclaim freedom upon you: freedom for the sword, plague and famine. From now on you are free (of My bonds), and abandoned. No longer am I your Master, to save you. — You shall be free and abandoned to the sword and to famine."

"Indeed, out of rebellion you too pursued [17] the ways of your sister Shomron. She rebelled against the Almighty and against the King of Ashur. You, too, rebelled against the Almighty and against the King of Bavel. She broke a covenant; you, too, broke a covenant. She put her trust in the kings of Egypt; so did you. Hence, I place her cup in *your* hand;[18] your sentence shall be like her sentence, and your judgment like hers. Shomron underwent three exiles; you, too, will undergo three exiles. She was under siege for three years; you, too, will be

---

13 הושע פרק ה, טו.   14 סדר עולם כו.   15 ירמי' פרק לד, ט.

16 ירמי' טו, ורש"י שם.   17 יחזקאל כג, לא.   18 שם.

besieged for three years. They ate the flesh of their sons and daughters; you, too, will eat the flesh of your sons and daughters." [19]

And thus the verdict was sealed . . .

Tzidkiyahu Breaks His Oath

"For an outright provocation of My anger (like a foul place, where a passerby holds his nose to avoid the stench [20]) has this city become to Me." (Hashem therefore planted the idea of rebellion in Tzidkiyahu's heart; to bring about their exile and punishment). Forthwith, King Tzidkiyahu rebelled against the King of Bavel, breaking his oath.[21] He rebelled against Nevuchadnezar by sending envoys to Egypt (to whom the Tribes had been shipping oil to gain their support in case of war), asking for horses and soldiers [22] to help him cast off the yoke of the King of Bavel.

Even though in response to his inquiry the Sanhedrin had absolved the king of his oath to Nevuchadnezar,[23]* his act was nevertheless a desecration of Hashem's Name. Hence, Hashem stated through the prophet Yechezkel:[24] "Shall he who does this, escape? Shall he who breaks a promise, be saved?" (One can be absolved of his oath only in the presence of the one to whom he had sworn.[25] There was furthermore the question of the profanation of Hashem's Name, since the gentiles would claim that Jews did not honor their oaths.[26]) "Therefore, — I swear, says Hashem, that precisely in the land of the King (meaning Nevuchadnezar) who had crowned him, whose oath he despised and whose treaty he has broken — there, in the midst of Bavel, will Tzidkiyahu die. Neither will Pharoh align with him in the war, not with a large mighty army nor with a multitude of men." For even though Pharoh too yearns to throw off the yoke of Bavel, yet he will not come to Yehuda's aid. "Cursed is the one who puts his trust in man and makes flesh his strength, and whose heart turns away from Hashem." [27]

19 סדר עולם פרק כו.   20 ויקרא רבה יב, ה.   21 מלכים ב' כד, כ.
22 יחזקאל יז, טו.   23 נדרים סה.   * תוספת דבר.   24 יחזקאל יז, טו.
25 ר"ן נדרים סה.   26 חידושי הרמב"ן נדרים ס"ה.   27 ירמי' יז, ה.

Furthermore, Pharoh has always been a "splintered reed" that pierces the hand of the person trying to lean on it for support.[28] — As for Tzidkiyahu who swore by Hashem and His Torah, and now broke his oath and his treaty, — "Shall he be acquitted?"

For eighteen years* before the destruction of the Bais Hamikdash, a Heavenly Voice was heard in the palace of Nevuchadnezar saying, "Evil servant: go, destroy the house of your Master, for His sons do not listen to Him!" But Nevuchadnezar was frightened. "God only wants to destroy me," he said, "as He destroyed Sancheriv the elder!"

The King of Bavel finally went. When he came to the crossroads,[29] one road leading to the desert, the other one to Yerushalayim,[30] he stopped. He tried all acts of divinations and looked for omens through all forms of sorcery. He shot arrows in the air, consulted the Terafim (idol images) and saw that he would succeed.[31] Ammon and Mo'av (Yerushalayim's evil neighbors) furthermore kept encouraging him with messengers, relaying the prophecies of Yehuda's impending destruction.[32] Yet, Nevuchadnezar was afraid, and did not go up to destroy the holy city.[33] When, however, Hashem gave it into Tzidkiyahu's heart and he broke his oath, Nevuchadnezar concluded: Had he broken only my covenant but not the one with his God, surely God would stand by and protect him, and I would have reason to fear him. Had he broken his oath to God and not to me, then I would also not fight him, as he did not sin against me. But now he broke both his covenant with me and with his God. He now has rebelled against his God and against me as well.[34]

In the ninth year of King Tzidkiyahu, on the tenth day of the tenth month (Teves) of the year, Nevuchadnezar King of Bavel and his armies finally marched up on the city of Yerushalayim. They encamped before the city, and built a siege-wall around her. Thus the city came under siege until the eleventh year of King Tzidkiyahu.[35] Trapped were

---

28 מ״ב יח, כא.   * תוספת דבר.   29 יחזקאל כא, כו.   30 יל״ש יחזקאל כא.
31 שם.   32 סנהדרין צו: 33 פתיחתא דאיכה רבתי.   34 אסתר רבה ג, א.
35 מ״ב כה, א.

not only the city's residents, but also the people of the other towns of Yehuda and Binyamin who had sought protection behind its strong walls. Anticipating Nevuchadnezar's onslaught, they had said: [36] "Why do we sit still? Let us band together and move into the fortified cities and be silent there." [37] — Hence, all of them together now came under siege in Yerushalayim.

In this hour of affliction Tzidkiyahu sent to Yirmiyahu pleading: "Pray for us to Hashem our God,[38] perhaps He will still spare this poor and desolate nation. Perhaps there still is mercy."

Egypt, the Splintered Reed

Meanwhile, the armies of Pharaoh sailed from Egypt to go up and help Yehuda. When the Babylonian armies heard about their coming, they hastily gave up the siege of the city. Tzidkiyahu and the people considered their flights an act of Heavenly Redemption. In His great compassion, they thought, Hashem once more had brought light to His people to save them from their oppressors, as ever since, throughout our long history.

Hashem said to Yirmiyahu: "Tell the following to the King of Yehuda who sent you to beseech me: The armies of Pharaoh which set out to help you have already returned to their country. Now the Babylonians too will return here, besiege this city, capture it, and set it on fire.[39] Do not deceive yourselves by saying: 'The Babylonians will flee our country, Oh! We are saved.' — Because Judgment has already been sealed, to bring upon you all these afflictions."

As soon as Pharaoh's armies set out in their ships, Hashem beckoned to the sea, and inflated hide pouches (resembling human skin) floated to its surface. The soldiers wondered and asked one another: "What are these?" They said: "These are our ancestors, who were drowned by the fathers of those to whose rescue we are rushing!" — Thereupon

36 ‏ירמי׳ פרק ח, יד.‏   37 ‏תנא דב״א פרק ל.‏   38 ‏ירמי׳ פרק לז, ג.‏
39 ‏שם פסוק ס.‏

the Egyptians turned back, and swept on the city of Azza instead.[40] And Judea waited in vain . . .

Since the Babylonian troops had fled Yerushalayim in their fear of the approaching Egyptian army, the Judeans reopened the city's gates. Yirmiyahu (who all the while had been praying that Yerushalayim be spared) now left the city and headed for the Land of Binyamin, to become part of its people [41] (since their wickedness was less than that of the nobles), and to convey Hashem's prophecies. — Among them was Yireya son of Shelmiya son of Chananya, a false prophet, who had been appointed to oversee the people who entered or left. Yereya was looking for a pretext to slander Yirmiyahu, and to take revenge on the prophet for having cursed his grandfather. He went to the city commanders and said: "This man has done us much harm. Now I have found him going over to the Babylonian side." — The commanders were furious with Yirmiyahu. They whipped him and put him in prison, where he remained for a long time.[42]

Honor for Father and Son

Great was Yirmiyahu's anguish. Ever since the days of Yoshiyahu son of Ammon, King of Yehuda, he had been prophesying without end. (As a youth and even before he was born, Hashem had already acknowledged and sanctified him.[43] He was even born circumcised.)[44] Forty years before the Destruction he already prophesied that which Hashem commanded him. — And out of a Father's love for His son he came, to save them. But the sons did not lend an ear. They refused to listen, and even degraded him. Enemy and traitor, they labeled him. Moreover, they suspected him of being the son of a harlot (who is forbidden to a Kohen), and even suspected him of adultery, for which he deserved to be killed.[45] Had not Hashem commanded him, "Do not take a wife"? [46] Thus the scoffers of that time derided him: "Is it possible for mortal man to live forty years without a wife?" [47]

40 סדר עולם כו.　　41 שם פסוק יב.　　42 יל"ש ירמי' כח.　　43 ירמי' א, ה.

44 יל"ש ירמי' רסא.　　45 בבא קמא דף טז ע"ב.　　46 ירמי' טז, ב.

47 ב"ק טז: בפי' מהרש"א.

Yirmiyahu lamented in his anguish: [48] "Woe unto me, mother, you indeed brought me into this world to be a man of quarrels, to bring strife to everyone. I have never pressed any one for payment, nor has anyone ever come to collect debts from me. Not for monetary claims (that I have against them, or they may have against me) have I quarreled with these people. Only out of love have I come to admonish them. — And now all my people curse me."

However, Yirmiyahu's prophecies were preciously different from those of the other prophets; and unlike those of Eliyahu or of Yonah son of Amitai. The prophet Yonah defended the honor of Bnei Yisrael, the *son*, (that no Divine wrath be kindled against the Jewish people, in wake of Ninveh's repentance), but not the honor of the Father. Hence Hashem spoke to him "a second time," but no more. — The prophet Eliyahu defended the Father's honor, but not the son's. He said: "I fought for the God of Hosts, because the Children of Yisrael violated Your covenant," but he did not plead that the children repent. Said Hashem: "I am not pleased with your prophecy. Anoint Elisha, son of Shafat, as prophet in your place." Yirmiyahu however, defended the honor of the Father as well as the honor of the son. He said: "*We* have sinned and rebelled, and *You* did not forgive!" Therefore his prophecies were doubled, as it is written: "And many similar things were still added on to them," [49] perhaps he will yet repent!

Yirmiyahu thus kept reproaching the Children of Yisrael, demanding the honor of Hashem. At the same time he never ceased praying for mercy for them, demanding also the honor of "the son" — even though they had thrown him into the pit. — Finally Hashem said to him: "Don't pray for this nation. Don't raise your voice on their behalf, as I do not listen when they call Me, because of their wickedness!" [50] — Yirmiyahu however was not deterred. He still kept upholding the honor of the children. "Woe! Hashem Elokim, the Righteous One of the world," he said. "The false prophets keep saying to them: 'You will not see a sword, you will not suffer hunger. For I shall give you

48 ירמי׳ פרק טו, י.   49 ילקוט שמעוני ירמי׳ לו.   50 ירמי׳ פרק יא, יד.

genuine peace in this place.' [51] — Do not reject Your children, for it is *they* who are misleading them." Said Hashem to Yirmiyahu: "There is a conspiracy among the men of Yehuda and among the inhabitants of Yerushalayim. They have reverted to the transgressions of their fore-fathers who refused to listen to Me, and they pursued idols to serve them. The House of Yisrael and the House of Yehuda have broken the covenant that I made with their fathers.[52] — Shall they go free?" ... Therefore, "what is my friend doing in My House, to keep on pleading for mercy on their behalf?"

Undeterred, Yirmiyahu continued to plead for the sake of both Father and son. "Although our sins testify against us, Hashem, act for the sake of Your Name. Because our errings were many, therefore we sinned against you. But still, You are the Hope of Yisrael, its Savior in times of distress. Why should You be like a stranger in the Land, like a wayfarer come to lodge? Why should You be like a bewildered man, like a mighty one who is helpless to save? Are You not Hashem, in our midst? Is Your Name not bestowed upon us? Do not abandon us,[53] if only for the sake of Your Name!"

Hashem replied, "Even if Moshe and Shmuel (both of whom were forced to plead for Yisrael) were to stand before Me, I would still not be with this nation.[54] — And even *they* never asked Me to remove My wrath before they had succeeded in making My people repent.[55] — If My people will hearken to My prophecies even now, fine. But what if they will not listen? ... Then, in hiding I will weep for your greatness which goes to naught, and for the haughty nations of the world who taunt you, saying: 'Where is their God?' And for My Name, which is being profaned among the nations. — But you, Yirmiyahu, you can no longer bring them back to Me.[56] For they have insulted God's messengers, despised His words, and scoffed at His prophets. They shouted at them.They unleashed their anger against them, slapped them,[57] threw them into the pit, and even slew some of them. Until Hashem's wrath mounted against His nation, till there was no remedy."

51 ירמי' יד, יג.   52 שם יא, ט.   53 ירמי' יד, ז, ח ו־ט.   54 שם טו, א.

55 רש"י שם, פסוק א.   56 רש"י שם.   57 דה"ב לו, טז.

— When one listens to the words of Torah, there is still a remedy for his illness.[58] But when one insults G-d's prophets, abuses the Torah sages, and even refuses to hear their teachings, there is no cure. — What's more, Yisrael has shown lack of appreciation for Torah [59] by failing to say the blessing over the Torah before beginning to learn.[60] How then could the light of the Torah now reach them, to cure and bring them back to the path of life? — "Do not pray for this people, to win favor for them!" [61]

Hashem's Prophet is Scorned

The commanders, upon hearing Yirmiyahu's prophecy that "the city would be delivered into the hands of Nevuchadnezar to capture it," [62] continued to heap insults on Hashem's prophet. They said to the king: "This man should be put to death, because he weakens the hands of the people and the soldiers who have stayed in the city, by speaking like this. His intentions are to undermine their efforts and break their spirit, so that they will stop fighting the enemy."

The nobles kept heaping scorn on the Prophet who (while being so loyal to Hashem) so fervently tried to save the people. — Until they turned the bitter into sweet, and the sweet into bitter, saying: "This man does not seek the welfare of this people, only their harm." [63] They said to the king: "Let this man be put to death! He anyway deserves to die, since he defiled the wife of his friend." [64] "And although we are not permitted to execute him (for lack of witnesses), halachically we are permitted to bring about his death." [65]

The King, however, was too weak to stand up to the princes. Without Tzidkiyahu's knowledge, they seized and threw Yirmiyahu into the pit of mire.[66] However, they did not intend to kill him directly, but only to cause him to die. They therefore lowered him by rope slowly, so that he started to drown in the mire by himself.[67]

58 יל״ש ד״ה לו.   59 ישעי׳ ה, כד.   60 נדרים פא.   61 ירמי׳ יד, יא.

62 ירמי׳ לח, ג.   63 שם פסוק ד.   64 בבא קמא טז: 65 סנהדרין פא:

66 ירמי׳ לח, ו.   67 סנהדרין שם.

When Baruch, son of Neriyah, aide to the King, heard what had happened he hastened (at the risk of his own life) to alert the King.[68] The King immediately ordered Baruch to take thirty men, (they were so weak from famine that thirty men were needed to do the work of three), to save the prophet. With ropes they carefully hauled Yirmiyahu out of the pit, saving him from certain death. — They then confined him to the Court of the Guards, among all those who were imprisoned there.

A Glimpse of Light

With the ramps surrounding the city and the Kasdim struggling to capture it, and judgment already pronounced upon Yehuda, — precisely then did the imprisoned Yirmiyahu envision the tidings of Redemption.[69] — Chanamel, his cousin, arrived in the courtyard, and Yirmiyahu purchased his field in Anasos (in the portion of Binyamin). He paid him the full price — seven Shkalim and ten pieces of silver, and duly signed the deed in the presence of witnesses. In view of all the Jews sitting in the Court of the Guards, Yirmiyahu gave orders to place the signed deed in an earthern vessel, "so it would last for a long time." "For thus spoke the Lord of Hosts! There will yet come a time when they will again buy houses and fields and vineyards in this land!"

When Yirmiyahu suddenly perceived Hashem's Fatherly Glimpse of light, he wondered and prayed: "Since now, in the midst of war, You commanded me to purchase the land (as if to nullify the evil of the Judgment), — can it be that even Yehuda and Yerushalayim may yet be saved, and You will thus have made a name for Yourself as of this very day?"

Then Hashem said to Yirmiyahu, "People will once again be buying fields for money, (written and signed in a legal deed, and attested by witnesses) in the Land of Binyamin and in the suburbs of Yerushalayim, in the cities of Yehuda and on the mountain heights, in the cities of the lowland and in the towns of the desert. — For I shall

68 פרקי דרבי אליעזר נג.   69 ירמי׳ לב.

cause their captivity to return, says the Lord." [70] Again, will there be heard in the cities of Yehuda and (these desolate) streets of Yerushalayim, the voice of joy, and the voice of gladness; the voice of the bridegroom, and the voice of the bride, the voice of those who say: "Praise the Lord of Hosts, for Hashem is good; His great love endures forever!" [71] — However you saw what this nation has done to Me. They turned their backs to Me, not their faces. Though I taught them from the earliest, they would not hearken to receive admonishment. Therefore this city has become a provocation of My anger and fury, for all the evil which Yisrael and Yehuda have done, — they, their kings and their princes, their Kohanim and their (false) prophets.[72] Therefore (like a father grieving over his son) go forth, tell them: Behold, I shall bring upon her a healing and a cure, — Only, through the hand of the King of Bavel I shall cure them, "through the sword, famine and pestilence" — while they linger in the land of their enemy! *There* I shall purify them of all their sins, and forgive all their iniquities committed against Me!

— Only *then* shall I return their captivity and have mercy upon them, — "to reveal to them the wealth of peace and truth." [73]

Tzidkiyahu's Worries

Tzidkiyahu, the righteous, was however, totally different from the nobles who surrounded him. Desperately trying to save his people, the King risked his life as well by summoning the prophet into the palace through the third entry of the Bais Hamikdash. Tzidkiyahu swore to Yirmiyahu in secret that he would never kill him, and pleaded, "Do not withhold a thing from me. Just tell me truthfully what Hashem says."

Undaunted, Yirmiyahu then relayed to the King the full prophecy: "Thus says the God of Yisrael: If you go out to meet the commanders of the King of Bavel (and accept the Heavenly Judgment), then you

70 שם פסוק מד.   71 ירמי׳ לג יא.   72 ירמי׳ פרק לב, פסוק לא ולב.
73 ירמי׳ לג, ו.

will live and this city shall not be destroyed by fire. But if you do not go out to meet the princes of the King of Bavel, you shall both perish. This city will be delivered into the hand of the Kasdim who will set it on fire and you shall not escape from their hands." [74]

Yirmiyahu kept beseeching the King to bring about glory not only for the Father but also for Yehuda His son. Time and again, he pleaded with the King: "Listen to the voice of Hashem in which I speak to you, so that all will be well with you, and you shall live! [75] For Hashem will not scorn forever, nor will His anger last forever. He only treats the people according to their doings, and pays them according to the work of their hands.[76] Thus for all those years in which they failed to go up to Yerushalayim for Aliyas Regel for the Festivals they now will go into captivity.[77] And for those seventy years in which you failed to let the soil fully rest her Sabbaticals and Yovel-years while you were dwelling upon her,[78]* accordingly, for seventy years the Land will reclaim its Sabbaths — while you languish in the land of your enemy. Then shall this land rest, and atone for its missed Sabbaticals. Now therefore bend your neck under the yoke of the king of Bavel. Serve him and his people, and you will live.[79] Accept My judgment and drink from God's Hand the Goblet of Wrath, to atone for your sins. — Until the day when He will redeem you! ... For when the seventy years of Bavel are completed, I will take heed of you and fulfill My good word toward you, — to bring you back to this place." [80] Then you shall return and dwell in this land securely, forever. Planted — not to be uprooted again. Built — not to be demolished, forever.[81]

Having forgiven you, Hashem will then in turn unleash His fury upon these pagan nations as well, — when *their* day of reckoning arrives. "Who would not fear You, King of the nations?" sighed Yirmiyahu.[82] Said the prophets to Yirmiyahu: "All the prophets called Him 'King of Yisrael,' Why do you call Him 'King of the nations?' " — Said Yirmiyahu: "I heard Him saying, 'I ordained you a prophet to the na-

---

74 ירמי׳ לח, יח.   75 שם פסוק כ.   76 ירמי׳ כה, יד.   77 גיטין פח.

78 ויקרא כו, לה.   * תוספת דבר.   79 ירמי׳ כז, יב.   80 ירמי׳ כט, י.

81 רש״י שיר השירים ה, ו.   82 ירמי׳ י, ז.

tions',[83] therefore I said: 'King of the nations.' Implying that if on His own children and grandchildren He has no mercy, will He have mercy on others? [84] Then *their* day will come, their day of calamity, when the Goblet of God's Wrath will be poured for the nations. — Now however, accept His Sentence upon you!"

Notwithstanding his righteousness, Tzidkiyahu did not humble himself before Hashem's Prophet.[85] He was concerned over the honor of the descendants of the House of David, and feared for his own life, that the King of Bavel deliver him into the hands of those Judeans who (heeding Nevuchadnezar's demand) had left the city to greet him,[86] and made peace with Bavel. Now they would scheme to torture him [87] in revenge. Also, Tzidkiyahu's hand was weakened, and he felt powerless to stand up to the princes of Yehuda and Yerushalayim. He thus dismissed Hashem's prophet, whose mission remained unfulfilled. Tzidkiyahu even commanded him not to mention his prophecy to the princes of Yehuda. For they had already despised [88] the words of Hashem, and made heavy the ears of Yehuda, *"the rebellious house,"* [89] so as not to listen. — Thus Yirmiyahu stayed imprisoned in the Court of the Guards, until the day Yerushalayim was captured.[90]

83 ירמי׳ א, ה.   84 שמות רבה כט, ט.   85 איכה רבתי ב.   86 מ״ב כה, יא.

87 ירמי׳ לח, יט.   88 ישעי׳ ה, כד.   89 יחזקאל יז, יב.   90 ירמי׳ לח, כח.

PART TWO

The Churban

Chapter One

GLOOM AND DARKNESS

Chapter One

GLOOM AND DARKNESS

AT THIS time Hashem's anger at His people reached the point where remedy was no longer feasible. Neither was there anyone in that generation who could ease and sweeten the bitterness of the sins.[1] — At once "The lion came out of his thicket." [2] And behold, the armies of the King of Bavel waged war over Yerushalayim. They encamped around the city, encircled it with bulwarks and set up ramparts to reach its walls. And while the city came under siege and distress, the Kasdim also attacked the other fortified cities in Yehuda which were still holding out.[3]

Starvation

In Yerushalayim itself there were countless strong and brave men who fought the Kasdim ferociously and inflicted upon them heavy casualties.[4] However, Hashem broke their staff of bread, forcing them now to eat their bread in carefully weighed rations and to drink their water by measure,[5] fearful and anxious about the morrow.[6] Yet the year was one of unmatched bounty; [7] the earth brought forth an abundance of produce, unparalleled since the beginning of time. But Hashem's curse rested upon them, so that the fruit of their soil and of their toil was eaten by strangers, in their very presence. — The Kasdim said: "We will wait until their bread and water supplies are exhausted and their strength depleted." — "Hashem poured out His anger like fire. He destroyed, and did not show pity." "He stripped His Mikdash as if it were a plowed garden. He caused His Place of Assembly to be forgotten, the Festivals and Sabbaths to be neglected in Zion. In His fierce indignation He spurned both king and Kohen." [8]

1 דניאל ט, יג; שמות רבה מ״ג, ג.   2 ירמי׳ פרק ד, ז.   3 שם לד, ז.

4 יל״ש תתרס.   5 יחזקאל ד, טז.   6 שם יב, יח.   7 יל״ש ירמי׳ מא.

8 איכה ב, ו.

Meanwhile, bread was becoming ever more scarce. The city was plagued by hunger, thirst and lack of all basic necessities. "All her people were sighing, searching for bread. They gave away their valuables for food, to keep themselves alive." [9] "Those that were raised in scarlet, now embraced the dunghills." [10] "The tongue of the suckling infant clung to its palate from thirst; toddlers pleaded for bread, but no one provided it for them."

Grief and sorrow engulfed the daughters of Zion when their young ones languished in the streets of the city, asking their mothers: "Where is grain and wine? . . . They fainted like wounded men in the broad streets of the city." — The daughters of Zion gathered in the market places and looked at one another saying: "Why did you come out into the marketplace, you, who never before stepped foot here?" And her friend replied: "Shall I conceal from you how harsh is the plague of hunger? I can no longer bear it!" . . . Clinging to each other, they wandered through the city in search of food, finding none. They finally leaned against the street pillars, embraced them, and died upon them. — "Like all those slain in the public squares of the city!"

And their infants, still living on mother's milk? — "They would come creeping on their tiny hands and feet. Each recognizing its mother would reach for her breast putting it to his mouth in the hope that some milk would come forth. — But the milk would not come. The infants then were seized and stricken, as indeed they poured back their lives into their mothers' bosoms!"

To add to the agony, the Kasdim in their ruthlessness also brought Uchbanin (a fruit whose sweet fragrance is particularly pungent), and roasted them over an open fire outside the Wall. The tantalizing aroma would waft into the city, penetrating the nostrils of those swollen by hunger. Their bellies would burst and they died an appalling death, — "Pierced by the produce of the field." [11] — "Making those slain by the sword even more fortunate than those felled by hunger."

Maddened by hunger, the people ate even the bitter grass of the field and the roots of the greens, from which many died as if pierced

---

9 איכה א, יא.   10 שם ד, ה.   11 איכה רבה ד, ט.

by sword. "The calamity of the Daughter of Zion grew as vast as the ocean, but there was no cure. Neither did the prophets find any vision from Hashem." [12] Her strength ebbed; her beauty waned, turned into neglect and the disgrace of death. Hashem brought upon them confusion and consumption, fever and pestilence. One third of the people died from the plague [13] and from every kind of disease and affliction not even mentioned in the Torah. They filled themselves with bitter grass and stuffed themselves with wormwood, for Hashem's anger was their lot. Their faces were darker than blackness, unrecognizable in the streets. Their skins hung on their bones, dry as wood, until they all dropped to the ground in the streets, young and old alike. The Kohanim, along with the sages, died in the city. They too had searched for food to keep alive; their bodies, like the holy stones, were strewn all over the streets. The sons of Zion, precious like pure gold, became mere shards of shattered earthen pottery ... Their calamity as vast as the seas.

Yet, Yehuda did not repent. "Her impurity still clung to her skirts." Though she was sinking rapidly, she did not consider her future. "The sin of My people became greater than the sin of Sdom which was destroyed within a moment." The daughter of Zion turned into a glutton, "My People became cruel," ... mothers ... upon the flesh of their sons and daughters, and men with the flesh of their friends.[14] "Mothers ate their children, their tender sucklings. The hands of merciful women cooked their own children, for food!" Said one to the other: "Today we will slaughter *my* son, tomorrow, yours!" — And they ate together, amid the siege and distress brought upon them by their enemies.

Yirmiyahu's Grief

Yirmiyahu meanwhile remained in the Court of the Guards, hopeful but helpless. The Heavenly gates of prayer had long since closed to his pleas, and no vision was forthcoming from Hashem. — Embittered,

---

12 איכה ב, ט.   13 יחזקאל ה, יב.   14 ירמי' יט, ט.

he lamented: "Cursed be the day on which I was born" (it was the ninth day of Av[15]). "Cursed be the man who brought tidings to my father saying: 'A son was born to you!'" (This had been Pashchar, son of Immar, a high-ranking officer[16] in the Beis Hamikdash who later had Yirmiyahu beaten and thrown into prison[17]). He even bemoaned the day of his conception.[18] "Why did I emerge from the womb to see only toil and grief and have my days consumed in shame?"[19] To whom can I be likened?[20] To a Kohen whose turn came up to administer "the bitter waters" to a Sotah. The unfaithful woman was brought before him, and he duly uncovered her head to expose her hair. When he handed her the cup of water to drink, he glanced at her. And behold, it was his own mother! — He broke into a wail: woe to me, Mother! I have tried to honor you, and here I shame you!

Thus did Yirmiyahu lament bitterly: "Woe unto me for your sake, Mother Zion! I had hoped to prophesy only good and comforting messages concerning you, but instead, I bring tidings of punishment! My days will be consumed in shame — as it will be said: 'In *his* days was Yehuda exiled.'"

The Day of Hashem's Fury

While Yirmiyahu languished in his grief, and Tzidkiyahu pursued righteousness, the wicked nobles of Yehuda, together with all the people, refused to take heed and repent "before darkness descended."[21] Courageously, the soldiers still remained at their posts while the fortress of Yehuda, its towers and high fortified walls still stood intact and strong. For three and a half years the Kasdim tried to breach the walls but failed, because Hashem was strengthening the people of Yerushalayim,— "perhaps they might yet repent."[22] With massive hammers (each weighing as much as the load carried by three hundred mules) the Kasdim battered the gates of Yerushalayim trying to crash them, but

15 חז"ל, הובא בספר סדר הדורות ג"א רצח, עי"ש.   16 ירמי' פרק כ, פסוק ב.
17 חז"ל, הובא ברד"ק ירמי' כ, טו.   18 שם כ, יד, ובראשית רבה, פרשה סד ה.
19 ירמי' כ, יח.   20 יל"ש ירמי' כ.   21 ירמי' כג, טז.   22 פתיחתא איכה רבה.

the hammers themselves shattered to pieces.[23] For eighteen years even Nevuchadnezar himself lived in fear of the G-d of Yisrael. He therefore stayed in Rivlah and sent his loyal aide [24] Nevuzaradan [25] against Yehuda and Yerushalayim. [26] Even "the kings of the earth and the inhabitants of the world at large refused to believe that an oppressor or enemy would ever enter the gates of Yerushalayim." — — And now Nevuzaradan too was seized by fear, and resolved to pull back and return to Bavel, — "lest the people of Yehuda do to me as they did to Sancheriv, King of Ashur!"

Alas, Yehuda's sins caused it to happen. — A Voice from on High spoke to him: "Attacker, son of the Attacker, arise and capture Yerushalayim! — The time has come for the Bais Hamikdash to be destroyed and for the Kodesh Hakodashim to be burned down!" [27] — The dreaded day of Hashem's fury had indeed arrived.

And Hashem did as He had planned. He destroyed, and did not spare. He cast down from heaven to earth the glory of Yisrael. He did not remember His foot-stool on the day of His anger, but cut off in fury every vestige of Yisrael's greatness. "He retrieved His Right Hand in the face of the enemy," that it would not again serve Yehuda as a protection and salvation. "He raised the banner of our oppressors causing our enemies to exult in our sorrow."

The Wall is Breached

In the eleventh year of Zidkiyahu (3338), on the ninth day of the month of Tamuz (with the city in the grip of starvation and its people without bread, — except for the nobles and soldiers) Nevuzaradan charged forward. With the back of his hammer he struck one single blow at the Wall.[28] — And the City was breached.[29]

At once, all the Commanders of the King of Bavel — brazen and haughty [30] — rushed forward. Hastily they sat down by the center gate (the middle one of the three walls surrounding Yerushalayim [31]).

26 איכה ד, יב.   25 סנהדרין צה: 24 יל"ש מ"ב, כה.   23 סנהדרין צו.

30 ירמיה לט, ג.   29 ירמי' נב, ז.   28 שם.   27 סנהדרין צו:

31 רד"ק שם.

There, each set up his seat, at the very entrance of the gates of Yerushalayim (as Yirmiyahu had prophesied [32]). Like a shepherd, shame-
lessly hanging his pitcher on the hook formerly used by his master.[33]

While the armies of the Kasdim were besieging the city, Tzidkiyahu
and all his military aides decided to escape secretly. They saw the
calamity descending upon them from Heaven, and the city falling into
the hands of the Kasdim. — Hurriedly they fled in the darkness of the
night through the gate between the two walls adjoining the Royal
gardens, into the tunnel [34] leading from the palace to the plains of
Jericho.[35]

Relying on Human Strength

When the distressed Bnei Yehuda saw the Wall of the City of David
breached, "the choicest of valleys" filled with Bavel's chariots and
her knights poised to storm the gates of Yerushalayim and enter the
city, they gathered all their weapons to resist their enemies. They assembled the people in front of the steadily increasing breaches in the
Wall. Then they collected the little water that still remained in the city.
They used part of it for mixing the lime to close up the breaches in
the Wall, while they filled the ditch they had dug between the walls
with the remainder to prevent the enemy from penetrating the city.*
They also surveyed the houses of the city, with stoic resolve demolishing
many of them to use the stones to fortify the Wall.

Alas, it was only to their weapons that they turned. If only they had
put their trust in the Almighty while doing all that was humanly possible
(as the righteous Chizkiyahu had done before, when he strenghtened
the breached Wall).[36] But the eyes of this generation were fixed only
upon armor. To Hashem Who had built and established Yerushalayim,
they did not return. They refused to acknowledge the L-rd Who had
long since chosen this city as His abode,[37] pretending that there was
no "rod of His wrath." "The House of Rebellion" thus profaned

32 ירמי' א, טו.   33 סנהדרין קג.   34 עירובין סא: 35 שם מ"ב, כה ד ו-ה.

* תוספת דבר.   36 דה"ב לב, ה.   37 רש"י ישעי' כב, יא.

Hashem's Name by imitating the ways of the nations surrounding them: to wage (their) war with armed force alone. Said Hashem, the L-rd of the H-sts: "Surely, this iniquity shall not be forgiven until you die." [38]

"For I know their inclination which drives them today," Hashem said, concerning this generation.[39] "I know your rebelliousness and stiff necked obstinance,[40] since despite all your afflictions, you still reject My rebuke, thus profaning My Name among the nations." — Therefore, repentance alone will not atone for your sins, nor will the Fast of Yom Kippur (when you mortify your flesh before Me), nor the bitter sufferings befalling you continuously. Only death will bring you salvation! [41]

Bnei Yisrael barricaded themselves in their homes. They rushed to the roof-tops to fend off their attackers.[42] Each of Yerushalayim's massive mansions alone was strong enough to withstand an onslaught for at least forty days.[43] — But Hashem had long since removed His protective shield from them,[44] rendering them helpless before the enemy.[45] — On the 17th day of the month of Tamuz Bnei Yisrael could no longer bring sheep into the city. The daily offerings of the *Korban Tamid* were discontinued,[46] — and all their courage abandoned them.

The Valley of Slaughter

On that same day, the inner Wall of Yerushalayim was also breached. The jubilant Kasdim haughtily swept into the city to loot and plunder. They disdainfully abused the Sons of Yehuda already consumed by hunger. Their swords brought bereavement in the streets, while terror gripped those inside the homes. The Kohanim were not revered, nor were the eldery spared. Young man and maiden, the elderly and the venerable, all were victimized by the Kasdim. (Other conquerors at least spared the elderly and the very young.) "Forward, let's wipe out

41 יומא מח.	40 סד״ע פכ״ז.	39 דברים לא, כא.	38 ישעי׳ כב, יד.
44 ישעי׳ שם, פסוק ח.	43 איכה רבתי פ״ב.	42 ישעי׳ פרק כב, א.
	46 ערכין יא:	45 תורת כהנים בחוקותי ז.

155

this people!'', they defiantly shouted. Joyfully, they crushed the young men. Like on a day of gathering, they trampled our gallant ones and crushed the imprisoned of the land. Among these were youths who eclipsed the very sun with their beauty.[47] — But "the enemy slaughtered all those precious to the eye."

The maidens of Zion too were grieving; their lot was especially bitter! While the hordes of Kasdim went after silver and gold to pillage the spoils, thousands of their soldiers and archers turned to the modest, genteel daughters of Yerushalayim [48] — to chase and defile them. They humiliated the women of Zion; the maiden of Yehuda were "trodden like grapes in a wine-press." [49] — Their hearts cried out to Hashem, and they wept before Him; "Master of the Universe, You have not spared us. Will You have no mercy on the Holiness of Your Great Name either?" [50] — And they lowered their heads to the ground.

Like a raging fire Hashem's wrath burst upon the Children of Zion. The Kasdim slaughtered and had no pity. They devoured Yisrael, — the aged and the young, men, maidens, children and women alike. They went on butchering without stop,[51] until they saturated the streets of Yerushalayim with blood. Blood mingled with blood. Yehuda turned into a travesty of death. Bnei Yehuda in their anguish cried: "We are doomed! Our days are finished. — The end has come!"

Attempting to flee the sword, many of the stricken reached the lands of Ammon and Moav.[52] They ran to these neighboring countries, and fled even to the distant land of Edom, their arch-enemy. In their fright the stumbling fugitives hid in forests and villages, in mountains and deserts. But their flight was cursed. Wherever they went, Hashem's fury was their lot, for "even those in distant places perished of pestilence." [53] Their strength depleted, they paid with their lives for their bread, falling by the sword in the desert. Feebled, they were constantly pursued, without respite. Their pursuers were swift, fleeter than the eagles. They jumped upon them on the mountains, and ambushed them in the desert. Bnei Yehuda had escaped from the sword, only to

47 סנהדרין צב: 48 יבמות טז: 49 איכה א, טו.   50 גיטין נח.
51 סנהדרין שם.   52 ירמי׳ מ, יא.   53 יחזקאל יב.

be slain by the sword. And those who were captured were wantonly abused by their captors. — Finally, they were killed heaps upon heaps.

Said Rabbi Yehoshua, son of Karcha: "An elderly resident of Yerushalayim told me: 'In this valley alone Nevuzaradan, chief of the Guardsmen, slaughtered two million one hundred thousand people. In Yerushalayim, on one rock alone, he slaughtered nine hundred and forty thousand'." [54]*

In their ruthlessness the Babylonians did not even spare infants and innocent sucklings. They were bent upon wiping out every remnant of the Jewish people.

With unparalleled sadism, they grabbed tender babies and shattered their heads against the rocks. — — Said Ula: nine measures (Kabin) of brains were found on one stone alone.[55] — — Said Rabbi Yehoshua, son of Levi: three hundred children were found tied together, suspended from one branch! [56]

Viewing all this, pride filled the Kasdim's hearts. They opened their mouths, hissed and gritted their teeth. They boasted: "We swallowed them up. This day which we had hoped for is ours. We witnessed it!" [57]

Tzidkiyahu Sentenced

Tzidkiyahu too, was made to drink the bitter goblet of Hashem's fury. All his armies dispersed, the last of Yehuda's kings tried to escape through the eighteen-mile-long tunnel leading to Yericho.[58] He fled in the darkness of night, his coat slung over his shoulder (to speed up his escape). He was exhausted, yet his sons kept hurrying him along. — But Hashem's net was spreaded out, ensnaring him.[59] Hashem caused a deer to run along the tunnel roof, on the outskirts of the city. The Kasdim chased after the deer and caught it at the tunnel's entrance in the plains of Jericho, at the very moment when Tzidkiyahu emerged from the cave.[60] They seized him and brought him to the King of

54 גיטין נז.   * תוספת דבר.   55 שם נח.   56 איכה רבתי ה, יד.
57 איכה ב, טז.   58 במדבר רבה ב, ט.   59 יחזקאל יב, יג.   60 רש"י שם.

157

Bavel in Rivla (Antuchia[61] which lies on the northwestern edge of Yisrael's border*). The King spoke to him harshly.[62]

Said Nevuchadnezar: "What made you rebel against me? — Which law should I apply to you? If it be the Law of your G-d — then you deserve the death penalty, for you swore falsely in His Name. If it be the law of my Kingdom, you must also be put to death for breaching your oath to the King."

Tzidkiyahu replied: "Kill me first that I may be spared the sight of the blood of my ten sons!" — But his sons pleaded: "Let *us* rather die first, that we may not see our father's blood being spilled on the ground!"[63]

The judgment of the thirty-two-year-old Tzidkiyahu lasted nearly four months. On the seventh day of Cheshvan[64]* the wicked king heeded the words of the ten sons, slaughtering them first, before the very eyes of their father — to increase his suffering. Afterwards Nevuchadnezar summoned the Great Sanhedrin to Rivla.[65] He accused them too of treason, saying: "*You* absolved him of his oath!" — He then stripped them of their power and they sat down on the ground, mute.[66] Then he slaughtered them too before Tzidkiyahu's eyes.[67] After this horrendous act, Nevuchadnezar revengefully persisted in his cruelty. He gouged out the eyes of the heartbroken king, and tossed them into the oven.[68] — Actually, Tzidkiyahu deserved to perish alongside his contemporaries for their combined sins, for failing to stop them from their wrongdoings though he had the power to do so.[69] However, the merit of having saved Yirmiyahu from certain death in the pit of mire now helped to spare him from death.[70] Nevertheless, G-d's earlier warnings came true: "I shall wreak My vengeance upon his head" — by blinding the eyes which are suspended in his head . . .[71] — And the sun of the dynasty of the House of David was eclipsed.[72]

At that moment Hashem degraded Yehuda's Kingdom and its rulers.[73] Nevuchadnezar took Tzidkiyahu, (the last king of the Davidic dynasty

61 סנהדרין צו. * תוספת דבר. 62 מלכים ב, כה, ו. 63 יל"ש מ"ב, כה.
64 שו"ע או"ח תקפ. * תוספת. 65 גדרים דף סה. 66 איכה ב, י.
67 ירמי' נב, ו. 68 יל"ש מ"ב, כה. 69 סנהדרין קג. 70 מועד קטן כח:
71 יל"ש יחזקאל יז. 72 פתיחתא דאיכה רבתי כג. 73 איכה ב, ב.

to occupy the throne of which it had been said: "Your house will be established forever" [74]), and treated him like a commoner. He bound the grieving monarch in chains, carted him off to Bavel, and imprisoned him until the day he died.[75] — Thus Tzidkiyahu drank the full goblet of punishment for all the generations, — to the last drop.[76]

Tzidkiyahu did, however, acknowledge the justice of Hashem's judgment. He moaned and wept, and cried out in anguish: "Behold, ye people! See what has happened to me! Yirmiyahu prophesied: 'you will go to Bavel, you will die in Bavel, but your eyes will not behold Bavel!' But I did not heed his words. And here I am in Bavel, but my eyes do not see Bavel [77] because Hashem's Hand has come down upon me."

Oppressors — all around

In the span of twenty-eight days (from the 9th of Tamuz — when the city was breached, until the 7th of Av), Yirmiyahu's bitter prophecies concerning Yerushalayim came to pass. The once tumultous and joyous city turned into a morbid "Valley of Vision" (whose rulers fled to far away places [78]). These were days of uproar and confusion, because "Hashem intended to destroy the walls of the Daughter of Zion." [79] The enemy kept tearing and razing, showering destruction upon the mighty Wall. Not only had Hashem commanded the Kasdim against Yaakov, but also its oppressors from all-around.[80] All of Yehuda's evil neighbors joined against them. Ammon and Moav, Plishtim and Edom, and even Ashur.[81] They all rejoiced together, exulting: He'ach! Hail the calamity of the people of Zion! "The House of Yehuda is now like all nations." [82] Hashem detests them; His love has departed from them. They too join now all the nations whom He has delivered into the hands of Nevuchadnezar.[83]

Even the people of Seyir rushed forward, their hearts filled with the rage they had long harbored against Yehuda; now their hate sur-

---

74 שמואל ב, ז, טז.   75 ירמי' פרק נב, יא.   76 סדר עולם פרק כח.

77 יל"ש מ"ב, כה.   78 ישעי' כב, ג.   79 איכה ב, ח.   80 איכה א, יז.

81 תהלים פג, ט, ובראשית רבה לז, ד.   82 יחזקאל כה, ח.   83 רש"י שם.

faced and the innermost hopes of their hearts were exposed.[84] Indeed, Hashem had made Seyir lowly and despised by the nations. They had neither language nor script of their own.[85] But in their evil haughtiness they continuously harmed and avenged themselves upon Yehuda. When Nevuchadnezar surrounded Yerushalayim, the Edomites came from Seyir and posted themselves at the crossroads, about a mile behind the Kasdim. There they stood, hurling insults at the Creator, and slaughtering all those who had escaped the sword of the Kasdim.[86] Yet it was not its own battle that Edom was waging, for this Churban was not meant to be their doing, but Bavel's. Furthermore, Edom's ambition was to be among the very first to destroy the holy city after it was breached.[87] — They joined the slaughter, spreading devastation on the Holy Mount. Yet they were not satisfied with "the sacking of their brother Yaakov." Indeed, their brazenness reached its peak on the very day of their brother's calamity, when Hashem brought upon His people the tragic Day of Yerushalayim. — Said Edom in his eternal hate: "Raze it! Raze it! Destroy it completely, — down to its very foundation!"[88]

Pagans in the Bais Hamikdash

As for the Almighty, the verse tells us:[89] "It was *He* Himself breaking down the walls, and shouting to the mountains!"[90] Throughout these twenty-eight days it was as if Hashem was bewailing and lamenting the downfall of his children who fell by sword; as if He, the Blessed One, shouted to the mountains, because of the voice of despair rising from His people — If only they would repent! . . .

In vain did He smite His children. They did not heed the lesson, and the nation did not return to the One Who struck it. "I am weary of reconsidering," said Hashem.[91] He hid His Countenance from them, and so they died by sword, hunger and pestilence. The time had come to destroy the G-dly Dwelling that stood in their midst.

84 עובדי' פסוק ו.   85 עבודה זרה דף י: 86 יל"ש עובדי'.   87 שם.

88 תהלים קלז ז.   89 ישעי' כב, ה.   90 תענית כט.   91 ירמי' טו, ו.

Said the Almighty: "As long as I dwell in My House, the nations cannot touch it. But I will turn away My eye from it and shall swear not to consider it until the time of Redemption! — Let the enemy come and destroy it!"

Immediately, Hashem swore by His Right Hand, and withdrew it before the enemy.[92] — It was the seventh day of the fifth month (Av). On that very day the enemy entered the Heichal and destroyed it.

The heart of the wicked commander then swelled with arrogance. But a Heavenly Voice issued forth saying: "Villain, why do you boast? If Heaven had not inflicted their woes, would you have ever been able to overcome them? It is a dead people that you slaughtered, a consumed Mikdash that you set to fire, milled flour that you have ground"...[93]

As soon as Nevuzaradan entered the Court of the Kohanim (where the Jews once had slain Zacharya, son of Yehoyada, the Kohen), he found this prophet's blood foaming and seething. Nevuzaradan was startled. He asked the Kohanim: "What kind of blood is this?" They replied: "It is the blood of the oxen, rams and sheep that was spilled here." At once he ordered that they bring the blood of some fresh offerings, but it looked different. Said Nevuzaradan: "If you tell me the truth, good. But if not, I shall rip your flesh open with iron combs!"

Replied the Kohanim: "Since the Almighty demands an accounting of this blood, we shall tell you.[94] But what can we say? We had a prophet in the days of Yeho'ash, King of Yehuda, who prophesied about the future destruction of Yerushalayim (describing all that you are doing to us today).[95] We rose up and killed him. For 238 years his blood has been seething without stop. We have smothered it with sand, and tried everything,[96] but the bubbling has not calmed down."

Said Nevuzaradan the villain: "I will appease it!" — He brought the members of both the Great Sanhedrin and the Small Sanhedrin, and slaughtered them over the blood, but it would not quiet down. He brought young boys and maiden and slaughtered them, but it still did

92 פתיחתא דאיכה רבה כ״ד.   93 סנהדרין צו: 94 יל״ש יחזקאל כה.

95 סנהדרין שם.   96 קהלת רבה ג, כ.

161

not rest. He brought small children from their teacher's house, murdered them over the prophet's blood before the eyes of their fathers and mothers, but it would not abate. He brought young Kohanim and butchered them over the blood, and it did not rest. He killed nursing mothers clasping their sucklings, yet the frothing refused to subside. He had already slaughtered 940,000 people, their blood surging up to the grave of Zacharya [97] — and still it would not calm down. — Nevuzaradan then approached the grave and said: "Zacharya! Zacharya! I have killed the best of them, do you want me to slaughter them all?" — At once, the Almighty signaled the Prophet's blood. It quietened down, and sank in the ground on the spot. — At that moment Nevuzaradan contemplated converting to Judaism.[98]*

Blood was then shed like water, blood mingling with blood. In anguish the Bnei Yehuda cried out to Hashem: "You wrote in Your Torah, 'do not take the mother together with the children,' but here mothers and children are both being dashed to pieces. You wrote in Your Torah: 'Do not slaughter an ox or sheep together with his son on the same day,' yet here parents and children are all being killed on the same day. — You wrote: 'When a man hunts a beast or a bird and slaughters it, he shall cover its blood with earth,' — and here blood is spilled throughout Yerushalayim, but there is no one to bury the dead.[99] We are treated not even like beasts or fowl."

The Almighty had already forsaken His Mizbe'ach, and abandoned His Mikdash. — He delivered the walls of its palaces into enemy hands.[1] — Thereupon, an angel descended from Heaven, placed his feet upon the Wall of Yerushalayim, and breached it. The angel then called out saying: "Let the enemies come and enter the House whose Master is no longer here. Let them plunder and loot it! Let them enter the vineyard and sever its vines, — its watchman has abandoned it!" [2]

Thereupon all the dignitaries of Bavel came, each establishing his chair in the Middle Gate (between the Gate of the Woman's Court

97 סנהדרין שם.   98 קהלת רבה ג, כ.   * תוספת.   99 איכה רבה א, לז.
1 איכה ב, ז.   2 יל"ש ירמי' כ.

and the Gate of the Heichal), the place where the Great Sanhedrin used to convene and dispense the Law to Yisrael. "At the site of justice, there was the wickedness" as the enemies haughtily set up a platform on the Holy Mount, to deliberate how to burn down the Beis Hamikdash — which had now been captured by pagan hands.[3]

The enemy stormed into the Heichal and roared, as they would do on their Day of Assembly.[4] The defiled ones rejoiced when they entered the Holy Beis HaMikdash, to destroy and to devastate. Their hands stretched out toward all of our treasures, to plunder silver and gold. They exulted over us and rejoiced over our tragedy. They opened wide their mouths against us, to insult and belittle us. — "For the Master was no longer in His house!" . . .

At that moment, the evil neighbors of Yerushalayim — the nations of Ammon and Mo'av (about whom Hashem commanded: [5] "They shall not come into your congregation") — rushed forward and joined the enemy. Everyone came to grab silver and gold, but the Ammonites and Mo'abites entered only to seize the Torah Scrolls, as if to flout the Command excluding them from joining the Jewish community.[6] — They then heaped blasphemy upon blasphemy. They surged forward into the Kodesh Hakodashim. When they saw the two Kruvim poised over the Holy Ark, they seized them, put them into a cage, and paraded them through the streets of Yerushalayim, shouting: "Did you not say that this nation does not worship idols? Look what we found, see what they worship! All faces are the same! [7] The House of Yehuda is like all the nations." [8] — And they hurled insults and blasphemy.

The Kasdim meanwhile looted all the precious vessels from Hashem's House. They smashed the majestic copper pillars (dating yet from the days of King Shlomo), shattered the copper stands and water basins, and carried them away — mere scraps of copper . . . They took the holy vessels (used for the Services) and all other utensils, large and small, from G-d's House. They also sacked the treasury of the Beis Hamikdash and the treasures of the king and his aides, plundering all

3 יל"ש שם.   4 איכה פרק ב, ז.   5 שם א, י.   6 איכה רבתי א, לח.

7 איכה פתיחתא ט.   8 יחזקאל כה, ח.

the coveted precious vessels. All these the heathens took and defiled,[9] and carried away to Bavel.[10]

While Hashem's House Burned ...

On the seventh and the eighth day of Av the heathens dined and wined and debased themselves inside the Beis-HaMikdash.[11] But since the final Judgment was already sealed, "Hashem destroyed as He had intended. He did not withdraw His Hand from devouring, and caused the Chail (a part of the Har Habayis) and the walls to lament. Together they languished." [12]

At that moment the Heavenly Prosecution dashed forward before the Almighty and said: "Master of the Universe! Shall this wicked man be allowed to stand and boast: 'I have destroyed Hashem's House, and burned down His Mikdash'? Said the Almighty: 'Then let a fire descend from Heaven and burn the House!' " [13]

Thereupon four angels descended, each holding a torch of fire, and they put these to the four corners of the Mikdash.[14] The day was the 9th of Av, — (the same infamous day on which, 889 years earlier in the desert, the Sons of Yisrael had wept in vain over the Land so "desirable, good and spacious." This very day was thenceforth designated to become a day of weeping for all generations to come[15]). It was also the turn of the Mishmar (Service of the week) of Yehoram. When the Leviyim on the platform were saying the Shir, out of their mouth issued[16] a verse of lamentation (from the Shir of the fourth day[17]): "He has turned their own iniquity against them; in their own wickedness *Yatzmisem*, He cuts them off." And before they managed to conclude, "*Yetzmisem* Hashem-Elokeynu" (which also implies a consolation, from the word *Tzimas* — i.e. "Hashem Elokim will bring them back, *together*"), the heathens came and captured them." [18]

9 בכורות נ.   10 מ"ב כה, יג.   11 תענית דף כט.   12 איכה ב, ח.

13 איכה רבתי א, מא.   14 פסיקתא רבה כז.   15 ערכין יא: 16 רש"י שם.

17 תהלים צד, כג.   18 תענית כט.

As the Day Waned

In the year 3338 (as indicated in the verse: "*Sha-lach,* Banish them from My sight! Let them depart!" — *Sha-lach,* numerical value 338),[19] on the ninth day of Av, before dark, they set fire to the House. Hashem had turned against Yaakov like a flaming fire consuming all around him." [20] The fire kept burning throughout the 10th of Av until sunset, destroying all but the walls of the Beis HaMikdash.[21] It was at the turn of the day, "when the evening shadows lengthened.[22] Darker than black were our eyes, for the crown of our head had fallen." The Beis-Hamikdash — our joy and delight for 410 years [23] — burned down. All the glory of Yisrael has departed, because we sinned!

When the Kohanim and Leviim saw the House engulfed in flames, they seized the harps and trumpets and leaped into the flames.[24] Immediately, groups of young Kohanim gathered, clutching the keys of the Heichal in their hands. They climbed to the roof of the Heichal and cried out, "Master of the Universe! Since we have not proved worthy as Your loyal custodians, let the keys be handed over to You!" — They tossed the keys upward toward the Heavens, and a Hand reached down and caught them. -- And the youngsters too leaped into the flames of the burning Beis-Hamikdash.[25]

While they all gave their lives sanctifying the Holy Name, the enemy poured its wrath on the remaining Kohanim (who had refused to leave the Beis HaMikdash) and burned them alive. Only Yehoshua son of Yehotzadak the Kohen Gadol [26] was left, — a firebrand saved from the flames.[27]

Moreover, the enemies seized untold numbers of our flowering youth and tied their hands behind them. As the youngsters wept over the destruction of Hashem's House, their delicate faces were burnt by the salty tears pouring down their cheeks like the scalded wounds of a boil [28] (fulfilling the verse, "And her tears are upon her cheek").[29] They too were slaughtered inside the Beis Hamikdash by the ruthless enemy

22 ירמי' ו, ד.   21 משנה פרה, פרק ג, ג.   20 איכה ב, ג.   19 ירמי' טו, א.

26 זכרי' ג, ב.   25 תענית כט.   24 פסיקתא רבה כז.   23 ע"ז ט.

29 פתיחתא דאיכה.   28 איכה א, ב.   27 ירושלמי תענית פ"ד.

who knew no pity. Lads and maidens, old men and women; no one was spared. For Hashem had delivered all of them into the hands of the enemies,[30] to destroy the remnant of Yisrael in its revenge.

Yehuda Destroyed

Hashem lashed out in His fury. He poured out His fierce anger, and kindled a fire in Zion which devoured its foundations.[31]

Six measures of anger were poured over Yehuda from on High. Anger and fury, rage and destruction, shattering and extermination — like the six Men of Destruction, each with his particular tool of devastation in hand, to kill and destroy, and to fill the courtyards with the slain.[32] — — The enemies thus burned down the House of Hashem, and the palace of the King. All the houses of Yerushalayim and all the castles, all the great buildings, the synagogues and Houses of Learning where they nurtured prayer and Torah study all were burnt down. The Kasdim furthermore demolished the fortified walls all around Yerushalayim, levelling them to the ground.[33] As if indeed they had wiped out the whole population of Yehuda and Yerushalayim as well, each and every one, as was decreed from on High. "Those who were to die naturally, died naturally; such as were for the sword, died by the sword; such as were for famine, by famine. And those who were for captivity, went into captivity"[34] (Each succeeding punishment in the verse was more severe than the previous one.[35]) — To punish them for the three heavy iniquities (idolatry, adultery, and murder) Hashem brought upon them three bitter decrees:[36] "Because of you the Beis HaMikdash will be plowed into a field; Yerushalayim will be heaps; and the Har Habayis a wooded hill."[37] Yerushalayim thus turned into "the Valley of Death"[38] as well as "the Valley of Vision". For within her walls were realized all the staggering Visions of the Goblet of Hashem's fury.*

30 דהי"ב לו, יז.   31 איכה ד, יא.   32 יחזקאל ט, ז.   33 ירמי' נב, יד.
34 ירמי' פרק טו, ב.   35 בבא בתרא ח: 36 יומא טו: 37 מיכה ג, יב.
38 ירמי' יט, ו.   * תוספת דבר.

The city, once full of people and the glory of Yisrael, she that was called "the beautiful landscape, the joy of all the world," — how did she become consumed by fire, mere heaps of serpents' dwellings?!

For Zion was left like a hut in a vineyard, like a night-lodge in a cucumber field, like a besieged city.[39] "She was transformed into destruction and wasteland, a butt for derisive hissing and curse.[40] For in the day of Hashem's wrath none escaped or remained. Those that I have cherished and nurtured, My enemy consumed." [41]

Nevuzaradan took Serayah the Kohen Gadol (who even then refused to move from the demolished Mizbe'ach), Tzefaniah his Second, and the three Amarkalim who were the keepers of the keys of the Courtyard of the Mikdash; also the high-officer who was in charge of the military, and those of the King's attendants who had not fled with the others; the scribe to the chief general and sixty common men, and he brought them all to the King of Bavel to Rivla. There the King had them beaten and put to death.[42]

Only 832 (numerical value of the words Eretz Yisrael) remained in Yerushalayim, formerly called "the city that teemed with people." They had survived "the sword, pestilence and famine," but had refused to flee the city.[43] These survivors, together with those who had obeyed Nevuchadnezar and made peace with him, as well as the masses of people in the cities of Yehuda which were laid waste, Nevuzaradan exiled to Bavel. Only some six thousand [44] of the most impoverished who had nothing left, he allowed to remain in the land. (As Hashem had given it into his heart.) He gave them fields and vineyards, and they became vineyard-keepers and wine processors.[45] But all other remnants of Yehuda, Nevuzaradan carried off with him on the long and bitter road to Bavel. Along the way the enemies loosened their bow-strings, tying with them the hands of the nobles of Yehuda.[45b] "My young men and maiden went into captivity," as Yirmiyahu had prophesied. — "He led them in darkness, with no light in sight.[46] Thus,

39 ישעי' פרק א, פסוק ח.   40 ירמי' פרק כה, פסוק יח.   41 איכה ב, כב.

42 ירמי' נב, כ"ד עד כ"ז.   43 שם פסוק כט.   44 ס' שלשלת הקבלה וסדר הדורות.

45 ירמי' נב, טז.   45b פתיחתא דאיכה כד.   46 איכה ג, ב.

850 years from the day their Fathers crossed the Yardein river to take possession of the inheritance of the Patriarchs (only two years short of the would-be irrevocable curse of "You shall utterly perish" [47]* at the end of 852 — the numerical value of "Venoshantem" — meaning when you shall become stale in the Land), Yehuda was exiled from its land.[48]

Not only mighty Bavel, but all other nations as well pounced upon Yehuda, like seventy wolves attacking one stray sheep. They banded together, united in their hatred of Hashem and His anointed people. Not only the powerful, but also the lowly nations surged forward from the four corners of the earth: They all took captives from the vanquished Judeans and carted them off to their faraway lands. — Amongst them were "the Exile of Yerushalayim which is in Sefarad" (Spain),[49] and the Yehudim from the land of Canaan, exiled as far as Tzorfas (France).[50]*

47 דברים ד, כה; גיטין פח.   *   תוספת.   48 ירמי' נב, כז.   49 עובדי' פסוק כ.
50 רש"י ומצודת דוד ואבן עזרא שם; ופי' אברבנאל; יחזקאל ה, ב.   *   תוספת.

Chapter Two

ON THE MOURNFUL ROADS OF ZION

Chapter Three

ON FOREIGN SOIL

Chapter Four

TIDINGS OF THE REDEMPTION

Heavenly Weeping
No Light in the Darkness
Among the Exiles
Belated Weeping
Mount Zion Desolated
Yishmael's Betrayal
By the Rivers of Bavel
Hashem's Wrath
Yet to Be Rebuilt

Chapter Two

ON THE MOURNFUL ROADS OF ZION

AS *THE* enemies wreaked destruction on earth below, they also caused grief in heaven above.[1] Even Angels cried outside, and the angels of peace wept bitterly; for the roads were laid waste and wayfarers had ceased traveling. "Hashem indeed had annulled His covenant (with His people), and despised its cities"; He ceased to consider His children as humans. — Said Hashem: "Since I no longer have an Abode on earth, I shall remove My Shechina from here and return to My original Dwelling in Heaven!"

Heavenly Weeping

On that day Hashem, the L-rd of H-sts, called for weeping, lament, hair-tearing, and the donning of sackcloth.[2] He Himself wept, saying: "Woe to me! What have I done? I allowed My Shechina to dwell on the earth below for the sake of Yisrael. Now that they sinned, I have returned to My original Abode. Have I not become a laughing stock for the nations, a mockery to My own creatures?"

The patron angel Metatron then appeared. He prostrated himself before Hashem, and said, "Master of the Universe! Do not weep! I will weep for You!" But Hashem replied: "If you do not let Me weep, I will enter a confine where you may not intrude, and *there* will I cry." [3]

For the catastrophe of Yerushalayim was even greater than that which had earlier befallen Shomron. Likened to a king who had two sons. Angry with one of them, the king seized a cane and struck him. The son writhed with pain and died. When the king lamented over the body of his dead son, he consoled himself with his remaining one. Some time later, he became angry with his second son. Again he grabbed a

1 ישעי' לג, ז—ח.   2 ישעי' כב, יב.   3 יל"ש איכה תתקצו.

cane and struck him, and he, too, died in convulsion. Said the desolate king, "Now I have no more strength to weep; call the mourners, and let *them* lament us — me and My children." [4]

Hashem said to the ministering angels, "Come, let us go together, you and Me, to My Dwelling, and see what the enemies have done to it." [4] Without delay He proceeded with the angels and Yirmiyahu before Him. When they beheld the Beis-HaMikdash, Hashem said, "Indeed, this was My Abode; this was My Dwelling Place. But the enemies have come and done with it as they pleased." [5]

Then Hashem wept. He cried out and said, "Where are My Sons? Where are My Kohanim and My Leviim? Where are they? Where are My mighty ones? What can I do now? How many times did I warn them to repent, only to have them refuse?"...

"To whom am I likened today?" Hashem said to Yirmiyahu. "Am I not like a man who escorted his son to his wedding only to have him suddenly die under the Chupah? And you are not pained, not for Me nor for My children? Go, call upon Avraham, Yitzchak, Yaakov and Moshe in their graves, for they surely know how to weep!" [6]

Approaching the graves of the Patriarchs, Yirmiyahu broke out in bitter lament. "Cherished bones, how can you slumber peacefully? Your children have gone into exile and their homes have been destroyed. Where are the merits of their ancestors to protect them in the lands of drought?" [7]

At once, the Patriarchs broke into weeping, bewailing the ruin of their children. Avraham placed his hand on his head, cried out and wept, "Have I been tested ten times in vain for their sake?" — Yitzchak cried: "Will you not credit them with the merits of that first Sacrifice which was performed through me? Shall my offspring now be ground to dust and wiped out?" — Following them came Yaakov, the youngest of the Fathers, and then Moshe the loyal Shepherd. — Until a Voice from on High called out saying: "This has been My Decree. And by right has it all befallen them!"

At that moment the Patriarchs huddled together and broke out in

4 שם.   5 שם.   6 שם.   7 רבי אלעזר הקליר בקינות לתשעה באב.

violent wailing. Said the Almighty: "Patriarchs of the world: why are you weeping?" — And Moshe the Shepherd broke in and pleaded: "Master of the Universe! Is there really no return for the children?"

Voice in Rama

Then, "A voice was heard in Rama, a lament and bitter weeping. Rachel weeps over her children. She refuses to be consoled over her children, because they are not there." [8] — And not with legal claims or arguments did Rachel come forward; not with force, nor even with the merits of the Patriarchs and Matriarchs. She came with a simple undisputable humane claim that stems from the utter tenderness and compassion of a Jewish mother. With this did she appear, crying before Hashem: "Master of the Universe! It is clearly known to You that Yaakov loved me dearly, and only for my sake did he labor for my father seven full years. But when the day of my heart's rejoicing arrived, my father put my sister in my place. Yet I suppressed my yearnings and restrained my love. I had pity on my sister lest she be not shamed. I therefore revealed to her the signs which I had made up with Yaakov. I showed kindliness and was not even jealous of her. And if I — mere flesh and blood and dust of the earth — was not jealous of my rival and did not put her to shame, — Oh King, Who are everlasting and all-merciful! Why was *Your* anger so fiercely provoked by the erroneous rivalry of idolatry which is without substance whatsoever, to have my children exiled, slaughtered by the sword, exposed to the enemy to do with them as he pleases — Shall *Your* mercy perhaps be less than the mercy of Your woman-servant of flesh and blood?"

At once Hashem's compassion was aroused and He responded: "For your sake, Rachel, I shall act! Withhold your voice from weeping and your eyes from shedding tears. There is reward for your deeds, says Hashem — and they shall return from the land of the enemy!" [9] — — with the coming of the generation that will again yearn for My Kingdom.[10]

8 ירמי' לא, יד.   9 שם פסוק טו, טז.   10 יל"ש שם.

173

No Light in the Darkness

Moshe the loyal shepherd then came forward and said: "Enemies: By your own lives, I put My oath upon you not to kill Bnei Yisrael with cruel deaths, and further, not to destroy them completely! Do not slay the son before the very eyes of his father or the daughter before the very eyes of her mother. For the Day of Reckoning will surely come, when the Master of the Heavens will demand of you a full accounting of your doings." [11]

But the Kasdim did not act thus. They tortured the father together with the son, the mother together with her daughter. They led them away in darkness with no light in sight, and showed them no mercy whatsoever. They placed their heavy yokes even on the aged, contrary to accepted universal custom. [12] They locked the young men into iron chains, with their hands tied behind their back.

When Nevuchadnezar, the wicked, lifted his eyes and saw them still marching erect, he called out to his servants: "Place heavy loads on their shoulders, until their bodies buckle under them!" As there were no millstones in Bavel, they placed millstones of crushing weight on the young men's necks who had to drag them to Bavel. [13]

The exhausted captives wanted to sit down and rest, but the Kasdim forbade it. [14] They trudged on, exhausted before the pursuer. They asked permission to pause to pray, but Nevuchadnezar had already ordered Nevuzaradan: "Their God accepts those who repent. His Hand is always stretched out to receive those who return to Him. After you have conquered them, do not give them a chance to pray, for they may yet repent and then their God will have mercy upon them." When one of the exiled still arose to pray, he was immediately seized, cut to pieces and tossed before the captives. Having no choice, the weary exiles thus continued their forced march, "chased to their very neck", [15] — unable to bring forth a prayer from their throats.

The exiles but wished to weep, "We are so ashamed to have abandoned the Land," but the enemies did not allow it. They hurried the

---

11 שם. 12 ישעי׳ מז, ו. 13 איכה רבתי ה, יג. 14 ילקוט תהלים קלז.
15 איכה א, ו.

captives on, beating them continuously. Only when the Kasdim themselves stopped to eat or to drink could the hungry and weary captives stop to weep and lament.[16] Their tears were their bread by day and night.[17] "For marked is the yoke of my sins in God's Hand, twisted like ropes around my neck. He has caused my strength to falter, delivering me into the hands of those whom I can not resist." [18]

Yirmiyahu is Lured Away

At the time when Yerushalayim was about to be destroyed, Hashem had said to Yirmiyahu: "Arise, go to Anasos and buy the field from your cousin Chanamel." Yirmiyahu then thought, "Perhaps the Almighty took pity on them. Or maybe Yehuda repented, and now they will again become involved in the study of the Torah." However, as soon as Yirmiyahu, "Hashem's friend," rose and left Yerushalayim, an angel descended and braced his foot against the walls of the city and breached them. At once the enemy burst in and destroyed Hashem's Dwelling, and turned Yerushalayim into ruins. Meanwhile Yirmiyahu, having carried out his mission in Anasos, turned back to the holy city. He lifted his eyes and saw smoke rising from the Beis-HaMikdash. Wishfully he thought, "Perhaps Yisrael has repented? They are bringing their offerings again, and this is the smoke of their Ketores" (holy incense). Drawing closer, however, he saw the walls breached and the Mikdash turned into mounds of stones. He screamed and cried out: [19] "Hashem, You lured me into leaving by sending me away on Your mission, and I let myself be lured. You forcefully caused me to leave Yerushalayim, and now You have won!"

Among the Exiles

Sobbing, Yirmiyahu took to the roads and searched the paths. "Which way did the sinners go?" he cried. "Which way did the strayed ones take? Let me go and perish together with them!"

---

18 איכה א, יד.   17 ילק"ש תהלים מב.   16 יל"ש איכה רבתי תתרכא.
19 ירמי' כ, ז.

Continuing on his way, Yirmiyahu saw a path full of blood stains and all the ground alongside soaked with the blood of the slain. Fixing his eyes to the ground he recognized the footprints of toddlers and small children who had gone into captivity, and he bent down and kissed them.

Meanwhile the exiles were approaching Rama. As soon as they reached it, they broke into bitter wailings. At once Mother Rachel, too, broke into bitter moaning to plead for mercy for them. "A voice was heard in Rama, lamentations and bitter weeping. Rachel weeps over her children." — Just then Yirmiyahu reached his brethren.[20] He embraced and kissed them. He wept with them and they wept with him. Said Yirmiyahu in his sorrow: "Woe to you, my brethren and my people that all this has befallen you, because you did not hearken to my prophecy." [21]

Relentlessly the captain kept driving the exiles forward, robbing them of their strength. But when the weary captives saw Yirmiyahu in their midst, they gathered strength. Slowly they continued their march.[22]

Having followed the exiles in order to be with them, Yirmiyahu voluntarily locked himself up in chains together with the young men.[23] When Nevuchadnezar saw the prophet among the exiles in Rama, he gave strict orders to Nevuzaradan, captain of the Guard, concerning Yirmiyahu.[24] "Take him away, and keep your eyes on him (but not on his nation). Don't do him any harm (but his people you may harm as you like). Grant his every wish (but not the wishes of his people)!"

As soon as Nevuzaradan released him from his chains, Yirmiyahu noticed a group of young boys in shackles. He went and pressed his head close to their heads, inside the chains, but Nevuzaradan came and took him away. Seeing a group of older men chained together, he came back and thrust his neck together with theirs, but again Nevuzaradan came and removed him.

Said Nevuzaradan to Yirmiyahu: You must be either a false prophet,

20 רש"י ירמי' מ, א.   21 פסיקתא רבתי כז.   22 פתיחתא דאיכה לד.
23 ירמי' מ, א.   24 פתיחתא דאיכה לד.

insensitive to pain, or desirous of bloodshed. A false prophet — because for years you kept prophesying that this city will be destroyed, and now that it is destroyed, you are bitter about it. Insensitive to pain — because I really do not want to harm you, but you are trying to harm yourself! Desirous of bloodshed, because the King ordered me not to harm you and you yourself are looking for ways to be harmed, so that the King will hear of it and kill me.[25] — And Nevuzaradan forcefully tore him away from the exiles.

Belated Weeping

Yirmiyahu insisted on staying with his brothers and did not move from them. Finally, the exiles reached the borders of our Land. The Captain of the Guard kept close watch over Yirmiyahu. He came over and asked the prophet: "Would you like to come along with me to Bavel, where I will keep a watchful eye on you, or would you rather return and stay here in the land of Yehuda?" [26]

Yirmiyahu's heart was heavy with grief for both his people and his country. Finally Hashem's Word came, helping him to decide. Said Hashem: "Yirmiyahu, if you will stay here in the Land of Yehuda, I shall go along with the exiles to Bavel. But if you go with them, then I will stay here in the Land." Yirmiyahu answered: "Master of the Universe! If I go with them, what can I do to help them? Better let their King and Creator go with them, for He can help them considerably.[27] Further, if I go with them to Bavel, there will be no one to comfort the impoverished remnant here in the Land." [28]

Nevuzaradan presented Yirmiyahu with food and gifts, and sent him off.[29] — And Yirmiyahu turned to part from his brethren. When the exiles lifted their eyes and saw Yirmiyahu leaving them, — they all broke out into weeping and cried: "Yirmiyahu, our master, are you really leaving us?"

Yirmiyahu answered in his sorrow: "I call upon the Heavens and

25 שם.   26 ירמי׳ מ, ד.   27 פתיחתא דאיכה שם.   28 יל״ש תהלים קלז.
29 ירמי׳ מ, ה.

Earth as my witness, had you only cried once — while still in Zion, you would not have been exiled!" [30]

Mount Zion Desolate

As Yirmiyahu made his way back alone through the mournful, desolate roads of Zion, he found chopped off fingers scattered about the hills. He gathered them, tenderly held them in his hand, and kissed them. Then he lovingly covered them with his robe and said: "My sons, did I not warn you? Did I not tell you: [31] Give glory to Hashem your God before it gets dark, yet before your feet stumble on the mountains of darkness!" [32] And thus Yirmiyahu, lonely, continued his journey, sobbing, "How pitiful you are, dearest of all countries!" [33]

It was concerning these very times that he had once prophesied: [34] "For the mountains I will take up a weeping and wailing, and for the meadows of the wilderness, a lament. For Yisrael's majestic hills turned into wilderness, and no longer is heard on them the voice of cattle." Because the people did not hearken to the words of Torah nor to the voice of prophecy. Therefore the bird of the sky as well as the beast, have all departed; they are all gone.[35]

Yirmiyahu continued along his solitary way, lamenting: [36] "Would that my head were water and my eyes a fountain of tears, that I might weep day and night for the slain of my people." For grievously broken is my nation,[37] my sons were not even eugolized or buried, remaining as dung on the surface of the earth [38] — mere feed for the birds of the sky.

Weeping, the prophet continued: "For the ruin of my people I am broken, possessed by gloom! [39] My eye waters down and does not cease, without intermission.[40] For He that would comfort and relieve my soul is far away from me. My children have become desolate, because the enemy has prevailed." [41]

30 יל״ש תהלים פרק קלו.   31 ירמי' פרק יג, טז.   32 סוף פתיחתא דאיכה.

33 פסיקתא רבתי.   34 ירמי' ט, ט.   35 שם.   36 ירמי' ח, כג.

37 שם יד, יז.   38 שם טז, ד.   39 שם ח, כא.   40 איכה ג, מט.

41 איכה א, יח.

Yirmiyahu kept crying in his sorrow: "My heart, my heart goes out to the slain; my innards twist in pain over the slaughtered!" Rivers of tears flowed from his eyes, over the calamity of his people and the exile of Hashem's servants; over the gloomy roads of Zion and her gates which stood deserted; over the desolate Mount of Zion, where foxes now prowl; [42] over the intrusion of Hashem's defilers into the Chambers of the Mikdash; the desecration of the vessels of the Heichal and the Mizbeach of incense; and over the holy Shulchan — empty and shamed. — For what does a Father have left after He has banished His sons . . ." [43]

Yirmiyahu kept walking and weeping, weeping and walking, — until he reached the home of Gedalyah, son of Achikam, in Mitzpah. There he remained among the people who were left in the Land. [44]

42 שם ה, יח.   43 ברכות ג.   44 ירמי' מ, ו.

Chapter Three

ON FOREIGN SOIL

SAD and bitter was the exiles' lot as they were led on to foreign soil. Ruthlessly the enemy kept driving and beating them, relentlessly breathing down their necks. They were driven from mountain to mountain — from one place to another on the long and twisting journey. For months, their feet and hearts were afflicted on dusty roads,* being consumed by drought by day and frost by night. — As they passed near the borders of the land of Yishmael, they pleaded with their captors: "Have mercy on us, and lead us through the land of Arav (Arabia) by way of our cousins the Yishmaelites. Perhaps they will have pity on us."

Betrayed by Neighbors

The Yishmaelites treacherously came forward to greet the captives. Offering different kinds of salty foods, they also brought out air-inflated leather flasks. "Let us drink first," pleaded the Jews. Replied the Yishmaelites: "First eat, then you will drink." Feeling reassured, the exiles ate first, then thirstily they put the flasks to their mouths to drink the water — but instead they swallowed only air, and their stomachs burst.[1] "All her friends dealt treacherously with her; they became her enemies.[2] They heard of her plight and they rejoiced." [3]

As the oppressed exiles were driven past the border of Mo'av and Ammon, these too joined in with insults against Hashem's nation. They taunted them: "Why do you weep? Are you not going home, to the house of your father? Did your ancestors not dwell on the other side of the river?" [4]

The Kasdim kept chasing the captives onward with Nevuzaradan roaring over his prey like a lion.[5] The exiles plodded on wearily, with-

---

* תוספת דבר.   1 איכה רבתי ב, ג.   2 איכה א, ב.   3 שם א, כא.
4 צפני' ב, ח ורש"י שם.   5 איכה רבתי פרק ה.

out strength, but their pursuers (contrary to the custom of all conquerors) kept hurrying them on, forcing them to run against their will.[6] They marched them naked like the beasts of the earth, to degrade them. And they became a laughing stock for all people.[7]

The people of Bari, an Arab tribe, came out to watch them and were shocked to see that the Judeans were nude. What did they do? They stripped their own slaves and maid-servants. They then offered the nude slaves to Nevuchadnezar as a gift and said to him, "It seems you are a king who likes nude people." — The wicked man took the hint and said to them: "Take their clothing and dress the Judeans." [8*]

Death From the Waters

From the day they had left Yerushalayim, the Kasdim kept driving the captives without respite, not even allowing them to sit down.[9] When they finally reached the Euphrates River, Nevuzaradan said to his soldiers, "Let them rest. Now that they have come this far, their God will no longer have pity upon them to rescind His decree." And thus the exiles said,[10] "By the rivers of Babylon, there [11] did we sit down" — for the first time.

At once, the exhausted captives rushed to quench their burning thirst from the waters of the Euphrates. Having been used to the pure waters (from mountains, rains, or springs) of Yehuda, many of them [12] died upon drinking from the polluted, foul-smelling waters of the Euphrates.[13] And there (when we finally did sit down), "We *also* wept" — for those who died by Bavel's water.

By the Rivers of Bavel

While the haughty Nevuchadnezar sat on the deck of his royal boat, with his high-ranking aides and dignitaries at his side, entertained by an array of musical instruments and musicians,[14] members of Yehuda's

---

6 יל״ש תהלים קלז.	7 איכה ג, ד.	8 יל״ש שם.	* תוספת.

9 יל״ש תהלים קלז, א.	10 תהלים פרק קלז, א.	11 פסיקתא רבתי כט.

12 יל״ש תהלים קלז.	13 פתי׳ דאיכה יט.	14 ישעי׳ מג, יד.

royalty, chained in iron shackles and nude, were marched down the bank of the river. Nevuchadnezar raised his eyes, and behold, even in misery and captivity, they had grace and dignified carriage, and a radiance was cast over them. He turned to his servants, "Why do these men walk so erect, without any load on them? Are you short of loads to burden their shoulders?"

Immediately the servants brought out Torah scrolls, sewed them into pouches, and filled them with wet sand from the river's bank.[15] They then loaded the heavy pouches on the prisoners' necks and shoulders, causing them to buckle under the crushing load. Cried the Bnei Yisrael, "By our neck we were chased!"

Only then did they lend an ear and open their hearts. — Indeed, Hashem's Hand had struck them sevenfold for their sins, making all the bitter visions of His Prophets come true. — And they acknowledged the Verdict, and bowed to the Divine Judgment: "Hashem is the Righteous, for we have rebelled against His commands!"[16] They wept bitterly and their cries reached up to the Gates of Heaven. Said Rabbi Acha bar Abba: "At that moment, the Holy One, Blessed be He, wanted to turn the world back into chaos. He said: 'Everything I created was only for the sake of this people. But now, of what use is the world to Me? I shall destroy it!'"[17]

Thereupon the angels entered and pleaded before the Almighty: "Master of the Universe! The whole world with everything therein is Yours. Is it not enough that You have destroyed Your Dwelling on earth? Must You now also destroy Your Dwelling in Heaven?!"[18] — Said the Almighty: "Do I need consolations? Am I not everlasting — the Omniscient, Who knows beforehand all that will happen; the One, Who knows all that will be at the End? Therefore, I say:[19] 'Desist! I shall bitterly cry! Do not hasten to comfort Me! I detest the consolations which you offer to comfort Me! Better go down and remove the load from My children!'"

At once, the "Malachim in attendance" descended and lifted the

15 תרגום איכה ה, ה.   16 איכה א, יח.   17 יל"ש תהלים קלז.   18 שם.
19 ישעי' כב, ד.

load off their shoulders; they, and the Almighty with them. As it says: [20] "For *your* sake I was sent down to Bavel." [21]

"For there, by the rivers of Bavel did we sit and weep" a *second* time (the first, when Yirmiyahu left them at the borders of the Land). Because their forefathers had wept needlessly in the desert once (when they rejected "the good, spacious and desirable Land"), their descendants now had to weep twice.[22] They furthermore cried doubly because while still in their land "they did two evils; they forsook Me — the fountain of life-giving waters — and they hewed themselves broken cisterns which could not contain waters." [23] And since they sinned doubly and were punished doubly, by right, they ought to be consoled doubly. Hence, you prophets, "Console My people, console them (doubly), says your God!" [24]

How Can We Sing?

Nevuchadnezar saw the captives weeping, and he said to the Levites: "Why do you sit there and weep? Prepare yourselves. And while we eat and drink, you will stand and play before me and the idols, the way you used to play before your God!"

Startled, the Levites stared at each other. "Is it not enough that we have caused the destruction of our Beis Hamikdash? Shall we now play our harps for this midget and for his idols?"

Hurriedly they held counsel, and hung their harps upon the willows growing on the banks of the river.[25] Overcoming their inhibitions they all then placed their right thumbs in their mouth, crushed them and bit them off. When their captors demanded of them: "Sing for us some of the songs of Zion," the Levites answered proudly: "How can we sing Hashem's song on foreign soil?" [26] They did not say, "We will not sing," but "how *can* we sing?" They displayed their fingers and said: "When we were bound, our fingers were cut off, — so how can we sing?" [27]

20 שם מג, יד.   21 יל"ש תהלים שם.   22 איכה רבה א.   23 ירמי' ב, כג.

24 יל"ש איכה א תתכ"ה.   25 תהלים קלז, ב.   26 קלז ד.   27 ילק"ש קלז.

Upon learning what had happened, Nevuchadnezar slew of them heaps upon heaps. Yet the Levites were gratified and delighted that they had not succumbed to their oppressors' demand to sing Hashem's song before the idol-pagantry.

At that moment the Almighty swore concerning Yisrael: "You overcame your natural inhibition and cut off the fingers of your right hands. I, too, having drawn back My Right Hand from before the enemy, shall not bring it foreward again (in its full glory) until I remember (to return) you." As said: "If I forget you, Yerushalayim, let My Right Hand forget its cunning." [28]

Chapter Four

TIDINGS OF THE REDEMPTION

JUDEA sat lonely and mute, accepting Hashem's Judgment. Saturated with shame,* she offered her cheek to those who struck her. She put her mouth to the sand in submission; perhaps there still was hope. — "For not forever will Hashem forsake us . . ."

In Anguish

The "exile of Zidkiyahu" then returned to the One Who had punished them, and their hearts cried out to Him. For who would have told the evil to descend, if Hashem had not so commanded? But it is not He Who causes the good or the bad to come. These are but the fruit of our own deeds and transgressions. For it is we who have rebelled. — Let us search and examine our ways, and let us return to Hashem. Let us lift our hearts on high, to the Almighty in Heaven. Even though You detested us, have You not already utterly poured Your anger upon us? [1] "You slaughtered on the day of Your wrath, and showed no mercy! You called my oppressors from around as on a day of solemn Assembly. You saw all their revenge, You heard their slander, all their evil schemes against me. And when they heard of my misfortune they rejoiced, because You brought it upon me.[2] Would that You bring upon them the day You have proclaimed to come, and may they become like me — like me in sorrow, but not like me when I will be comforted.[3] Repay them, O Hashem for the deeds of their hands. Bring unto them affliction of the heart. Let Your curse be upon them. Pursue them in anger, and destroy them from under Your skies."

And the children beseeched their Father in Heaven: "Behold Hashem and look down; to whom have You done all this?" — "Draw us back to You, Hashem, and we shall return. Renew our days as of old!" [4]

* תוספת. 1 איכה ה, כב. 2 שם א, כא. 3 פסיקתא, פיסקא "אנכי אנכי".
4 איכה ה.

Wrath Upon the Nations

Even in time of anger, Hashem listened and saw all. From on High He roared and wept over His Abode and His Children who were no longer there. He heard the cries and screams of those who stumbled, and He saw their tears. For the heathens mistreated and tortured them cruelly, out of pure wickedness. They doomed them to pain and shame, to ridicule and slander, to scorn and curse. For "I Hashem raged only a little, but they in their wickedness helped to increase the affliction." [5]

Yet before the Churban and Exile, Yirmiyahu had already prophesied the tidings of recompensation and Redemption. Therefore, Hashem turns a sword against the nations, "the full goblet of His fury" readied in His Hand to make them drink thereof." "And they shall drink and stagger and be crazed," when "Hashem pays them back according to their deeds and for what their hands have wrought. For Hashem has a reckoning with the nations, and toward His servants He will relent." "When the seventy years are completed, Hashem will punish Bavel for her sins, and turn her into an everlasting desolation,[6] a land of waste and hissing, without inhabitants." "I will intoxicate her princes and her wise men, her governors, deputies, and her mighty ones. — And they will slumber a perpetual sleep, never to awake, says the King, whose Name is the Lord of Hosts!" [7]

Not only with Bavel, but with the other nations too, has Hashem designated a day of reckoning; with our evil neighbors who rejoiced at our calamity and came running to inflict damage and ravage Hashem's Holy Mountain.

The Goblet of Fury, therefore, will also pass to Egypt, "the very fair heifer." She too will become a wasteland, devoid of all settlers. "For the day of their ruin will arrive, the designated time of their reckoning.[8] The same applies to the despised Plishtim, to Aza and Ashkelon,[9] to cut off from Tzor and Tzidon every remainder. So will Mo'ab and her cities also be captured, and she will no longer pride herself on her city of Cheshbon; for I strongly detest the haughtiness

---

5 זכרי' א, טו.   6 ירמי' כה, יב.   7 שם נא, לז.   8 ירמי' מו, כא.
9 שם מז, ה.

of Mo'av, the overly proud nation. Her brazennes, arrogance and self-glorification I saw. Therefore I shall pour My fury over Mo'av, and from Elala until Yahatz their voices will shriek.[10] Mo'av will perish as a nation, because she glorified herself over Hashem. — Also in Rabba, the city of the Sons of Ammon, shall I sound the trumpets of war, and she will turn into heaps of rubble.[11] — I shall further spill My fury upon all the kings of the north, from near and from afar."

Also, against the people of Edom Hashem would remember the Day of Yerushalayim. Said Bnei Yisrael before the Blessed One: "You say to us 'remember,' but we are prone to forget. — Would that *You* remember, as there is no forgetfulness before You!" [12]

Edom will therefore become a wasteland; Batzra and all her towns will turn into perpetual ruin! "From the noise of their fall the earth will quake, and the shriek of her cry will be heard to the Sea of Suf." [13] Therefore, "rejoice and exult — for the moment — Daughter of Edom, dwelling in the land of Utz! For to you too will the cup pass. You too will be drunk and will vomit." [13b] — — Praised be He Who will repay you your just desert, for what you have done to us! "Praised is He Who shall seize your infants and dash them against the rock!" [14]

Upon Eilam too I will stretch out My Hand, and I will set up My Throne to judge her. "I will bring evil upon her, the fury of My anger, says Hashem. And I will send the sword after them, till I have consumed them." [15] For Hashem will call the sword against all the inhabitants of the world, to make them pay according to their deeds and for what they have wrought; because they hungrily devoured My people ... And *then,* all those you have slain and who are now slumbering, — "they will arise and live! ..." [16]

A Delightful Child

"Ephraim is My precious son",[17] the Almighty had testified yet earlier about Yehuda; he is Mine and precious to Me, even though he lacks

---

10 שם פרק מח, לד.   11 שם שם מט, ב.   12 מדרש שוחר טוב, קלז ח.

13 ירמי' פרק מט, כא.   13b איכה ד' כ"א.   14 תהלים קלז, ט.   15 ירמי'

מט, לז.   16 "ציון עטרת צבי" לר' יהודה הלוי.   17 ירמי' לא, יט.

the maturity to honor Me. For is he not "a delightful child?" (An expression used for a toddler of 2-3, or a child of 4-5.[18]) Although there is surely a lack of fear and respect for his father in this youngster, and although he does not know yet how to speak well, and only loose chatter and incomplete words come from his lips, yet his chatter and nonsense ring sweet and are a delight to his father's ear. — The same is with My unruly, naughty son Yisrael, even though he has sinned.

"For whenever I speak of him," even if it be rebuke and punishment,* "I remember him ever more," so that even at the time of anger, My love gets the upper hand. "Therefore My innards moan for him," while treating him like a father who must discipline and mete out punishment to the son who is his heart's delight. For indeed, he is My dear son, and I shall not forsake him; not in this world, nor in the world to come.[19] Therefore, "I shall always remember him still more." — The more I remember him, the stronger becomes the remembrance, and the more My innards keep moaning for him. — "I will surely have mercy on him, says Hashem!"

Yet to Be Rebuilt

"Therefore I am with you," says Hashem, "to save you. For I will make a thorough end of all the nations where I have scattered you, but I will not make an absolute end of you. I will chastise you in judgment, yet I shall not destroy you utterly." [20] Says Rabbi Shmuel son of Nachman: Both a harsh decree and a great forgiveness were extended to Bnei Yisrael on the day the Beis Hamikdash was destroyed, as it is written: "Your iniquity, Daughter of Zion, has ended. He will exile you no more." [21] For there is a reward for your labor, as well as for your afflictions. "With weeping shall you come and with prayers shall I bring you, and they shall return from the land of the enemy." "There is hope for your future, says Hashem, and the children shall return to their own borders." [22] Because all who consume you, they themselves

18 ויקרא רבה פרשה ב, פיס' ג.   * תוספת דבר.   19 ויקרא רבה פרשה ב, ב.
20 ירמי' ל, יא.   21 ילקוט שמעוני סוף מ"ב.   22 ירמי' לא, טו—טז.

shall be consumed, and all your oppressors will go into captivity. I shall bring shame on those who plunder you, "but to you I shall bring balm, and heal you from your wounds, says Hashem." "I shall build you again, and you will be rebuilt, O! pure Maiden of Yisrael. You shall again be adorned with your timbrels, and dance forth with the merriful. You will yet plant vineyards on the mountains of Shomron, and the planters who plant will reap the fruit." [23]

For Hashem will surely have mercy upon His people, and He will sign a new covenant with the House of Yisrael and the House of Yehuda. "I shall give My Torah unto their midst, and inscribe it into their hearts. I shall be their God, and they shall be My people." [24] And then "I will return to Yerushalayim with compassion; My House shall be rebuilt in it, says the Lord of Hosts." And a builder's plumb line shall be stretched forth over Yerushalayim [25] to measure her wall, — its length and width.

23 ירמי' לא, ג—ד.   24 שם פסוק לב.   25 זכרי' א, טז ורש"י שם.

Chapter Five

THE REMNANT OF YEHUDA

Chapter Six

THE EXILES IN EGYPT

Chapter Five

THE REMNANT OF YEHUDA

HARD as those times were, yet the Almighty revealed even then to the exiles that His Fatherly compassion and His benevolence had not ceased. Although Yehuda had been banished, in her misery, Hashem had left her a little remnant; Nevuchadnezar had permitted some of the most impoverished to remain in the Land of Yehuda. He now appointed over them as governor Gedalyahu son of Achikam (the son of Shafan the scribe [1]), who, following Yirmiyahu's advice, went over to the camp of the Kasdim yet before Yerushalayim was conquered.[2] By order of the King, Yirmiyahu was to stay with Gedalyahu and board in his house. Thus the Prophet dwelt in midst of the people who had remained [3] in Yehuda and who so badly needed him and his consolation. With him was his disciple Baruch ben Neriyah whom Hashem had spared on the day of His fierce anger, because he had put his trust in Hashem in risking his life to save Yirmiyahu from the pit of quicksand.[4]

Gedalyahu ben Achikam

News of Gedalyahu's appointment reached the ears of Yehuda's former army commanders who, together with some of their men, had managed to escape the burning city of Yerushalayim and hide in caves and forests. They soon learned that the King of Babylon had appointed Gedalyahu (whose father, Achikam, had yet been one of King Yoshiyahu's top officials) ruler of the land, and that he entrusted to him the Remnant of impoverished men, women and children,[5] as well as the unfortunate daughters [6] of the King of Yehuda, all of whom he had not banished to Bavel. Encouraged, they now joined Gedalyahu in Mitzpah: Yishmael son of Netanyah, of the royal family: Yochanan

1 מ״ב כה, כב.   2 ירמי' לט, יד ורש״י שם.   3 שם לט, יד.   4 שם לט, יו.
5 שם מ, ז.   6 שם מא, י.

son of Kore'ach, an army commander; his brother Yonathan; Serayah son of Tanchumas; the sons of Eifai of Netofat and Yizanyahu, son of the Ma'achati; they and their men. They took possession of some of Yehuda's cities and settled there.

But the spirit of the weary settlers was still very low. Moreover, the soldiers feared that Nevuchadnezar would return to punish them for having revolted and waged war against him. "Perhaps we should leave the country and save our lives?" they said. But Gedalyahu swore to them and their men, "Be not afraid to serve the Kasdim. Stay in the land, serve the King of Bavel, and all will be well with you. As for myself, I am staying in Mitzpah to protect you against the Kasdim who might return, so that they will not harm us. Do not fear them. Have faith in the Almighty and gather the wine, the dried figs and the oil which have been left here and there in the land still from the days of the siege. Store them in your vessels, and stay in the cities you have seized." [7]

The army commanders listened to Gedalyahu, they and their men. Even those who had fled to Moav, Ammon, Edom, and other neighboring lands soon learned that the King of Bavel had indeed left a remnant of Yehuda, with Gedalyahu, the righteous and pure hearted son of Achikam, over them.[8] So they returned from wherever they had escaped and confidently came to Gedalyahu in Mitzpah, about six thousand men in all.[9] And they gathered a bounty of dried figs and wine.[10]

The Children then became aware of the Father's mercy. For had He not graciously shown them a ray of light, by not allowing all of Yehuda to be banished and the Land to become thoroughly devoid of its sons? — They took it as a good omen. It gave them hope for a better morrow. Indeed, they said, Yehuda is not yet destroyed!

A Base Jealousy

However, the jealousy of our scheming neighbors was our undoing. Since years gone by, these little nations had been rejoicing at any sign

7 ירמי׳ מ, י.   8 ר״ה יח: 9 ס׳ שלשלת הקבלה.   10 ירמי׳ מ, יב.

of calamity befalling us. And like Bavel the haughty one they, the low and degraded ones, hurried joyfully to kill and destroy the people of Yehuda. The pitiful, small, impoverished Remnant on Yehudah's soil was now like a thorn in their eyes. They therefore plotted to destroy it, to wipe out their memory forever, to slaughter and take possession of their land.

Baalis, King of Ammon, secretly sent a message to Yishmael ben Natanya, instigating him to murder Gedalyahu. Yishmael (a former high-ranking official to the King of Yehudah) was jealous of Gedalyah's standing, and craved the position for himself. Although on his mother's side a scion of the royal family, he was ineligible for kingship, since on his father's side he was the sixteenth generation of a freed slave.[11] Besides, he was the wicked son of a wicked father,[12] deceitful and blood-thirsty. Yishmael therefore let himself be instigated to murder the righteous and innocent Gedalyahu.

Excessive Humility

The plot became known to Yochanan ben Kore'ach and the generals who were in the field. They hurried to Gedalyahu in Mitzpah and said to him: "Do you know that Baalis King of Ammon has sent Yishmael ben Natanyah to murder you?" But Gedalyahu refused to believe them.[13]

Yochanan, however, was apprehensive about Gedalyah's life and about the welfare of "the remnant of Yehudah." He came to Gedalyah a second time and spoke to him in secret. "Take it to heart! Yishmael has arrived here to kill you. He is pursuing you. I will go and kill him first, before he has a chance to murder you (as is halachically right). Not a soul will know about it. Why should he kill you for naught and cause all the people who have rallied around you to disperse, and the remnant of Yehuda to be lost?" [14]

Said Gedalyahu to Yochanan: "Do not do such a thing! You are lying about Yishmael!" (For in his righteousness he would not believe

11 ירושלמי הוריות ג, ח. 12 מגילה טו. 13 ירמי' מ, יד. 14 שם פסוק טו.

195

that Yishmael would conspire to kill an innocent brother and thereby bring annihilation to the last remnant whom Hashem had spared in the Land.)

Gedalyahu, however, spoke out of excessive humility. He should have paid attention to Yochanan's words.[15] Although he suspected Yochanan's warnings to be only slander, nevertheless he should have been on guard, for there was reason to be suspicious of Yishmael, who had only recently returned from Ammon, the enemy's land. This matter further concerned not only Gedalyahu's life, but the future of the whole impoverished remnant in the Land. Gedalyahu, however, was overly righteous, bringing tragedy upon all of them.

Yishmael's Treachery

Fifty-two* (the numerical value of "Gedalyah") days had passed since the Almighty started bringing some light to the remnants of Yehuda who were under the protection of Gedalyahu.[16] But on 3 Tishri,[17] (the day after Rosh Hashana) Yishmael ben Netanyah, together with some of the remaining former aides of King Zidkiyahu (who were also jealous of Gedalyahu's high position), and ten others of their men came to see Gedalyahu in the city of Mitzpah. Neither Yochanan ben Koreach nor his loyal army officers were in town at the time. And Gedalyahu and Yishmael's men "ate bread there together." [18]

Gedalyahu in his innocence was not even suspicious of these men who were actually seeking his life. "Together" — with love and friendship he shared his bread with them. While Gedalyahu was sitting innocently at the table, they suddenly attacked their host, and Yishmael cruelly slew him with his sword.[19]

The bloodthirsty schemers then went and slaughtered the other people, "survivors of the sword" who were with Gedalyahu in Mitzpah. They also killed the Babylonian military whom Nevuchadnezar had left with Gedalyahu. Only some of the common folk and women and

15 ילקוט שמעוני ירמי' מא.   *   תוספת דבר.   16 סדר עולם פכ"ו ור"ה יח:
17 ב"בית יוסף" או"ח סי' תקמט איתא שבר"ה נהרג גדלי'.   18 ירמי' פרק מא, מ.
19 שם פסוק ב.

children remained in the city, being yet unaware of the innocent blood that had been spilled in the house of Gedalyahu.

On the following day, the deceitful Yishmael continued to spread terror. He noticed a group walking the road, — eighty men who had come from Sh'chem, Shiloh and Shomron. They were mourners of Zion and Yerushalayim, shaven of beard (because upon hearing of the Beis Hamikdash's destruction, they mournfully cut off their grace, the beards), with rent clothes (following the Halacha pertaining to one who sees the cities of Yehudah in ruin),[20] and their flesh gashed (like the open ruins of Yerushalayim). They were yearning to see the Mikdash (although the House was not there anymore), as they always had done. They carried offerings and incense to be placed on the ruins of the shattered Mizbeach.[21] — Making a mockery of all their noble intent and feelings, Yishmael treacherously went out to them from Mitzpah, appearing mournful and weeping. As they met, he said to them, "Come with me to Gedalyahu ben Achikam in Mitzpah!" As the dismal mourners followed him innocently into the city, Yishmael and his men callously murdered them, treating their blood even worse than that of a deer or a hart. They tossed their bodies into the pit (dug yet by Assa son of Aviya King of Yehuda, when Baasha King of Yisrael besieged him[22]), filling it up now with the corpses of the slain.[23] (Though Assa had built the pit for Yehuda's welfare, but because he sinned by relying on Haddad King of Edom, his pit now became the place of atrocity. Because from on High the beneficial is brought about through a worthy one, and adversity through the guilty[24]).

Only ten of the men were spared. They had pleaded with Yishmael: "Do not kill us, for we have treasures hidden in the field — wheat and barley, oil and honey — which we stored up from the blessing that rested on the produce of the land in the year of the exile."[25] In return, the greedy Yishmael spared them.[26]

20 מועד קטן דף כו ע"א.   21 פי' מצודת דוד, ירמיה פרק מא, פסוק ה.
22 מ"א טו.   23 ירמי' מא, ט.   24 ספר חסידים מה.   25 יל"ש ירמי' מא.
26 ירמי' מא, ח.

The Churban Completed

Not satisfied with all his atrocities, Yishmael now tried to extinguish the last "Remnant of Yehudah," that which not even Nevuchadnezar, the wrecker, had contemplated. The traitor imprisoned the King's daughters and all the people still left in Mitzpah. Rising early on the third day of the massacre, he forced his captives along on the road leading to the land of Ammon, to settle there among our enemies, — his advisors. As soon as the news of Yishmael's atrocities reached them, Yochanan ben Kore'ach and the army heads gathered all their men and swiftly chased after Yishmael. Yishmael hurried on his way, forcing the imprisoned onward to the point of exhaustion, the faster to reach the land of our evil neighbors. The pursuers caught up with him near the large water pools of Giv'on. Seeing them, the captives slipped away from their fleeing captors, and turned back to their rescuers. Yishmael, however, with eight of his men, escaped across the border into Ammon.[27]

Despite their miraculous escape, the survivors remained heartbroken and bitter. For it was a day of utter tragedy and confusion, as the death of the righteous Gedalyahu was equal to the burning of Hashem's House.[28] Hashem in His mercy had placed him in the Land to protect the poor remnants, but now that this Tzadik was murdered, it seemed that the Almighty had completely removed His mercy from them.

Upon this fateful day the frightening Churban came to be complete. Therefore the prophets designated the day of Gedalyahu's slaughter as a day of fasting and weeping for all generations, like the grievous fast-day of Tisha b'Av. For on 3 Tishrei [29] the remaining "spark of Yisrael" was extinguished, causing the dispersion to be complete.[30]

Gripped by Fear

In the aftermath of Gedalyahu's slaughter, the exiles' spirit sunk to its lowest as they dreaded Bavel's reprisal. "Now Bavel will strike us to

27 שם. 28 ראש השנה דף יח ע"ב. 29 זכרי' פרק ז, ה ור"ה דף יח ע"ב.
30 רמב"ם הל' תענית ח' ב'.

avenge the Kasdim who were killed in Mitzpah and the death of
Gedalyah whom the King of Bavel himself had appointed over the
cities of Yehudah." Thereupon Yochanan and the generals took the
small group of survivors and set up camp in a place once occupied
by Shimon ben Barzilay of Gilead (when he returned from his duel
with Avshalom [1]), near Beis El. From there they planned to make their
way down to Egypt, to save themselves from the Kasdim.[2]

Although they considered their escape a matter of life and death,
they still hesitated to descend to Egypt, the most defiled and corrupt
of all the countries. They turned to Yirmiyahu who was secluded in
his mourning. All the army commanders, together with Yochanan ben
Kore'ach and Yezanyah ben Hoshayah and all the people, the young
and the old, they all approached the Prophet and said: "Let our plea
now be accepted before you and grant us favor, even though we have
sinned and did not listen to you. Pray to your God (not "our God",
for we sinfully rejected Him) on behalf of this small remnant, for we
are left a few out of many as your own eyes can see; That Hashem,
your God, may show us the way to follow and what we should do."
Replied Yirmiyahu, the loyal prophet, "I heard you. I will pray to
Hashem your God, as you request. Whatever Hashem answers I will
relay to you. I shall not withhold a thing from you." [3]

They stood before Yirmiyahu shame-faced, like a thief who is caught.
For forty years they had not heeded the prophet's pleas and warnings,
(If only they had listened, before their whole world turned black upon
them!) Would he now believe their promise to obey him?

Hence they continued to speak and to promise faithfully to accept
the Heavenly judgment. "May Hashem be a true and faithful witness
between us, if we do not act according to whatever Hashem tells us
through you. Be it for good or for bad, we shall obey the Voice of
Hashem, *our* God (as from now on we are acknowledging Him again).
So that it may be well with us as we obey the voice of Hashem, our
God." [4]

1 שמואל ב יט.   2 ירמי׳ מא, יז.   3 ירמי׳ מב, ד.   4 שם פסוק ו.

199

Prophecy Delayed

A partition of iron seemed to separate the last remnant from their Father in Heaven. He did not lend an ear to the plea of His Children who had strayed and were now filled with fear. In vain did they turn to Him now during the Aseres Yémei Téshuvah, seeking Him when He was close and easily reached.[5] — To them He was not available to hear their plea and prayers. And His prophecy was not forthcoming.

They soon realized that Hashem was still angry with them. The days were passing, and still, there was no response. Yirmiyahu remained absorbed in prayers, but still he received no prophecy for them. Days came and went. — Unquestionably, Hashem had turned His Back upon them.

Finally, On Yom Kippur there was forgiveness. After ten days' waiting, Hashem's Word finally came to Yirmiyahu. Joyfully, the prophet called Yochanan ben Kore'ach, the army commanders and all the people, from small to great, and delivered Hashem's message to them:[6] "If you stay and dwell in this Land, then I will build you and not tear you down; I will plant you and not uproot again, for I have reconsidered the evil I have brought upon you." As to your fear of the Kasdim: "Be not afraid of the King of Bavel, for I am with you, to deliver you and save you from his hands. I will grant you mercy by arousing his mercy towards you. And he will return you (and all your exiled brothers) to your own soil!"

"But if you say: We shall go down to Egypt where we will see no war nor hear the battle trumpet of war, nor be hungry for bread, and there will we dwell and live by the "laws of nature" like all the nations around us, — then the very sword which you feared will overtake you there — in the land of Egypt. The hunger you dread will cling to you there. No remnant of yours shall remain or escape from the evil which I shall bring upon you. — You shall become a curse and horror, affliction and shame. And you will never see this place again."

5 ישעי' נה, ו.   6 ירמי' מב, י וכו'.

Fear of the Judgment

But weariness had already entered their hearts, and they did not heed Yirmiyahu's words this time either. Their faces reflected their innermost thoughts against Hashem and His prophet. Being aware of their feelings, Yirmiyahu warned them once more: The choice is no longer yours! Had you not sent me to plead before the Almighty, your sin in going to Mitzrayim would have been unintentional. However, having asked and received Hashem's answer, you now will be willfully transgressing His command, misleading yourselves, not me. Therefore know clearly, that you shall die by sword, hunger and pestilence, in the very place where you are headed to settle.[7]

But the prophet's words did not penetrate; their ears and their hearts refused to believe. "Is the Almighty so indulgent," they asked, "as to simply forgive our misdeeds and all our transgressions, and dismiss our rebellion against Him? — After He has already abandoned His Mizbe'ach, emptied His Mikdash, and destroyed without pity, will His love for us now become stronger than in the past, that we may say: under His wings and Special Protection will we dwell in His land, and we will live?"

Baruch ben Neriyah

It was Azaryah son of Hoshayah who disheartened them and weakened their spirits even more.* Together with Yochanan ben Kore'ach and all the men who refused to listen, he defiantly said to Yirmiyahu: "You speak falsehood. Hashem our God did not send you to tell us. 'Don't go to Mitzrayim to live there.'[8] No evil has ever come from the Almighty, and He would not command us to stay in this land under the vengeful sword of the enemy. Neither would these words have originated with you. It is only your disciple, Baruch ben Neriyah, who instigates you against us.[9] He does not care if the Kasdim kill or deport us to Bavel. Baruch is only concerned with his own good, and with the

---

one thing he has craved all his life — that the spirit of prophecy descend upon him."

"Has Baruch ben Neriyah not been complaining to the Almighty throughout, crying: 'Woe to me, for Hashem has been adding misery to my suffering. He singled me out from among all the disciples of the prophets. Yehoshua served Moshe, and the Ru'ach HaKodesh rested upon him. Elisha served Eliyahu, and the Ru'ach HaKodesh rested upon him. Why am I different from all the disciples? I am worn down by my sighs, but "Menucha" (meaning prophecy [10]) I have not found yet.[11] Am I not the disciple of the prophet Yirmiyahu, from whom I learned and received the Mesora of Torah?[12] Then why have I not merited prophecy?' "

The men continued, "It is prophecy that your disciple Baruch ben Neriyah craves. And since prophecy cannot commence except in Eretz Yisrael, he therefore keeps inciting you against us with falsehoods, saying: 'You may not go to dwell in Mitzrayim.' [13] But this is not what Hashem, your God, has commanded you, and this we have not promised you in advance."

As for Baruch ben Neriyah, what was Hashem's reply to him? "That which I had built, I have been destroying! That which I had planted, I have been plucking up! And you, Baruch, are seeking greatness for yourself? Don't My prophets always receive their visions only in the merit of Yisrael? Thus it was even with Moshe — the Father of all Prophets. All the thirty-eight years in the desert (from the time of the sin of the Meraglim onward) during which Bnei Yisrael were as if "in Niduy" (a form of decreed segregation), the words of Prophecy were not forthcoming to Moshe.[14] And now, when the whole land is being punished with abandonment and destruction; the House of Yisrael, 'My vineyard' which I had built and planted in a most fertile hill [15] I have been tearing up and destroying, as it became unsuitable and unworthy to Me; — and *you* seek greatness for yourself?"

"Do not ask for it, son of Neriyah! Of what use is the fence, when

10 במדבר יא, כו.   11 ירמי' מב ויל"ש.
12 הקדמת הרמב"ם ליד החזקה.
13 ירמי' מג, ג, בפי' אברבנאל.   14 תענית לו: 15 ישעי' ה, א.

the vineyard is no more? What need for a shepherd, when the flock is gone? Indeed, Yisrael sinned and disgraced themselves. Because of them, I am bringing calamity upon *all* flesh. And if Yisrael is not there, what need is there for prophecy? — It is enough that I have spared your life in all the places where you have been going,[16] that you be not caught up in the people's sins and their punishment."

The people, however, clung to their suspicion that Yirmiyahu had been instigated by Baruch ben Neriyah to command them to remain in the land of the prophets, even though the king of Bavel would surely take revenge and kill them. They refused to heed Yirmiyahu's pleas.

Yochanan ben Kore'ach and the army chiefs gathered the whole Remnant of Yehuda, the men, women and children (who meanwhile had returned from the neighboring lands), as well as all the people left by Nevuzaradan, and the King's daughters. They took them and Yirmiyahu with his disciple Baruch — against their will — and went down to Mitzrayim.[17] Thus, by their own counsel and refusal to heed Hashem's Word, they ("the remaining spark of Yehudah") themselves caused the banishment from the Land to become complete and final.

16 יל"ש ירמי' מב.   17 ירמי' מג.

Chapter Six

THE EXILES IN MITZRAYIM

FLEEING from the Babylonians, the weary remnant of Yehuda finally came to Tachpanches in Mitzrayim.[1] This was the second time (the first came in the time of Sancheriv King of Ashur, as it is written, "Woe to those who go down to Mitzrayim for help"[2]) that Bnei Yisrael disobeyed Hashem's commands: "For as you have seen Mitzrayim this day, you shall not see them ever again, for ever"[3] and "you shall not return this way anymore."[4] And both times they stumbled and fell.

Prophetic Warnings

Hashem's message came to Yirmiyahu in Tachpanches. "Take in your hands some large stones and hide them in the mortar of the brick work, at the entrance of Pharoh's house in Tachpanches — in the presence of men of Yehuda — and tell them: Thus says Hashem, the Lord of Hosts, the God of Yisrael, 'Behold, I will send and take My servant Nevuchadnezar the king of Bavel (from whom you are trying to escape), and I shall set up his throne upon these stones that I have hidden, and he will spread his royal pavillion over them. He will come and smite the land of Mitzrayim; to deliver those who are for death, to death; such as are for captivity, to captivity; such as are for the sword, to the sword. And in the houses of Mitzrayim's idols, I shall kindle a fire and consume the idols made out of wood; the others, Nevuchadnezar will capture. For Nevuchadnezar, who has proclaimed himself a deity, will come and pay back Pharoh, who boasted: *'Mine is the Nile, and I created myself!'* Nevuchadnezar will wrap up the spoils of the land of Mitzrayim (on whose futile help you are relying),

1 שם פסוק ז.   2 ישעי' לא, א.   3 שמות יד, יג.   4 דברים יז, טז.

204

as a shepherd wraps his garment around his shoulders." [5] And Mitzrayim will no longer be to you a safeguard recalling transgressions as you turn to her.

A Mizbe'ach for Hashem

But the exiles did not hearken to Yirmiyahu. They mistrusted him, saying: "Hashem has abandoned His Mitzbe'ach. He rejected His Mikdash, and He cast us away from His Presence, — no longer to be His nation!" They settled down in the cities of Migdal, Tachpanches, Nof and the province of Patros,[6] and strayed after pagan-worship. Yet they found in Mitzrayim five cities whose people spoke the language of the Bnei Yisrael of Kena'an, were loyal to Hashem, took their oaths only by His Name,[7] and even had a Mizbe'ach built for Hashem. (These were the descendants of the masses of captives from Mitzrayim and Kush whom Sancheriv had taken along on his three-year siege of Shomron.[8] Upon Sancheriv's miraculous defeat at the gates of Yerushalayim, Chizkiyahu freed all the captives. Having witnessed Hashem's great miracles, they now believed in Him and upon returning to Mitzrayim they started bringing offerings to Hashem.[9]) The newly-arrived Bnei-Yehuda began also to bring offerings and incense on this Mizbe'ach erected for Hashem on foreign soil. Their women, however, strayed. For, besides serving Hashem, they also poured wine libations and burned incense in worship of the sun and other celestial bodies.[10]

Yirmiyahu at once reproached the women for their transgressions, and for provoking Hashem's anger through their worship of "foreign deities, whom neither they nor their forefathers ever knew." "You are destroying not only your own lives but also the lives of every man, woman and suckling, for Hashem will turn His attention to punish you! From child to adult you will all die. From all this remnant of Yehuda who have come to dwell in Mitzrayim, not a survivor will

---

5 ירמי' מג, יב.   6 ירמי' מד, א.   7 ישעי' יט, יח.   8 סנהדרין צד:
9 סדר עולם   10 ירמי' מד, ח וכו'.

return to the Land of Yehuda which you long for — they will never return!"

Idolatry

The exiles truly had not come to settle down in Mitzrayim; they only yearned to return to the Land of Hashem, and dwell there in His shade. Their hearts longed for the day of redemption when all the exiles would be ingathered in mercy. But now they felt lost, depressed, helpless and frightened. — And as they strayed after worthlessness, they themselves became worthless.

They confronted Yirmiyahu for his reproach, saying, "Have then our women acted without our knowledge? It was indeed with our knowledge, and for *our* benefit! Are we perhaps more worthy than our fathers, our kings and princes who, while dwelling in the cities of Yehuda, poured wine and burned incense to the heavenly galaxy? And they did it in the King's Palace, at a time when the Almighty's eyes were fully fixed upon His nation and land, from the year's beginning till its end. Even with His Special Providence they felt in need of the heavenly bodies. How much more so we, here, in the land of the gentiles when Hashem has turned away from us. — Indeed, we are like one who has no God.

Moreover, our fathers lived in abundance and knew no hardship; we are in want of everything. From the day of Yerushalayim's destruction, when we stopped pouring wine and burning incense to the heavenly galaxy, our people fell by the sword, and hunger decimated us. And now that we are in the land of the gentiles, and Hashem has withdrawn His Hand and Divine Protection from us, we too are now ruled by the celestial bodies and the signs of the Zodiac — like all the peoples of the earth." [11]

Replied Yirmiyahu, "How short-sighted you are! Your slain are not the slain of the sword, and your dead are not the fallen of wars.[12] Is it then because you ceased to burn incense to the heavenly bodies that

11 ירמי׳ מד; בראשית רבה מד, יב. 12 ישעי׳ כב, ב.

this evil has befallen you? On the contrary, it is precicely because you burned incense and sinned against Hashem. You did not hearken to His voice and did not walk in the ways of His Torah. — *That* is why this evil has befallen you."

"I beseech you, do not emulate the ways of the gentiles. Do not fear the signs of the Zodiac! [13] For long ago, since the days of your father Avraham, Hashem has lifted you "outside" — above the dome of the Heavens; forever beyond the realm of these celestial bodies' dominion.[14] Hence, why should you delve into astrology? Why study the customs and ways of the gentiles,[15] which are not Yaakov's lot? — And now you dare even say, 'we will continue to do it, to pour wine-libations and burn the incence?' "

But their ears were stuffed, incapable of hearing. They only kept repeating, "The Almighty has already rejected us from dwelling in His Estate! Hence our ways on earth now are just like those of all the other nations." They therefore turned to the idols for salvation and support, like all the nations of the earth to whom the Almighty indeed had assigned the signs of the Zodiac. They too now prepared "sacrificial cakes" and "images" for the idols,[16] out of hope that they might assist and sustain them in their dispersion. — Until the day when Hashem would have mercy upon them and return them to their Land, once again under His Divine Protection, like a father guiding his beloved son.

Once more, Hashem sent Yirmiyahu to warn them; perhaps this last Remnant of Yehudah would yet repent. But they did not, and Hashem would not indulge them any longer because of the gravity of their abominations. Said the Almighty,[17] "We shall see whose word shall endure, Mine or theirs!"

But the last Remnant of Yehuda continued to stray after the idols, sinking lower and lower — until their day of Judgment arrived.

---

13 ירמי' י, ב.   14 בראשית טו, ה' ורש"י שם.   15 ילקוט שמעוני ירמי' י.

16 ירמי' מד.   17 ירמי' מד, כח.

Tzor Falls

In the twentieth year of Babylon's reign, Hashem incited Nevuchadnezar to besiege the powerful, merry city of Tzor ("with horses, chariots and horsemen and a multitude of people." [18]), as she had grown arrogant in her riches and beauty, boasting, "I sit a Godly way of sitting, (high up) in the heart of the seas," [19] and because she had rejoiced, exclaiming: "Hurrah! the Gates of Yerushalayim (where all trading nations used to enter) are shattered! Now all of them will turn to me for trade. I shall be filled from the ruins of Yerushalayim, 'the destroyed one'."

For three years Tzor (Tyre) was held under siege by the King of Bavel, and in the twenty-third year of his reign she was finally delivered into his hands. He devastated her beauty, plunging her into a split of the earth,[20] turning her into a bare rock upon which the fishermen spread their nets, — never to be rebuilt.[21] Having captured Tzor, Nevuzaradan turned East to the small number of the Bnei Yehuda who were in Ammon, Mo'ab and the other neighboring territories of Yehudah — 745 people in all, and carried them with him to Bavel.[22]

Mitzrayim Destroyed

In the twenty-seventh year of Nevuchadnezar's reign (3346) (the eighth year after the burning of the Beis HaMikdash), Hashem gave him the land of Mitzrayim. "The lion came and broke her mighty arms,[23] cutting down people and beasts." The Egyptians ran for their lives, dispersing among the nations.[24] Nevuchadnezar did away with her masses, plundered her possessions, grabbed her spoils — making them a prize for his armies. Hashem also sent locust against them — into the bounty of grains stored in their homes and fields [25] in which they had placed their security. The land became filled with the dead, and Mitzrayim's pride and strength vanished. Mitzrayim became a wasteland; and her cities, ruins for forty years. Hashem then will return the captivity

18 יחזקאל כו, ז.   19 שם כח, ב.   20 יל״ש יחזקאל כח.   21 יחזקאל כו, ד ו־ה.
22 ירמי׳ נב, ל.   23 יחזקאל ל, כב.   24 שם פסוק כג.   25 ס׳ שלשלת הקבלה.

of Mitzrayim, to remain however a low kingdom — never again to exalt herself over other nations.[26]

It was then that the bitter prophecies of Yirmiyahu concerning Bnei Yehuda in Mitzrayim were fulfilled. — The day turned dark in Tachpanches.[27] For Yehuda's exiles in Mitzrayim were also completely wiped out by sword and famine.[28] They fell and died by the thousands and tens of thousands.[29] Not a survivor was left out of the whole bewildered, destitute remnant who had followed false reasoning and leaned on Mitzrayim, "the splintered reed." Only Yirmiyahu and Baruch ben Neriyah survived, together with a small number of Judeans [30] who had not turned away from Hashem and whenever taking an oath would say, "As truly as Hashem lives." These Nevuchadnezar carried away to Bavel,[31] fulfilling the verse, "They shall come to Bavel, and there they shall stay until the day when I shall remember them." [32]

Yehuda's Desolation

The Land of Yehuda meanwhile lay waste, bereft of its sons and daughters who had gone into captivity. It was *then* that the Land observed its years of rest, making up for all those Sabbaticals and Jubilees which were not duly observed when her children were still dwelling there. The Land now atoned for her Sabbaticals by being devoid of her children, while they in turn atoned for their sin by being dispersed in their exiles. — While desolation kept spreading throughout the Land.[33]

At that dark hour our evil neighbors rejoiced and rushed to take possession of the abandoned "desirous Land." — While Hashem stood aside, not being zealous for His desecrated Place — "on the day foreigners captured their wealth and strangers entered its gates and cast lots over Yerushalayim; [34] to split and divide her amongst them."

26 יחזקאל פרק כט, טו.   27 שם פרק ל, יח.   28 ירמי' פרק מד, כז.
29 ס' "סוד מישרים" הובא באוצר התפלות סדר י' ימי תשובה ובספר "יסוד ושורש העבודה".
30 ירמי' מד, ברד"ק ובמצודות.   31 סדר עולם כו ורש"י קהלת יב, ו, ובאברבנאל,
הקדמה ליחזקאל.   32 ירמי' כז, כב.   33 ויקרא כו.   34 עובדי' פסוק יא.

But they too would soon feel the fulfillment of Hashem's Prophecy: "Desolate will be your enemies dwelling in the Land." [35] For as much as they tried to cultivate and settle the Land, they did not succeed. Our enemies did not find gratification in our desolate land and they were unable to hold on and make it their homestead.[36] For seven full years, sulphur and salt consumed the whole land, and for fifty-two years no bird was ever seen flying overhead in the Land of Yisrael.[37]

— "While *you* were in the land of the enemy." [38]

35 ויקרא כו, לב.   36 רש"י ורמב"ן שם.   37 יומא נד.   38 ויקרא כו, לד.

PART THREE

The Babylonian Exile

Chapter One

ENCOUNTER OF THE EXILES

Chapter One

ENCOUNTER OF THE EXILES

IT WAS a long, torturous journey for the captives of Yehuda who had been marched into exile. From Yerushalayim, "the light of the world," they had been brutally taken to descend into faraway Bavel, the land of darkness.[1] To their necks they were pursued;[2] they labored, but were given no respite. For five months the Kasdim tormented the humiliated Bnei Yehuda on their agonizing march, and withheld from them bread and water. The strength of the exiles ebbed. Their skin shriveled on their bones, and became dry as wood.[3] They were like those long since dead. — Until they finally arrived in Bavel.

With Yehoyachin's Exiles

The jubilant and haughty Nevuchadnezar (Nevuchad Netzar[4]) marched at the head of his army into his capital Bavel, dragging along the blinded King Tzidkiyahu and the captives of Zion. Like all the people, the exiles of Yechonyah came out to greet the victorious king. They, too, were duly dressed in festive white garments. However, underneath they had donned black clothes of mourning.[5] — Eleven years had passed since they, together with Yechonyah, the King of Yehuda, had been exiled to Bavel.[6] Throughout these years they had nursed the hope that their brethren who remained in Yehuda would repent, so that Hashem would have mercy upon the wretched nation and limit its banishment to their own small exile. But now their brethren, like themselves, had been banished from Zion and Yerushalayim.

True, the exiles of Yehoyachin had long been aware that Hashem's outstretched sword was poised against their brethren. Already in the

---

1 איכה ג, ה.   2 שם ג, ב.   3 איכה ד, ח.   4 סנהדרין דף צה ע"ב.
5 פתיחתא דאיכה רבתי כג.   6 מ"ב כו.

ninth year of King Tzidkiyahu, on the tenth day of the tenth month, Hashem had revealed Himself to Yechezkel ben Buzi, who was with them in exile, saying:[7] "Son of man, write down the name of the day; this very day the King of Bavel has encircled Yerushalayim!" Warn "the bloody city"[8] that "I, too, will increase the blaze, heap on the wood, kindle the fire.[9] Because I have been purging you (from your impurity), but you have not been purged."[10] Therefore, "speak to the House of Yisrael. Thus says Hashem: 'Behold, I will profane My Mikdash — the pride of your strength, the delight of your eyes, the longing of your soul. And your sons and daughters whom you have left behind (in Yerushalayim) shall fall by the sword!'"[11] But though the exiles knew that Yerushalayim had come under siege, they were confident that Hashem's kindliness surely had not ended. The Exile of Yehoyachin would not believe that the day of Hashem's wrath would ever come. And when it happened, they were unaware that it was already taking place. For the Almighty concealed from them the day of the Destruction.

Day of the Tidings

Only now, five months later, did the tidings reach them. "It came to pass in the twelfth year (of the exile of Yehoyachin), in the tenth month, on the fifth day of the month: the fugitive, having escaped from Yerushalayim, came to Yechezkel saying: 'The city has fallen!'"[12]

However, it is he whom Hashem loves that He reproves; like a father rebuking his son, to teach him and guide him in the ways of the righteous, so He made them aware that only He The Blessed One had brought all the evil upon them for all their iniquities and transgressions. Therefore, even before the refugee arrived, bringing with him the bitter tidings, Hashem had already spoken to Yechezkel.[13] The evening before, Hashem's Hand was on the prophet and He opened his mouth so that

7 יחזקאל כד, א-ב.   8 שם פסוק ו.   9 שם פסוקים ט, ו-י.   10 שם פסוק יג.

11 שם פסוק כא.   12 יחזקאל לג, כא.   13 שם פסוק כב.

Yechezkiel would not remain mute, unable to rebuke the Bnei Yisrael who still kept insisting: "We have not sinned."

"Son of Man," Hashem spoke to him, "those dwelling in the waste places of the land of Yisrael keep saying, 'Avraham was only one, and he inherited the Land; but we are many, so to us surely the Land was given'." [14] They further say: Avraham, who was given only one Mitzva (circumcision), [15] inherited the Land, we, who were given many Mitzvos, are surely given the Land as an inheritance. [16] Avraham, who worshiped but the only God, inherited the Land; we, who worship also many of His heavenly forces and also the celestial bodies that He created, His angels and the Sarey-Maalah (superior angels), His servants (who are also part of His Royalty [17]) — we surely deserve to inherit the land. [18]

Hashem's Word came again to Yechezkel: [19] Therefore, speak to them: thus says Hashem: you eat your food smeared with blood (of those whom you killed for their money) and raise your eyes to your idols and shed (innocent) blood, thus disregarding even the precepts commanded the gentiles) — shall you inherit the land?...[20] "As I live, says Hashem, so I shall do as I had envisioned; I will turn the Land into outright wasteland and desolation, and the pride of her strength will cease. The mountains of Yisrael will be blighted, without a passerby. — And I have revealed all this to you now, before the fugitive arrives in the morning, so that they shall know that I, Hashem, have laid the Land waste for all the abominations they have committed." [21] Hurry now, hasten to tell My people the bad tidings, even though they will not believe it. But when it reaches them, "they shall know that a Prophet has been in their midst."

The next morning (on the fifth of the month of Teves 3339) the fugitive from "the Valley of Death" arrived. Then the exiles of Yehoyachin learned that the city which had been the joy of all the world had been captured and Hashem's nation had fallen by the sword; that "all her beauty was marred when her crown was removed. And that

---

14 שם כד.   15 בראשית יז.   16 יל"ש יחזקאל לג.   17 שבועות דף מד.
18 ילקוט שם.   19 יחזקאל שם.   20 ילקוט שם.   21 יחזקאל שם פסוק כט.

the defilers of Hashem had made their way into the innermost confines of the Mikdash."

Faced with the bitter tidings, their hearts sank and their hands became feeble. Stunned by sorrow, their spirit grew faint, their knees dripped with water and groans wracked their bodies:[22] It had indeed come to pass![23]

Bitter indeed was the day in which rejoicing ceased and happiness darkened, — as if they too now beheld the Churban with their very eyes. And then they believed it.

They proclaimed the day of the tidings as a day of fasting and mourning, like the day of the burning of the Mikdash itself[24] — that very Day of Hashem's Fury, in which He cast the glory of Yisrael down from heaven to earth. For like their brethren, they too now became inconsolable mourners of Zion. "For our heart's joy ceased, and our dances have turned into mourning. The crown of our heads has fallen. — Woe to us, for we have sinned!"[25]

Cheers with Laments

When the exiles reached the city of Bavel, — mourners came out to greet mourners.[26]

However, the exiles of Yechonyah, being already in Bavel under the rule of Nevuchadnezar, were obligated to honor the king. Thus, they had to display their loyalty to "the welfare of the Kingdom in whose borders they dwelt," as Yirmiyahu had commanded them: "Seek the peace of the city into which I have exiled you, for in its peace you will have peace."[27] Thus, they too, like all the people, came out clad in festive white as if rejoicing at Bavel's victory; but underneath they wore black[28] because their hearts were humble with mourning for the destruction of Hashem's House.

Slowly the staggering exiles, some in shabby rags, some nude, came closer and closer. How frightful was their sight, and to what could they

---

22 ברכות נח: 23 יחזקאל כא, יב.   24 ר"ה י"ח: 25 איכה ה, טז-יז.
26 קהלת רבה יב.   27 ירמי' כט, ז.   28 פתיחתא דאיכה רבתי כג.

be likened?[29] Who could tell what they really were — humans or demons? — For their flesh and skin were wasted, their bones broken.[30] Darker than black was their appearance, beyond recognition in the streets.[31]

When the staggering exiles finally came close, Yehoyachin's exiles walked about the streets in full mourning.* Anxiously they approached the captives: "What happened to Father? What happened to Mother? What happened to my brother?" — And the newly arrived but replied:[32] "Whoever had to die, died. Whoever had to be captured, was captured. Whoever had to fall by the sword, fell by the sword!" — The exiles of Yechonyah broke out in lament. In their mourning each was slapping his hip with one palm in grief, while raising the other hand as if glorifying Nevuchadnezar and singing praises to him.[33]

"Woe, My Brother!"

When the wretched, weary captives met with their brethren, the exiles of Yehoyachin, their spirits suddenly revived. The two exiles comforted one another.[34] And although they all mourned, they felt strengthened as one cried out "Oh, brother!" and the other replied, "Oh, my brother!"

At this moment the worn-out exiles came to realize that Hashem's Fatherly Mercy had not ceased. Had He not, out of compassion, first driven part of the Judeans to Bavel, to smooth the way for them now (like a dressing prepared in anticipation of the wounds to come)? For Hashem indeed showed kindliness to Bnei Yisrael, having exiled Zidki-yahu and his subjects to Bavel while the Exile of Yehoyachin was still alive.[35] Thus the multitude of the "Exile of Tzidkiyahu," were coming not to the dark "wilderness of gentiles," but to their own flesh and blood, to their sages and their own Sanhedrin. They realized they were now coming to the great "Chorosh and Masger,"[36] those Torah giants who had preceded them in exile by eleven years to prepare for them

---

29 איכה ב, יג.   30 שם ג, ד.   31 שם ד, ח.   * תוספת.   32 ירמיה טו, ב.

33 קהלת רבה יב, ח.   34 פסיקתא דרב כהנא פיסקא טז.   35 גיטין פח.

36 מ"ב כד, יד.

Houses of Learning and places to dwell in captivity. For these learned men of Yehoyachin's Exile would now teach Torah to them, the impoverished remnant of the people, who were driven into exile only after the great ones.[37]

Moreover, since the time of the very first exile (that of Yehoyakim in 3320), Hashem had placed respected officials from amongst their fellow Judeans in the Royal Palace: Daniel with his companions, Chananya, Mishael and Azarya. Through them Hashem now steered the king's heart to do favor with the exiles. For they all were brothers, the sons of Yehuda, each helping the other, and encouraging one another: "Keep strong!"

Only upon the blinded King Zidkiyahu did Hashem pour out His fury.[38] Tzidkiyahu thus emptied the goblet of bitterness of all the generations together.[39] And Nevuchadnezar held him imprisoned until the day of his death.[40]

A Day of Persuasion

At that point the exiles of Yehoyachin humbly made peace with the Heavenly verdict, as did those of the Ten Tribes who were there with them. For the very day of the encounter when the two exiles met was to become "a day of persuasion," — as they all became forever persuaded of Hashem's supreme righteousness. Since the day when the Ten Tribes had been exiled (3205) and the Tribes of Yehuda and Binyamin were left untouched, the Ten Tribes kept questioning, "Why has He banished us, but not them? It is because they are the members of His Palace; because His Mikdash was built in *their* portion?! — Could there indeed be favoritism?" [41]

However, erringly they had questioned the measure of Hashem's justice all these 134 years. The Tribes of Yehuda and Binyamin simply had not yet sinned as much as their brethren in the Kingdom of Yisrael, and their cup of transgressions was not yet full. When it did fill up,

37 רש"י גיטין שם.   38 יחזקאל יז, כ.   39 סדר עולם כה.   40 ירמי' נב, יא.
41 פתיחתא דאיכה רבתי ו.

He at once banished them too. Now all of the exiles together exclaimed: "He is our God! This is our God! Indeed, He is powerful and true! Even to the members of His Household He shows no favoritism." [42]

Sanctification Through Justice

On that Day of persuasion Hashem proved to the Tribes of Yehuda His trustworthiness.[43] Since now in Yehudah Hashem had made known the measure of His justice, "His Name became great among all of Yisrael." [44] — They all humbly accepted His judgment.

Even to the nations of the world the tragic day of Yehudah's calamity became a day of persuasion. For they too watched Hashem's ways of meting out justice, and had seen His strong Hand come down upon His nation. At the time when the Ten Tribes were exiled but not Yehudah and Binyamin, the heathens too claimed, "He is partial to them, because they are the members of His Dwelling!" However, when later Yehuda too strayed [45] and sinned and was banished, the nations of the world conceded: Indeed there is a Judge, there is justice in Yehuda! There is a God Who sits in judgment [46] even over His own children and His Household! Thus His Name was sanctified and feared throughout the world.

Justice with Mercy

Hashem's strict justice was nonetheless full of mercy. For although the verdict of exile had been sealed, the Almighty did not drive them out in the rainy winter season that they not perish from the cold on their torturous journey.[47] Neither did He exile them to the land of Edom (the brother of their father Yaakov). For He understands Bnei Yisrael's ways, and He knows their fitting place.[48] The Almighty knew that the Bnei Yehuda would not be able to endure the gruesome edicts of Edom who would decree upon them Shmad (total assimilation), forbidding

---

42 שם.   43 הושע ה, ט.   44 תהלים עו, ב.   45 הושע ה, ה.

46 במדבר רבה יג, ד.   47 תנחומא תזריע ט.   48 איוב כח, כג.

them to engage in Torah study and fulfill the Mitzvos. Therefore He exiled them among the Babylonians who were not as ruthless.[49]

Moreover, Bavel was not a completely alien land; it was as if they were driven back to the home of their father. It was from the city of Ur Kasdim, in ancient Bavel, that Avraham their forefather had begun to spread light to the whole world.[50]* From Bavel they originated, and to Bavel He returned the Judeans. — Like a woman, having disgraced her husband, being sent back by him to the house of her father.

Throughout the long journey Nevuchadnezar had treated the Judeans cruelly as if he wished to destroy them completely. But as soon as the exiles reached Bavel, Hashem turned the heart of Nevuchadnezar ("My servant") to do good to His people.

Only for the sake of His Judgment had Hashem made Nevuchadnezar ruler of the world, in order to chastise Yehuda.[51] And seventy years of exile were decreed upon them to atone for their sins only, but not to bring upon them extinction.[52] "For Hashem's eyes are upon the transgressing Kingdom." Only the erring *Kingdom* He will destroy from upon the surface of the earth; however, "I shall not destroy the House of Yaakov, said Hashem." [53] Had they, their kings, nobles and Kohanim only lent an ear to the words of Yirmiyahu [54] — even at the very last moment — to come forward and greet the officers of the King of Bavel and to accept Hashem's Judgment, then neither sword, pestilence nor hunger would have overtaken them, ever. And even after they were exiled, no sooner had they reached the Euphrates river than Nevuzaradan, chief of the armies, commanded his soldiers: "Henceforth let them rest." [55]

Although "the prisoners of Zion" were vanquished in battle and treated like slaves, immediately upon reaching Bavel they were granted rights like all those under Nevuchadnezar's rule, and were permitted to settle wherever they wished. They settled in the various cities throughout the country: in Tel-Aviv near the banks of the river Kvor,[56] Tel

---

49 פסחים פז: 50 פסחים פז: ורש"י שם. * תוספת. 51 תוספתא בבא קמא ז, ב.
52 חבקוק א, יב. 53 עמוס ט, ח. 54 ירמי' לח, יח. 55 פסיקתא רבתי כט.
56 יחזקאל ג, טו.

Melach, Tel Charsho, Kruv, Idoiy, and Imar,[57] in Kosifyo [58] and Hutzel, in Nahardeyah [59] and Fum Nahara,[60] and elsewhere — just like all inhabitants of the land.

However, they had arrived utterly impoverished and in want of everything, carrying the "shame of hunger" among the gentiles.[61] Not even the most basic necessities (such as waterflasks, blanket and food-dish [62]) had they prepared for exile, for they had kept insisting: "The prophecy envisioned by Yechezkel is meant for the distant future.[63] It will not happen soon." And now in exile, how were they to draw water without a vessel? Or in what bowl could they knead their dough from the meager bits of flour that would come their way? [64]

In search of food, the shamed exiles turned into beggars, going from door to door. Until Nevuchadnezar was urged to take their plight to heart, and for a period of twelve months he gathered the poor of Yisrael and fed them daily.[65] (see "Nevuchadnezar's Charity").

For Hashem's mercy was increasingly and constantly with them. Even the mere choice of Babylon as the site of Exile was an act of mercy. For Hashem knows the ways of Torah and those that study her, as well as the fitting location for Torah to flourish.[66] And even though Yehuda had to be banished from the Holy Land and become estranged from the holy tongue spoken there, yet they were not entirely detached from Holiness. Hashem banished them to Bavel whose Aramaic tongue was close to the language of the Torah [67] so that Torah would not be forgotten from the Bnei Yisrael.[68] — Furthermore, there had never been date-trees growing in Bavel. Only forty years before Yehuda was to be exiled, dates were planted there, as the dates train the tongue for Torah-study.[69] (Dates then became so abundant, that three basketfuls sold for one zuz [70]). — So that Bnei Yisrael could dedicate themselves to Torah.

57 עורא ב, נט. 58 שם ח, יז. 59 מגילה כט. 60 קידושין עב:

61 יחזקאל פרק לו, ל. 62 איכה רבתי א, כב. 63 יחזקאל פרק יב, כז.

64 יל"ש יחזקאל פרק יב, ורש"י יחזקאל יב, פסוק ג. 65 סוטה דף כא, ורש"י שם.

66 רש"י גיטין י"ז. 67 פסחים פז: 68 רש"י שם. 69 ירושלמי תענית פרק ד, ה.

70 פסחים פח.

Chapter Two

IN THE DARKNESS OF BAVEL

Chapter Two

IN THE DARKNESS OF BAVEL

THAT a nation and kingdom be driven from their land and exiled into captivity — has happened in the course of world history. But that a nation and kingdom be cruelly profaned, stripped of its royal garb, its priests and nobles, sons and daughters, murdered in the wide open streets, its people driven into captivity in the faraway lands of the enemy — and yet, its spirit would not fall, and it would neither be spent, to intermingle nor assimilate to be swallowed up by the powerful conqueror who had dragged it into captivity — this happened only to Yehuda "a nation unique on earth."

Unassimilated

Indeed, the exile of Yehuda was unlike any other exile. When gentiles are banished from their homeland, they are not truly in exile, for they eat of the bread of their captors and drink of their wine. But Bnei Yisrael who do not eat of their captors' bread or drink of their wine and do not intermarry to take from their sons and their daughters — theirs is truly an exile.*

But this is precisely what helped them to preserve and retain their unique identity. Because they did not eat from the bread of the gentiles or drink of their wine, and because they completely seperated themselves from the impurity of the nations and did not intermarry, *therefore* they remained "Yehudim" (one who does not worship images), even in the land of the enemy — and like a nation within a nation.

Babylon's Origins

Still, Yehuda did not find rest in that foreign land. They were like lost sheep,[1] uprooted from Hashem's Portion, — from Yerushalayim the

* איכה רבתי ד, יז.   1 ירמי' ג, ו.

magnificent, from Mount Carmel and the Baashan, from the Mountains of Ephraim and the Gilead. And they now descended to Bavel, the land of darkness; [2] the land of depths,[3] called Shin'or ("emptied out"), because there all the dead of the Mabbul (Flood) were emptied out [4] (So that whoever ate from her soil, was considered to be eating insects and creeping things).[5]

From the very beginning, still from Adam it had been decreed that Bavel was to become an inhabited land,[6] adorned by the splendid, tall palm trees on the banks of her rivers.[7] Even the Euphrates was at this time still flowing in its original river bed, unchanged since the time of Creation, so that whoever saw it would say: "Blessed is He Who has made the works of Creation." [8] Yet only now did Bavel turn into a powerful empire whose men "shall hold the bow and javelin. They are cruel, and show no mercy." [9]

The Babylonians (Kasdim) were an ancient people descended from Chom, one of the three sons of Noach, "from whom the nations divided in their lands, each after his tongue, after their families, in their nations." [10] The roots of Bavel's kingdom too were in the earliest days of kingship on earth — the kingdom of "Nimrod son of Kush son of Chom,[11] after the Mabbul, in the land of Shin'or." "He was the first to be a mighty man (a king) on earth. He was a mighty hunter before Hashem," — in that he ensnared men with his words, and instigated them to revolt against their Creator.[12] It was in this vast plain of Shin'or that the people then started to build for themselves a city and a tower whose top would reach into the Heavens.[13] Why then was it named Bavel? Because "it was there that Hashem mixed up ("Balal") the language of the whole earth and from there He scattered them over the surface of the earth." [14]

All these years, however, Bavel was under the rule of Ashur. For Ashur had refused to follow Nimrod who knew his Creator and yet rebelled against Him.[15] When Ashur, son of Shem [16] (the righteous)

5 שם.	4 שבת קיג: וב"ר לז, ד.	3 ערכין דף לד.	2 ע"ז דף כו.
9 ירמי' נ, מב.	8 ברכות נט:	7 שם ורש"י סוטה מו:	6 ברכות לא.
13 שם יא, ד.	12 שם פסוק ט.	11 שם, פסוק י.	10 בראשית י, ה.
	16 בראשית י, כב.	15 רש"י בראשית י, ט.	14 שם פסוק ט.

saw his children listening to Nimrod and rebelling against their Maker by building the Tower,[17] he immediately left that place. He then built the great city of Ninveh [18] (as well as Rechovot Ir, Kolach, and Resen), which was to become the capital and the glory of Ashur's empire. Until, with time, the measure of the sins of Ashur's kingdom was filled. Her glory fell down, and Bavel regained its independence. — The hour of Bavel arrived.

An Inferior Kingdom

Mighty Bavel, however, was actually a low and inferior kingdom. The people of Bavel, Ninveh, and all the lands under the Kasdim's rule were descendants of Kesed son of Nachor, the brother of Avraham [19] — "the nation that was not," [20] not worthy or deserving of being one. (Would that they had not been at all! [21]) For they were a stupid and ignorant people, more so than the other nations, so that the Almighty Himself — so to say — was sorry for having created it.[22] They were a bitter, impetuous people,[23] embittered, cruel and recklessly wild. But it was Ashur that built and firmly established Bavel, gracing her with grand castles, massive fortresses, palaces and towers.[24] — And, through Ashur, Bavel eventually reached glory.

Bavel was further a land of poor, arid soil, which caused a lot of hardship. Of the ten measures of poverty that descended into the world, Bavel took nine.[25] Even in her rains there was no blessing, for just as the people of Bavel spoke falsehood, so were her rains false [26] and disappointing. She dwelt however upon many waters,[27] on the banks of the Euphrates river which had split off from the river coming out of Eden from the East.[28] Thus the Euphrates eventually became the source of all her riches and great treasures.[29]

---

19 בראשית כב, כב.	18 בראשית שם, ויונה ג, ב.	17 רש״י שם פסוק יא.
23 חבקוק א, ו.	22 סוכה נב:	21 רש״י סוכה, נב:	20 ישעי׳ כג, יג.
27 ירמי׳ נא, יג.	26 תענית ט:	25 קידושין מט:	24 ישעי׳ שם.
	29 יל״ש ירמי׳ נא.	28 בראשית ב, י, יד.

Bavel's Rise

As the destined hour of Bavel's reign arrived, Hashem lifted to Power this lowly nation which suddenly "went to distant lands to take possession of dwellings which were not theirs." From lowliness they turned into the terror of the world, causing all the nations to fear and tremble before them. Justice and eminence were dispensed by Bavel,[30] for kings and judges were theirs now — spreading burden and fear throughout the world.[31] Their horses were fleeter than leopards, and sharper than wolves at evening.[31] Their horsemen spread out in ever increasing numbers. From afar they came flying, like vultures hastening to devour.[32] Bavel became "the hammer of the world,"[33] shattering and pulverizing all.

For the mighty Kasdim were out only after violence, — robbing and plundering[34] — not even after the glory of victory or conquest. They destroyed and burned down the cities they conquered without leaving a survivor, striving hurriedly to return to their homeland in the northeast. Thus did this one bitter, impetuous nation swallow many nations, gathering captives like dust.[35]

Haughtiness

With growing power, haughtiness and flattery descended to Bavel.[36] The Kasdim's heart swelled in conceit. They scoffed at kings and derided them, (as they did to Yehoyachin and Zidkiyahu, Kings of Yehuda, whom they shamed and treated like plain commoners) while they heaped scorn upon princes.[37] They mocked at strongholds and fortified cities, heaping earth around them and conquering them by way of the ramps they had built.[38] Not one was able to withstand them.

With increasing success came increasing conceit. In utter self-glorification, they denied Hashem, claiming: "Our power is derived from our idols.[39] It is not the work of Hashem." At the peak of their power Bavel

---

30 חבקוק א, ו, וז.   31 רש"י שם.   32 שם פסוק ח.   33 ירמי' ג, כג.

34 חבקוק שם.   35 שם.   36 קידושין מט: 37 חבקוק שם פסוק י.

38 שם.   39 שם פסוק יא.

therefore turned more and more to their idols. They worshiped Bail, Navo,[40] and Merodach.[41] Until Bavel turned into a land of carved idols, its people going wild after their fearful looking deities.[42]

Bavel's greed too grew as wide as the Shéol (grave) and like death itself [43] which knows no satiety; like the Angel of Death who never has his fill of killing. She thus "amassed for herself all the nations, gathered unto herself all the peoples." [44]

Mount of Destruction

At this time, all the sciences (their foundations and principles, as well as the books of wisdom which had been with the Bnei Yisrael through all generations) were removed to the land of the Kasdim.[45] With its newly acquired books of wisdom, the mighty city of Bavel (the pride of Kasdim's glory) became the envy of all the kingdoms.[46] She turned into "the delicate and luxurious one, dwelling securely and saying: "I am the one, and there is none besides me." [47] This "Mount of destruction" [48] felt secure in its unparalleled, massive, fortified walls and its tall gates,[49] its princes and warriors, its sorcerers who worked magic since their youth,[50] and astrologers who read the positions of the stars, foretelling the future from the new moon.[51] Until in her wildness she felt secure even with her wickedness, claiming: "No one sees me." [52]

Bavel built palaces and castles, with the multicolored portraits of Kasdim (painted with vermilion) carved in the walls.[53] Her governors and haughty deputies dressed exquisitely. Her horsemen, enchanting young men,[54] everything about them bespeaking arrogance. Heavy belts girded their loins, and colorful turbans arrogantly flowed down from the back of their heads — all an image of high rank and nobility.[55]

Bavel indulged ever more in her harlotries [56] and gratifications, thriv-

---

40 ישעי' מו, א.   41 ירמי' נ, ב.   42 ירמי' נ, לח.   43 חבקוק ב, ה ורש"י שם.

44 שם.   45 ס' הכוזרי מאמר א, ס"ג.   46 ישעי' פרק יג, יט.   47 שם מז, ח.

48 ירמי' נא, כה.   49 שם פסוק נח.   50 ישעי' מז, יב.   51 שם פסוק יג.

52 שם פסוק י.   53 יחזקאל כג, יד.   54 שם פסוק יב.   55 שם פסוק טו.

56 שם פסוק יד.

ing on the gold of the conquered lands and their taxes. She, "the Empress of the kingdoms," [57] became "the praise of the whole earth," [58] and nations flocked to her in a steady stream.[59] "The tender and delicate," they called her,[60] and she was full of tumult and clamor.[61] — Until Bavel profaned all the nations and their monarchs through her sinful foulness.[62]

Built with Blood

Oppressive and loot-thirsty was Bavel. "Madheyva," the golden one she was called,[63] but with derogatory connotations, (*M'dod-haveh,* measure and bring more; [64] or *Me'od haveh,* bring a lot [65]) for she was forever commanding the vassal nations to bring her more and more. "Traitor and robber," too, she was called. For she was treacherous even toward nations with whom she lived in peace,[66] — as she robbed them and trampled upon the treaties she had signed with them. In her wrath she attacked nations and dealt them incessant blows. She subjugated the nations with angry, unrelenting persecution, with the staff of the wicked and the sceptre of the tyrants.[67] She filled herself up with the spoils of plundered cities and lands, and wallowed in the blood of the slain. She built her towns with blood, and established her cities with iniquity.[68]

Throughout this vast pleasure-seeking Empire of Bavel, the stones seemed to cry out of the walls and the rafters of wood answering them:[69] "We are stolen. All of us are robbed, soaked and defiled with the blood of the slain." — For Bavel murdered, and afterwards inherited the spoils.

Into this Bavel — as deep as the grave,[70] now descended the Daughter of Yehuda who was fairer than white. Could she find peace there? ...

57 ישעי' מז, ה.   58 ירמי' נא, מא.   59 שם פסוק מד.   60 ישעי' מז, א.

61 ירמי' נא, נה.   62 שבת דף קמט: 63 ישעי' יד, ד.   64 שבת דף קנ.

65 שם.   66 ישעי' כא, ב ורד"ק שם.   67 ישעי' יד, ה-ו.   68 חבקוק ב, ח ו-יב.

69 שם פסוק יא.   70 פסחים פז:

From Light into Darkness

As the exiles of Yehuda entered the large cities of Bavel through the glorified walls of her fortified castles that towered into the sky, bitterness overtook them. For these were the cities of the enemy, the pride of the devastators who relished the blood of our slain and mocked at their victim's agony. And this unperturbed enemy now dwelled confident and secure,[71] while the roads of Zion were desolate and all her gates abandoned. — While Hashem's city lay humiliated as deep as the lowest of graves.[72]

Only when darkness of the night covered them, the sons of Yehuda gave vent to their hurt. They broke into weeping; tears streamed down their cheeks.[73] For as vast as the ocean was Yehuda's calamity; who would find her a cure? She had become trash and refuse among the nations,[74] cheap as an earthenware pitcher, the work of a craftsman's hands.[75] For "the Crown was cast down, and all help had ceased. Only wrath was poured over her since she had left Yerushalayim." [76] "A sword was drawn, as she was abandoned for slaughter. Satiated only with bitter herbs and the waters of bitterness," could she now eat or even relish food?

What glory could Yehuda altogether find in those castles and fortresses of Bavel, dark and depressing as the grave? Or to what could she compare their seeming grace and starkness, as she recalled Zion, the epitome of beauty? — For "the exiles of Yerushalayim remembered all its delights of bygone days." [77] Not only her Mikdash and its magnificent vessels; not only Yerushalayim with its walls, suburbs and palaces; they longed even for the deserts of Eretz Yisrael in which it is better to lodge than in the castles of foreign lands.[78] They yearned even for the graveyards of Yisrael, which are more precious than the palaces of Bavel.[79] In exile, she even wondered about Chevron, the choicest of graves.[80]

And what delight could the exiles of Yehuda find in the ways of

71 איכה א, ט.   72 פזמון "ד' ד'" לתפילת נעילה ליוהכ"פ.   73 איכה פר' א, ב.

74 שם ג, מה.   75 שם ד, ב.   76 מלשון הקינות לט' באב.   77 איכה א, ז.

78 ב"ר, ח.   79 סנהדרין צו: 80 "ציון הלא תשאלי" לר' יהודה הלוי.

Bavel and her gratifications, in all her haughtiness and conceit, which spelled only extortion, injustice and bloodshed? . . . "Defiled! Defiled one," called her the Children of Yehuda "Begone! Move away! Do not touch us," in these defiled lands of the nations. For the Judeans' tongue turned mute and their mouth closed. Not one of them was able to utter any words of Torah in the darkness and defilement of Bavel.[81] No one was able to expound upon his study [82] as had been the custom before, when the air of their dear Holy Land was the breath of the soul.[83]

Many of them now lowered their heads, and their spirits sank. "My way is hidden from Hashem," lamented the children of Yaakov, "My judgment is being overlooked by my God." [84] Some even gave up in despair, exclaiming: "My future and my expectations from Hashem have perished." [85] He will no longer return to live in our midst.[86]

Dialogues of Despair

Some of the men of Yehuda came and sat before the prophet. "Repent," the prophet said to them. The men replied: "When a slave is sold by his master, or a woman is divorced by her husband, are they still bound to each other by any ties? Did Hashem not chase us out of His home [87] (like a man who divorced his wife, or a master who sold his slave)? He furthermore cast us into the land of the heathen, a dweller of which is compared to the Godless,[88] and whose very dust of the earth lures one into pagan worship.[89] What does the Almighty still demand from us, and what binds us now to His Mitzvos and His Torah? Did He not sell us to Nevuchadnezar, whose slaves we are now — like all the kingdoms on earth existing solely by plain destiny of nature?

"Do Tshuva (repent)!" the prophet said. "Consider: your forefathers sinned — and where are they now?" To which the people of Yisrael devised yet another convincing answer, retorting, "And your prophets who did not sin — where are they?" (Thus it is written,[90] 'your fathers:

---

81 פתיחתא דאיכה רבתי כא.   82 קהלת רבה פר' יב.   83 ר' יהודה הלוי שם.
84 ישעי' מ, כז.   85 איכה ג, ח.   86 שם ד, טו.   87 סנהדרין קה.
88 כתובות קי.   89 שיר השירים רבה ה, ג.   90 זכרי' א, ה.

where are they? And the prophets — will they live forever?' [91])" Indeed, all this is not wrought by Hashem!"

Despite their argumentation, the men of Yehuda eventually admitted their error. For the prophet further told them Hashem's word: [92] "Indeed, My words and the statutes which I had ordered My servants, the prophets, to prophesy — did overtake your fathers, (but not the prophets) and they repented and admitted saying, 'Indeed as the Lord of the Hosts intended to do to us according to our ways and doings, so has He dealt with us.'" And then they also admitted: We have sinned. [93]

Hashem continued delivering His answer to His bewildered Children. Said the Almighty to the prophet: "Go forth, speak to Yisrael. [94] Where is the document of your mother's divorce with which I sent her away? To whom of My creditors have I sold you? Behold, you have been sold for your own iniquities, and only for your transgressions was your mother sent away. Not for the sake of divorce or the act of selling, but only until the time when you will take heart to repent from your sins." [95]

"Neither have you been delivered into the power of Nevuchadnezar, King of Bavel!" That is why it says, [96] 'Nevuchadnezar, My servant.' For it was foreknown to Hashem that Yisrael would claim that they were sold to Nevuchadnezar, — therefore Hashem had long before called him "My slave." "Now when a slave acquires possessions, to whom do he and his possessions belong if not to his master?" [97]

Said the Almighty: "Who made Me into a sexton of these idol-worshippers? Who sold My sons to them in slavery? It was Yisrael's sins which caused this to Me, [98] so that they might atone there for their wrongdoings. But why did I first subjugate all the countries and nations under Nevuchadnezar and the Kasdim? This too, have I done for the honor of Yisrael: lest the nations of the world say: Hashem delivered His Children into the hands of a lowly nation. [99] Only for the sake of

91 סנהדרין דף קה.   92 זכרי' א, ו.   93 סנהדרין שם.   94 ישעי' נ, א.
95 סנהדרין שם.   96 ירמי' מג, י.   97 סנהדרין שם.   98 ילק"ש פנחס תשע"א.
99 שם.

your own honor have I given to Bavel all this power and glorious might, — and you still say: 'Hashem has forsaken us?' "

Yechezkel ben Buzi

It was to Yechezkel ben Buzi that Hashem now gave of His Spirit, and he prophesied to Yehudah, and also to the gentiles who had rebelled against Him! [1] Yechezkel was a prophet, the son of a prophet.[2] Why then was he called *"Ben Buzi,"* "the son of a scorned one?" It was because his parents, pious and righteous people practicing benevolence and kindliness, let themselves be abused all their lives for the honor of the Almighty and for the honor of Yisrael, His People.[3]

At the age of twenty-five Yechezkel was exiled with King Yehoyachin, together with the "Chorosh and Masger." For five years thereafter he was imprisoned,[4] and in the fifth year of Yehoyachin's exile, Yechezkel began prophesying (3332).

Prophecy on Foreign Soil

Before Hashem had chosen Eretz Yisrael, all countries were equally suitable to receive prophecy. But after Eretz Yisrael was selected, all other countries were disqualified.[5] However, for the love of His Children (which upsets all rules), the Shechinah went along with them to Bavel.[6] There He was with them in their suffering.[7] And there, in the land of the enemy, He sent them His prophets, to arouse them to repent.[8]

However, Hashem would not relinquish the honor of Eretz Yisrael. Therefore the beginning of Yechezkel's prophecy still had to start only there.[9] Thus it was that upon returning to the Land of Yehudah ("on 5 Tammuz, in the fifth year of King Yehoyachin's exile" [10]), his first prophecy came to Yechezkel: "Son of Man, you dwell in the midst of the House of Rebellion, whose members have eyes for vision but

---

1 יחזקאל ב.   2 מגילה ט.   3 תנא דבי אליהו רבה פרק ו.   4 סדר הדורות ג"א שטז.

5 יל"ש יחזקאל א.   6 ישעי' מג, יד.   7 תהלים צא, טו.   8 תורת כהנים בחקותי ח.

9 יל"ש יחזקאל א, ורש"י יחזקאל א, ב.   10 יחזקאל יב א, ב.

do not see, ears to listen but do not hear — because they are a House of Rebellion. Now, you Son of Man, provide yourself with utensils for exile, and go into exile in daytime, before their eyes. Exile yourself from where you are into another place in their sight. Perhaps they will realize that they are a "House of Rebellion." [11] Thus Yechezkiel began prophesying [12] to them of the final exile of Tzidkiyahu. Once his first prophecy had come to him in the Holy Land, Hashem continued to speak to him after his return to Bavel, even though he was on foreign soil. [13] As it says: "Hayo Haya," Hashem's Word came to Yechezkiel Ben Buzi the Kohen, in the land of the Kasdim. [14] "Hayo Haya" — Twice: once before, in the Holy Land, and now again on foreign soil. [15]

Therefore here, in the land of exile, [16] Yechezkel — in his prophecy — was like a villager (one who had never yet faced the King, nor seen the splendor of the capital, the palace or the royal household) who suddenly was made to gaze at Royalty. Now that he merited to behold but a glimpse of it, he stood in awe and marveling (as if indeed he saw all the King's glory and splendor). And his mouth opened as if indeed pouring out all of Hashem's praises.

Although for the sake of His People Hashem spoke to His prophets on foreign soil, yet it was only at a clean, undefiled spot by the water.* He also spoke to them in Bavel's uninhabited plains, [17] somehow deemed fit for prophecy like Eretz Yisrael in its purity. Nevertheless, foreign soil caused Yechezkel's prophecies to be rather occluded. (like looking through an unclear, misty mirror) a prophecy full of riddles and parables. [18]

Only out of boundless mercy to His people had the Almighty given them a prophet when they were stubborn, stiff-necked, and a House of Rebellion; [19] and the prophet had to stand up to their stubborness. Said Hashem to Yechezkel, "Behold, I made your face hard against their face, and your forehead strong, to withstand their forehead." [20]

---

11 יחזקאל פרק יב, א-ב. 12 רש״י יחזקאל פרק א, ג. 13 תרגום שם.

14 יחזקאל שם. 15 יל״ש יחזקאל א. 16 חגיגה יג: * תוספת דבר.

17 יחזקאל ג, כב. 18 רש״י יחזקאל א, א. 19 שם פרק ב. 20 שם ג, ח-ט.

"Convey My Words to them, whether they listen or not, since they have been rebellious [21] and do not wish to listen to Me."

Yechezkel was also called "Ben Buzi" (Son of Shame), because the people demeaned him,[22] saying: "He is a descendant of Rachav the harlot." For his contemporaries were light-headed; [23] they did not fear or tremble before Hashem's Word that came to them through His prophet. Because of their slander, Hashem Himself distinguished him, illuminating his sacred lineage: "Yechezkel Ben Buzi, *the Kohen*." [24]

"Like all the Nations"

With fatherly mercy Hashem kept admonishing His Children and sending His prophet again and again; hopefully, they would listen! Ever since the seventh year of the exile of Yehoyachin, Hashem had forewarned them through Yechezkel, His untiring loyal prophet not to err by considering themselves sold or divorced.

In the seventh year on 10 Av (4 years before the Beis Hamikdash was destroyed), some of the most righteous [25] and distinguished elders [26] of Yehoyachin's exile came to inquire of Hashem, and seated themselves before Yechezkel.[27] They erred however, as they contemplated throwing off Hashem's yoke.[28]

Said the elders: Ever since the days of our forefather Avraham, there was a covenant between us; He was our God, and we were His people. Now, for the first time, He has driven us out of His homestead and cast us off to another land. Let us now inquire of Him. If He makes Himself accessible to us, then He is our God as He always was and we are His people. But if He does not listen to all our pleas and answer our demands, we shall no longer be punished for our transgressions, as He is not our God, and He does not wish us to seek Him. For this will indeed prove that He has sold us, and that there is no further link binding us; — like a slave sold by his master, or a woman divorced by her husband.[29]

21 שם ב, ז.   22 ילק"ש פנחס תש"ע, תשע"א.   23 פתיחתא דאיכה רבתי טו.

24 יחזקאל א, ג.   25 יחזקאל כ, א.   26 רד"ק שם.   27 סדר עולם.

28 ויקרא רבה.   29 רש"י שם.

(Not only these elders, but even Yirmiyahu himself had already spoken in a similar vein when he asked Hashem: "Do You really detest Yehuda? Have You indeed despised Zion? Why have You smitten us, leaving no cure for us?" [30] Like the king who angrily sent his wife away, and her chaperone pleads her cause, thus spoke Yirmiyahu to Hashem: "Do You really detest Yehudah? If You still intend to return to her, why have You smitten her with no prospect of cure? And if You do not intend to come back to her, why didn't You divorce her and free her to marry another,[31] so that the House of Yisrael may now be like all the nations, like all the families of the earth, worshiping and putting their trust in wood and stone.")

Now Hashem's Word came to Yechezkel: "Son of Man, speak to the Elders of Yisrael and say to them: 'Thus says Hashem: 'Have you come to inquire of Me? As I live, I shall not make Myself accessible to you.' " — Will *you* speak justice with them, Son of Man; will *you* judge? [32] Will you argue with them?

Like a rock, like massive iron was Yechezkel as he argued with the Elders of Yehuda. "Thus says Hashem: [33] Ever since I chose Bnei Yisrael when they were in Mitzrayim, already then I made Myself known to them by letting My Shechinah dwell among them, and through Moshe, Aharon and Miriam, My prophets, whom I had sent to them. Already then I lifted My Hand in an oath saying: 'I am the Lord, *your God*.' I also swore to take them out of Mitzrayim and bring them into the land I explored for them, a land flowing with milk and honey, a land more desirous than any other. For this land that I have explored is more precious to Me than all others. So are Bnei Yisrael more precious to Me than all nations. I will bring Bnei Yisrael, the precious, into the land that is precious.[34] When I further gave them the laws and the statutes of My Torah — My "tool" [35] for two thousand generations, written in black fire on white fire [36] which had been My daily delight,[37] I made known to them the laws they must fulfill and through which they would find life. I further gave them My Sabbath

30 ירמי׳ יד, יט.　　31 יל״ש שם.　　32 יחזקאל פרק כ, ב, ד.　　33 שם.
34 במדבר רבה כג.　　35 משלי ח, ל.　　36 ריש מדרש תנחומא.　　37 משלי שם.

as a sign between Myself and them.[38] For by giving them My day of rest as their day of rest, I have sanctified them unto Me [39] (like a king, who, wishing to honor his beloved attendant, decides to clothe him in garments resembling his own, and wraps him in the very cloak worn by the king.) However, of one thing I warned them, and I made it a condition with them in Mitzrayim through Aharon, My prophet: [40] Each of you must cast away the abominations which your eyes behold. Do not defile yourself with the idols of Egypt. Only then will I be Hashem, your G-d! [41]

"But your fathers did not heed My warning. They rebelled against My command and refused to listen. They sinned in the desert, and even later in the good, spacious and precious land. They did not cast away the idols and images, even while I was bringing them forth from Egypt. My hatred remained subdued for close to nine hundred years, ever since the exodus from Egypt.[42] My love for them covered up their sins. Moreover I was concerned lest My Name be profaned in the eyes of the pagans. I had mercy upon My people, and desisted from destroying them: perhaps their children would yet keep My laws and observe them.

"Now you came and sinned even more than your fathers. Upon every high hill and under all thick-leaved trees you slaughtered to your idols, pouring out the provocation of your offerings, like all the nations surrounding you. — Shall I now be accessible to you to fulfill your needs and wishes?

"As I live!" — says Hashem Elokim. — "I will *not* make Myself accessible to you!" [43]

"It Shall Never Be!"

Still, the Elders of Yehuda were confused and lost as they had come to inquire of Hashem. Yechezkel therefore continued to speak justice and argue with them.

---

38 יחזקאל כ, יב.   39 רש"י שם.   40 רש"י שם.   41 שם פסוק ז.

42 רש"י שם פסוק ה.   43 שם פסוק לא.

"That which enters your mind, that which you say: 'let us be like the pagans, like the families of all lands, to worship wood and stone,'[44]— *it will never be*! For ever since the first Covenant when I took you out from beneath the dominion of the dome of the sky. You, O' House of Yisrael, have never been like all the nations, to exist merely by the laws of nature. Nor will you ever be!"

"For not because you were sold did I bring upon you all the evil, nor have you become like a divorcee, who is no longer bound to her former husband. Only like a widow, Yehuda has become.[45] — Like a widow, who, even in her widowship, is still called that man's widow. Furthermore, you are not even a real widow, only "Ke-almanah," *like* a widow; that is, a woman whose husband went overseas, but who intends to return to her.[46] — You are not cast away from before Me and turned free, nor have I removed My yoke and commandments from you, as it enters your mind to say: 'From now on we shall no longer be supervised by Hashem's special Divine Providence. Henceforth we shall be subject but to the 'happenings of time' and the position of the celestial bodies, from which our whole success springs — like all the families of the globe'."

— "That will never be!"

With Outpoured Wrath

"As I live," says Hashem Elokim — "with a mighty hand and with an outstretched arm, and with outpoured wrath will I be King over you.[47] On this day, as it always has been. Somehow or other, I will always be your King,[48] even in the lands of your exiles. Despite your unwillingness, and even against your wish: My reign over you will stay forever." [49]

As for all your sufferings? They have come only to reprimand you, and to mete out a Father's punishment to His son who was led astray.

44 שם פסוק לב.   45 איכה פרק א, פסוק א, ועיין חידושי מהרש"א ברכות דף נח:
46 רש"י איכה פרק א, א.   47 יחזקאל פרק כ, פסוק לג.   48 הושע פרק יג.
49 תורת כהנים בחוקותי ח.

From all the families of the earth I have lovingly known only you. Therefore I punish you for all your wrongdoings.[50] The heathens I do not even hasten to punish for their sins, in this world.[51] Only with you do I act so strictly. Only from you do I hasten to exact pay in this world for My every judgment against you, — because of My love!

Therefore, thus says Hashem, the Lord of Hosts: "I will purify them and test them. For what else can I do for the (guilty) Daughter of My people? [52] I shall take you into the wilderness of the nations, and *there* shall I talk justice to you face to face [53] — not through a judge or a messenger. I will cause you to pass under the rod (like a shepherd passing his flock under his rod, scrutinizing each one of them). And I shall bring you back into the bond of the Covenant, never to be released. And I will continue to test you and purify you. I will purge the rebels from your midst and those who sin against Me.[54] But you, O House of Yisrael, you shall return and repent, because of the Covenant and because of My love! I will then gather you from the lands in which you are scattered, and I will be sanctified through you in the eyes of the nations when I lead you unto the Soil of Yisrael which I had sworn to give to your fathers. For on My holy Mount, on Yisrael's Heights, *there* shall you worship Me, and there shall I be appeased, and there will I again be accessible to you. And you will know that I am Hashem when I act with you for the sake of My Name, not in accordance with your evil ways, O House of Yisrael.' Thus says Hashem." [55]

This was similiar to the answer given by the Almighty earlier to Yirmiyahu on the same question of Yisrael's rejection,[56] when He said: "Go back to your teacher Moshe, the master of all the prophets. Already then I assured him:[57] 'Notwithstanding all that, when they will be in the land of their enemies, I will not detest them; nor will I abhor them, to destroy them completely, to annul My Covenant with them. For I am Hashem, their God'," — forever.

50 עמוס פרק ג, ב.   51 סוטה דף כא. ורש״י שם.   52 ירמי׳ פרק ט, ו.
53 יחזקאל כ, לה.   54 שם.   55 יחזקאל סוף פרק ב.   56 יל״ש ירמי׳ יד.
57 ויקרא כו, מד.

The Heavenly Merkava

On the first day of the Shavuos Festival,[58] Hashem revealed to Yechezkel the Merkavah [59] (the Holy Throne of His Shechinah). By the River Kevor, Yechezkel was shown that the Shechinah dwelled with them even in midst of the exile.[60] "The Heavens opened, and I saw Godly visions;"[61] the likeness of the Throne, and the likeness of the four living creatures, the Ofanim and the Chayos. All this glory and all this splendor was shown to him there, so that the Children would behold the Father's glory and realize that He had not forsaken them. They might then understand and take it to heart.

To what may this be compared? To a king whose wife and sons sinned against him. As punishment, the king banished them from his palace. Some time later he summoned one of his sons and said to him: "Come, let me show you your home, the house that I had built for you and your mother." — Thus after Hashem showed Yechezkiel the heavenly Vision, He said to him: "Son of Man, all this is My glory of which I have bestowed more upon you people than upon all the other nations of the world. Did your banishment now lessen this glory? Or has the house I built for your mother become less precious? Do you think there is no one to serve Me now? I have nine hundred and six thousand of ten thousands of "Angels of Attendance" standing before Me, sanctifying My Great Name daily from sunrise to sunset as they exclaim: 'Holy! Holy! Holy!' And from sunset until sunrise they say: 'Blessed be the glory of Hashem, from His Place.' — So it is not to Me that you have caused harm, but only to yourselves. Why then do you still act unseemly and unworthy, spurning the punishment that comes upon you?"[62]

Through Distance — Closeness

Nevertheless, Hashem reconsidered bringing the evil,[63] and He did not carry out His resolve to make Himself unapproachable. As soon as the

---

58 זוהר חדש מד, ע"א.   59 רש"י יחזקאל פרק א, פסוק ג.   60 זוהר חדש שם.
61 יחזקאל א, א.   62 תנדב"א פרק ו.   63 יחזקאל כ, ד.

exiles but lent an ear to listen and resolved in their hearts to return to Hashem, He made himself accessible to them, long before the years of exile and retribution were even completed.

For out of compassion for them, Hashem had exiled them to the land of Bavel, where no bodily servitude to the king was thrust upon them. Only with taxes and tributes did Nevuchadnezar rule over them,[64] but he did not decree harsh edicts against them as other countries would later on do. Furthermore, they remained strictly under the king's personal charge, subject neither to the whims of the princes nor to all the lowly peoples whom he had vanquished and gathered under his rule. — The governor of Meshan (Nevuchadnezar's son-in-law), for one, sent word to the king, "How is it that of all this huge captivity that you brought with you, you have not sent any to us that they may serve us as well?" Said Paltiyahu ben Beniyahu to the king: "We, the distinguished sons of Yisrael, will stand before you and serve *you* here; let our slaves be dispatched there." Thus Nevuchadnezar sent to his son-in-law, not the sons of Yehuda, but their slaves. When the exiles saw that they were not degraded to become slaves to slaves,[65] they eventually found peace of mind in Bavel. They bent their ears to listen, and pondered their lot.[66]

Following their banishment from Hashem's good and spacious land, their eyes and hearts eventually started to open. For hadn't the precious Three — the Land of Yisrael, the Beis HaMikdash, and the Dynasty of David (all of which had been given to them conditionally) been taken away from them with one stroke, because of their sins? And all that remained to them now was the Torah and the covenant with Aharon the Kohen, which had not been given on condition.[67] For now they had neither king nor kingdom, country nor state. Only the Torah and its Mitzvos remained with them and these constituted their whole life. Only these now united them, breathed life unto them, and preserved them as a nation!

Thus, *through distance came closeness.*[68] Precisely because Hashem

64 במדבר רבה טו.

65 קדושין דף ע"ב: ורש"י שם.

66 מנחות דף קי.

67 יל"ש תהלים קלב.

68 יל"ש ירמי' ל.

had pushed them away, therefore they now suddenly strove to come closer. They returned to Him with their whole heart. They again observed the Mitzvos, laws and teachings which Hashem had commanded them, the whole covenant He had signed with them.

Their very stay in Bavel became beneficial. For they now saw the man-made idols of Babylon from up close — her richly bejeweled images [69] which, once having fallen did not rise, and erected did not move; they saw all the fresh produce offerings being served there become stale in front of these corpses.[70] They then detested their own deities and cast them away — until in the very darkness of Babylon (whose very dust seduced people into idolatry,[71]) precisely there the Bnei Yehuda cleansed themselves of the foulness of idol-worship.[72] (True to Yechezkel's prophecy:[73] *"There* you will know that I am Hashem"). And the exiles did this openly in front of the pagans who watched and came to testify: "Indeed, the Bnei Yehuda reject and detest idol-worship!" So that, from then on, whoever rejected worship of idols was called by them a Yehudi.[74].

Waymarks

And so the exiles dwelt in the land of their captivity. They built houses and inhabited them, planted gardens and ate their fruit, just as Yirmiyahu had prophesied.[75] They married and raised families. They took wives for their sons and they gave their daughters away to men, and these in turn had sons and daughters. They multiplied in exile, and did not decrease in number. They further sought peace for the city they were exiled to and prayed to Hashem for its welfare, since in its peace they, too, would have peace.[76] They found their livelihoods, and many of them grew rich in "the land of their misery." Some of them were even appointed by Nevuchadnezar to high posts.[77] As many fields became the property of the sons of Yehuda who settled there in a

69 דניאל ג, א.   70 אגרת ירמי' בכתובים אחרונים.   71 שיר השירים רבה ה, ד.

72 שיר השירים רבה ה, ג.   73 פרק כ, מב.   74 מגילה יג.   75 ירמי' כט, ה-ו.

76 שם.   77 תנא דבי אליהו רבה פרק ה.

permanent way,[78] the Sages ordained statutes to govern their settlement on foreign soil, patterned after the statutes that had previously been ordained in the Land of their Fathers.[79]* They even forbade the raising of goats and sheep, lest these graze and damage the fields of others.

They instituted in Bavel both the ten conditions which Yehoshua and his Beis Din (Court) had lain down — for the general benefit of the people — when he partitioned the land,[80] as well as the edicts which had been enacted later on by King Shlomo.[81] All these were now duly observed in faraway Bavel, according to the Halacha pertaining to a country in which Bnei Yisrael settled.[82]

Even though the Bnei Yehuda established their homes in Bavel, they stayed separated from the natives. "Yehudim," they were called, as they were like a nation within a nation. They remained strangers, and even at the very beginning of the Babylonian Rule they only wished: May we soon see its end! [83] — They yearned only to return home, to "the realm of the Covenant."

Even the remembrance of the Mitzvos pertaining to Eretz Yisrael (which were lost to them now) were of some comfort to them. Even preserving the distinction of the animals which they used to bring as offerings in the Mikdash gave them strength (for the Kedusha [holiness] of the Beis HaMikdash had not ceased with its destruction). They therefore ate in Bavel only the flesh of fish and fowl, deer and gazelle, but not the flesh of cattle and sheep from which they had brought offerings on the Mizbe'ach.[84] Said Bnei Yisrael: When the Beis Ha-Mikdash was standing we offered their fat and blood, and we were granted forgiveness. Here now is our own fat and blood and our lives. May it be Your Wish that *they* atone for us, and that You accept our prayers instead of the Korbanos.[85]

While dwelling in distant foreign cities, the Bnei Yisrael kept track of the places and cities of their origin. "We are residents of Eilam,"

78 בבא קמא פ. ושם ברש"י ותוס' ויש חולקים. 79 שם. * תוספת דבר.
80 ב"ק דף פא ע"א. 81 שם. 82 שם ורמב"ם הל' נזקי ממון פרק ה, ג.
83 ריש פתיחתא דאסתר רבה. 84 דניאל י, ג בפי' ר' סעדי' גאון. 85 במד"ר יח, כא.

"Residents of Beis Lechem," "Men of Anassos," "Residents of Horo-mo," etc.[86] Throughout their long sojourn in the land of their captivity, they made sure to remember whence each of them came, so that each would be able to return to his former city and homestead, on that great day of "the return of Zion and Yerushalayim," when Hashem would finally gather them and bring them back to holy soil.[87]

Also to preserve the purity of their families and of the unbroken chain of their lineage did they keep vigil. For were they not all the seed of Avraham, Yitzchak and Yaakov, some of them Kohanim, some of them Leviim and the others Yisraelim — but all of them assigned to perform their specific service. The Kohanim had been assigned to do Service in the Mikdash, each according to the "House of their Fathers" and with their specific Mishmar (Weekly Watch), while the Leviim had served as Meshorerim (singers) and Gate Watchers. Keeping the charge of the Mikdash and the Mizbe'ach, each had been performing his specific Service and assignment.[88] And if they took no measure to remember now, how would their children and grandchildren know to which Service or assignment they must return, on the day when Hashem brought back the captives of Zion?

They even took upon themselves to continue the charge of Trumos and Maasros,[89] which were commanded "a statute forever," [90] like the everlasting covenant of salt,[91] although the Torah did not require its fulfillment outside the land of Yisrael. For had not the neglect of these Mitzvos been a cause of the very exile? [92] Moreover — since the bitter day of Hashem's anger when "Our dance turned to mourning," [93] there were no longer Kohanim doing Service, nor Leviim singing on the Duchan (platform) and no Yisraelim in their Maamados (weekly stand-in Shift). No longer are offerings being brought, nor is anyone apportioning and donating his Trumos. How should all of these be forgotten in exile? Should these Mitzvos not even be remembered in expectation of the exile's return to Yerushalayim?

86 עזרא פרק ב.   87 שם פסוק א.   88 במדבר פרק יח, ה.   89 שם.
90 שם יח, יט.   91 שם.   92 שוחר טוב נז, ב, ורות רבה ד, פסוק "והנה בועז".
93 איכה ה, טו.

By special temporary ordinance they were therefore commanded by the prophets among them:[94] "Set Trumos and Ma'asros aside from your wheat and new wine,[95] and give them to the Kohanim and the Leviim, as you always did." Thus the Kohanim in Bavel were now eating Trumah (which may be consumed anywhere).[96] This would further help them to prove their lineage as Kohanim, when Hashem ultimately returned the captivity of His people.[97]

Even the precepts of Shmita (the cessation of working the land, every seventh year, for the transgression of which they were exiled [for 70 years]) they now scrupulously observed in Bavel, of their own free will![98]* The pagans even ridiculed them for it: "Fools! In your own land you did not keep the Sabbaticals, and now in exile you do?"[99]

In their yearning to return to their Land, the exiles thus set themselves guideposts and markers on the road of Torah[1] and Mitzvos. ("Like the bitter, wild dates"[2] [of their forefathers], fruit totally unfit for consumption, but planted only as markers along the roads) to help them remember and recognize the road their fathers had marched enroute from the Holy Land to Bavel, so that they might in time come and return from Bavel to Yerushalayim on the very same road of their fathers — on the day when they will joyously sing praise[2b] and say: "We were like dreamers."[3]

The Calendar (Lu'ach)

In their yearning for the Holy Land and the Services on the Holy Mount (now desolate and mournful), all that mattered to the exiles in this world was the Destruction of Hashem's House. (And how could they ever forget!) So that all of their calculations and dealings and even the reckoning of their months and years now revolved around the Churban.

---

94 ידים ד, ג ורע"ב שם.   95 אבות דרבי נתן.   96 במדבר יח, לא.
97 קדושין סט: 98 רש"י איכה א, ז; רמב"ם הל' שמיטה ויובל י, ה.   * תוספת דבר.
99 רש"י שם.   1 עירובין נד: 2 ירמי' לא, כ ורש"י שם.   2b תהלים קכ"ו א'.
3 שם.

246

Ever since leaving Egypt — the Bnei Yisrael counted their months from the date of the Exodus. The month of Nissan [4] (when they went out) became for them "The first of the months of the year." [5] The years, too, they counted from the Exodus (as it is written: [6] "In the second year of their Exodus from Mitzrayim." "In the fortieth year of Yisrael's Exodus from Mitzrayim." [7]) Even after they entered the Land, they continued counting from the Exodus, as it is written: [8] "It came to pass in the 480th year from the Bnei Yisrael's Exodus from the Land of Mitzrayim."

This method of counting from the Exodus continued until the Beis HaMikdash was built (2928). Thereafter, they counted from the date of its construction. (As it is written: [9] "It was at the end of twenty years from when Shlomo built the House of Hashem.") Now, when the Beis HaMikdash was destroyed (3338), they said: "Since we were deemed not worthy of counting from its construction, let us count from its destruction," as stated in the verse, [10] "In the fourteenth year after the city had been captured, etc." [11] — counting the years and months from the Destruction of the House. [12] They even began to count events that befell other nations from the time of the Churban! Thus it is written: [13] "In the second year [14] of Nevuchadnezar's reign he dreamt dreams."

Increasing Sorrow

Even in their grief and mourning, the House of Yisrael was unlike all the nations. Normally grief diminishes with the passing of time, and affliction is gradually forgotten. Yisrael's mourning for Zion however, grew ever more intense. It continuously became harder to bear, as bitter tidings kept coming one after the other.

When Tzidkiyahu's exiles first set out on the long torturous and cruel journey down to Bavel, Hashem still left some survivors in the

---

4 שם כג, טו.   5 שמות יב, ב.   6 במדבר א, א.   7 במדבר לג, לח.

8 מלכים א, פרק א.   9 דברי הימים ב׳ ח, א.   10 יחזקאל פרק מ, א.

11 מכילתא דרבי ישמעאל, ריש פרשת בחודש השלישי.   12 ילק״ש דניאל פרק ב.

13 דניאל ב, א.   14 סדר עולם, ועיין רש״י שם בדניאל.

Land,[15] as if to ease the exiles' mourning and lighten their grief. Indeed, the spark was not yet entirely extinguished, they felt. Even in desolation and banishment the glory had not disappeared entirely. Nevuchadnezar appointed Gedalya ben Achikam as Governor over this poor Remnant of Yehuda; [16] and Yirmiyahu the prophet, having left the exiles at the border, returned through the mournful roads of Zion to be with him, to console and lift up the spirits of the poor Remnant whom Hashem had left in the Holy Land.[17] Thus also the sorrow of the exile of Tzidkiyahu was somewhat mitigated.

Hardly had they settled down when, on the heels of the fugitive's tidings that "the city was stricken," [18] the tragic news* of Gedalyahu's slaughter reached them. The grieving exiles learned that the horrible murder had extinguished the last remaining spark of Yehuda, sealing their banishment.[19] For in fear and confusion the last Remnant had fled to the land of Egypt, "the splintered reed."

The bad tidings grew even worse with Yechezkel's prophecy concerning Mitzrayim and all its inhabitants.[20] In the twelfth year of Tzidkiyahu's reign (the first year after the Churban [21]), on the first day of the twelfth month, Hashem's Word came to Yechezkel: "Son of Man, raise lamentations over Pharoh, King of Egypt, as I have cast My net over him. By the sword of Bavel will I turn Mitzrayim into waste and desolation, and smite all those who reside therein.[22] The small Remnant of Yehuda who fled for their lives to Mitzrayim will be wiped out together with the masses of Egypt and all her pride. They too will die by sword, hunger and pestilence. None shall remain or escape." [23]

Fast Days

The exiles in Bavel remained in grief and mourning. Not only when the prophets told them to do so, but they voluntarily added days of lamentation and weeping. How could they not add to them?

---

15 ירמי' לט, י.   16 מ"ב כה, כב.   17 סנהדרין קג.   18 יחזקאל לג כא.

* תוספת דבר.   19 רמב"ם הל' תענית פרק ה, ב.   20 יחזקאל פרק לב.

21 שם פסוק א ומצודת דוד.   22 יחזקאל שם.   23 ירמי' מב, יז.

Not only the 9th of Av, the very day of Hashem's wrath and fury —
but even the other days of calamities still pained their heart. They
discerned between the weeping of one night and that of a different
night, between one wilderness and another. They remembered the 10th
of Teves, when Nevuchadnezar first laid siege to Yerushalayim;[24] the
9th of Tammuz, when the city's walls were breached;[25] and the 3rd of
Tishrei, when Gedalyahu was slain and the Churban became complete.[26]
The Bnei Yehuda voluntarily[27] turned these days into a time of fasting,
weeping and lamenting to arouse their hearts to repent for their sins
and the sins of their fathers. So that truly they all might become good.[28]*

Since they accepted these fast days upon themselves and their
offspring as well, it became an obligatory tradition for all of Yisrael[29]
to fast on these four days[30] — not to allow themselves any respite from
mourning, nor to let their eyes ever stop weeping,[31] — refusing to give
Hashem a respite either.[32] "Until He would look down and behold
from Heaven;[33] until He returns to establish Yerushalayim again as a
focus of praise on earth."[34] — And then peace would flow to them like
a river, from the Hand of the Almighty.

Most severe was "the Fast of the Fifth Month", when Hashem's
Dwelling was set ablaze. That day became one of weeping and bitter
lamentation, of rolling oneself in dust, as when one suffers a personal
loss.[35] On that day the Elders of Zion sat mute on the ground. They
put ashes on their heads, and donned sackcloth. The maidens of Yerushalayim lowered their heads to the ground,[36] as if they had lost the
betrothed of their youth.[37] They called on the lamenters, who raised
lamentations over them, just as had been prophesied years earlier (yet
in the days of Yehoyakim), by Yirmiyahu in the Sefer of Eichah.[38]

The 9th of Av (Tish'a B'av) was designated as the day of Fast, for
it was on the 9th day (at sunset) that the enemy set fire to the Beis
HaMikdash, to lament the calamity brought about by our sins.[39] Un-

24 מ"ב פרק כה, פסוק א.   25 מ"ב פרק כה, פסוק ד.   26 שם שם פסוק כה.
27 זכרי' פרק ח שם בפי' ר' אברהם אבן עזרא.   28 רמב"ם הל' תענית ה, א.
* תוספת.   29 זכריה פרק ה, יט.   30 שם.   31 איכה פרק ב, פסוק יח.
32 ישעי' סה, יז.   33 איכה ג, נ.   34 ישעי' שם.   35 ירמי' ו, כו.
36 איכה ב, י.   37 יואל א, ח.   38 ירמי' לו, ד.   39 תענית כט.

like the other days of mournful fasts (which are only from dawn to evening), on Tisha B'av they fasted from evening until the following evening, submitting themselves to the five afflictions which Hashem decreed for the Fast of Yom Kipur. They refrained all day from eating and drinking, washing, anointing the body, wearing shoes, and abstained from marital relations [40] (Some even refrained from greeting one another all day.)

For Hashem had filled them with bitterness; [41] how could they even eat or drink? How could they greet their brethren with "Peace be unto you!" on the very day when peace itself had deserted them? [42] How could they possibly forget Yerushalayim and the Day of Yerushalayim, unless they also forgot their own right hand? [43] — How could they divert their heart from the mourning which burned in their bones like a fire sent down from the Heavens? [44]

Accepting the Verdict

Along with mourning, came shame. "We are ashamed that our Land cast us out for our sins," [45] they cried as they recalled their earlier evil ways,[46] which had caused the downfall of their glory and brought about this bitter exile of Yehudah and Yerushalayim. Together, they lamented and sighed: Why has all this befallen us? "Why was the Land destroyed, to become like a wilderness, without even a passerby?" [47] And each tried to answer, one way or another.

They themselves then decreed a sentence of death and destruction upon themselves, for all their sins and abominations.[48] "Hashem is Righteous," they admitted; "All His Ways are Justice." And now, as always, His Judgment is tempered by Mercy! And shame covered their faces. — Said the Kneses Yisrael: "When I dwelt in peace in the Land of Yisrael, I thought I would never stumble; but when I sinned, — You removed Your Shechinah and I became frightened. In exile therefore I cry out to You, saying, 'What benefit is there in spilling my blood,

---

40 שם ל.   41 איכה פרק ג, טו.   42 שם ג, יז.   43 תהלים קלו ד.

44 שם איכה א, יג.   45 ירמי' ט, יח.   46 יחזקאל לו, לא.   47 ירמי' ט, יא

48 שם.

250

when I am lowered into the pit? Hear, Oh! Hashem, and show me favor; be You my help. — And send me Your good word.' " [49]

As Yehuda's shame and T'shuvah grew, so did Hashem's compassion for their return, like a merciful father, to his children.[50] Said Hashem, "In Yerushalayim you did not keep the commandments, but now in exile, you do?!" [51]

Then Hashem too, regretted, so to speak, the banishment of His sons and daughters.[52] "Now that My children repented," said Hashem, "what am I doing here?" "My People have been taken away for naught!" [53]

Under the Prophets' Guidance

In His mercy, Hashem then sent them His prophets, to encourage them and raise their spirits on foreign soil. His Words were conveyed by Yechezkel, as well as by Yirmiyahu and his disciple, Baruch ben Neriyah, after both had been exiled to Bavel by Nevuchadnezar (3346) following the destruction of Mitzrayim.[54] Presently, the old, beloved prophet Yirmiyahu restored the exiles' spirits. "Our father Yirmiyahu," they called him,[55] and he, like a father, rebuked and taught them.

Now the Bnei Yehuda no longer turned after the kings who throughout had been causing them to stumble and transgress. Neither did they follow the princes of Yehuda nor her arrogant, money-seeking governors but only the sainted, devoted prophets of Hashem.

Not only Yirmiyahu and Yechezkel, but of the forty-eight prophets and seven prophetesses who are mentioned to have prophesied to Yisrael since the days of the patriarchs,[56] eight were sent during the seventy years between the destruction of Yerushalayim and the rebuilding of the Second Beis Hamikdash. And to comfort His People they were sent. To console them as well as Yerushalayim itself, fulfilling the historic, all-encompassing consolation: "Nachamu, nachamu Ami, says your God," which Yeshayahu long before had prophesied.[57] — "Nacha-

49 מדרש תהלים ל, ו.   50 תהלים קג, יג.   51 יל"ש מ"ב כד.   52 סוכה נב:
53 ישעי' נב, ה.   54 יחזקאל ל, כב וכו'.   55 ילק"ש תהלים קלו.   56 מגילה יד.
57 ישעי' מ, א.

mu nachamu, Ami," be doubly comforted My People,[58] "will say your God."

Double Prophecies

But what caused Yeshayahu to merit these prophecies of consolation more than all his fellow-prophets?

Said Yeshayahu: "As I was pacing my House of Study I heard the voice of Hashem, saying: "Whom shall I send? Who will go for us? [59] I sent Amos ("the burdened") and they called him a stutterer." (He was called Amos, because he stuttered and was "burdened" by his tongue). Said the Bnei Yisrael: Has Hashem discarded all His world, and let His Shechinah (Divine Presence) rest precisely upon this stutterer? — "I sent Michah, and they slapped his cheek, as it is written:[60] With a rod they smote the cheeks of a judge in Yisrael. Now, whom can I send; who will go for us?" [61] — And Yeshayahu replied: "Here I am. Send me!"

"My sons are troublesome and rebellious," said Hashem to Yeshayahu. "Are you ready to suffer their whippings and abuses?"

Said Yeshayahu: "Even so, I have bared my back to the smiters, and my cheeks to the pluckers.[62] — But I am truly not worthy to convey Your message to Your children, even though they have sinned."

Said Hashem: "Yeshayahu, you love righteousness and hate wickedness.[63] — You love to prove the righteousness of My People and hate to point out their wrongdoings. Therefore, I have anointed you with the oil of gladness, over your companions. All your fellow prophets began prophesying by transference from another prophet; ("Eliyahu's spirit rested upon Elisha." [64] "Hashem took of the spirit that rested upon Moshe and gave it to the seventy Elders" [65]). But you will derive your prophecy directly from the Almighty: "The spirit of Hashem was upon me, for He anointed me to bring good tidings to the humble. He has sent me to mend the heart-broken; to proclaim freedom to the

58 פסיקתא דרב כהנא, פסקא "נחמו נחמו". 59 ישעי' ו, ח. 60 מיכה ד, יד.

61 פסיקתא שם. 62 ישעי' נ, ו. 63 תהלים מה, ח. 64 מ"ב ב, טו.

65 במדבר יא, כה.

captives, and the opening of the jails to the imprisoned." [66] Moreover, all the prophets prophesy simple, singular prophecies; yours, however, will be double: "Awake, O! awake!" [67] "Take heart O! take heart!" [68] "Rejoice, I will rejoice." [69] "I, I am your Comforter!" [70] "Comfort, O! comfort, My People, will your God say." [71] — for the sake of the all-encompassing, final, double consolation.

When the Bnei Yisrael heard Yeshayahu saying: "Nachamu! Nachamu, be doubly comforted My People," they said to him: Do you tell us these tidings on your own, perhaps? Replied Yeshayahu: "Your God will say". It is *your God* Who says this.

Continued the Bnei Yisrael: "Our Master, Yeshayahu, have you perhaps come to comfort only that generation in whose time the Beis HaMikdash is destroyed?" Replied Yeshayahu: "I have come to comfort *all* generations." It was not prophesied, "Said Hashem," but "Hashem *will say*" — for all future generations.

Eight times Yeshayahu prophesied to them saying: "Hashem will say," * and accordingly, eight prophets arose to comfort Bnei Yisrael after the Destruction of the Beis HaMikdash: [72] Yoel, Amos, Tzefanyah, Yirmiyahu, Yechezkiel, Chagai, Zacharyah, Malachi. — Would that they be comforted!

The Bnei Yehuda, however, were too confused by the prophets' words to accept them. "Why do you comfort us in vain?" they asked them. "Has not our harp turned to mourning while we dwell here in a place of hollowness, carrying a yoke too heavy to bear?[73] Why then do you comfort us for naught? Even your answers spell falsehood and lies." [74] Said the Bnei Yisrael to its prophets, "Why, your very words need clarification; they contradict each other." [75]

Came Hoshe'a to the exiles to console them and said, "Hashem sent me to console you." They replied, "What have *you* got? Which prophecy have you brought us?" Said Hoshe'a, "I will be as the dew to Yisrael. It will blossom like a rose, and strike its roots like the Levanon." [76]

66 ישעי׳ סא, א.   67 שם נא, ט.   68 שם פסוק יז.   69 שם סא, י.
70 שם נא, יב.   71 פסיקתא שם.   * תוספת.   72 פסיקתא דרב כהנא, פיסקא "נחמו".
73 קינות לט׳ באב.   74 איוב כא, לד.   75 פסיקתא שם.   76 הושע יד, ו.

Replied the exiles, "Yesterday you told us:[77] 'Ephraim is smitten, their root is dried up; they shall bear no fruit. Even if they bring forth children, I shall slay the beloved fruit of their womb.' And now you tell us this? Which should we believe, the first or the second?"

Came Yo'el and said to them, "Hashem has sent me to console you." They said to him, "What prophecy do you bring us?" He replied, "It shall come to pass on that day, that the mountains will drip with nectar, and the hills shall flow with milk. All the river-beds of Yehuda shall flow with water, and a well-spring shall come forth from the House of Hashem and it shall water the Valley of Shittim." [78]

Countered the exiles: "Yesterday you told us:[79] 'Awake ye drunkards and weep! Howl, all you drinkers of wine, because of the sweet liquid that is cut off from your mouth.' And now you are telling us something different! Which should we believe, the first or the second?"

Amos then came to console them, and he said, "On that day I shall raise the Sukah of David that is fallen." [80] But here, too, the exiles found his last prophecy contradicting the first one. And so it was with Michah and Nachum, Chabakuk and Tzefanyah, Chagai and Zecharyah.

Finally, Mala'achi (the last of the Prophets) came and said to them, "Hashem has sent me to console you." They said to him, "What prophecy have you brought us?" He replied: "All the nations shall praise you for you shall be a land of desire, says the Lord of Hosts." [81] But as before, they replied,[82] "Yesterday you told us, 'I have no desire for you nor will I accept an offering at your hand', and now you are telling us this! Which shall we believe, the first or the second?"

Until the prophets turned to Hashem and said: "Master of the Universe, Yerushalayim refuses to be consoled." — Said the Almighty, "Nachamu, nachamu, Ami," (to be read "Imi" — with Me). Me and you, let us go together and console them.

"Console, O console," doubly! — Console them, you heavenly beings, console them, those down on earth. Console them, those living;

77 שם ט, טז.   78 יואל ד, יח.   79 שם א, ה.   80 עמוס ט, יא.

81 מלאכי ג, יב.   82 שם א, י.

console them, those who have died; Console them in this world, and console them in the World to Come! Console them for the Ten Lost Tribes, and console them for Yehuda and Binyamin. — Console My people! O console! [83]

The Great Beis Hakneses

Not only His prophets, but even His Shechina was with the exiles in Bavel. For their sake He too, was sent to Bavel.[84] For the Bnei Yisrael are precious to Him. Wherever they were exiled, His Shechina went with them.[85]

But where did the Shechina have its dwelling place in the depths and darkness of Bavel? In the Beis Hakneses of *Hutzal* (adjoining the Beis Hamidrash of Ezra, the scribe, below the city of Naharde'a [86]), and in the Beis Hakneses of *Shaf Veyasiv* in Naharde'a.[87]

When the first masses of exiles were driven out with Yehoyachin, King of Yehuda in the year 3328, they took with them stones of Yerushalayim and some of her soil (fulfilling the verse [88] "for Your servants hold her stones dear, and cherish her very dust."). For they loved the stones of the Holy Land and its dust,[89] even to cherish and kiss them.[90] — And as if even in exile their country was still with them.

Throughout their arduous journey, the mourning captives watched over all these pieces of stone and every speck of sand which they had taken along, more than one watches over treasures of silver and gold. Now, being uprooted ("De'shaf") from Hashem's land, and having settled ("Ve'yasiv") in faraway, alien Babylon, they later built from these stones and holy soil a Beis Hakneses in Naharde'a.[91]* This had been their intention from the very beginning — the reason they took all the effort to carry and protect them, all the way from Yerushalayim till Bavel.[92]

In this cherished place of prayer the exiles would gather, as if in

83 פסיקתא שם.　　84 ישעי' מג, יד.　　85 מגילה כט.　　86 ספר הערוך, ערך שף.

87 רש"י מגילה שם.　　88 תהלים קב, טו.　　89 רש"י שם.　　90 אבן עזרא תהלים שם.

91 רש"י מגילה שם.　　* תוספת.　　92 רש"י תהלים שם.

the holiness of Yerushalayim itself, (Even in later generations some of the greatest made every effort to frequent and pray in this Beis Hakneses of Shaf Veyasiv, in order to merit holiness and special higher wisdom.[93]) For the place itself was of hallowed soil, like the very Gates of Zion. Not only the Torah which they studied here, but even the walls and the very dust of this Beis Hakneses were sacred, like the land of their fathers from which they had been banished. And between these walls (put up by mere dear and cherished love) the Shechina came to dwell with them.

Said Hashem, "My children are engulfed in grief. Shall I dwell in comfort?" [94] — Therefore, He too, moved away (Shaf) His Shechina from the Mikdash in Yerushalayim, and settled (Ve'yasiv) with them in Bavel; [95] sometimes in the Beis Hakneses of Hutzal, sometimes in the Beis Hakneses of Naharde'a.[96] There He was to them "a Mikdash me'at" ("a bit of a Mikdash") in the land to which they had come.[97] Although only "a bit," yet it had a measure of the very holiness of the Mikdash in Yerushalayim.

Thus out of Hashem's anger came to them favor; out of enragement, mercy; out of distress, relief; out of downfall, arising; out of darkness, light; and out of estrangement, a renewed closeness.[98]

And after it had been said to them, "You are not My people," it will yet be said, "You *are* the Children of the living God!" [99]

93 מגילה שם.   94 פסיקתא דרב כהנא "ותאמר ציון".   95 רש"י עבודה זרה מג:

96 מגילה שם.   97 יחזקאל יא, טז.   98 ילק"ש ירמי' ל.   99 הושע ב, א.

Chapter Three

'I HAVE NOT DETESTED THEM'

Chapter Four

MIRACLE-MEN

Chapter Three

'I HAVE NOT DETESTED THEM'

WHILE Nevuchadnezar "My servant"[1] allowed the Bnei Yehuda some respite in the land of their exile, his arrogance and haughtiness grew ever more.

Haughtiness

Hashem had made him the ruler of the whole world.[2] All the nations and kingdoms served him,[3] (even the sinful kingdom of Yehuda). His wife Shemirmith too ruled a dominion of her own.[4] But "He remained ever forcefully demanding. His endless desires left no righteousness in him." [5] He was filled with anger and greed, eager only to conquer. At no time did he ever say, "I have enough with all that I have acquired." [6] Even though Hashem made him king over the whole world, and called him "The head" [7] and "The lion," [8] (since his roar frightened all the peoples of the earth,[9] "being awesome and fearful" [10]), he was not satisfied and found no gladness in his power.[11] (Like all wicked men, who are never satisfied with their lot). Moreover, Nevuchadnezzar was of a most short stature [12] and fat as a barrel, and his voice chirped like a raven.[13] He considered himself a most inferior man.[14] He would look at himself and wonder, "I am a king?" [15]

The Terrifying Dream

In the second year from the day in which Nevuchadnezar had revealed his wickedness by entering the innermost of the Mikdash in Yerushalayim and destroying it,[16] he dreamt a dream. From on High he was

---

1 ירמי' מג, י.   2 מגילה יא.   3 שם כז, ר־ז.   4 אסתר רבה ג, ב.
5 חבקוק פרק ב, ד.   6 רש"י שם.   7 דניאל ב, לח.   8 ירמי' ד, ז.
9 מגילה דף י"א.   10 חבקוק פרק א, ז', ויל"ש שם.   11 יל"ש חבקוק ב.
12 תנא דבי אליהו רבה פרק לא.   13 ויקרא רבה לג, ו.   14 יל"ש שם, ב"זית רענן".
15 יל"ש שם.   16 יל"ש דניאל ב.

shown his innermost thoughts — the reflection of his heart's desires for the glory of his kingship — with which he was obsessed all day.[17] In the dream he saw himself as the golden head of the awesome image which was shown to him. That very day, the start of the decline of Bavel's Kingdom was decreed.[18]

The dream came right at the beginning of the night.[19] The king awoke with a racing pulse. His heart pounded like a bell and his sleep was gone [20] for the rest of the night.[21] He was doubly shaken, since upon awakening both the meaning and the dream itself eluded him.[22]

Terror-stricken, the king summoned his magicians and doctors, the sorcerers and astrologists, as he was desperate to recall the dream and learn its meaning. "May the King live forever!" they greeted the bewildered Nevuchadnezar. "Repeat the dream to your servants, and then we shall tell you its meaning."

"The dream has escaped me," [23] replied Nevuchadnezar. "Besides, were I to tell you the dream, you would fabricate a meaning. So *you* be the ones to tell me the dream as well as its interpretation.[24] If you do not, you shall be rent asunder, and your houses will be turned into dunghills and shame." [25]

His aides were shocked. No king had ever made demands that required prophecy.[26] Full of fear, they answered the king, "What you ask in nigh impossible to fulfill. No one could tell you the dream, for the angels who dwelt among men are no longer with us.[27] As long as the God of the Universe dwelt among people in Yerushalayim, angels and prophets used to reveal that which is hidden. Were one of the descendants of Aaron the High-Priest still to stand before you, performing the holy Service, he would put on the Urim Ve'Tumim and reveal your dream.[28] Now, however, there is no one in the whole world who can reveal it to you."

Nevuchadnezar flew into a rage. "So great was the Temple, yet you advised me to destroy it?" [29]

17 פי׳ ר׳ סעדי׳ גאון דניאל ב, ג.   18 רש״י שם.   19 בראשית רבה פט, ה.

20 דניאל ב, א.   21 ב״ר שם.   22 יל״ש, דניאל ב.   23 דניאל ב, ה.

24 תנחומא מקץ ב, גם בפי׳ ר׳ סעדי׳ דניאל ב, ט.   25 דניאל ב, ה.   26 יל״ש שם.

27 דניאל ב, יא.   28 ילק״ש שם.   29 שם.

Being furious, the King ordered all of Bavel's wise men slain. At once the decree went forth throughout the land, and all the wise men were seized, Daniel and his companions among them.[30] It was Daniel then who came up with a sensible and clever advice to Aryoch, the chief guardsman, whom the king had appointed executioner of the wise men of Babylon.[31]

Judean Youths

Although Daniel was still very young at the time,[32] Hashem had endowed him with unusual wisdom and understanding. It was already a great dignitary who stood before the king.

Daniel had come to Bavel yet in the first stage of Yehuda's exile, in the days of King Yehoyakim.[33] It was in the third year of Yehoyakim's rebellion that Nevuchadnezzar besieged Yerushalayim, and Hashem delivered the king of Yehuda into his hands. Nevuchadnezar seized also some of the sacred vessels of the Beis Hamikdash and carried them off to the land of Shin'or. He furthermore ordered Ashpenaz, the chief of his officers, to bring from Yehuda children from the royal seed and from the nobles — "youths without blemish, good-looking, skilled in all wisdom, with a fine grasp of knowledge and understanding of sciences, who are able to stand and serve in the king's palace." He ordered them taught the scripts and language of Bavel (which is easy to master).[34] The king supplied them with their needs and provided them with daily fare from the royal table, with the delicacies of which he himself partook and the wines which he drank. He ordered them trained for a period of three years, so that some of them should be worthy of serving the King.[35]

Daniel and His Companions

Nevuchadnezzar planned all this with a dual purpose: to weaken and ruin Yehuda's Kingdom, and at the same time to further strengthen

30 דניאל שם.   31 שם.   32 סדר הדורות.   33 דניאל א, ב.

34 חולין כד.   35 דניאל א.

the power of his mighty Bavel. Thus it was that he exiled the cream of Yehuda's youngsters to his own land.

Among the exiled youngsters were Daniel, Chananya, Mishael and Azarya.[36] They were of royal seed,[37] and blessed with the six [38] royal virtues of David Hamelech:[39] they were indeed good-looking, knowledgeable in all areas of wisdom, and without a blemish — in that, never in their lives had they needed any medical care.[40] They furthermore possessed the strength to stand in the King's palace with perfect control over their bodily needs, and the ability to refrain from laughter, conversation and sleep, out of fear of the King [41] — although they were children and although they had just been taken away from their homeland and from the serenity of their parental homes.

The Kasdim taught the youngsters of Yehuda all of Bavel's wisdom, its language and script. Striving to lead the children of Yehuda's Royal House unto the ways of the wise men of Bavel and its princes, they gave Daniel and his companions names after the different deities, as was customary in Bavel.[42] Daniel was named "Beiltshatzar."[43] "Beil" for Bavel's idol, "*Shatzar*," meaning wisdom in Aramic.[44] Chananya, Mishael and Azarya were called Shadrach, Meishach, and Aved N'go.

Daniel was only fifteen years old,[45] yet at this crucial hour his courageous resolve stood all of them by. (It was the She'ma that continuously strengthened him. For by daily reciting it devotedly, he dedicated himself to fulfill its words with all his heart and soul.[46]) It was to this that Hashem alluded: "Thus the children of Israel will eat their bread unclean among the gentiles whither I will drive them." He courageously was determined [47] not to defile himself with partaking of the food of the Royal table; not with the King's own sweet delicacies, nor with his drinks of wine or oil.[48] Within the walls of Bavel's proud, high-rising castles (built solely for the fulfillment of bodily desires and gratifications, and filled with every material object coveted by man), the young Daniel had the strength and self-control to deny

36 שם.   37 שם.   38 ישעי' פרק יא, פסוק ב.   39 סנהדרין צג:
40 שם.   41 שם.   42 דניאל פרק א.   43 דניאל שם פסוק ז.
44 רש"י שם.   45 פי' אבן עזרא דניאל, ד.   46 ר' סעדי' גאון, דניאל א, ח.
47 דניאל שם.   48 יל"ש דניאל א'.

himself all the pleasures and delights that Bavel offered. None of their delicacies or drinks entered his mouth for fear they would defile his soul (Even if the particular food or drink was not specifically prohibited as Neveilah or Treifah). Daniel therefore, only strived to isolate himself completely, in body and spirit, from the abomination of Bavel. For not like sitting serenely at a parents' table was dining in the land of the gentiles, hence B'nei Yisrael were in need of great vigil and special separation in order to retain their purity.

With this resolve, Daniel refused to see Hashem's words as a decree. He said: "It is only to test us that Hashem decreed upon us that we will eat our bread unclean. Let us do what we are supposed to, and He will do as He wishes!" [49] And he insisted on not being defiled with unclean bread.

And Hashem granted Daniel favor and mercy before the chief officer in charge of the youths' training [50] who became very apprehensive. For would he not pay with his life should the boys, lacking food, look pale and thinner than other boys their age? [51]

Said Daniel, "Please test your servants for ten days (these happened to be the ten days of T'shuvah, from Rosh HaShana to Yom Kippur [52]). Just give us some seeds to eat and water to drink, and that shall be our total fare." [53] (The eating of seeds, he knew, would cause bad breath which would repel Nevuchadnezar, so that he would not approach and defile them bodily,[54] the way he defiled all his princes and servants.[55])

"Can you, princes, keep back from bread and wine for ten days?" [56] asked the officer. "Yes, we can! We are the descendants of Avraham, who was put to test with ten trials, and withstood them all. Perhaps his merits will help us now." [57]

The chief officer agreed to their wish, and put them through a test ten days. At the end of the ten days, Daniel and his three companions looked even better and healthier than all the other children in the palace who had partaken of the king's food.[58] From that day on, the

49 תנחומא פ׳ וירא כא.   50 דניאל שם פסוק יא.   51 ר׳ סעדי׳ גאון שם יב.

52 פי׳ ר׳ סעדי׳ גאון שם יב.   53 דניאל א.   54 ר׳ סעדי׳ שם.   55 שבת קמט:

ור׳ סעדי׳ גאון, דניאל א, יב.   56 תנחומא שם.   57 שם.   58 דניאל א.

steward took the food and wine alloted to the four youths for himself, while serving them only seeds and water.[59] Daniel thus became the first who strictly separated himself from all (even Kosher) food cooked by gentiles, and even from their drinks, followed by his three companions and eventually also by all of Yisrael.[60]

Hashem granted the four heroic youths of Yehuda knowledge and understanding in every field of wisdom. Daniel however excelled,[61] being wise even in his Fear of Heaven.[62] He thus merited even greater wisdom: Hashem's spirit rested upon him; a spirit of knowledge and understanding; a spirit of counsel, insight and strength; a spirit of deep wisdom and Fear of Hashem.[63] He came to understand the meaning of all visions and dreams, and how to explain and interpret them.[64]

At the end of the three years designated by the king (Daniel was then eighteen), the youths were brought before the throne. The King engaged them in discussions touching on all fields of wisdom, and found them to rank the highest among all the exiled royal youths of Yehuda. Immediately Nevuchadnezar ordered that only Daniel, Chananyah, Mishael and Azaryah should henceforth stand before him and serve him. The King quickly discovered that in any matter requiring knowledge, insight, and sound judgment, he would find the four young men of Yehuda tenfold more knowledgeable than all the magicians and sorcerers of his entire kingdom with Daniel even surpassing them all. — Daniel was to retain his high position in Babylon until the first year of the reign of King Koresh.[65]

The Dream Revealed

Daniel was thirty-four years old when Nevuchadnezar dreamt his dream.[66]* And in his wisdom Daniel saved himself, his three friends, and all the wise men of Babylon, after Nevuchadnezar had decreed death upon them all.[67] With logic, Daniel pleaded before Aryoch, the chief

59 שם. 60 ע"ז דף לו. 61 ברכות דף נה. 62 רש"י קהלת ח, א.
63 רות רבה פרשה ז וישעי' פרק יא, ב. 64 ברכות שם. 65 דניאל פרק א.
66 פי' אבן עזרא דניאל א, ד. * תוספת דבר. 67 דניאל ב.

guardsman who, upon the King's command, was about to execute all the wise men. "Why has the King's decree gone out in such haste, leaving the wise men no time to find an explanation of the dream?"

Bringing his pleading before the King, Daniel was granted time to find an interpretation of the dream. He then returned to his home to pray to Hashem. He also asked Chananyah, Mishael and Azaryah to help him, by beseeching Hashem [68] to show them a solution to this enigma, so that they would not die together with all those sinners.[69]

Hashem, however, does not do a thing unless He reveals His secret to His servants, the prophets.[70] He grants knowledge to the wise and wisdom to those who have understanding.[71] And then in a vision at night, Daniel's pleas were answered. Whereupon, filled with gratitude, Daniel exclaimed, "Blessed be Hashem's Name forever and ever, for wisdom and might are His. He is the One who alters times and seasons, and it is He who deposes kings and establishes kings." And he thanked Hashem Who in His mercy revealed now to His servant, both the king's dream and its meaning.[72]

At once Daniel went to see Aryoch who rushed him into the king's presence. "Daniel Beiltshatzar, can you tell me the dream I have dreamt, and its meaning?" the king asked. "I cannot!" answered Daniel. "The secret which the king has asked, no wise men, conjurers, magicians or sorcerers could ever reveal. But there is a God in Heaven, Who reveals secrets. It is He who made known to the king what shall be at the End of Days.

"While on your bed you were engrossed in thoughts of what would happen in latter days.[73] Therefore in your dream you saw a statue in the shape of a mighty person before you. Indeed, the image was huge, and its appearance was frightening. Its head was of pure gold, its chest and arms of silver, its belly and hips of brass, its thighs of iron, its feet part iron and part clay. While you were looking, one stone broke loose — not by hands, but by itself. It struck the statue at its feet, which were of iron and clay, and shattered them to fine pieces.

68 שם.   69 ילקוט שמעוני שם.   70 עמוס ג, ז וילקוט שמעוני שם.

71 דניאל ב, כא וסדר עולם פרק ל.   72 שם.   73 שם.

Then they all crumbled into pieces (the brass, the iron, the silver and the gold) and became like the chaff of a granary in summertime's threshing, carried away by the wind, leaving no trace of their former existence. The stone that smote the statue then became a great mountain and it filled the whole earth.[74] — Now this is the dream. And we will also tell you its meaning."

The Four Empires

"Hashem has shown you the fate of the four empires that will rule after you.

"For it is a mighty, powerful and glorious empire that Hashem has given to you. Every dwelling-place of people, beasts of the field and birds of the sky — Hashem has entrusted them all into your power, that you may rule them. You are the Statue's head of gold, first in time and importance.

"Succeeding you, another empire (Persia and Media) shall arise, inferior to you, as silver is inferior to gold. After this one, a third empire (Greece) will arise — like brass, which will rule over all the earth. The fourth kingdom (Rome and Yishmael[75]) will be as strong as iron which crushes and subdues all things, and indeed, it will shatter and crush all those other kingdoms. However, it will be a split empire, at once weak and strong, like the statue's feet and the toes which were part clay and part iron.

Then, in the days of this Fourth Empire, the God of Heaven shall establish a Kingdom which shall never be destroyed, nor shall its reign be left to another nation. This Kingdom shall smash to pieces and consume all these other kingdoms, and it will stand forever — just as you saw the stone that had broken loose by itself from the mountain, not by human hands, nor by armies or physical strength, yet it smashed to pieces the iron, the brass, the clay, the silver, and the gold alike. This will be the Kingdom of the Moshiach, which will endure forever." [76]

74 שם.   75 רב סעדי' גאון, דניאל ב, מא.   76 שם.

The Wicked Crowns the Righteous

Upon seeing that Daniel had described the dream correctly and inter-preted it truthfully, (which no one in his whole empire had been able to do), Nevuchadnezar bowed down on his face, prostrated himself before Daniel and ordered sweet offerings of meal and wine brought before him, in order to deify and worship him.[77] But Daniel refused forthwith, since he who is being worshiped incurs punishment just as the one who worships him.[78]

Nevuchadnezar was amazed. Here stood a mortal who rejected glory for himself, and refused to become a deity to the King, the ruler of the whole world. He then said in bewilderment: "Indeed, it is true, Elokim is the God of all gods, and the Master of all masters. It is He who reveals the hidden, so that you were able to reveal this secret to me!"

Then the king elevated Daniel even more, showered him with lavish gifts and appointed him ruler over the whole land of Babylon, and master over all its wise men, its governors and its high officials. Thus the exiled Sons of Yehuda became "the great among the nations" — that is, wherever they went, they became the high officers of their masters.[79]

Daniel, however, did not consider his elevation to the high post a result of his own merit; he attributed it equally to the merit of his three companions who, together with him, had beseeched the Almighty for a solution to the mystery of the dream. He therefore requested that they too be granted a share in the rule of the land. The king agreed and appointed Chananya,[80] Mishael and Azarya to oversee the royal affairs in the land of Babylon.[81] And they served as lords in the palace of Bavel's king, as Yeshayahu had prophesied to King Chizkiyahu long before.[82]

So it came about that the wicked crowned the righteous.[83] Nevuchad-nezar, the unclean and defiled, clothed Daniel, the pure and holy, in garments of purple and royalty.[84] And Daniel was seated in the Gate of the King.[85]

77 ילק"ש דניאל ב.   78 שם.   79 סנהדרין כד.   80 דניאל א, ז.   81 שם.

82 מלכים ב' כ, יח.   83 חבקוק א, ד.   84 יל"ש חבקוק ג.   85 דניאל ב, מט.

Unfortunately, all the benevolence of the wicked man was but harmful to the righteous Daniel. By crowning the righteous and being kind to him, the wicked merit even more power, and furthermore, benefit from the Tzaddik's wisdom and good counsel. Having merited even greater power, the final judgment is not decreed upon the wicked (as Daniel's later advice to feed the poor helped Nevuchadnezar to merit more power for himself). Hence Torah-fulfillment weakens [86] — as people seeing the glory and successes of the evildoer are inclined to follow his ways. The evildoer on his part furthermore uses the very power given him from on High to incite the people against their Creator. Concerning this the prophet Chabakuk [87] inadvertently sinned when beseeching the Almighty, as he complained: "Since the evildoer crowns the righteous, the Judgment emerges distorted." [88]

Grand Spectacle of Revolt

The ways of the wicked, however, are not constant. While in distress, they humble themselves; but as soon as the affliction passes, they return to their evil ways.[89] As soon as the Almighty revealed to the haughty Nevuchadnezar the impending decline and fall of his kingdom, and that at the End of Days, the eternal Kingdom of Hashem will reveal itself to all, Nevuchadnezar at once plotted to make the Bnei Yisrael forget Hashem [90] and cause them to fall through idolatry, so that they would never inherit the Eternal Kingship.[91]

Nevuchadnezar made a huge statue of gold (in the likeness of the image he had seen in his dream, except that its whole body was now of gold rather than just its head), sixty cubits high and six cubits wide, and he placed it in the Plain of Dura in the region of Bavel.[92] He stood it up, but it fell down. He stood it up anew, and it fell down again, because of its tremendous height. It did not stand until they brought forth all the gold and silver they had taken from Yerushalayim and poured a base over its feet, thereby fulfilling the verse:[93] "Their

86 חבקוק א, ד.   87 יל"ש חבקוק ג.   88 חבקוק א, ד.   89 שמות רבה יב, יט.

90 רות רבה, פרק ד.   91 ילק"ש דניאל לז.   92 דניאל ג, א.   93 יחזקאל ז, יט.

silver they will throw in the streets and their gold will belong to the unclean (that is, idols[94])." Then Nevuchadnezar sent orders to gather the satraps, the prefects, the governors and all the rulers and officials of all the countries to come and celebrate the dedication of the Statue.[95]

It was not an ordinary thing the aged Nevuchadnezar had in mind for his statue,* but a spectacular day, a spectacle of worship for all the kingdoms and countries together, the likes of which the world had never seen. All this would happen amid the blasts and sounds of an orchestral setting of all the finest and most melodious instruments, which no eye and ear could even perceive. So that all the people of the world would come and stand bewildered and marvel at the majesty and beauty of the grandiose statue to which all this belonged; the music, the beauty and power. And by witnessing and acknowledging the unique splendor of the statue, Nevuchadnezar would make all the peoples of the world as one, rebelling against their Creator.[96] (This Statue indeed had power, though misleadingly so.[97] How? The wicked Nevuchadnezar had taken the golden Tzitz [head plate] of the Kohen Gadol and put it into the mouth of the Statue, and it was really the Tzitz that was heard speaking from its mouth.[98])

When the satraps and governors and all the officials of all the countries arrived, they gathered in front of the Statue. Then the proclamation went forth loud and strong: "To all you nations, peoples, and tongues! Be gathered and stand ready before the Statue.[99] And when you hear the blast of the horns, the whistles and the harps, the flutes and violins, the bagpipes and all the other sounds of music (a mighty and serene sound, never yet equalled), you are all as one to fall on your face, and prostrate yourselves before the golden image. Whoever fails to do so will be thrown at once into the flaming kiln!" [1]

After the proclamation was issued the king's officials (on orders from the King) selected three men from each nation. The Sons of Yehuda amongst them, because the Almighty had placed a cruel man over them to test them.[2]

94 ילק״ש שם.   95 דניאל פרק ג, א.   * תוספת דבר.   96 שם.
97 שיר השירים רבה ז, יד.   98 שם.   99 בראשית רבה סח, יג.   1 דניאל שם.
2 שה״ש רבה ז, ח.

Aiming specifically to induce the Bnei Yehuda to worship idols, Nevuchadnezar set up his Statue purposely in the Plain of Dura, where the Bnei Ephraim had fallen after having prematurely left the land of Egypt.[3] He reckoned that upon seeing the withered bones of their fallen brothers, the hearts of the exiles would melt in fear. And when the Babylonians selected the delegates, they chose the greatest and most honored from among every nation, as befitted the alleged honor of the Statue. Thus Chananya, Mishael and Azarya were the three selected from Yehuda.

To Disgrace the Statue!

However, the three chosen youths were bewildered and confused, uncertain of the nature of the Statue itself. If it was made for idol-worship, they reasoned, then they had to either flee or let themselves be killed, but not pay homage to it. If, however, it was only a monument to the King, then they could either flee or pay homage, but they were not obliged to let themselves be killed. Even if the Statue was somewhat related to idolatry, they still would not be obliged to die, as they were the only Jews attending the spectacle, and the command of Kidush Hashem pertains only when ten Jewish men [4]* are present. On the other hand, they reasoned, since the majority of the Bnei Yehuda erringly considered the Statue to be an idol,[5] perhaps it would be worthwhile to sacrifice their lives for the sanctification of Hashem's Name.

The three of them went to see Daniel. "Our Master Daniel," they said, "Nevuchadnezar has set up a statue and selected three representatives from every nation, and from among Bnei Yisrael he has chosen us. What do you advise us to do? Should we bow to it, or not?" —

Replied Daniel, "You have the prophet before you, go to him!"

Immediately they went to Yechezkel, the prophet, and repeated their question, "Shall we bow down or not?" Replied the prophet, "My

---

3 סנהדרין דף צב: 4 תוס' ע"ז דף ג, ד"ה "שלא השתחוו".   * תוספת דבר.
5 שיר השירים רבה שם בספר "ענף יוסף" ו"עץ יוסף", ו"נמוקי יוסף" למסכת סנהדרין.

Master Yeshaya taught me: 'Hide for a little while, until the fury subsides.' Better flee and go into hiding while the wrath of the evil decree passes."

Said Chananya, Mishael, and Azarya, "Do you want us to flee so that all the nations present will not even be aware of our absence? Then they will claim: 'All the nations of the world (including Bnei Yisrael) bowed down and paid homage to the Statue,' thus causing His Holy Name to be profaned the world over?"

"If so, what would you like to do?" asked the prophet. They replied: "We would like to openly disgrace the Statue by being present and *not* prostrating ourselves before it. Then everyone will say: 'All the nations bowed to the Statue, except for Bnei Yisrael!' "

Said the prophet: "If such is your intention, wait until I consult the Almighty." Yechezkel went and said to Hashem, "Chananya, Mishael and Azarya wish to give their lives for the Sanctification of Your Name. Will You stand by them, or not?"

Replied Hashem: "I will not stand by them! Why — having caused Me to destroy My Dwelling, to set My Palace aflame, and to exile My sons among the heathen, — do you now come to seek Me? As truly as I am the One, I will not make Myself accessible to you!"

Tears rolled down the prophet's face. He wept, lamented and bewailed himself, "Woe to us! Lost is the Remnant of Yehuda! Only those three chosen were left of Yehuda and now this is the reply given to them?"

Weeping all the way, Yechezkel returned to the young men of Yehuda. "What did Hashem tell you?" they asked him. — "I shall not stand with you," he answered.

But their love for Hashem was stronger than death.[6] And they said to the prophet: "Regardless of whether He will save us or not, we shall give our lives for the sanctification of His Name!" [7]

(What was it that stirred Chananya, Mishael and Azarya to submit themselves to the flaming kiln, rather than flee for their lives, as the prophet had advised them? They learned it through the rule of "in-

6 שיר השירים ח, ו. 7 שיר השירים רבה שם.

271

ference from minor to major," from the frogs in the Egyptian plague. Of the frogs, who were not commanded to sanctify His Name, it is written:[8] "They will come into your house ... into your ovens and into your kneading troughs." When is the trough placed near the oven? When the oven is hot. Yet, the "frogs entered the hot, burning ovens, although they too could have fled for their lives. — We, who have been commanded to sanctify Hashem's Name, how much more so!")[9]

As soon as the three young men had left, Hashem appeared to Yechezkel and said to him, "Do you really think that I will not stand with them? Of course I will save them! For thus said Hashem Elokim:[10] For this now I will yet make Myself accessible to the House of Yisrael! But leave them now. Let them continue undeterred in their simple wholesomeness."[11]

Only to test them had Hashem acted thus, to bring out their deeper inner strength. Said Hashem, "I shall see whether Chananya, Mishael and Azarya will stand the test, as their forefather Avraham stood up for Me. And if the threesome will stand before Me (straight) as a palm tree, like the clusters of grapes deriving their growth from the vines, — the Patriarchs — I will redeem all of the House of Yisrael because of their merit."[12]

When the representatives of all the nations assembled in the Plain of Dura following the King's command, Chananya, Mishael and Azarya were among them. What did they do? They decided not to stand together in one place (like the representatives of all nations), but to scatter themselves among the vast gathering, one here and one there, so that all the people would notice and witness their doings. Then, moving around they sanctified His Holy Name, continuously proclaiming aloud, "Whether the Almighty will save us or not, to the golden statue you have erected, we shall not bow!"

Awesome and breathtaking was the spectacle of all the world's notables standing there, in the open plain, facing the gigantic statue! When they heard the blasts and sounds of music of this greatest or-

---

8 שמות ז, כח.   9 ילק"ש דניאל ג.   10 יחזקאל לו, לז.   11 ילק"ש שה"ש שם.
12 תרגום שיר השירים ז, ט.

chestra ever assembled, the representatives of all the nations instantly fell on their faces and as one, all world together prostrated themselves before the huge golden statue, — an act like never before in history. Only three among them, the selected sons of Yehuda, proudly remained standing erect, straight as a palm tree, sanctifying His Holy Name by loyally displaying utter derision and scorn for the Statue as well as for the one who had erected it.[13]

Said Hashem, "I had said I would go up the palm tree and take hold of its leaves.[14] I had envisioned that *all* of the tree, *all* of Yisrael together as one, would sanctify My Name. But I have found only this one palm twig of Chananya, Mishael and Azarya."

That same night the prophet Zecharya had a vision in which he saw a man, riding a *red* (as blood) horse, standing among the Hadasim (myrtles, signifying the righteous) in an abyss (Bavel)![15] — For at that moment Hashem wanted to turn the whole world into blood. But when He watched Chananya, Mishael and Azarya, He felt pacified.[16]

13 שם ילקוט שמעוני. • 14 שיר השירים ז, ט. • 15 זכרי׳ א, ח. 16 סנהדרין צג.

Chapter Four

MIRACLE-MEN

UPON seeing the Judean youths in their proud defiance, the Kasdim, in their zeal, rushed to the King and cried out to him: "There are men here of Yehuda whom you appointed to oversee the affairs of the province of Babylon — your gods they do not worship, and to the golden statue you set up, they did not bow.[1] They just turned all your plans to naught!"

Immediately, the enraged Nevuchadnezar summoned Chananya, Mishael and Azarya and said to them, "Are my decrees of no value that you did not bow to the Statue? Why, while still in your own land,[2] you turned already after idol-worship. Even then you used to send and buy from us nails, hair and bones of the idols[3] and now you refuse to worship my god and to prostate yourselves before my golden statue?[4] Have you been exiled here for the sole purpose of making mockery of my idols?"[5]

Mighty Men

As one, Chananya, Mishael and Azarya replied, "Indeed, we shall obey the word of the King!"[6] For the Almighty had admonished the Bnei Yisrael: "I adjure you that if a kingdom issues harsh decrees upon you, do not revolt; obey the word of the king. However, if a kingdom decrees that you disobey the Torah and its commandments, do not obey. Tell the king, 'I will obey you in all matters concerning you, but pertaining to Hashem's commandments to which He adjured us on Mount Sinai, we shall not listen to you. For decreeing to prevent us from observing the Mitzvos is intended only to make us deny the

4 דניאל ג, יד.   3 ויקרא רבה לג.   2 במדבר רבה טו.   1 דניאל ג, יב.

6 קהלת ח, ב.   5 ילק״ש דניאל ג.

274

existence of Hashem.'[7] We therefore shall obey the Word of the King of all kings, the Almighty,[8] and all that He adjured us to do." (Hence, the Sons of Yehuda now called Bavel's ruler[9] "Nevuchadnezar," not "King Nevuchadnezar," as if to say: "You are king over us in matters of taxes, tributes, excises and head taxes. But to engage us in idol worship, you are plain Nevuchadnezar, equal in rank to a dog").[10]

At once, the king issued orders to repeat[11] the giant spectacle of the previous day, in all its splendor and beauty. So that upon again hearing the sound of all the musical instruments from the world over, the three youths of Yehuda, too, would prostrate themselves before the golden Statue, like all the nations of the earth. — And this day they would be forced to bow to the king's statue, tomorrow to genuine idols.

In his rage the king furthermore shouted: "Did not Yirmiyahu warn you long ago,[12] 'Upon the nation and kingdom that will not place itself under the yoke to serve Nevuchadnezar, King of Bavel, I shall bring sword, hunger and pestilence until I have them destroyed by him?' If you fulfill the first part of the verse, fine. — If not, I will fulfill its second part: 'Until I have them destroyed.'[13] If you are ready, upon hearing the sound of the orchestra, to bow down to the Statue I made, you will be free. If not, you will at once be thrown into the flaming kiln. And where is the God who will save you from my hands?[14] Have I not burnt down His Dwelling and exiled His People? In His own House He was not able to stand up against me — in mine He will?"[15]

With unmatched courage (sanctifying Hashem's Name in the very palace of the King) Chananya, Mishael and Azarya stood up to the King and replied: "Indeed. But there is our God whom we serve. He has the power to save us from the flaming kiln, as well as from your hands,[16] just as He saved our forefather Avraham from the flaming kiln of Nimrod. However, Avraham was righteous and worthy of having miracles done for him, but we are sinners. Still, regardless whether

7 תנחומא נח י. 8 ויקרא רבה פרשה לג. 9 דניאל פרק ג, פסוק טז.

10 במדבר רבה, ויקרא רבה שם. 11 רש"י דניאל ג, כו. 12 ירמי' כז, ח.

13 ויקרא רבה לג. 14 דניאל ג. 15 תנחומא ס' צו ב. 16 דניאל שם.

He saves us or not, let it be known that your idols we will not worship and to your golden statue we will not bow!" [17]

"I Am a Wall"

Nevuchadnezar was so enraged that his face became disfigured. He shouted orders to immediately rekindle the fire in the kiln and to increase its heat sevenfold.[18] Said Nevuchadnezar, "These are powerful men, they dare to speak to me with defiance." And he commanded his strongest soldiers to seize and chain the three youths, to have them thrown into the flaming kiln.[19]

At this historic moment Hashem was hoping and waiting for the youths of Yehuda. Why, of all the human beings He had created, none but these had remained thoroughly faithful, and they were few in number and weak? Indeed, like "that little sister of ours" of Shir HaShirim. "What shall we do with our little sister on the day when she is spoken for" [20] — on the day when nations pass cruel edicts against her? Said Hashem: "If Chananya, Mishael and Azarya will make their deeds stand up, enduring like a wall, I shall save them, and build from them the world. But if their deeds will be transient only, like a door revolving on its hinges, I will only adorn them with a cedar plaque, and their glory will be only temporary."

At that fateful hour the Jews in Bavel were found to be loyal before Hashem,[21] as the three young men declared before Him: "I am a wall — we are setting up Mitzvos and good deeds like a wall! 'And my breasts are like towers' — we are ready to raise in Your world clusters of righteous people like us. For they will learn from us and from our deeds, until the end of all generations." [22]

Said Hashem, "Today I shall be praised through them before all the nations of the earth! Today I shall bring back their dead to life. Today I shall take revenge and punish their enemies! I am the Lord — the Judge, to mete out punishment. I am the Trustworthy to reward the loyal." [23]

---

17 שה"ש רבה שם.   18 דניאל יג, יט—כ.   19 רש"י שם.   20 שיר השירים ח, ח.
21 שמות רבה טו, טז.   22 שה"ש רבה ח.   23 ילק"ש אחרי, סימן תקצא.

That night was the Eve of Yom Kippur [24] which was also the Eve of Shabbos. And while the king's servants rekindled the fire, Chananya, Mishael and Azarya found themselves omens, verses, which they recited throughout the night.[25] "Not for our sake, Hashem, not for our sake!" intoned Chananyah.[26] Said Mishael, "To Your Name bring glory!" [27] And Azarya concluded, "For the sake of Your kindliness and truthfulness." [28] And together, they chanted: "Why should the gentiles say: 'Where is their God?' " [29]

In the Flaming Kiln

Having recited the verses repeatedly throughout the whole night, they embraced them as good omens. Ready to descend into the kiln, they put their trust in Hashem's Name and on the Almighty.[30] Immediately with day-break, the king's strong-bodied soldiers grabbed the youths and bound them tightly. "God is with me, I am not afraid," Chananya cried out. "Do not fear, you, My Servant Yaakov," Mishael continued. And Azarya concluded, "Hear oh Yisrael, Hashem our Lord, Hashem is one!" [31]

The three young men further came wrapped and dressed in their beautiful festive garments, as usual,[32] so that even now they would not appear bewildered or scared.[33] They wished only to shame their enemies who, seeing them, would say: "Look at the Sons of Yehuda. They dress up in their best garments as if it were their wedding day, when they march out to fulfill the will of their Creator, letting themselves be burnt in the flaming kiln."

In their zeal and haste to carry out the king's command,[34] the soldiers failed to be careful about themselves. And when they threw Chananya, Mishael and Azarya into the flames, they themselves were consumed by the intense heat which surrounded the flaming kiln.[35]

24 שה"ש רבה ז, יד.   25 שמות רבה ט.   26 תהלים קטו, א.   27 שם.
28 תהלים שם.   29 שם פסוק ב ופסחים קיח.   30 מדרש תהלים לא, א.
31 זוהר ס' אחרי.   32 דניאל שם.   33 רש"י סנהדרין צג: 34 שה"ש רבה ז, יד.
35 דניאל שם.

As soon as Chananya, Mishael and Azarya fell into the flaming kiln (actually it was as if they willingly threw themselves into it),[36] Hashem commanded the Angel Gavriel to go down and save them.[37] He heated up the outside of the kiln and cooled its inside, making for them a miracle within a miracle.[38] To them the fire now became but a guiding star, a clear bright light that does not consume at all.[39]

An Awesome Sight

When Nevuchadnezar saw the Angel Gavriel, all his limbs began shaking. He shouted, "Why, this is the same angel whom I saw in the battle of Sancheriv! He then looked like a small conduit of fire, yet he consumed the whole army of Ashur." [40]

The King stood trembling. Bewildered and wondering he exclaimed before his advisors, "Did we not throw three men into the fire, and they were tied up in ropes?" — "True," they replied. "So it was."

"Lo, I see four men walking in the fire, and they are free from their bonds," [41] the king exclaimed. "And the shape of the fourth is like the angel of God, just like the one I saw long ago."

All the while, the angel Gavriel was walking behind the three, like a disciple following his master [42] (as the righteous are even greater than the angels). For these were truly miracle-men.[43] The ropes in which they had been bound were burnt, but they themselves were strolling unscarred in the midst of the flames. — And Hashem was waiting for them to come out of the fire.[44]

Immediately, Nevuchadnezar approached the opening of the fiery kiln and shouted: "Shadrach, Meishach and Aved N'go, servants of the Supreme God, you may now come and step out! [45] He has freed you already, and He made miracles for you."

"Indeed, we would not leave without the king's permission," they replied, so that no one would say, 'They escaped from the kiln.' "Furthermore, we do obey the king's command." [46] — And out of respect

---

36 דניאל ג, כז וילקוט שמעוני שם.   37 שמות רבה יח.   38 שוחר טוב קיז, ג.
39 שה"ש רבה זו, יג.   40 ילק"ש דניאל ג.   41 דניאל ג, כה.   42 ילקוט שם.
43 זכרי' ג, ח.   44 ב"ר פח, ז.   45 דניאל ג, כו.   46 קהלת ח, ב.

for the Kingdom, they said,[47] "At the king's command we were thrown in, and at the king's command we shall come out." [48] And when the king called upon them, the three came out of the kiln.

"Praise Hashem, all nations!" [49] intoned Chananya. "Laud Him, all the peoples!" [50] joined him Mishael. Concluded Azarya, "For His kindliness was overpowering us." [51] And Gavriel added after them:[52] "Hashem's truth endures forever, Halleluyah." [53]

At once, all the notables of the nations, the satraps, the prefects, the governors and royal advisors gathered around and gazed at the three men who were untouched by the fire; whose hair was not even singed; whose beautiful garments were not charred, and who did not even smell of smoke and fire.[54]

Miracles Upon Miracles

Six miracles occurred that very day.[55] The kiln which was dug deep in the ground floated upwards to ground level, so that the three Judeans could emerge easily; the kiln cracked and part of its walls collapsed, so that the onlookers could see what was happening within; the extreme heat caused the lime in the kiln to melt and flow afar, consuming the soldiers who had thrown the three men into the fire; the golden statue turned over and fell down on its face; four nations were burned (i.e. their kings and men who helped throw the threesome into the kiln). (Hence at the gathering before the golden Statue [56] seven nations were mentioned, later only three [57]); and the prophet Yechezkel revived the dead in the Plain of Dura.

Our Sages tell us:[58] at the very moment when Nevuchadnezar threw Chananya, Mishael and Azarya into the flaming kiln, Hashem said to Yechezkel, "Go, resurrect the dead in the Plain of Dura." As soon as he revived them, some bones emerged and slapped Nevuchadnezar's face.

47 מכילתא דר' ישמעאל, סדר בא, פרשה יג.   48 תנחומא נח.   49 תהלים קיז, א.
50 תהלים שם.   51 שם פסוק ב.   52 שם.   53 פסחים קיח.
54 דניאל שם.   55 סנהדרין צב, ורש"י שם.   56 דניאל ג, ג.   57 שם ג, כז.
58 סנהדרין צב:

279

"What are these?" Nevuchadnezar wondered. He was told: "The friend of these three is now reviving the dead in the Plain of Dura."

Indeed, all these miracles took place in the merit of the three young men who were still from that early "Exile of the Youngsters." For even during Bnei Yisrael's sojourn in the land of their enemies, "I have not detested or rejected them, to exterminate them." [59] I did not detest them in the days of the Kasdim, as I gave them Chananya, Mishael and Azarya.[60] And because of *their* sake those miracles came to happen.

For these "Anshei Moffes" were indeed exemplary, as well as miracle men.[61] They went into the flaming kiln to set an example ("Moffes"), so that a miracle ("Moffes") may be performed with them.[62] Thus either way Hashem's Name would have been sanctified through them; whether Hashem would bring about a miracle to save them in front of all the world or have them burned for the Holiness of His Name — either way His Name would be sanctified throughout the world! [63] Hence, in the very beginning, they did not heed Yechezkel's words when he told them in Hashem's name that He would not save them, wishing to sanctify His Name through their death.

The Withered Bones

How did Yechezkel revive the dead in the Plain of Dura? — On the day that Nevuchadnezar the wicked assembled all the nations before the Statue to incite them to revolt against Hashem, "Hashem's Hand was upon me, and His Spirit carried me out and He placed me in the midst of the Plain, which was full of bones." [64]

The Spirit of Hashem carried Yechezkel out, and forced him to go unwillingly (as if he were in a trance) to the plain where that very day, all the delegates of all who dwell on earth had gathered, to pay homage to the Statue. Yechezkel however was at the other end of the long plain, which extended from the river of Aishel until Rabbassi.[65]

59 ויקרא כד, מד.   60 מגילה דף יא.   61 זכרי' ג, ח.   62 ב"ר נו.

63 נמוקי יוסף לסנהדרין פרק בן סורר ומורה.   64 יחזקאל פרק לז, פסוק א.

65 ילק"ש יחזקאל לז, שעו.

The plain was full of the bones of the Bnei Ephraim who had mis-calculated the date for the promised Exodus from Egypt. They had left Mitzrayim prematurely (in the year 2418), and on their way to the land of Kenaan they were slain by the people of Gaza.[66]*

Resurrection

To encourage both Yechezkel and the Bnei Yehuda, the Spirit (of prophecy) brought the prophet down to this distant place, to show that the withered exiles, too, would yet return to life and arise, together with the dead of long ago, to make their exit on the Day of Redemption. — — Indeed, they merited all this because of the deeds of the three miracle-men, who at this very moment sanctified Hashem's Name at the other end of this vast plain before the whole world's communi-ty.[67] And it happened through the prophet, Yechezkel, son of Buzi. "And the Spirit led me all around the bones [68] (since Yechezkel was a Kohen, forbidden to defile himself with the impurity of the dead) and behold, they were very, very many on the surface of the plain, and they were completely dried out.

"Then Hashem said to me, 'Son of man, can these bones come to life?' I replied, 'Hashem Elokim, only You know!' " [69] (Thus implying that he did not believe and had doubts whether the withered bones of Yisrael were worthy of being resurrected.[70] Yechezkel therefore was later on punished. His bones were not buried in the purity of the soil of Yisrael.[71]).

"Hashem said to me, 'Prophesy over these bones and say to them: O dry bones, hear the Word of Hashem!' " — for everything depends on your listening and trusting His Words.[72]* "So I prophesied as I had been commanded. And... there was a noise, and behold, a rattling." It was the noise of the bones which started moving. For indeed, the withered dry bones did hearken to the Word of Hashem. They drew

66 יחזקאל פרק לז, ב.   * תוספת דבר.   67 ילק"ש פר' אחרי סימן תקצא.

68 יחזקאל לז, ב.   69 שם.   70 קהלת רבה ד, ג.   71 ילק"ש יחזקאל לז.

72 שם מפרשים.   * תוספת דבר.

together from the places where they had been scattered, each bone with its matching bone, at the place where they had been joined in life.[73]

"And as I looked, behold, sinews were upon them, and flesh had come up, and then skin was drawn over them. But there was no breath in them. Then Hashem said to me, 'Prophesy to the Spirit, prophesy, Son of Man! Say to the Spirit: Thus says Hashem Elokim: Come, oh, Spirit, from the four sides of the world where the souls (of these bodies) have been wandering. Blow breath, Oh, Spirit, into these slain, that they may live.' — And as I prophesied as He had commanded me, the Spirit entered into them. They came to life and rose up to their feet, an exceedingly large army." [74]

As soon as they stood up, they said Shirah. What was their Shirah? "Hashem brings death, and He gives life!" [75] — He brings death with righteousness, and He revives with mercy.[76*] — And the resurrected took wives, and fathered sons and daughters.[77]

"Then Hashem said to me, 'Son of Man, these bones are the whole House of Yisrael. They say: 'Our bones are dried out (since the sap of Mitzvos has gone out of them [78]); our hope is lost, we have been cut off and shall not live to see the Day of Consolation!' Therefore prophesy, and say to them: Thus says Hashem Elokim: Behold, I will open your graves and raise you from your graves, O, My People; and I will bring you to the soil of Yisrael. And I will put My Spirit into you, and you will live; I will settle you on your own soil, and you will know that I, Hashem, have spoken and performed' " [79] this sign before your eyes on that Yom Kippur of the three miracle-men in the Plain of Dura.

While Daniel Left

Where was Daniel when his companions were being thrown into the flaming kiln? Why was he not cast in together with them? —

73 יחזקאל שם.   74 שם.   75 סנהדרין דף צב: 76 סנהדרין צב:
* תוספת דבר.   77 שם.   78 שם.   79 יחזקאל לז.

He had gone away.[80]

And three concurred in this decision: Hashem, Daniel, and Nevuchadnezar. Hashem had said: "Let Daniel go away from here so that people shall not say: 'In his merit the three were saved'" (And they will fail to realize that the three are also miracle-men).

Daniel had said, "Let me go away from here, so that I shall not be subjected to the verse:[81] 'The images of their idols you shall burn in fire' if Nevuchadnezar in his wrath decides to have me (whom he worships as a deity), perish in fire." And Nevuchadnezar had said, "Let Daniel go away from here, so that people should not say of me, 'Look, he burned his own god in that fire.'"

Unwanted Praise

Seeing that Chananya, Mishael and Azarya had not been burnt nor even absorbed the smell of fire,[82] Nevuchadnezar at once rose to his feet to acknowledge Hashem in the presence of all the nations. "Blessed is the God of Shadrach, Meishach and Aved N'go," he exclaimed. "He sent His angel to save His servants who relied on Him and disobeyed the king's order and offered their lives, in order not to bow to none but their own God.[83] Therefore it is decided by royal decree that any nation, tribe or tongue who speaks anything amiss against the God of Shadrach, Meishach and Aved N'go would be cut to pieces, and his house would become fully disowned and be turned into a dunghill. Because there is no other God who could save through such a rescue." [84]

Thereupon Nevuchadnezar appointed the three great men as governors of the province of Babylon. And He sent out letters to all the lands, extolling the Name of the fearful and awesome God, saying:[85] "From Nevuchadnezar the King, to all the nations, peoples and tongues, who dwell on earth; may your peace be ever greater. — It behooves me to relate the wonders and miracles that the Supreme God performed with me. How great are His wonders, how mighty His miracles. His King-

80 ילק"ש דניאל ג.   81 דברים ז, כה.   82 שה"ש רבה ז, יד.   83 דניאל ג, כח.
84 שם.   85 שם.

dom is an everlasting Kingdom, and His reign is for all generations." [86]

Nevuchadnezar went on to laud and praise the King of the Heavens.[87] All the praise that King David had spelled out in his Tehillim, the wicked king now summarized in one single verse.[88] Had not an angel appeared and slapped his mouth to stop him from pouring out more praise, this evildoer (who had destroyed the Beis HaMikdash) might have disgraced all the hymns and songs of praise of the Sefer of Tehillim [89] of King David (who had laid the foundation for the erection of this very Mikdash.)

For all his praises were not welcome. Said Hashem, "Yesterday you exclaimed, 'Who is the God that will save you from my hands,' [90] and now you sing tribute and praises? I have no desire for either you or your praises!" [91]

Spittle of Disgust

The delegates of all the nations who had remained duefully assembled after having festively gathered, first to pay homage to Nevuchadnezar's Statue, and again the next day in their futile attempt to induce also the Judeans to bow down to the Statue; having returned (the following day) and witnessed Chananya, Mishael and Azarya walking unharmed out of the flaming kiln, they were thoroughly shaken. The whole concept of idol worship suddenly disintegrated before their eyes,[92] and all the world now saw how futile and empty it all was.[93] — They all then rushed over to the three Judeans, slapped their faces and taunted them: "Why, having such a great God, yet you bow down to statues?" [94]

At once the Bnei Yisrael called out and proclaimed: "Yours, Hashem, is the righteousness, and ours is the shamefacedness as of this day." [95] Whereupon the three miracle-men walked away. And from the time Chananya, Mishael and Azarya emerged from the flaming kiln, their names were never again mentioned in the Scriptures.[96] Where did they go? — Some say that once their task was accomplished,[97] there was no

86 שם. 87 דניאל ד, לד. 88 ויק"ר סוף יג, ה. 89 סנהדרין צב:

90 דניאל ג, טו. 91 מדרש שוחר טוב ח, י. 92 סנהדרין צג: 93 רש"י שם.

94 ילק"ש דניאל ג. 95 דניאל ט, ז. 96 בראשית רבה נב. 97 ילק"ש זכרי' ג.

longer any need to mention them. Another opinion is that after meriting all these miracles, they left their place and went to Yehoshua ben Tzaddok, the Kohen Gadol, to study Torah,[98] and had nothing further to do with the affairs of the exiles. Others say that they died through the evil eye that the people cast upon them because they had merited such great miracles. Rabbi Elazar Hakohen says: They drowned in the spittle [99] of the assembled nations who spat at them and said, "Why, you have such a great God, yet you worshiped idols in your homeland?" Until Chananya, Mishael and Azarya were drowned in the mass of the despising spittle. — And again the Bnei Yisrael proclaimed and said, "Yours, Hashem, is the righteousness, and ours is the shame-facedness, as of this day." [1]

Like the Patriarchs

Even though the three of them did not father any children,[2] Hashem had long before alluded to them when he testified, saying:[3] "I shall give them in My house and within My walls, a monument and a name, better than sons and daughters ... An everlasting name that will never be cut off." — And from them, all the House of Yisrael will learn how to sanctify Hashem's Name.

"Descent leads to rise." Because they themselves descended into the flaming kiln they arose, and the existence of the whole world was ensured because of them.[4] Hence, the act of these three miracle men was like the deeds of the three Patriarchs who illuminated the whole world like the rising sun.[5] For, in the dark abyss of Babylon, these three too, crowned Hashem and sanctified His Name. Hence the whole world was reset and rebuilt upon them.[6]

The Statue Falls

Nevuchadnezar also tried to entice Daniel. Said the King, "How come you don't bow to the Statue which possesses power and is the ruler of

98 סנהדרין צג. 99 שם וילק"ש זכרי' ג, ז. 1 דניאל ט. 2 סנהדרין צג:
3 ישעי' נו, ה. 4 שוחר טוב. 5 שמות רבה טו, ו. 6 שה"ש רבה ח, י.

all? If you would only come to observe its actions (the statue actually spoke, as Nevuchadnezar had placed in its mouth the Tzitz of the Kohen Gadol), you would surely wish to prostrate yourself before it!" [7]

Said Daniel, "Would you permit me to ascend and kiss the Statue's mouth through which it so wondrously speaks?" Thereupon Daniel raised himself to the face of the Statue and adjured the Tzitz, "I am a human being, a messenger of Hashem; see to it that no desecration of Hashem's Name comes through you. I decree that you follow me!" And as he pressed closer to kiss it, he sucked the Tzitz out of the Statue's mouth. [8]

When Daniel descended, all the musical instruments were still gathered, the orchestras played as before, but now the Statue was doing nothing; it was unable to show its power. Then, in the darkness of the night, [9] a wind came and threw the Statue down. The same wind resurrected the dead in the Plain of Dura. [10]

The heathen nations, having witnessed the wonders done by Hashem to Chananya, Mishael and Azarya, seized the Statue (the misleading object of their worship) and smashed it to pieces. These they shaped into bells and rattles, which they hung around the necks of their dogs and donkeys. Upon hearing the sounds of their rattling, they would say, "Look what we were bowing to!" — Thus was fulfilled the verse, [11] "Beil bows down, Nevo stoops, their idols are upon the beasts and upon the cattle!" [12]

Because Hashem brought light into the world through the miracles of Chananya, Mishael and Azarya, His Name became great in the world. [13] The erring Kasdim reached understanding, [14] and many of them converted to Judaism. [15]

---

7 שה"ש רבה ז, יד.   8 שם.   9 הגדה של פסח.   10 שה"ש רבה ז, ח.

11 ישעי' מו, א.   12 שה"ש רבה שם.   13 שם א, ג יג.   14 ישעי' כט, כד.

15 שה"ש רבה שם.

Chapter Five

THE LOWEST OF MAN

Chapter Six

A NEW SPIRIT

Chapter Five

THE LOWEST OF MAN

AFTER the universal revolt of the heathens ended in failure and Hashem's manifestations of miracles ceased, the haughty Nevuchadnezar at once returned to his former self (like a dog returning to his vomit). What is more, since he had been privileged to witness Hashem's wonders, he now proceeded in his wrongdoing with more zeal than before. The older he grew, the more demented he became. "Tifsar" (Tipesh-sar),[1] they called him now; great in years,[2] yet stupid. Finally, out of his power, success, and immense wealth he came to proclaim himself a deity.[3] Reasoned the wicked man, "All of mighty Babylon is not worthy of me; the whole earth is not worthy of me! I shall ascend into Heaven, above God's stars will I raise my throne.[4] I shall set myself apart from all human beings, as none is worthy of me.[5] I will ascend above the heights of a cloud." "I will make myself a small cloud to dwell on," and "I will be like the Most High." [6]

A Heavenly voice rang out: "Wicked son of the wicked, grandson of the wicked Nimrod who incited the whole world to revolt against Hashem. What is a man's lifespan? Seventy years. — Behold, from the earth to the first Rakiya (heaven) is a five hundred year walk. The breadth of each heaven is a five hundred year walk, and so is the distance between one heaven and the next. Since there are seven heavens, that makes fourteen times five hundred years. Above these are the Heavenly Chayos (special angels). The feet of the Chayos are equal to all that, and the ankles of the Chayos are again equal to all that. Above all that, comes the Kisai HaKavod (Throne of Glory). The feet of the Throne is equal to the sum of all that preceded it, and the Kisei HaKavod itself equals everything together. — The King, Mighty

---

1 ירמי' נא, כז.   2 בראשית רבה צ, ג.   3 ילק"ש ירמי' מד.   4 ישעי' יד, יג.

5 ילק"ש שם.   6 ישעי' וילק"ש שם.

and Eternal, High and Supreme, dwells above them all, — and you have said, 'I will ascend above the heights of the cloud, I will be like the Most High?' [7] Indeed, you shall be brought down to She'ol, into the depths of the pit." [8]

"Moreover, you wish to set yourself apart from all people — therefore the people will separate themselves from you!" [9]

The Tree Felled

That year Nevuchadnezzar dreamt a second time. He had been peacefully at rest in his palace. Suddenly he had a dream that troubled him and filled him with fear. As with his first dream, he decreed throughout his dominions [10] that all the wise men of Babylon be gathered, but no one was able to interpret the dream for him. Finally, Daniel was summoned.

"Beiltshazar, head of the sorcerers," the King said to Daniel,[11] "I know that the Spirit of the Holy God rests with you, and no secret is hidden from you. I will tell you my dream, so that you might interpret it.

"As I was lying in my bed, I saw a tree standing in the center of the earth.[12] Its height was great, yet it kept growing and getting stronger. It reached the sky, and it was visible to the ends of the earth. Its branches were beautiful, its fruit abundant, enought to feed all the people. In its shade wild beasts found shelter, and on its branches dwelt the birds of the sky. And all flesh was fed from it.[13]

"Still lying on my bed I then saw an angel, who is forever awake and holy, descend from the heavens and shout in a strong voice, 'Chop down the tree, cut off its branches, shake off its leaves and scatter its fruit. Let the beasts flee from its shade and the birds move away from its branches. However, leave the stump of its roots in the ground, (to be anchored down with chains of iron and copper amid the grass of the field) so that it does not move from its place. By the dew of heaven will he be washed, and with the beast alike will be his portion of the

---

7 חגיגה יג.   8 שם.   9 ילק"ש ישעי' י.   10 דניאל ד.   11 שם.

12 ר' סעדי' גאון שם.   13 דניאל שם.

greens of the field. Let his heart be changed from a man's, and let a beast's heart be given to him. Seven years shall this decree pass over him, mandated by the Angels of Wrath and Anger, with the approval of the Superior Angels. So that all the living may know that the Supreme One rules the Kingdom of Man and gives it to whomever He wishes. He even sets up over it the basest of men.'

"This is the dream that I saw, and all the wise men of my empire have not been able to interpret it. But you are able to, because the spirit of the Holy God rests with you." [14]

For a while Daniel stood appalled and silent, his thoughts bewildering him. He pretended to tremble in fear of having to make known the interpretation.[15] Said the king, "Let not the dream and its interpretation bewilder you."

"My Lord," said Daniel. "Let this dream come true on those who hate you, and its interpretation on your enemy."[16] (Sounding as if indeed he meant Nevuchadnezar to be freed from it). Actually, "My Lord," was addressed to Hashem, as Daniel lifted his eyes to Heaven and prayed, "My Lord, let this dream and its interpretation come true on Nevuchadnezar, Your enemy."[17]

Then he began the interpretation: "The huge and growing tree which you saw, — is you, O King, who have become so great and powerful. Your greatness has been constantly augmented until it reaches to heaven, and your dominion to the four ends of the earth. You then saw the Angel of Destruction descend from heaven and shout: 'Chop down the tree; destroy it!' — He meant you."[18]

"The edict of the Supreme One has been issued against you, O King. You will be driven from mankind, and your dwelling shall be with the beasts of the field. You shall be made to eat grass like oxen and be washed by the dew of heaven. Seven years will pass over you thus (because you destroyed His Sanctuary which took seven years to build [19]). In that interval you will come to understand and acknowledge that the Supreme One rules the Kingdom of Man and gives

---

14 שם.   15 שמות רבה ל, כד.   16 שם.   17 שם.   18 דניאל ד.
19 רש"י שם.

power to whomever He wishes. However, the stump of the trunk and the roots of the tree will remain in place, meaning, that your kingdom is to endure and will be returned to you in due time, after you understand and realize that *He*, the One in Heaven, rules the earth." [20]

Nevuchadnezar's Charity

As Daniel interpreted, so it was to happen.[21] At this moment however, Daniel's advice stood the king by. Said Daniel, "O King, let my counsel be acceptable to you. Absolve your sins through charity, and your iniquities by compassion for the poor, so that your peacefulness may be extended." [22]

Daniel acted with the best of intentions. Having watched the poverty-stricken lowest of the exiles reduced to begging, in utter hunger, he tried to find them some relief. He therefore advised the king, "These poor men whom you have exiled are hungry and thirsty; feed them!"

Nevuchadnezar took Daniel's advice. He opened up his treasuries, and for twelve months he was preoccupied with dispensing Tzedaka.[23] All those months he daily gathered the poor of Yisrael and fed them from his treasury.[24] As long as he provided for them, he merited that his kingship be safeguarded for him.

Daniel, though meaning well, was nevertheless punished for having given this advice. He should have prayed instead that Hashem provide for the poor, so that the Bnei Yisrael would not have to depend on Nevuchadnezar their enemy.[25] Furthermore, he should not have offered to the wicked the Mitzva of Tzedaka (the domain of Avraham Avinu) by saying: "Absolve your sins by charity." [26] Moreover, Daniel had effectively counseled his enemy how to undo the decree of the Supreme One, thus disarming the Measure of Justice. — Hence it was decreed upon Daniel to be thrown into the lions' den.[27]

---

20 דניאל שם.   21 שם פסוק כד.   22 שם.   23 ירושלמי סוטה ג, ד.

24 סוטה כא.   25 שמ"ר ל, כד; "עץ יוסף" שם.   26 שם.   27 ב"ב ד.

Among the Beasts

All of Nevuchadnezar's seeming benevolence, however, was not for the sake of kindliness, but only to perpetuate his rule.[28] With the close of the twelve months, as he was strolling the grounds of his palace (his dream long forgotten [29]), he heard the tumult and the pounding of the poor at the gate. "What is all the noise of this crowd in my ears?" he asked. His servants replied, "It is the poor to whom you allotted daily provisions."

In a loud voice, the king haughtily retorted, "Is this not the great Babylon which I have built up to be my royal house? With my great strength I built it, for the glorification of my splendor. Had I wasted my treasures to provide for these poor, how would I have built all these palaces? And from where would all my glory have come? — Henceforth I shall not provide for them." [30]

He had not yet finished uttering the words from his mouth when, behold! a Voice descended from Heaven: This is meant for *you*, King Nevuchadnezar! — your kingship has departed from you.[31]

Instantly the Heavenly decree was imposed upon Nevuchadnezar, the haughty dwarf. Madness seized him,[32] and he was driven away from all men. He ate grass as cattle, and his naked body was wet with the dew of the heaven. His hair grew long like eagles' feathers, and his nails resembled those of wild birds.[33] Animals and beasts saw their likeness in him, and chased after him.[34]

Seven full years passed since Nevuchadnezar had disappeared, during which time no one knew where he had wandered away, — while his son occupied his throne.[35] — When the term of the decree had reached its end, he regained his human mind.[36] Then he realized and understood.

Raising his eyes toward heaven, Nevuchadnezar blessed the Supreme One. He praised and exalted Him "Who lives forever; Whose rule is eternal, and Whose Kingdom stands in all generations. It is *He* Who

28 שם: 29 תנחומא פרשת משפטים ד.   30 דניאל שם ושמ"ר פר' כד.

31 דניאל פרק ד, כח.   32 ר' סעדי' גאון דניאל ד, ל.   33 דניאל שם.

34 ילק"ש ירמי' מד.   35 ילק"ש חבקוק א.   36 דניאל ד.

exercises His Will at once among the hosts of Heavens and the in-habitants of the earth — and there is none who can stay His Hand or say to Him, "What doest Thou?" [37] Because all the inhabitants of the earth together are totally insignificant, nonentities."

Only for a global ruler like Nevuchadnezar was it befitting to express such praises. Had another man expressed them, one could say, "In all his life he has not ruled even over two flies, who is he to say: [38] 'All the earth's inhabitants are like nothing?' " But for Nevuchadnezar, who ruled the whole world, [39] it was befitting to say it. [40]

As soon as Nevuchadnezar praised Hashem, his human mind was fully restored, and he returned to the glory of his throne. He was even granted additional power in the wake of his further praises of the King of Heaven, "all of Whose works are truth, Whose path is justice, and Who humbles those who walk proudly." [41] He would ride a male lion with a snake tied to its head, thus fulfilling the verse: [42] "Even the beasts of the field have I given (Nevuchadnezar) to serve him." [43]

Terror of the Earth

Soon after, Nevuchadnezar returned to his former strength and haughti-ness, in the usual manner of the wicked. While they are in distress, they humble themselves; as soon as the affliction passes, they immediately return to their corruption. [44]

And so this tiny dwarf (even among dwarfs he was considered short) tyrannized and oppressed all nations, forever demanding and collecting more and more money. He oppressed the people, causing them grief and distress, while burdening them with his yoke. He robbed people's possessions, to build and beautify his own palace. He destroyed con-quered cities and carried off the timber and stones to mighty Bavel, to build his city and his palace. In the center of his palace he erected a huge massive tower in which to take refuge, should the enslaved nations revolt and rise up to kill him. [45] He mocked their kings, cap-

37 שם. 38 דניאל שם. 39 ירמי' כח, דניאל ב. 40 קה"ר ג, יא.
41 דניאל שם. 42 ירמי' כז, ו. 43 שבת קנ. 44 שמות רבה יב, ז.
45 חבקוק ב, ט ורד"ק שם.

riciously casting lots to determine each one's turn to serve his abominations and bodily perversions.[46] For to defile himself was his lust, to plunder and gather captives like sand.[47] And all the world did not find rest or repose.

Till joy disappeared from people's lives. And throughout this wicked man's reign one could not hear spontaneous laughter issuing from the mouth of the people.[48]

46 ישעי׳ יד, יב.   47 חבקוק א, ט.   48 ילק״ש שמעוני ישעי׳ יד.

Chapter Six

A NEW SPIRIT

HOW did the strayed sons of Yehuda fare in the darkness of Bavel? —
Indeed, Hashem did not remove His Mercy from them. He even admonished Bavel: "Stop issuing evil decrees against My Children. Stop
burdening them! How else can Yaakov measure up when he is small [1]
and has no strength to stand?"

Eyes of the Congregation

Furthermore, from among their own brethren Hashem sent the Bnei
Yisrael prophets to become "the eyes of the congregation," to guide
them in all their needs and problems. For the Bnei Yisrael were not
like other nations who worshipped stars and the constellations, and
made their oars [2] (their leaders) of the oaks of faraway Bashan. Like
a boat whose mast comes from one place and its anchor from another,
these nations were ruled by kings and officers who came from different
lands. (Samla of Masreika ruled in Edom,[3] and Shaul of Rechovot
Hanahar after him,[4][5]).

Not so the Children of Yisrael. From their own midst sprang their
Kohanim and Leviim, their kings and prophets, their teachers and
rebukers. Their own spiritual leaders have always shown them the way.
just as the eye guides all the limbs of the body.[6] And there were many
prophets among them: Yechezkel, as well as the aged Yirmiyahu and
his disciple Baruch ben Neriya. They were there to encourage and
teach the exiles, and prevent them from stumbling and wrongdoing.

As the days of their sojourn in Bavel extended, the Bnei Yehuda
became increasingly disgusted with the land's idolatry and abominations. The seventy years between the first and second Beis HaMikdash
were to them like one long night. And in their distress they beseeched

1 עמוס ז, ב.   2 יחזקאל כז, ו.   3 בראשית רבה פג.   4 בראשית לו, לו.
5 שם לו, לו.   6 שה"ש רבה ז, ט.

Hashem, and begged: "Guardian of Yisrael, what will become of the night? [7] Guardian, what of this night?" [8]

Ever since the days of Yechonya's Exile there were those among them in whose hearts burned a passion, strong as death itself. They were gripped by a yearning and hope. "Let us be strong and go up," they said. "Let us return to the land of our fathers!" [9] But it was the fatherly Yirmiyahu whose words shielded them, like a wall of copper.[10] For he conveyed Hashem's words to His Children, that it had been decreed that our Land should lie waste and our cities remain destroyed, that they must serve the king of Bavel for seventy years.[11] But "by placing their neck under the yoke of Bavel's king and serving him and his people, they would live!" [12] For not for naught had they been exiled, and not in vain would they be redeemed. Indeed, "there is hope for your future, and there will be a reward for your deeds" and your exile. Upon the completion of the seventy years of Bavel the Sons would return to their borders.[13]

The Future Mikdash

At that time Yechezkel ben Buzi helped his brethren even more than the other prophets. Hashem sent through him His many prophecies, to admonish them for their sins and to rebuke their leaders as well for failing to keep watch over their flock. (Thereby causing the flock to lead their shepherd).[14]

Yechezkel also brought them words of comfort and tidings of the Day of Hashem's Revenge over the heathen nations who had taken possession of His land.[15] "For only like a woman's days of impurity were Yehuda's ways [16] before Me," said Hashem. They were like the unclean woman who eventually attains purity, and whose husband looks forward to the day of her purification, yearning to return to her.[17]

However, too pained were the exiled Sons of Yehuda who had been

7 ישעי' כא, יא.   8 תנא דבי אליהו סוף פרק ל.   9 הקדמת הרמב"ם לפירוש המשניות.
10 ירמי' כט.   11 שם כה, יא.   12 שם כז יב.   13 שם לא, טו—טז.
14 יחזקאל לד.   15 שם לו.   16 שם פסוק יז.   17 רש"י וילקוט שמעוני שם.

banished from their comfort and splendour, to feel consoled now even by the prophet's assurances that the Shechina was still with them even in Bavel.[18] Therefore, Hashem sought to console them by showing Yechezkel, in the midst of Bavel's darkness, a vision of the final, ever-lasting Beis Ha-Mikdash.

In the fourteenth year after the destruction of the city (3352), on Yom Kippur, the day of the very beginning of that Yovel year,[19] when slaves go out from bondage to freedom,[20] Hashem's Hand was upon Yechezkel. In the Godly vision he was brought into Eretz Yisrael and placed on a very high mountain on whose southern side stood something like the structure of a city.[21] And behold, there was a man whose appearance was like the appearance of copper, and a thread of flax in his hand, carrying a measuring rod. And the man said to Yechezkel, "Son of Man, behold with your eyes and hear with your ears, and put your heart to all that I will show you. For in order to be shown, you were brought down here! And relate all that you see to the House of Yisrael." [22]

Then the angel showed him the structure of the Mikdash of the Future, its walls and chambers, halls, gates and entrances, and he measured their length and width in cubits. He was also shown the courtyards and their offices, and the fences and pathways running through them. Then, suddenly, behold, the Glory of the God of Yisrael came from the East with a sound like the rushing of great waters, and the earth lit up with His Glory.[23] A spirit lifted up Yechezkel and brought him into the inner court, and behold, the Glory of Hashem filled the house! Then he heard One speaking out of the house: "Son of Man, this is the site of My Throne and the place of My foot-stool, where I will dwell in the midst of the Children of Yisrael, forever."

"Tell the House of Yisrael of this Mikdash, and let them be ashamed of their sins which caused the first Beis HaMikdash to be destroyed. Perhaps they will take heed to return to Hashem. And as they become ashamed of all they have done, make known to them the shape of the

---

18 זוהר תחילת שמות.   19 ויקרא כה, ט ו־י.   20 רד״ק יחזקאל א, א.

21 יחזקאל מ, א—ב.   22 שם פסוקים ג—ד.   23 שם פרק מג.

House and its structure, its exits and entrances, all its forms, its ordinances and its whole design. Make known to them all its laws, drawings and teachings, and write it down before the eyes of the people, that they may preserve its whole shape and all its ordinances" (to make them when needed). Let them learn it from you so that they know them when the final day arrives.[24] And when they learn and engage in this study (even though they cannot practice it now) I will consider it as if they actually engaged in its construction.[25]

Then, when they merit it, they again will settle brotherly in the Land, according to the inheritance of the Twelve Tribes of Yisrael.[26] Across the borders of Yehuda, from the East coast to the West coast heave offerings will be brought, and the Beis HaMikdash will stand in the midst of Yerushalayim, My Holy City. From this day and onward [27] it will not be known by any name ever, only "Hashem shamma," Hashem is there. Do not punctuate it "shamma," but "shma," her name. "Hashem Shma," *Hashem* is her name.

Fortunate is the city that bears the name of its King.[28]

The Crucible of Poverty

Unlike the man who returns to Hashem out of love is the one who repents out of affliction.[29] — Bavel was a place of affliction, because out of ten measures of poverty that descended on earth Bavel took nine.[30] Affected in many ways by Bavel's darkness and by its poverty, the exiles were thus purified and tested in "the crucible of poverty." [31] Theirs was a life of starkness and deprivation. Bare and bereft were they driven from Yerushalayim, and they now were in want of everything.[32] Even in death [33] in the land of Bavel they were deprived of everything.[34] They were dying in anguish, unable even to remove the filth from the bodies, deprived of bath and light, as they lacked even oil for lighting. (As only sesame oil [35] was available in Bavel). Neither had

27 יחזקאל מח.	26 יחזקאל מז.	25 ילק"ש יחזקאל מג.	24 רש"י שם.
30 ישעי' מח, י.	29 ילק"ש זכרי' א.	28 פסיקתא דרב כהנא פיסקא "שוש אשיש".	
33 תהלים יח, ה וילקוט שמואל ב כב.	32 שמ"ר ל, כד.	31 קידושין דף מט:	
	35 שבת כו.	34 רש"י ישעי' לג, ט.	

they sufficient water [36] or fire-wood to warm up the bathhouse.[37] Even bodily elimination was problematic. Since the soil of Bavel was water-soaked they could not dig ditches near their dwellings, hence they had to go out a distance into fields. So that even in these matters they prayed to Hashem for assistance.[37b]

Only of the pagans' taunts they had aplenty. The heathens kept embarassing and deriding them, saying, "The God of these people once punished Pharoh, Sisro and Sancheriv and others like them, but now it seems He has grown old." [38]

Of all the evil neighbors of Yerushalayim who oppressed her, Ammon and Mo'av were the worst. "For Hashem had commanded against Yaakov her oppressors all around," [39] and when the Bnei Yehuda were exiled, the Kasdim sent along Ammonites and Mo'abites to be constantly near them. Indeed, they did not allow the House of Yaakov any peace in their captivity but oppressed them even in Bavel, as for example the all-Ammonite city of Humanya which oppressed the impoverished Bnei Yehuda [40] living in the neighboring city of Fum N'hara.[41] Furthermore, in Bavel there were good places and bad places. There were whole cities whose residents were completely amoral,[42] and there the captives of Yehuda were forced to mingle with them and then learned from their ways.

Moreover, there was more flattery and arrogance in Babylon than in any other country. This haughtiness expressed itself in poor Torah knowledge, because due to haughtiness one does not serve his teacher as required and he fails to understand fully what he has learned, thus many of them remained poor in Torah.[43] Even Daniel, the greatest of that generation, since he resided in the corrupt Province of Eilam (in Bavel), merited only to study but not to teach Torah.[44]

False Prophets

A further menace plagued the exiles in Bavel: the false prophets. Not

36 קהלת רבה פרק יב וילקוט שמעוני ישעי' מד.   37 ב"ר ל"ז ד, ופרש"י שם.
37b ברכות ח, י.   38 ילק"ש יחזקאל פרק לה.   39 איכה א, יז ורש"י שם.
40 רש"י יבמות דף טז ע"ב.   41 קידושין עב: ורש"י שם.   42 קידושין ע ועב.
43 קידושין מט: ורש"י שם.   44 קידושין מט:

only then, but ever since the first exile of Yechonya, there were those who went around Bavel prophesying falsehood in Hashem's Name, words that He had never relayed to them.[45] Ach'av son of Kolaya and Tzidkiyahu son of Ma'asiya were the most corrupt and perverted of the false prophets. They fooled the people and presented themselves as prophets.[46] They seduced the wives of their friends and of the officers of Bavel, all supposedly in the name of Heaven. Until in the end, Hashem delivered them into the hands of the king.[47]

It all came about when Ach'av and Tzidkiyahu went to the daughter of Nevuchadnezar. Acting as agents for each other, both in turn spoke to her. Ach'av said, "Thus said Hashem, 'Submit to Tzidkiyahu'." And Tzidkiyahu said, "Thus said Hashem, 'Submit to Ach'av'." She went and informed her father. He said to her, "The God of these people abhors adultery. If they come to you again, send them to me." When they came to her, she sent them to Nevuchadnezzar. He asked them, "Who told you it is permissible?" They replied, "Hashem!" Said Nevuchadnezar, "But I asked Chananya, Mishael and Azarya, and they told me it is forbidden." They replied, "We too, are prophets like them. To them Hashem did not give this message, to us He did."

Said the king, "Then I will put you to a test, as I did with Chananya, Mishael and Azarya." Said the false prophets, "They were three; we are only two. Hence we do not have as many merits as they had, to save us." Said Nevuchadnezar, "Select a third one; whomever you want." They answered, "We choose Yehoshua the Kohen Gadol," for they reasoned that his many merits would surely protect them as well.

After Yehoshua was summoned, Nevuchadnezar at once seized the three and threw them into the fire. Ach'av and Tzidkiyahu were burned like roasted grains, while Yehoshua the Kohen Gadol was unharmed; only his clothes were charred,[48] (as the prophet Zecharya says in his vision: "Hashem showed me Yehoshua, the Kohen Gadol ... is he not a brand plucked out of the fire?"[49])

Said Nevuchadnezar to Yehoshua, "I know you to be a righteous man. Why then, has some of the fire touched you, whereas it did not

---

45 ירמי׳ כט.   46 ילק״ש ירמי׳ כט.   47 שם.   48 סנהדרין צג.
49 זכרי׳ ג, א—ב.

touch Chananya, Mishael and Azarya at all?" Said Yehoshua —
"They were three, and had many merits, but I am only one!" Said
Nevuchadnezar, "But Avraham your forefather was also only one, yet
the fire did not touch him when Nimrod threw him into the kiln."
Answered Yehoshua, "Avraham had no wicked men with him, hence
no permission was given to the fire to consume. With me however,
there were wicked men, and permission was given to the fire to do its
work." Hence the parable used afterwards: two dry pieces of wood
together with a moist one may yet be kindled.[50] (Actually however,
the charring of his cloths was a punishment to Yehoshua, because
his sons had married women unbefitting to Kohanim and he had not
prevented them [51]).

The end of those two wicked men furthermore gave rise to the curse
later heard among the exiles in Bavel: "May Hashem make you like
Tzidkiyahu and Ach'av, whom the king of Bavel burnt in fire." [52]
And from then on, the Sons of Yehuda were careful to lend an ear
only to the true prophets of Hashem whom He sent to them in the land
of their exile.

Forgetting Torah

Along with all the physical suffering that is caused by the hardships
of wandering on foreign roads is the interruption of Torah-study. Even
Yirmiyahu, the aged prophet, was interrupted in his intense learning
because of his journey's hardships.[53] "Thus the pitcher got broken at
the fountain" [54] — the pitcher of Baruch ben Neriyah was broken
at the fountain of Yirmiyahu. First Yochanan ben Keréach had taken
them forcefully along to Egypt. Later (upon the destruction of Egypt)
Nevuchadnezar exiled them to Babylon, and they further interrupted
their Torah-Study because of the hardship of the wanderings.[55]

In the year 3350, Baruch ben Neriyah received the Mesorah of the
Torah from his Rebi Yirmiyahu, in Bavel.[56] Yirmiyahu, in turn, had

50 סנהדרין צג. 51 שם. 52 ירמיהו כט, כב. 53 רש"י קהלת יב, ו.

54 שם פסוק ו. 55 רש"י שם. 56 שלשלת הקבלה.

received it from his Rebi, the prophet Tzefanya; Tzefanya, from the prophet Chabakuk and his Beis-Din; Chabakuk, from the prophet Nachum and his Beis-Din; and so on all the way back to Moshe Rabbeinu, who had received it from Hashem Himself.[57] Although Yirmiyahu lived yet many years afterwards, the pitcher of Baruch was already broken because of the afflictions of hardships and poverty. No longer was Baruch ben Neriyah able to draw Torah from the fountain of Yirmiyahu.

The exiles of Yehuda too shared their anguish, for many Halachos had been long forgotten in the tribulations of their journey. However the distinguished scholars of Yechonya's Exile stood them by, as Hashem had exiled these to Bavel earlier for the good of those who would come later.[58] Among them were the Chorosh uMasger, the great scholars of the Sanhedrin (so rich in Torah and learning[59]) who now stood ready to lead the masses of the newly arrived exiles.[60] For they all were heroic men waging the battles of Torah, and when they sealed the Halacha no one could ever reopen it.[61] Even in the land of their captivity, Hashem stood in the midst of the Sanhedrin, to teach and enlighten them.[62] The Chachamim thus were able to clarify and bring back all that had been forgotten in the afflictions of their trying journey into exile.[63]

Furthermore, the prophets Yirmiyahu and Yechezkel stood them by with their Torah teaching. Although Yirmiyahu did not prophesy to them in Bavel, and Yechezkel prophesied only during the fourteen years following the Churban, yet they preserved and handed down their prophecies in writing. Shortly before his death,[64] Yirmiyahu, with Ru'ach Hakodesh, recorded his own Sefer Yirmiyahu as well as Melachim and Eichah.[65] Hence their eternal words remained with the House of Yisrael for all generations. — Thus, in the days of Daniel, Hashem appeared to the Bnei Yisrael as a Sage teaching Torah to his People.[66]

57 הקדמת הרמב״ם ליד החזקה. 58 ירמי׳ פרק כד, ה. 59 תנחומא נח, ג.

60 ירמי׳ פרק כד, א. 61 סדר עולם פרק כה. 62 תרגום שיר השירים ו, ב.

63 סוכה מד, ורש״י שם. 64 בבא בתרא טו. ורש״י ד״ה כתבו ישעי׳. 65 שם טו.

66 ילק״ש דניאל ז.

Repentance

In the depths of Bavel Hashem gave His people a new understanding, to learn to know Him. Out of estrangement came a new closeness. For in their utter destitution, when all these sufferings came upon them, they confessed their own sins and the sins of their fathers; their betrayal of God. And then, in the land of their captivity, they returned to Hashem.[67] They found Him, because they sought Him with their whole heart and soul. And this poor, storm-tossed people (whom the nations had already considered forever uprooted) now found a new heart and a new spirit.

The exiles once more engaged in Torah-study and crowned their Creator in the land of their exile. They established houses of learning [68] for the constantly growing number of students, so that Torah was not cut off in Bavel. They studied not only the Sefarim of the Torah, Prophets and Kesuvim, but as well dwelt on the reasonings and discussions of the Oral Halacha.[69] (They all even became now as well versed in the laws of Gittin as they had been before, in Eretz Yisrael [70]) * And they learned to follow His Statutes and Ordinances, so that they would be His people and He would be their God.[71]

However, henceforth their study [72] was conducted in Aramaic, which is close to the language of the Torah [73] and easy to master.[74] The Torah itself had given recognition to Aramaic by making use of it in the Sefarim of the Torah, Prophets and Kesuvim.[75]* (The Books of Daniel and Ezra were partially written in Aramaic). Though exempted in exile from observing the Mitzvos pertaining to the Holy Land,[76] the exiles kept all the other Mitzvos scrupulously. They treasured them close to their heart, even in their dispersion.[77] Those Mitzvos in turn made the exiles stand out,[78] and set them apart from the other nations.

67 רמב"ן דברים ד, ל.   68 תרגום שה"ש ו, ב.   69 תנא דבי אליהו רבה פרק כג.

70 ב"ק פ. וגיטין ו. ותוס' שם.   * תוספת דבר.   71 יחזקאל פרק א, כ.

72 ילק"ש דניאל א.   73 פסחים פז: 74 חולין כד.   75 ילק"ש דניאל תתרס.

* תוספת דבר.   76 קדושין לז. וירושלמי שביעית פרק ו.   77 קהלת רבה יב.

78 ילק"ש ירמי' לא.

All Set Apart

Indeed, in all their ways and doings the Bnei Yisrael remained different from the other nations. Even the calculation of their months and years were different from Bavel's. They continued to set their months and ordain the leap-years by the ruling of the Sanhedrin (as instructed in the Torah [79]), just as they had done before, in Yerushalayim. Because after the Chorosh and Masger were exiled, those who had remained in the Land ordained the leap-year in Yehushalayim by resolution of a plain Beis-Din. After no one was left in the land, they started the ordainment of leap-years in Bavel.[80] Thus Yirmiyahu ordained a leap-year outside of Eretz Yisrael, as did also Yechezkel and Baruch ben Neriya.[81] For they were the ones who had securely preserved the secret of the leap-year calculations.[82]*

Not only in their Holidays and Festivals, but in all their ways and doings the Judeans differed from the Kasdim. In plowing and seeding, in planting trees and harvesting grains, in cutting their hair and in shaving; in the ways of eating, drinking and dressing, — in everything they were totally different from their neighbors. Not only in the explicit laws which they were commanded in the Torah Shebichsav (The Written Law), but also in the minute details of the boundless Torah She'b'al-Peh (the Oral Torah) as well, which was handed down to them from generation to generation since Moshe Rabbeinu received it at Sinai. Hence they continued (even in exile) to be "a people that dwells alone, and is not reckoned among the nations."

The Torah scholars in Bavel were even more set apart. For the sake of Yisrael's honor they dressed differently even from their own brethren. For the Bnei Yisrael had merited three types of vestments; those of the Kehuna (priesthood), the Royal Garb, and the Mantle of Torah. Upon their banishment to Bavel, Nevuchadnezar removed from them the vestments of Kehuna and Royalty.[83] Therefore, the Chachamim in Bavel were exeedingly careful about preserving the remaining Mantle

---

79 שמות יב, ב.   80 פדר"א ח.   81 ירושלמי הובא בתוס' יבמות קט"ו, ד"ה אר"ע
ובפד"א פ"ח.   82 שמות רבה טו, כ.   * תוספת דבר.   83 פתיחתא דאיכה
רבתי יב.

of Torah. They dressed in pure white, resembling God's angels; [84] in particular, the angel who appeared as "a man clothed in white linen." [85]

Furthermore, they were concerned with the unprecedented problems of dispersal and exile. When a wise man lives in his own town, he is known to the people and they honor him accordingly. But now, uprooted and unknown strangers, the Chachamim were especially careful to distinguish themselves by their appropriate garb,[86] to preserve the honor of Torah.

In their festivities too, the Sons of Yehuda separated themselves from the nations in whose midst they now dwelt. They would not participate in the pagan celebrations or rejoice in their joys. Only the holidays and festivals prescribed by the Torah were the source of their rejoicing.[87] Moreover, the exiles were all poor; food and drink was scarce, and throughout the year they found no rest from their labor. Only with the arrival of the Festivals, did joy come into their homes. That is why the Bnei Yisrael used to rejoice in their Festivals [88] now in Bavel even more than they had rejoiced before, in Eretz Yisrael.[89]

The "Conditional" Sanctuary

And Hashem was to them a "Miniature Sanctuary" in the distant land of Bavel.[90] With immense sacrifice the impoverished exiles built themselves Batei Kneses (Synagogues) in every place to which they were driven. These became the gathering places which they frequented daily — as if indeed they entered the beloved Gates of Zion and Yerushalayim themselves. And *there* they poured out their hearts "in the Presence of Hashem."

The sanctity of these synagogues now was however different. They were not subject to all the laws of fearful reverence that governed the Great Mikdash in Yerushalayim. Because these houses of prayer in Bavel were from the outset built with the explicit understanding that their sanctity would be only temporary.[91] For when the Day of Re-

---

84 קידושין דף עב.   85 יחזקאל פרק ט, ב.   86 שבת קמה: ורש״י שם.

87 דברים טז, יד.   88 שבת קמה: 89 רש״י שם.   90 יחזקאל יא, טז.

91 מגילה כח: ותוספ׳ שם.

demption (promised by the Prophets) speedily arrived, and the Children would return to their own borders, the sanctity of these synagogues would anyway cease.

Said the Kneses Yisrael (Gathering of Yisrael) to Hashem, "I am asleep, but my heart stays awake [92] — I am asleep concerning the Beis HaMikdash (which was destroyed), but my heart is awake in the synagogues and in the houses of study. I am asleep with respect to the Korbanos (which are no longer), but my heart is awake with Mitzvos and Tzedaka. I am asleep with respect to the commandments pertaining to the Holy Land, but my heart is awake (and eager) to fulfill them. I am asleep with respect to the Ultimate Day (which remains unknown), but my heart is awake awaiting the Redemption. — Even if I am asleep with respect to the hope of the Redemption, my heart is awake, being aroused and assured that Hashem will redeem me." [93]

92 שה"ש ה, ב.   93 שה"ש רבה שם.

Chapter Seven

DOWNFALL OF THE WICKED

Chapter Eight

THE END OF BAVEL

Chapter Seven

DOWNFALL OF THE WICKED

NOTWITHSTANDING all his power and haughtiness Nevuchadnezar acted fairly towards the people of Yehuda. He did not burden them
with a crushing yoke, as was the delight of other kings who prided themselves with their cruel treatment of the helpless captives fallen into their
hands. However, in his boundless haughtiness the king never showed any
mercy toward the noble and great ones. He never even opened the
gates of their prisons.[1] Whoever was thrown into jail in his times,
would never come out again.[2] After all these years he even did not
show any mercy to Yechonya and Tzidkiyahu, the Kings of Yehuda,
who languished in jail — the blind Tzidkiyahu for 26 years, and Yechonya his nephew (who had preceded him) for 37 years.

Nevuchadnezar's Death

Nevuchadnezar's reign lasted forty five years,[3] and he lived longer
than any world ruler in history. Then Hashem broke the staff of the
wicked.[4] In the 37th year since the exile of Yehoyachin, on the 25th
day of the twelfth month,[5] Nevuchadnezar, the mighty dwarf, died
(3364).[6] His glory descended with him to the grave, as he was buried
with all royal pomp of majesty, amidst the din of his psalteries.[7]

Only then did the world quiet down, and people burst into jubilation [8] — for the oppressor was stilled, and his extortions had ceased.[9]
The kings of the world relaxed from the constant sorrow and fears [10]
that Nevuchadnezar had caused them. They shouted and cried out,
"you, too, became weak, as we are; you, like us, are mortal. Worms
are spread underneath you, and worms are your cover." [11] Even the

---

1 ישעי' יד, יז.   2 ויקרא רבה יח, ב.   3 מגילה יא: 4 ישעי' יד ה.
5 מלכים ב' פרק כה, כז.   6 סדר עולם כח.   7 ישעי' פרק יד, יא.
8 תנא דבי אליהו סוף פרק ל, ע"ש.   9 הקדמת הרמב"ם לפירוש המשניות.
10 שם פסוק ג.   11 שם יא.

cypresses rejoiced at his death, together with the cedars of Levanon. For since Nevuchadnezar had been laid down, "the chopper" would no longer go up to destroy the Levanon.[12]

The nether world, however, shuddered at his coming.[13] The moment the villain descended to Gehinom, all who were there flared up, saying, "Have you come to rule us, or to be weak as we are?" Thereupon a heavenly voice rang out,[14] "Are you better than others?Lie down with all the unclean ones!"[15] Then Gehinom also quieted down, and everyone in it burst into jubilation.

A Trampled Corpse

After Nevuchadnezar's death, the nobles wanted to crown his son Evvil Merodach, in his place, but he refused to be king. He said to them, "When madness took hold of Nevuchadnezar and he lived among the beasts of the field for seven years, I listened to you and ruled in his place. When he returned to his throne he took revenge and threw me into jail. Perhaps now he is still alive and will return to kill me?"[16]

The next day,[17] all aides and ministers gathered and dragged Nevuvadnezar's corpse out of the grave, to prove to all that he was dead, and to annul his evil decrees.[18] Thus, instead of glory the haughty Nevuchadnezar now got his full measure of disgrace.[19] It was not even granted to him to lie in honor, with other kings alike. — For he had corrupted his own land with tyrannical enslavement, and slain innocent commoners and wise men alike.[20] Therefore they all hated him, and threw him out of his grave like a discarded twig.

Whoever saw his corpse dragged around, contemplated and wondered, "Is this the man who shook kingdoms and made the earth tremble? Is he the one who turned the world into wasteland, destroyed its cities, never opened the house of the prisoners,[21] and ruled with an iron fist over all of Hashem's creations?"[22]

12 פסוק ח.   13 פסוק ט.   14 ילק"ש ישעי' יד.   15 ישעי' יד, ד ושבת קמט:

16 ויק"ר יח, ב.   17 רש"י וילק"ש שם.   18 ילק"ש חבקוק א.   19 חבקוק ב, טז.

20 ישעי' יד, כ, ורש"י שם.   21 שם פסוקים טז—יז.   22 ילק"ש חבקוק א.

Now all of Nevuchadnezar's enemies rushed to the scene and joyfully pierced the corpse with the swords,[23] thereby fulfilling the verse:[24] "You are thrown out of the grave dressed in the garment of the slain, pierced by the sword."

Then, all the people knew that the lion — scourge of the earth — was dead. They threw him back to the stones of the pit, like a blood-covered carcass, trodden underfoot.[25] And on 27 Adar, his son Evvil Merodach, was crowned in his place [26] (3364).

A Peaceful End

At this time King Tzidkiyahu too was relieved of his misery (the merit of having saved Yirmiyahu from the lime-pit [27] stood by the blind king). As soon as Nevuchadnezar (his enemy) died, Evvil Merodach released Tzidkiyahu from prison, where he was chained for almost half his life. Tzidkiyahu thus lived to witness his enemy die in his lifetime; while he himself was freed.[28] The sons of Yehuda joyfully greeted their King, who for twenty-six years had been chained in copper-shackles. But, that very same day this last of the Kings of Yehuda died. The exiles eulogized him, crying, Woe, our lord; Woe that King Tzidkiyahu died, he who drank the sediments of the cup of punishment of all the generations. And in their mourning they burnt his bed, together with his personal articles, in a pyre, according to the custom at a king's funeral.[29] Thus came true the verse,[30] "You will die in peace, and with (royal) burnings, like your fathers, the kings who were before you."

Evvil Merodach, the new king, gave honor to Hashem and to His chosen people, Yisrael. He also remembered Yechonya, King of Yehuda, when he ascended the throne. For great is the power of exile; it atones for all sins,[31] and 37 years had now passed since Yechonya went into exile. Also, he had the merit of having subjected himself to Nevuchadnezar, accepting the yoke of Bavel's king as Hashem had commanded

23 ילק"ש חבקוק א.   24 ישעי' יד, יט.   25 שם.   26 מ"ב כה, כז.
27 ילק"ש ירמי' לד.   28 ילק"ש שם.   29 עבודה זרה יא.   30 ירמי' לד, ה.
31 ילק"ש ירמי' כא.

313

through the Prophet Yirmiyahu.[32] Moreover, Yechonya had truly repented in prison, so that Hashem forgave him all his former transgressions,[33] and he merited to live in peace after all the years of misery. For one who lives in comfort may yet be subject to distress, and he who is in distress should not give up hope of a better tomorrow.[34] Tzidkiyahu, who had lived well and reigned a long time even after Yechonya was exiled, merited only to die peacefully, but not to return to better days. Yechonya, who lived in distress all of his days, merited to dwell in comfort — when "Hashem sent the prisoner out from the pit in which there was no water." [35]

On the 27 Adar (the day that Evvil Merodach ascended to the throne), he freed Yechonya, King of Yehuda, from prison.[36] Unlike his father Nevuchadnezar, he even treated him royally. He spoke to him reverently, gently and comfortingly.[37] He exchanged his prison-garb for royal attire, and set his throne above the thrones of the other kings who were with him in Bavel. Thenceforth, Yechonya had his meals always in the king's palace,[38] as he was granted his provisions daily, by the King of Bavel, as long as he lived.

Moreover, miracles had also been made for Yechonya, even in his prison dungeon. He had been destined to die childless,[39] but since in prison he fulfilled the laws of family-purity (which he had not kept in Yerushalayim), he merited that his wife (who was allowed to visit in prison) bore him a son.[40] The child was named Asir She'altiel,[41] *Asir*, meaning imprisoned, for his mother conceived him in prison; *She'altiel*, meaning "I asked him of God." As he was conceived in answer to the king's prayers that the Royal House of David be not cut off.[42]

Hashem further blessed She'altiel (he had six sons,[43] and thus the seed of David's House was not cut off from Bnei Yisrael), and the Sages assigned him a high position in Bavel after the death of his father

32 מלכים ב, פרק כד.   33 ילק"ש מ"ב, כד.   34 סדר עולם פרק כח.
35 זכרי' ט, יא יולק"ש מ"ב, כד.   36 מ"ב כה, כז.   37 מצודת דוד שם.
38 ירמי' פרק נב, לב לד.   39 ירמי' פרק כב, ל.   40 ילק"ש מ"ב, כד.
41 דברי הימים א' פרק ג, יז.   42 רד"ק שם.   43 דברי הימים א' פרק ג, יח.

Yechonya.[44] Yet neither royalty nor glory ever returned to Yehoyachin, son of Yehoyakim, or to his sons. For the power of the kings of Yehuda was already weakened, because they had followed in the ways of the kings of Yisrael. Only through the generosity of Evvil Merodach was Yehoyachin returned to a life of comfort in the last years of his life, and he was like a prince to his people in the land of their exile.[45] He remained under the protection of the King of Babylon, — and through the latter's splendor there was glory for him, too.

44 סדר עולם זוטא.   45 ס׳ שלשלת הקבלה.

Chapter Eight

THE END OF BAVEL

THE rule of Evvil Merodach lasted twenty-three years. He was a decent, kind monarch, and the world was at peace during his reign. The exiles of Yehuda too, were at peace, though increasingly impatient already with the long years of captivity. With them were their sons and daughters and the grandchildren born to them in Bavel who had never yet seen the Land of Yehuda or the Holy City, but who yearned for Hashem, praying, — "When will I come and be in the Presence of Hashem?"[1] Bnei Yisrael kept pleading, "Master of the Universe, when will You return to us the glory of ascending for the Three Festivals and seeing the Shechina?"[2]

Awaiting Redemption

Like a watchman in midst of the siege, the Prophet Chabakuk then stood guard for his brethren. He raised his voice to Heaven and decried the injustice.[3] He drew a circle, stood himself in its center and declared: "I will not move from here, until I hear Hashem respond to my question: Why does He tolerate the successes of the wicked Kingdom of Bavel?[4] And how shall I answer those who argue with me and question Hashem's ways?"

Hashem indeed replied to Chabakuk, "Write down the vision, make it clear on tablets, so that the reader may easily understand. For there is still a vision for the appointed time. It speaks concerning the End, and it will not deceive. Though it may tarry, wait for it, for surely it will come — it will not delay!"[5] — And this verse now cut and tore into the inner depths of the people's hearts.[6] One may think Yisrael is waiting, but not Hashem. However, long before, it was already written,[7] "Therefore Hashem is waiting to bestow His Grace upon you,

1 תהלים מב, ג.   2 ילק״ש תהלים מב.   3 חבקוק א—ב.   4 רש״י חבקוק ב, א.
5 שם ב—ג.   6 ילק״ש חבקוק ב.   7 ישעי׳ ל, יח.

and He is rising to have compassion on you, for He is the God of Justice." But if He was waiting, and they were waiting, what was holding back the redemption? Midas Ha'Din (The attribute of Strict Justice), was holding it back! — But if it was held back, why were they waiting? In order to receive reward, as it is written,[8] "Praiseworthy are all who wait for Him." [9]

As the Sons of Yehuda were waiting and hoping for His redemption,[10] Hashem in His kindness and great mercy made them find tranquility on foreign soil. Then Evvil Merodach died, and he was succeeded by his son Belshatzar (3386).* Bavel now returned to the days of the wicked, haughty Nevuchadnezar and his corruptness. It was as if Belshatzar was not the son of the decent Evvil Merodach, but of the wicked Nevuchadnezar. (As it is written,[11] "Nevuchadnezar, his father.") For by his ascension to the throne the wicked followed the wicked one, a destructor followed another destructor, a haughty one followed a previous one,[12] thereby returning peaceful Bavel to the horrendous days of Nevuchadnezar, his father's father.

Stirrings of the Heart

While in the land of their enemy, the sons of Yehuda subdued their stubborn heart to Hashem, and with time, their sins were almost atoned for. The end of the exile decreed upon them was drawing nearer. — "I slumber in Bavel," Bnei-Yisrael said, "but my Heart (Hashem) is awake" [13] — to redeem me! [14] Indeed, Hashem had already planted the seed for the return of Yisrael's glory.

The year that Belshatzar ascended the throne, the power of the kings of Persia began to rise, and that same year the downfall of Babylon was decreed.[15] In a nighttime vision Hashem appeared to Daniel and gave him the prophecy concerning Persia and all the other empires, their rise and their downfall. Until the End of Days when the kingship of the world will be given over to Yisrael.

---

8 ישעי׳ שם.   9 ילק״ש חבקוק ב.   10 סנהדרין קיא: * תוספת.

11 דניאל פרק ח, ב.   12 ילק״ש דניאל ד.   13 שיר השירים פרק ה, ב.

14 שה״ש רבה ה, ד ב״עץ יוסף״ שם.   15 יחזקאל כט, כא ורש״י שם.

The Four Beasts

In his vision [16] Daniel saw the four winds (from the four directions of the sky) blowing, and they stirred up the great sea. Then, from the sea, four huge beasts emerged successively, one diverse from the other. The first was like a lion, and had eagle's wings (the Empire of Babylon). Then its wings were plucked off, and it disappeared from the earth. The second beast looked like a bear (in the Kingdom of Persia people ate and drank and were padded with flesh like a bear), and it would rule after Bavel. It was followed by a third beast, rising from the water. This one looked like a leopard, and had four wings on its back, and also four heads (representing the Empire of Greece, which split into four, and issued various cruel decrees against Yisrael).[17]

In a vision of the following night [18] Daniel saw a fourth beast, more powerful, fearful and awesome, as strong as all the other three together,[19] emerging from the sea. Its huge teeth were of iron, its nails of copper. It devoured and crushed everything to pieces, and trampled the remains with its feet. — This fourth beast was different from all the other beasts preceding it. It had ten horns, and behold, a small horn sprang up among them. (That is the Kingdom of Yishmael, which would be scattered among the Romans [20]) And while Daniel watched, thrones were set up, and the Heavenly books opened. And the Lord of Hosts rose and sat in Judgment over all kingdoms.

Daniel saw Hashem's fury rising upon hearing the haughty words which the small horn spoke. The awesome beast was slain and its body was destroyed and consumed by fire. The other beasts, too, had their patron-angels subdued and power removed, yet their lives were prolonged "for a season and a time." Then, in the clouds of the heavens a human shape appeared (the Mashi'ach), and came before Hashem. And the kingship which until then had been in the hands of the beast-like empires, Hashem now transmitted to this man to whom indeed ruleship, glory, and kingship befit. All the nations then will serve him, for his reign is the everlasting reign; it will never cease nor be destroyed.

16 דניאל פרק ז, ורש"י שם.   17 ויקרא רבה.   18 ויקרא רבה יג, ה.
19 רש"י דניאל ז, ז.   20 ר' סעדי' גאון דניאל ז, ח.

The fourth beast (the fourth future empire) was indeed different from the other beasts. It would wage war against Yisrael, the Holy People, and be victorious and conquer them. It would speak words against the Most High One, of scorn and revulsion. (As the wicked Titus later did.[21]) It would further oppress and ruin Bnei Yisrael to wrench them away from their faith. And under this rule the holy Sons of Yisrael would be subjected "until the time and the times and half a time." [22]

Daniel was shaken. His thoughts bewildered him, and the radiance of his face dimmed. He saw the four beasts, each different from the other, thus would the hate of each of them towards Bnei Yisrael take a different form. Every empire ruling the world therefore hates the Bnei Yisrael and enslaves them.[23] Yet, far off is the day of His coming, and who would even know it. — Hence, the words only cut deep into his heart.

The events of the End of Days were thus hidden and sealed, not to be revealed. Daniel recorded for himself all he had seen in the prophecy, but he passed on only a vague outline of the vision to his brethren.[24] He but guarded the matter in his heart.[25]

Another Vision Concealed

In the third year of Belshatzar's rule, when the Bnei Yisrael almost completely atoned for their sins, the prophecy again came to Daniel.[26] And behold: A ram was standing before the river, and it had two horns (symbolizing the kings of Media and Persia — who were like a pair). The horns were high, one taller than the other (Persia's rule lasted longer than Media's), and the latter one came up last. Daniel saw the ram going westward, northward, and southward, and no beast could stand before it. It did as it pleased, and grew big. From the west came a young he-goat (this was Greece) which grew exceedingly large. It flung the ram to the ground and trampled it. When at its mightiest, its great horn was broken and a vision of four horns came up in its

21 גיטין נו.   22 דניאל ז, כה.   23 דניאל ז, כה.   24 דניאל ז, א.
25 שם פסוק כה.   26 דניאל ח.

319

place. Out of one of those came forth a lowly horn (the kingdom of Rome) which grew so high that it reached the hosts of the heavens, and it cast down to the earth the Bnei Yisrael (who are likened to the stars) and trampled them. Against Hashem it then hurled its blasphemy and curses. Through it the daily Korbanos would be banned for a time, the Mikdash destroyed, and Truth (the Torah) cast down to the ground. For as long as the Bnei Yisrael themselves cast words of the Torah to the ground, this Kingdom would issue evil edicts, and succeed.[27] For as long as God's children are enslaved to them, it is as though His Right Hand is enslaved together with them.[28]

Daniel heard one of the holy ones (an angel) ask, "How long will last this vision that the daily offerings be banished and the (idol) transgression (of desolation) taking its place? How long will the Mikdash and the heavenly hosts as well be trampled underfoot?" And an angel replied, "Till Nightfall and Morning, two thousand and three hundred (years), then the holiness will be rectified," [29] — that is, the sins. When Yisrael's sins will be atoned, to annul the decree of being trodden down.

Alas, the Bnei Yisrael did not merit to have the End of Days clearly revealed to them. As the angel was speaking to him, Daniel fell into a deep sleep, face to the ground. The angel touched him and put him back upright, to convey to him what will happen at the End of the indignations (of the Galus). — "But as for you, Daniel, obscure the vision; do not clarify its details. For it will happen only after many more days." [30]

Daniel was heart-broken and crushed by the frightful vision he had been shown the second time. He took ill for a year, and remained devastated over the vision. He was also shocked and dismayed over the complacency of Belshatzar,[31] considering that the day of Hashem's revenge was at hand, and his ruin soon to come.[32] Belshatzar's rule was about to be cut off, but he did not perceive it at all, and was not

27 ילקוט שמעוני דניאל ח.   28 ילקוט שמעוני תהלים תתפ״ה.   29 שם ח, יד.

30 פסוק כו.   31 שה״ש רבה ג, ד.   32 ישעי׳ יג, ו.

even disturbed. In his complacency he but pursued his lowly gratifications and self-indulgence as usual.

Daniel quietly sealed the tidings in his heart and went about his service to the king as before, without anyone noticing or suspecting a thing.[33] — Until the day of Hashem's revenge against Bavel finally arrived.

Hashem's Day

In Belshatzar's third year (3389) — which was the seventieth year from King Nevuchadnezar's ascent to the throne (3319) — Hashem brought His punishment upon Bavel, as He had once brought it upon Ashur (Assyria).[34] Suddenly Hashem unleashed upon Bavel and her inhabitants a wind of destruction.[35] For "in those days and in that time the iniquities of Yisrael were searched for, but did not exist; and the sins of Yehuda, but they were not to be found," for Hashem had forgiven those whom He had left as a remnant.[36] — At once a nation from the North swept down on Bavel, "the destructive mountain," to pay her back for all the evil she had done to Zion.[37]

Ever since the beginning of Nevuchadnezar's reign, Wrath had been amassed against Bavel, to descend upon her when her time arrives — the time of reckoning. On the day that Nevuchadnezar entered the Beis HaMikdash in the days of King Yehoyachin (3327),[38] on that very day his arch-enemy, Darius the Mede, was born.[39] However, Hashem does not bring punishment upon a people until the hour of its dismissal.[40]

Darius later slipped out from under the yoke of King Belshatzar, to revolt against him. He was sixty-two years old when he struck at the peaceful, unsuspecting capital of Bavel,[41] together with Koresh, [42] his son-in-law from Persia — both powerful kings. From the northeast Hashem aroused these strangers ("His designated" and appointed ones[43]), suddenly to scheme against Babylon. To bring about her

33 דניאל ח, כז.   34 ירמי' נ, יח.   35 שם נא, א.   36 שם נ, כ.

37 שם נא, כד.   38 מלכים ב' כד, יג.   39 ילק"ש דניאל תתרסד וסדר עולם כח.

40 סוטה ט.   41 דניאל ו, א.   42 רש"י דניאל ה, א.   43 ישעי' יג, ג.

destruction, Hashem's revenge for His Dwelling.[44] Powerful Eilam also joined forces with them,[45] and with great waves of men they came upon Bavel by way of the frightful desert [46] to her west. They swept through the wastelands like whirlwind, raising storms of dust.[47] The noise of their multitudes was heard in the mountains, the tumult of nations encamped together.[48] "They clutched bow and spear, for they were cruel and merciless. Their sound was like the roaring sea, and they rode horses. Warriors, all lined up for battle against you, oh, Daughter of Bavel!" [49] And towards him whom Hashem commands it the archer will bend his bow.[50] His smart arrow will not fail.[51]

From all sides simultaneously they attacked mighty Babylon, but her warriors fought back. In the furious battle countless men fell.[52] The armies of Persia and Media hurled their stones and ceaselessly arched their bows not sparing their arrows, none of which missed their mark. — For Bavel had sinned against Hashem.[53]

The very day of the attack marked the completion of the full seventy years of Babylon's Kingdom which the exiles had been counting, its days and years. And then they saw and realized: "Indeed, this is the day of revenge against Bavel! Hashem has incited traitor against traitor, and wrecker against wrecker, for their day has arrived, their end has come." He has come upon thee, "mountain of destruction," to destroy you! [54]

However, the very hour of Bavel's downfall had not yet arrived. "The Guardian of Yisrael neither slumbers nor sleeps." He guards their goings and their comings:[55] Yisrael's goings out of one empire, and their coming into another. He watches, lest one nation trespass the boundaries of another nation. That not one kingdom should encroach upon the reign of another, not even by a hairbreadth. If its time to fall comes by day, it will fall by day; if its time to fall is at night, it will fall at night.[56]* And being that this whole last day of the seventy years was still within the realm of Bavel, Belshatzar was victorious.

44 ירמי' נא, יא.   45 ישעי' כא, ב.   46 שה"ש רבה ג, ג.   47 ישעי' כא, א.

48 ישעי' יג, ד.   49 ירמי' נ, מ"ב.   50 שם נא, ג.   51 שם נ, ט.

52 שה"ש רבה ג, ד.   53 ירמי' נ, יד.   54 שם נא.   55 תהלים קכא, ח.

56 ילק"ש ישעי' כא.   * תוספת.

Notwithstanding their bravery, the besieging armies of Persia and Media were forced to flee, with Belshatzar, King of Babylon, winning the battle of the day.[57]

Between one Drink and Another

However, Belshatzar, the haughty chopper, did not see it that way. "My strength saved me," he boasted. "Babylon's massive walls were my help." — And, — he miscalculated — by one day only.[58] He reckoned that the prophesied seventy years of Bavel's empire were completed already on that very day, but instead of being destroyed, he now (*after* the seventy years) emerged victorious over his enemies. Hence, the words of the prophet were null and void. — Bavel certainly would not be destroyed . . .

The army-scouts rushed to the palace reporting to the king, "The enemies' armies have abandoned the siege. They all fled; not a man remains!" [59] At that moment Babylon's joy was boundless. The King and the military went into a frenzy, drunk with victory. Only the Sons of Yehuda did not share in the joy of the heathens. Their heart was bitter. Why, Bavel almost fell — but it did not fall.

As evening came, the king made a grand feast for a thousand of his officers and dignitaries, to celebrate the day's victory. In his haughtiness he made this a very special feast,[60] as though he had defeated not only the armies of Persia and Media, but Hashem's plans for Babylon as well. — That night was the cherished night of Pesach,[61] the hour guarded by Hashem as the time of His Children's redemption. Said the evildoer to Bnei Yisrael, "With how many sieves did you sift your Omer, which you sacrificed before your God in Yerushalayim?" "Thirteen," they replied. He then ordered his flour sifted through fourteen sieves, to show that his feast was greater than God's.[62]

The tables were set, the candlesticks were lit, and they ate and drank.[63] The king drank wine, matching a thousand of his officers. The wine then caused Belshatzar to err a second time on that day; he

---

57 רש"י דניאל ה, א.   58 שיר השירים ג, ד.   59 ספר יוסיפון פרק ג.

60 דניאל ה, א.   61 שה"ש רבה ג, ד.   62 שם.   63 ישעי' כא, ה

failed to distinguish between the seventy years of the kingship of Bavel and the seventy years of the exile to Bavel. For had then Yirmiyahu prophesied of "seventy years of Bavel's Kingship?" He had spoken only "of Bavel," [64] which actually means Yehoyakim's exile to Bavel [65] in the *second* year of Nevuchadnezar's reign. (leaving the count of seventy from that time on [3320], still one year short). The wicked king, however, erringly reckoned the seventy years of Bavel's kingship (from the start of Nevuchadnezar's reign [3319]) as having been completed then (3319 to 3389). And since the Sons of Yehuda had not been redeemed yet, he reasoned, that they never will be.[66]

The king then ordered the vessels of the Beis Hamikdash brought before him — the golden and silver vessels which Nevuchadnezar had taken from the Heichal in Yerushalayim. By touching them, the uncircumsized Kasdim [67] had already desecrated their holiness, but the arrogant Belshatzar went even further. He defiantly made personal use of the vessels of the King of kings. He and his lords, his queen and his concubines,[68] all now drank brazenly from the holy vessels, and so did his she-dog, who was dear to him as a concubine.[69] While they drank their wine from the consecrated vessels of the Mikdash, they furthermore extolled their gods of gold and silver, copper and iron, wood and stone, to whom they attributed their greatness and victories. (For Belshatzar was not like his grandfather Nevuchadnezar, who had run three steps for the honor of Hashem, whereby he had merited and was granted the three generations of Bavel's Royalty.[70]) Now the wine dealt treacherously with him; he was conceited and could not be satisfied.[71] Even to the members of his own household he was not acceptable. His house and dwelling would not last.[72]

At that moment the Divine Verdict was pronounced that Belshatzar and his seed would be uprooted from this world.[73] And, between one drink and another — one empire displaced another.[74]

---

64 ירמי' כט, י.   65 מגילה יא: 66 שם.   67 ילק"ש דניאל ה.

68 דניאל ה, ג.   69 ילק"ש נחמי' ב.   70 סנהדרין צו.   71 חבקוק ב, ה.

72 רש"י שם.   73 ילק"ש דניאל ה.   74 שיר השירים רבה ג, ד.

The Writing on the Wall

At once judgment had come to the world for its evil, and to the wicked for their iniquity.[75] That night the inhabited world was cast in darkness.[76] For the stars of the heaven and its constellation did not illuminate it with their light.[77]

Just then, the fingers of a man's hand came out of the heavens and started writing on the wall of the king's palace, facing the candelabrum in front of the table. When the king saw the palm of the hand writing,[78] the color of his face changed, and his thoughts terrified him. The joints of his loins loosened and emptied themselves out of fear, while his knees shook and knocked one against the other.[79]

The king cried aloud to bring in the wise men of Bavel — the sorcerers, the astrologers and the conjurers. Said the king to them: "Whoever would decipher the writing and explain its meaning would be vested with royal purple. His neck would be graced with a golden chain, and he would rule one third of the Empire."

Three lines were written on the wall:

מ מ ת ו ס
נ נ ק פ י
א א ל ר ז

But the wise men and even the Judeans present,[80] could not read the Holy Hebrew letters, since, at that moment, an angel had changed the letters back to the Ashuri script[81] (see chapter "Ashuri Script"). Seeing that none of the wise men was able to decipher the writing,[82] the king became frantic, and the color of his face changed even more. The lords too, were alarmed and perplexed.[83]

The queen, seeing the king's fear and apprehension, entered and said, "May the king live forever! Is there not in your empire a man in whom rests the light and wisdom of the Holy God, who understands to interpret dreams and explain riddles, and whom Nevuchadnezar had appointed head of all the wise men of Babylon?"

75 ישעי' יג, יא.   76 עמוס ה, כ.   77 שם פסוק י.   78 דניאל ה, ה.
79 דניאל ה.   80 שם.   81 רש"י סנהדרין כב.   82 פי' ר' סעדי' גאון דניאל שם.
83 דניאל ה.

Where was Daniel, "Hashem's beloved", on that fateful night? He had secluded himself, to fast and plead for mercy over the destruction of the Beis HaMikdash.[84] He was deeply shaken by the defiance and the blasphemy of the evildoer. He was shocked at the complacency of that wicked man for whom the table was set and candelabra lit[85] — with only one small step between him and death.

Daniels' Interpretation

The guards patrolling the city found the aged Daniel, and brought him before the King, who described to him the event and promised him the reward for deciphering the hand-writing.

Daniel looked around, and lo, the treasured vessels from Hashem's Dwelling in Yerushalayim — which he himself had never laid eyes on — were here, defiled by the unclean. At once, he acted as if capriciously towards the king. And in the midst of Babylon's sinful festivity he detached himself from all around him, longing only for the supreme delight of Hashem's love,[86] and he proudly despised all the mundane rewards promised him by the King.

Facing Belshatzar, Daniel said boldly, "Your gifts, keep to yourself, and your rewards give to another. I have no desire for them. Moreover, your gifts are the gain of stolen property, and the treasures of the wicked do not make for success.[87] But the writing I shall read before the king, and its interpretation I shall also tell."

At that moment Daniel, the one, stood up against the king, the one.[88] And through Daniel who was from the Tribe of Yehuda which is compared to a lion,[89] came the downfall of Bavel, the third beast of the Vision, which looked like a lion.[90]

"Listen, O King!" said Daniel, "To your grandfather, the eternal God gave a kingship, power, glory and splendor. But this great power made him haughty. His heart swelled with pride and he wantonly persisted in doing evil, until finally, Hashem cut off his glory. Now you, his son, came, and you likewise pride yourself over the Lord of

84 שה"ש רבה ג, ג.   85 שם ישעי' כא, ה.   86 שה"ש רבה ז, ה.   87 שם.

88 ב"ר צט, ב.   89 בראשית מט, ט.   90 דניאל ה, כח.

the heavens. You praise and extol your idols which neither hear nor see, nor know a thing — but Hashem, in whose Hand your soul rests, and whose power is behind all your dealings, to Him you have not even paid homage. Therefore the hand has been sent out before Him, and it has written this message.

This now is the text of the writing, carved on the wall of the very palace of your haughtiness:

Menei, Menei, Tekeil, Ufarsin

And this is its meaning: *Menei*, Hashem has calculated the end of your kingship, and found its time completed. *Menei,* — Hashem again rechecked the end of your kingship, and it has indeed been completed. *Tekeil*, you have been weighed before Him on the scale, and you were found to be wanting every measure of righteousness (that might have extended the final date). *Ufarsin*, your kingdom has been broken to pieces, and it was given to Media and Persia." [91]

Thus the aged Daniel, who sixty-nine years earlier had been exiled with the youngsters of the first Exile of Yehoyakim (over whom the Kasdim had boasted, "We have destroyed them! We have swallowed them up"), this same Daniel now stood up, on the day of Hashem's revenge against Bavel, to interpret and to explain to the King of Bavel its end — his imminent death.

Belshatzar's Death

Overcome by deathly fear, Belshatzar sought to flatter Daniel in order to arouse his compassion, so that he would pray to Hashem to annul the decree.[92] He dressed Daniel in royal purple, placed a heavy golden chain on his neck,[93] and pronounced him ruler over a third of the empire — the end of which however, had already been counted by Hashem. — Said Daniel to the king: "The decree has already been sealed!"

Upon hearing the interpretation of the handwriting, Belshatzar sum-

91 דניאל ה.   92 ר' סעדי' גאון שם ה, כג.   93 שם פסוק כט.

moned all the generals of his armies and said to them, "To prevent that no people or nation may rebel against us, let us attack them first!" [94]

Said the Almighty, "To all you have sent to escape fear and prevent your fall into the grave, but to Me you have not sent? Upon your life, through those who are with you and in whom you have placed your trust will your punishment come!" [95]

At once, Hashem instilled a new spirit in the hearts of the Medes and Persians. Like lions they rushed back from the Pride of the Yarden and laid siege again to the mighty fortresses of Bavel.[96] Bavel's scouts stood watch on its walls straining for any sound of an approaching enemy, as they were unable to see because of the blackness of that night. Suddenly they heard the thunder of vast armies, pairs of galloping horsemen, chariots, donkeys and camels; [97] and they all carrying with them the weapons of their fury.

When Bavel's king heard their report, he became weak with fear. Frightened, he commanded his loyal guards at the gates: "Whoever will be found outside this night, let his head be cut off, even if he says he is the king." [98]

Terror-stricken, the king's intestines were gripped by trembling, like a woman with birth-pangs.[99] Trying to conceal his agony, his bowels kept emptying themselves from great fear as he sneaked outside. The watchmen grabbed him in the darkness. "Who are you?" they shouted. "I am the king," he replied. Said they, "Has not the king commanded us that even if a person says he is the king, we are to cut off his head?" Thereupon they picked up a candelabrum and cracked his skull with it. Belshatzar writhed in pain that whole night, to fully complete the term allotted to him from on High. Only near dawn, life departed from him, as it is written,[2] "On that night, Belshatzar, king of the Kasdim, was killed. [3] One of his chamberlains chopped off Belshatzar's head and secretely carried it to the camp of Darius and Koresh, the kings of Media and Persia.[4]

94 שה"ש רבה ב, ד.   95 שם.   96 ירמי' ג, מד.   97 ישעי' כא, ז.
98 שה"ש רבה שם.   99 ירמי' שם.   1 ישעי' כא, ג.   2 דניאל ה, ל.
3 שה"ש רבה שם.   4 ס' יוסיפון.

The Night of Bavel's Fall

That night Hashem brought punishment upon the statues and the carved idols of Bavel as well.[5] He put to shame Beil, the supreme idol of Bavel, causing it and its base to stoop over.[5] Merodach (considered the second) was smashed to pieces, and all of Bavel's images were shattered.[6] The Kasdim, whose hands had not wearied or tired during all those seventy years, now for the first time weakened. "For strangers came upon Bavel and emptied her land.[7] Her foundations crumbled, her walls were broken down.[8] The land quaked and writhed in pain and fear.[9] Bavel's warriors stopped fighting; they sat idly in their fortresses. They turned to each other in amazement, gazing at their enemies whose faces seemed to them like flames of fire. Their strength failed them; they became like women.[10] One runner ran to meet another, one messenger to inform another, to tell the king of Bavel that his city was taken on every side; the river crossings were seized, the thickets burned, and the soldiers were panic-stricken,"[11] — for Bavel had suddenly fallen and was now destroyed.[12]

Hashem's Day had arrived — a day of cruelty and wrath, to lay the land desolate and destroy its sinners.[13] Ruthless hordes overran the Land of Bavel; they were cruel and had no pity. They did not value silver; gold was not their delight;[14] only to slaughter and destroy "the Mountain of Destruction." Hence all hands became feeble, and every man's heart melted.[15] Belshatzar, the insolent one, had stumbled and fallen, and there was no one to raise him up. The enemy kindled a fire in Bavel's cities, and it consumed all about.[16] Some were slaughtering, and others plundered. The stabbed fell in the land of the Kasdim, the pierced lay in her streets.[17]

Hashem had called the sword upon the Kasdim, upon its inhabitants, dignitaries and wise men. The enemy's sword was poised against the sorcerers who but invented falsehoods and were proven to be liars.[18] Those who were found were pierced, whoever was caught

5 ירמי' פרק נא, נב; ילק"ש ירמי' ו.   6 ירמי' נ, ב; ישעי' כא, ט; יל"ש ירמי' מו.
7 ירמי' פרק נא, ב.   8 שם נ, טו.   9 שם נא, כט.   10 שם נא, ל.
11 שם פסוקים לא—לב.   12 פסוק ה.   13 ישעי' יג, ט.   14 שם פסוק יז.
15 שם פסוק ז.   16 ירמי' נ, לב.   17 שם נא, ד.   18 שם.

fell by sword. Their infants were smashed before their eyes, their homes were plundered, their women ravished.[19] Thus Hashem repaid Bavel and her people for all the evil they had inflicted upon Zion.[20]

On that night "the hammer of the whole earth" was cut asunder and broken. Bavel became a desolation among the nations.[21] "Shamed be your mother; she who gave birth to you has been greatly disgraced." For the ultimate end of the nations is a desert, desolation and a wilderness.[22] A great outcry was heard from Bavel, the sound of massive destruction from the land of the Kasdim. Her roar had been like that of the mighty waters, but Hashem plundered Bavel, and all her great tumult has ceased. For Hashem is the Lord of all retribution. He surely avenges.[23]

While Bavel's glory was at its peak and she had fortified herself at the very height of her might,[24] precisely then did Hashem cause plunderers to come upon her. All at once the land of the Kasdim turned into spoil, and all that plundered her now, felt gratified; [25] as she had done, so they did to her.[26] "The envy of the glorious kingdoms" she was still called (as if she were still at the dawn of her ascent to power and splendor), and precisely then came Bavel's Night. Her massive walls were shattered, her tall gates were consumed by fire, — as she, the Mighty Bavel fell.[27]

The armies of Persia and Media too were astonished at the miraculous speed of the events. "How could it be?" they wondered. Only the morning before, the attackers had deserted their field of battle, and suddenly that night, the fortified kingdom of Babylon had already fallen into their hands?

The report of the hand writing on the wall and Daniel's interpretation of it reached the ears of the annihilators of Bavel. They also heard of all that had happened in the palace of the King of Bavel, and his shame and disgrace in death. Darius and Koresh then knew that it had all been the work of God's Hand.[28]

Only the Sons of Yehuda remained unscathed in that "night of

19 ישעי׳ יג, טו.   20 נא, כד.   21 ירמי׳ נ, כג.   22 שם פסוק יב.

23 שם פרק נא, נו.   24 שם פסוק נג.   25 שם נ, י.   26 נ, טו.

27 שם נא פסוק נח.   28 ספר יוסיפון.

Bavel," for their loyalty to Hashem saved them from the sword of Persia and Media.[29] Indeed, Yisrael and Yehuda had not been widowed of their God.[30] Even in exile, the Lord of the Hosts, their Mighty Redeemer, acted. He fought their battle, when the day of their redemption came; the day the seventy years of Bavel's Empire were completed (3389),[31] to bring about the downfall of Bavel "the destructor," which would never rise to power and glory again.

On the night of her downfall the Almighty intoxicated Bavel, her princes and wise men, her governors, deputies and mighty ones. Together they drank the poisonous goblet, which made them stagger. And they were put to perpetual sleep, — never to awake again.[32]*

29 רד"ק חבקוק ב, ג.   30 ירמי' נא, ה.   31 שם ג, לד.   32 שם נא, נז.
* תוספת.

PART FOUR

The Kingdom of Media

Chapter One

UNDER THE RULE OF DARYAVESH

Chapter One

UNDER THE RULE OF DARYAVESH

AFTER Belshatzar was killed by his servants, the time arrived for the ministers "to anoint a shield," and choose a new king.[1] — Said Daryavesh (Darius) to Koresh, his son-in-law, "you reign first, as you are worthy of kingship." [2] Replied Koresh: "Did not the prophet say, 'the kingdom will be split and given to Media and Persia'? — *first* to Media (that is Macedonia [3]), and afterwards to Persia?" — At once, Darius the Mede, took over the kingdom [4] (3389).

Why Darius first? In order to place a villain after a villain, a wrecker after a wrecker, a haughty one after a haughty one.[5] Because of his haughtiness and cruelty he was chosen to be the tool of Hashem's wrath, to fill the land of Bavel with corpses; to fufill Yirmiyahu's grave prophesies in this one year of Daryavesh's rule.

Heralds of Revenge

When the exiles saw Hashem's revenge from Bavel, (the revenge for both the destruction of His Heichal and the exile of His chosen people), they saw the fulfillment of the harsh prophecies of Yeshayahu ben Amotz in which he clearly envisioned Babylon's downfall.[6] They witnessed Bavel's sudden collapse (when between emptying one cup of wine and another, one kingdom entered the realm of another kingdom [7]) and became aware of Yisrael's sudden Salvation.

At once the Bnei Yehuda burst into praise: "Come, let us relate in Zion the deeds of Hashem, our God." [8] — At that moment the tumult started among the exiles. There were those who now (on their own) fled from the foreign Bavel [9] and hurried to return to the Land of

<hr>

1 ילק״ש ישעי׳ כא.   2 ילק״ש אסתר תתרמט.   3 יומא י.   4 דניאל ו, א.

5 ילקוט דניאל ד.   6 יט, א.   7 שה״ש רבה ג, ד.   8 ירמי׳ נא, י.

9 שם ג, כח; ורד״ק שם.

335

Yehuda, to relate in Zion Hashem's revenge for the Heichal. For they longed to reach out and speak to Zion's heart and appease its ruins.

But the designated term of the seventy years of Judea's exile was not yet completed, and the land had not yet atoned for its missed Sabbaticals through the matching years of desolation. Counting from the Exile of Yehoyakim (3320), one year was still missing (to complete the seventy years of Bavel).[10] Came the wicked, arrogant Darius and completed it.[11] Fulfilling the verse, "And the floods of the wicked frightened me."[12]

The Ministers' Conspiracy

Darius was sixty-two years old when he ascended the throne of Bavel.[13] Since he was ruling a foreign people, he endeavored through wise planning to strengthen and assert his rule over the vast Bavel. He therefore relied heavily on the advice of Daniel who served him well.[14] The king appointed 120 satraps over his empire and over them three viziers, of whom Daniel was one. The satraps were to advise the viziers, in order not to cause the king any disturbance in the affairs of his kingdom. Daniel however distinguished himself above all the satraps and ministers, because a spirit of outstanding wisdom was vested in him. Until the king decided to make him ruler over all of his empire.[15]

Being jealous, the ministers, however, did not rebel against Darius, the cruel foreign king who had filled their land with the blood of the slain, but plotted only against Daniel, the righteous Jew. Had they been able to rise against the One Above and "cast off His bonds," they would have done so. But because they were powerless to act against Heaven above, they plotted against Daniel on earth, below.[16]

In their jealousy, the ministers, viziers and the satraps tried to entrap Daniel and to accuse him with respect to the affairs of the kingdom, but they could not find any fault with him. Said the plotters, "We will not find any pretext against Daniel, except with respect to the Torah of his God."[17]

10 דהי"ב לו, כא.   11 ילק"ש דניאל תתרסד.   12 תהלים יח, ה; וילקוט מלכים דף סד.

13 דניאל ו, א.   14 ספר יוסיפון.   15 דניאל שם.   16 שוחר טוב סד, א.

17 דניאל ו, ו.

They all assembled before the King, pretending to be concerned with his welfare and honor only, and slyly exclaimed, "O, King Darius, may he live forever! We, the viziers, the satraps, the counsellors and the governors, all the advisors of your kingdom came together in counsel, to strenghten and secure the Empire of the king who only now came to rule us from a different country. Every king issues decrees and makes laws but, all your life you have never yet issued any edicts; hence you are not a King.[18] Therefore let the king for the first time issue a royal edict (which by law cannot be revoked), that for the next thirty days whoever makes petition to any deity or man save to you, O, King, — shall be thrown into the lions' den."

Darius, accepting at face value their counsel, allegedly for his personal welfare and the strengthening of his empire, did not realize that they were scheming only to murder an innocent righteous man. And the king signed the decree of prayer prohibition.[19]

Daniel Prays

Daniel at once realized that only because of him the prohibition against prayer had been decreed against all of mankind,[20] yet he went up to his house to pray. In his attic (which was his House of Prayer)[21]* he had windows facing the direction of Yerushalayim, as King Shlomo had declared,[22] "They will pray to You from their lands, towards Yerushalayim, the city which You have chosen, and to this House which You built for Your Name."[23] For even though it is destroyed, the eyes and heart of Hashem are there always. Three times daily, evening, morning and after noon,[24] Daniel would fall on his knees, facing Yerushalayim to thank God, and plead that He have mercy on Yisrael and be available to them in their time of affliction.[25] Although he was not yet commanded to pray three times daily and certainly not to give up his life for his prayers, Daniel refused to change any of his customs which he had practiced since childhood in

18 שוחר טוב פרק ס"ד.   19 דניאל שם.   20 ר' סעדי' גאון שם ט, יא.

21 עירובין כא, ורש"י שם.   * תוספת.   22 מלכים א, ח.   23 דהי"ב ו, לד.

24 תהלים נה, יח.   25 שמות רבה טו, ז.

the Land of Yehuda, even before being exiled in the days of Yeho-yakim.[26] Now, when he went up to his house, he prayed:[27] "O, Hashem, hear my voice in my prayer; from the fear of the enemy preserve my life!" [28]

Before the King

The ministers and satraps lay in wait around Daniel's house, while he prayed, imploring Hashem:[29] "Preserve me from the secret council of the wicked, from the tumult of the evildoers!" They noticed a young girl playing outside, and asked her about Daniel's doings.[30] She said to them, "He is on his knees, praying to his God." Thereupon they entered and found Daniel praying and pleading to Hashem.[31] Daniel was not frightened by their presence, his heart did not tremble, and he calmly finished his prayers. Then the ministers fell upon him. They seized him and brought him before Daryavesh.[32]

As they gathered again before the king, they made their accusation: Being from the sons of Yehuda, Daniel does not even care that the King's decree be enforced, hence he is not concerned with the existence of the King's empire either. Not once, or by chance, but three times a day did he plead his petition before his God, completely disregarding the King's decree. (But they did not even realize that just as Daniel was loyal to his God, so was his God loyal to him.[33])

When Darius heard their accusation, he instantly saw through their evil scheme. He was sorely distressed, for he was very fond of Daniel, and his death would be very hard on him. The king tried to redeem Daniel for money, but could not, for an edict passed in accordance with the laws of Media and Persia, could not be recalled. He then tried to save Daniel by dismissing their claims. Said the King to the ministers," "I do not believe you!" [34]

That whole day the king tried every measure to save Daniel from their hands. Worriedly he said to himself, "Even for so righteous a

26 ברכות לא.   27 תהלים סד, ב.   28 שוחר טוב שם.   29 שם פסוק ג.
30 ר' סעדי' גאון, דניאל שם; גם בספר יוסיפון.   31 דניאל ו.   32 ס' יוסיפון.
33 שם.   34 ילק"ש תהלים סד.

man it is impossible to be saved from all those lions." For this was the Royal Den, housing 1464 lions.[35] Moreover, the ministers had issued orders to withhold all food from the lions and starve them that whole day, so that they would jump upon Daniel and tear him apart instantly.[36] Darius argued with his aides all day long, until close to sunset. When the time came for the Mincha Prayer, Daniel turned his face towards Yerushalayim, saying: "Why, because of these wicked men I shall refrain from praying?" He thereupon fell on his knees, and said his prayers before their eyes.[37]

At once they all stepped forward and triumphantly said to the king, "Have you not said to us, 'I do not believe you?' Now you have seen it with your own eyes!" The king could no longer save him. He was compelled, by the law of Media and Persia, to execute Daniel.

The Lions' Den

Towards the evening the king finally ordered Daniel thrown into the lions' den. Yet, he still hoped for the Tzadik to be saved. He raised his voice and blessed [38] Daniel in the presence of all his ministers: "May the God whom you have always served, save you now!" [39] Moreover, in his anger the king made a firm condition with the satraps and ministers, that should Daniel indeed be saved, all of them would be thrown into the lions' den instead.[40]

The king was also concerned lest Daniel later be murdered by those who were jealous of him. Why indeed should the king have been so concerned? The God who had created the Yam Suf (Red Sea) on condition that it was to split for the Sons of Yisrael; the fire to cool off for Chananya, Mishael and Azarya, and the lions not to harm Daniel — would He not have made a condition with the thrust of a stone or another weapon not to bring harm to a man who was so righteous? Yet the king continued to worry about Daniel's safety. Said Darius: From the lions' den it is impossible to save him, for the edict

35 ילק״ש שם.   36 ס׳ יוסיפון.   37 ילקוט שם.   38 ילק״ש דניאל ו.

39 דניאל שם פסוק יז.   40 ילקוט שם סד.

has already been issued. Let me save him from being hurt by people, and if the miracle comes, let it come! [41]

Upon the king's orders they brought a large stone and placed it over the opening of the pit. (The stone was miraculously brought down from Eretz Yisrael, as there were no such stones to be found in Bavel.[42]) The King put a double seal on the stone, one with his own signet and another with the signet of his ministers. Thus nobody would be able to remove it from the pit's opening, and no enemy could secretly throw a stone or an arrow against the pious Daniel,[43] whom the King hoped would somehow emerge alive.[44]

As Daniel descended into the lions' den, he implored mercy from Hashem, Who is called "The Lion." [45] Said Hashem, "Let a lion come down and save a lion from the mouth of a lion." [46] Instantly the angel who is "the Arye debei Ilahi," [47] ("the heavenly lion") came down and saved Daniel (who was from the Tribe of Yehuda which is likened to "a lion").[48] Instantly the front teeth and the molars of the lions cleaved to each other (unable to open or move), out of fear of the heavenly angel and of Daniel who seemed to the lions like a lion himself — and they did not harm him.[49]

That night was the first night of Pesach.[50] Daniel spent that whole Night-of-Vigil in the frightening lions' den, putting his trust in Hashem.[51] The prophet Habbakuk brought him his meal and all that was required for celebrating the Seder. They ate and drank together, and blessed Hashem.[52]

Hashem Acknowledged

After Daniel was cast into the lions' den, the distressed king returned to his palace and retired for the night without partaking of the royal meal. The musicians who customarily played the harps and violins were

---

41 רש״י דניאל ו, יח.   42 ילק״ש שם.   43 תהלים סד, ה.   44 דניאל פרק יח.

45 הושע יא, י.   46 במדבר רבה יג, ד.   47 ילק״ש שם.   48 בראשית מט, ט.

49 במדבר רבה שם.   50 שמות רבה פר׳ יח, ט.   51 מדרש תהלים לא, א.

52 ר׳ סעדי׳ גאון, דניאל ו, כג.

not allowed to entertain him; neither were the maidens who usually performed for the king,[53] as he remained angry and worried. The king thought to himself, "Why did this tribulation come upon me? Why should this man die by *my* hands?" [54]

Throughout that long night the king remained bewildered. Sleep escaped him.[55] He kept wondering, "Has a miracle occured for Daniel or not?" — At dawn, (yet before sunrise) the king arose and excitedly rushed to the lions' den. Upon approaching the covered opening he cried out sadly, "Daniel!" But Daniel did not answer, for he was saying the morning *Shema*.[56]

Unable to believe that the Tzadik had perished, the king called out a second time, "Daniel, servant of the Living God, was the God Whom you constantly worship able to save you from the lions?"

Daniel replied, "May the King live forever! Hashem sent His angel, who closed the mouths of the lions, and they have not harmed me, for He has found some merit in me. Even against you, O, King, I have not committed any wrong when I prayed to the Supreme God, for you too, are obliged to honor Him just as I am." [57]

Darius was overjoyed, and Daniel was promptly pulled out of the den. No injury or wound was found on his body. Said the ministers to the king, "The lions were satiated, therefore they did not devour him." [58] Replied the king, "If so, you go and spend the night with them and we shall see if they are satiated." [59]

Immediately, all those who had spoken ill of Daniel were seized and thrown into the lions' den — they, their children, and their wives. Before even reaching the floor of the pit, — while stll in the air — the lions leaped up at them and tore them apart. They devoured them and gnawed and chewed their bones to shreds.[60]

And Daniel the Tzadik rejoiced in Hashem, in Whom he had trusted, and all the upright of heart glorified Him.[61]

53 דניאל ו, יט, ובפי' ר' סעדי' גאון שם.   54 ילק"ש שם.   55 דניאל ו.
56 ילק"ש שם.   57 דניאל שם וילקוט שם.   58 ילק"ש שם.   59 שם.
60 דניאל שם.   61 תהלים סד, א.

"Fair as the Moon"

At the moment it was acknowledged that Hashem is in the midst of Yisrael.[62] Darius wrote a letter to all the peoples and tongues on earth, saying, "Great peace be unto you! I have issued a decree that throughout my dominions all should fear and tremble before the God of Daniel, for He is the Living, Everlasting God; His kingdom is a Kingdom which will never be destroyed, and His reign will be till the End of Time. He is the One Who liberates and rescues, and He performs omens and miracles in heaven and on earth. *He* saved Daniel from the mouths of the lions."

The lions' den was not the only tribulation that came upon Daniel. Six afflictions passed over him in his lifetime, and he withstood them all: The exile of Yehoyakim, the exile of Yechonya, the exile of Tzidkiyahu, the time when Daniel and his companions were summoned to be slain in connection with Nevuchadnezar's dream,[63] the throwing of Chananya, Mishael and Azarya into the flaming kiln, and now the lions' den.[64] During each and every one of these trials Daniel sanctified Hashem's Name before all the world, and his righteousness was reflected and shone like the brightness of the dawn, so that even the gentiles acknowledged Hashem and lauded Him.

Daniel's radiance was "fair as the moon" [65] which disperses the darkness, — illuminating the stark night of Media's rule. And Hashem granted him an eternal name, never to be erased [66] — the Sefer of Daniel, which bears his name.[67] Daniel further was successful in the royal service of Darius (and of Koresh, his successor), and he became great and famous throughout the world.[68]

Beseeching Hashem

Daniel "the beloved man" was not concerned with self-glorification however, but only with helping his brethren. (How could he ever enjoy fame and status in the land of the enemy?) And at the height of his

62 במדבר רבה יג, ד.   63 דניאל פרק ב, פסוק יג.   64 ילק"ש עזרא ה.
65 שמות רבה טו, ז.   66 ישעי' נו, ה.   67 סנהדרין צג: 68 סוף דניאל ו.

glory, Daniel immersed himself in the Holy Scriptures, to study and analyze the count of the years of which Hashem had spoken in His prophecy to Yirmiyahu: "To complete seventy years to the ruins of Yerushalayim." But even he erred and failed to grasp the meaning of the words.[69]

He erred by commencing the count of seventy from his own exile and that of the youngsters, in the early days of King Yehoyakim. Said Daniel: "Yirmiyahu prophesied,[70] 'When seventy years of Bavel will be completed, I shall redeem you.' Now, since the start of our exile (3320) until the slaying of Belshatzar is one year less than seventy." Now Darius came and completed the seventy years, — so why then has the redemption not yet come? And why has Hashem not shown us a light to go up and rebuild the Beis HaMikdash in Yerushalayim in the portion of Yehuda?[71]

Daniel beseeched Hashem with fasting, sack-cloth and ashes, to atone for the sins of Bnei Yisrael which were holding back the set time of the redemption. As Daniel prayed, he confessed their sins. He began: "I implore You Hashem, the Great and Fearsome. (He dared to omit "the Mighty." [72] Said Daniel, "Pagans enslave His children — where is His might."? [73] But "the Fearsome" he did say, for Hashem had wrought awesome miracles in the lions' den and in the flaming kiln.[74]). You keep Your covenant and kindliness to those who love You and keep Your commandments. We have sinned, and have commited iniquities, and have done wickedly; we have revolted and turned away from Your Laws; we have not hearkened to Your servants, the prophets, who spoke in Your Name to our kings, our ministers, and the common people. Yours, Hashem, is the righteousness, but ours is the shamefacedness, as of this day. Hashem, You carried out Your warnings to us and to the judges who judged us, by bringing upon us and upon Yerushalayim a great calamity, the likes of which never before occurred under heaven. — And now Hashem, consistent with Your Righteousness, I beg, have Your anger and wrath removed

---

69 ‏דניאל ט.‏   70 ‏דניאל ט, כג.‏   71 ‏מגילה יב.‏   72 ‏שמות רבה מג, טו.‏
73 ‏יומא סט:‏   74 ‏מדרש שוחר טוב יט, ב.‏

from Your city, Yerushalayim, Your Holy Mount. Because of our sins and the iniquities of our fathers, Yerushalayim and Your People are put to shame before all the nations about us, and Your great Name is profaned by them. And now, our God, hear Your servant's pleas. Let Your Face shine on Your desolate Sanctuary, for *Your* sake! Bend Your ear, My God, and listen! Open Your eyes, see our ruins and the city that bears Your Name! For not for our righteousness do we submit our supplication to You, only because of Your great Mercy. Hear, O, God! Forgive, Hashem! Hearken and act, delay not! For Your Sake, O, God. For Your Name is proclaimed upon Your city and Your people." [75]

Seventy Years — Twice

While Daniel was entreating Hashem and confessing the sins, the angel Gavriel (who had already appeared to him once before, in the days of Belshatzar),[76] approached him in swift flight, saying, "At the beginning of your pleas, Daniel, God's Word was sent out. For you are triply precious: You are precious before Hashem, praised by the heavenly host, and admired by the people of your generation down on earth.[77] — Hashem has therefore sent me to bestow upon you special understanding.[78]

"Seventy Sabbatical years were decreed for your people and your holy city, to eradicate sin, end the transgression, atone for iniquities, and to bring in everlasting righteousness, to fulfill vision and prophecy, and to anoint the Holy of Holies.* Be known therefore and understand, two seventy-year periods were decreed upon them: seventy years of the exile of Yehuda, and also seventy years of the ruins of Yerushalayim! The seventy years of the exile of Yehuda start with the first exile — in Yehoyakim's time (3320), and with the end of the one full year of Darius' reign they will have been completed (3390). The seventy years of the ruins of Yerushalayim, however, begin with the destruc-

---

75 דניאל ט, ד—יט.   76 דניאל ח, ט.   77 ילק"ש דניאל.   78 דניאל ט.
* תוספת דבר.

tion of the Beis HaMikdash (3338). Now, until the arrival of one called "His anointed" (that is King Koresh), who will commence to rebuild the Holy City and the Mikdash, a set time is given to their exile — seven *full* Shmitah cycles. (Actually 52 years passed from the Churban until King Koresh; still, only the seven full Shmita cycles of 7 years each were mentioned, but not the final 3 years which amounted only to a part of a Shmita-cycle.) Thus eighteen more years were needed for the completion of the seventy from the Churban of Yerushalayim (3338, till 3408).

The angel Gavriel then also made known to Daniel the years of the Second Beis HaMikdash: Sixty-two Sabbaticals, amounting to four (Koresh) will come (3390), a time is set for the existence of the Second Beis HaMikdash: Sixty-two Sabbaticals, amounting to four hundred and thirty-four years. To these are added four more years, only half a Shemita, hence not included in the 62 Shmitos count. Altogether four hundred and thirty-eight years; eighteen years still until its Construction (3390 to 3408) and standing 420 years. Hence from the destruction of the First Beis HaMikdash till the destruction of the Second (for the destruction of the Second Beis HaMikdash was already included in the edict of the destruction of the First [79]) seventy Sabbaticals, or 490 years (7×70), will pass. (i.e. seventy years from the destruction (3338) until its rebuilding (3408), and standing four hundred and twenty years.) [80]

Then a nation of patricians (the Romans) will sweep the land, destroy its animal and meal Korbanos, and raise their idol abominations instead. "Until at the End of Days total destruction and complete ruin will come down upon this evil nation and its despicable idols," as prophesied for the days of Mashiach, the King. [81]

Fall of Edom

Not only through Daniel, but also through His other prophets Hashem had spoken of the distant "day of Edom." Already in the days of

79 ילק״ש עמוס תקמז.   80 סד״ע פרק כח.   81 סוף דניאל ורש״י שם.

Ach'av, King of Yisrael, the prophet Ovadya had prophesied about Edom, the dreadful fourth beast which would persecute and harm especially the Bnei Yisrael. For close indeed is Hashem's Day against all nations,[82] also against Edom. He will annihilate the wise men of Edom and banish wisdom from the Mount of Eysav. As they have done, so shall be done to them: full recompense for all their deeds. The House of Yaakov will be a fire, the House of Yosef a flame, and the House of Eysav stubble; they shall kindle them and devour them:[83] "Then redeemers will ascend Mount Zion to judge the Mount of Eysav, and the kingdom shall be Hashem's." [84]

Why was Ovadya chosen to prophesy upon Edom? Because Ovadya was a proselyte from Edom. Said Hashem, "From their own people I will bring it against them.[85] Let Ovadya, who dwelt among two evildoers (King Ach'av and Queen Izebel) but did not learn from their evil deeds, come and punish the wicked Eysav, who dwelt among two righteous people (Yitzchak and Rivka) but did not learn from their good deeds." [86]

Then the day will come when Hashem will thrust His Hand over Edom.[87] With the mere turn of the Hand He will punish them. Like eggs in a person's hand. The moment he turns his hand, they fall and break of themselves.[88]

Anticipation

Meanwhile, the Sons of Yehuda bore the yoke of the king of Media.

Why was his country called Madai (Media)? Because it acknowledged ("Modai," from the root Modeh, Lehodot) the existence of Hashem, and admitted His power to carry out His Will.[89] The kings of Media were basically incorrupt and simple-hearted, and Hashem accused them only for the pagan worship which their forefathers had passed on to them; [90] they were likened to a rabbit which is distinguished by the signs of both purity and impurity at the same time.[91] Although

---

82 עובדי' טו.   83 עובדי' שם.   84 שם כא.   85 סנהדרין לט:
86 שם.   87 יחזקאל כה, יג.   88 ילק"ש יחזקאל שם.   89 אסתר רבה א, ח.
90 אסתר רבה סוף פרשה א.   91 ילק"ש משלי דף קמה.

346

the Bnei Yehuda were under their yoke, Hashem had granted compassion in the hearts of the Medes, so that they burdened the Judeans only with light labor [92] — since the Heavenly Angels stood by them to strengthen and protect them.

At the time of Babylon's fall, the "heavenly overseers" of Media had asked Hashem for permission to intensify the burden of their rule over the Judeans, but the angels Gavriel and Michael interceded on their behalf. All this was now told to Daniel [93] by the angel, in the first year of Darius' reign. The angel also told him of the impending rise and fall of the Kingdom of Persia; [94] of the mighty Kingdom of Greece, which would be shattered and scattered to the four directions of the heavens; [95] of the king of the South and the king of the North; of the edict of Shemad (to force the Bnei Yisrael to abandon their faith), and the Deliverance through the Chashmonaim; of the awesome Roman Empire, and the destruction of the Second Mikdash. With the passage of time, said the angel, even the knowledgeable will tremble in their efforts to explain and pinpoint the set time of the End. For it will be a time of affliction, the like of which had not yet been since the day Yisrael became a nation, until that very day.[96]

Daniel listened, but did not comprehend. He wondered: "Hashem, what will be the end of all this?" [97] And the angel replied, "Go, Daniel, to your end, and rest with the righteous in your (eternal) world. You then will arise to your destined portion, at the End of Days! For closed up and sealed are these events, until the time of the final redemption, and there is no one with us who even knows. Even the holy and wise will not understand, until the time when it comes. — But 'Praiseworthy is he who anticipates it, and it surely will reach him.' " [98]

Media's Rival

In that dark night of Bavel, the sons of Yehuda were filled with hope and anticipation. They searched for that which their soul loved, but they did not find it. They then longingly gathered before Daniel

92 רש"י דניאל י, כ.   93 דניאל פרק יא, א ורש"י שם.   94 פסוק ב.

95 פסוקים ג—ד.   96 פרק יא ו-יב, א.   97 דניאל יב, ח .   98 שם יב.

and said to him, "Our teacher Daniel, all the dread prophecies of Yirmiyahu have already come upon us. Only this good one:[99] 'At the completion of seventy years of Bavel I shall redeem you,' only this one has not yet been realized!"[1]

Said Daniel, "Bring me the Sefer of Yeshaya!" He began reading until he reached the verse,[2] "The burdensome vision of the desert of the Sea, as storms in the South sweep on." He said to them, "If it is called 'sea,' why does it say 'desert,' and if it is desert, why the sea? Because the grievous vision refers to the four kingdoms which are compared to beasts,[3] each different from the other; and so are their blows and edicts different from each other. If you are unworthy, they will be like beasts of the desert. But if you are meritorious, they will become like beasts of the sea, which, as soon as they emerge on to dry land, perish."[4]

"Successively, one after the other, they will ascend, in the proper order and at the set time. So far, Bavel (competitor of Eilam) has already been devoured and disappeared. And now that all the sighs of her subjugated have ceased,[5] 'Go up Eilam; besiege Media!' For Media's competitor too already has been created.[6] Darius, the Mede, too, will drink the cup of wrath, as his competitor Koresh (Cyrus, who will take over the kingdom from him) already has been readied. For "As soon as Media's beast comes up to dry land, she will die."

Bavel's Final Punishment

When Daryavesh finished his one-year rule (completing the count of seventy years of the Exiles), the prophesied final punishment of the haughty defiled Bavel came. After the tidings of Belshatzar's death and Bavel's downfall in "that year of tidings" a second frightening tiding was now heard in the land of the Kasdim. For *two* punishments were grievously prophesied upon her.[7]

At that time, Hashem's decree caused Bavel suddenly to be laid

---

99 ירמי׳ כט, י.   1 שה״ש רבה ג, ד.   2 ישעי׳ כא, א.   3 דניאל ז.
4 שה״ש רבה שם.   5 ישעי׳ פרק כא, פסוק ב.   6 שה״ש רבה שם.
7 ירמי׳ נא, מו ורש״י ישעי׳ יג, יט.

waste, as if by itself. Bavel's empire (which embraced all the countries she had subjugated and ruled), "the envy of the nations, and glory of the Kasdim's might," suddenly became as Sodom and Amora after Hashem overturned them.[8] Bavel turned into an arid, barren land in which no man would dwell, nor a wayfarer pass.[9] Wild screaming beasts crouched in the land; the houses filled with eagles and owls. Ostriches made it their dwelling place; goat-shaped demons their dancing floor.

The wide stretches of Bavel turned into heaps, a dwelling-place for jackals, a waste and a hissing, without inhabitant.[10] Hashem cut off from Bavel name and remnant (of rulers), son and grandchild.[11] She totally lost reign and kingdom. Even her language and script went into oblivion, as the Kasdim started to use the language of another nation.[12] And, at this time, all sciences and books of wisdom were taken from Bavel and transferred to Persia.[13]

Proliferated with ponds and pools of water, Bavel became the habitat of beasts and wild birds. And Bavel's evil neighbors suffered along with her. For when the curse came down upon Bavel, her neighbors too, were accursed.[14] She went down to the grave, to the depths of the pit.[15] Like a stone cast into the Euphrates River.

— — — Thus sank Bavel.[16]

"Blessed be He!"

The sons of Yehuda lived through all the ongoing, but their hearts did not turn faint.[17] For they witnessed Hashem's reckoning and His revenge, the day of recompense against Bavel and its inhabitants. Then they took up the Prophet's message, "Go out of her midst, my people. Let each person save himself" from the land of exile.[18] "For the violence done to me and my flesh is now upon Bavel," said the settlers of Zion, "and my blood is upon the Kasdim.[19] Nevuchadnezar, King

8 ישעי׳ יג, יט.   9 ירמי׳ נא, מג.   10 שם פסוק לז.   11 ישעי׳ יד, כב.

12 מגילה י: 13 ס׳ הכוזרי מאמר א, סג.   14 ברכות נח.   15 ישעי׳ יד, טו.

16 ירמי׳ נא, סד.   17 ירמי׳ נא, מו.   18 שם פסוק מה.   19 פסוק לה.

of Bavel, devoured me, crushed me, and he turned me into an empty vessel. He swallowed me like a sea-monster, filling his belly with my delicacies." [20] — "So let Bavel now be forgotten, let us turn her out from every heart."

Only for the sake of good tidings shall we talk and tell the peoples about Bavel. As a symbol of miracles we will hold her high, to relate her fate to the nations. For mighty Bavel was conquered, her idol Beil shamed, the image Merodach broken in pieces. All her figurines were ridiculed, her abominations shattered,[21] when Hashem's venegeance took revenge for us.

Forever shall we now bless and thank Hashem for having laid Bavel waste. With fivefold blessing shall we thank Hashem for Bavel and its ruins.[22]

Upon beholding the soil of Bavel, one now says, "Blessed is He Who has destroyed the wicked Bavel." One who sees the ruins of Nevuchadnezar's palace says, "Blessed is He who has destroyed the house of the wicked Nevuchadnezar!" One who sees the lions' den or the kiln says, "Blessed is He Who performed miracles for our ancestors in this place." One who sees the idol Markoolis says, "Blessed is He Who shows patience with those who transgressed His Will." One who sees the most cursed and devastated place of Bavel from which dust is taken [23] says, "Blessed is He Who speaks and acts, Who decrees and also fulfills." [24] — Even centuries later the great sages of Yisrael would gather dust from the soil of Bavel in their garments and toss it to the wind, to fulfill the verse,[25] "I will sweep her out with a broom of destruction." [26]

Media's Exit

With the demise of Bavel, Darius the Mede completed his one-year reign over the conquered empire, thus concluding the seventy years of Yehuda's exile in Bavel. Then (as Yirmiyahu had prophesied) for the

23 עיין רש"י שם.   22 ברכות נז: 21 ירמי' ג, ב.   20 פסוק לד.

26 ברכות נז: 25 ישעי' יד, כג.   24 שם.

second time in that year, the Bnei Yehuda saw the fulfillment of Hashem's "good tidings in the land." Suddenly one world-ruler displaced another.[27]

Darius, King of Media, was slain in battle, and the throne passed to his son-in-law Koresh [28] (3390), who was destined to build the Second Beis HaMikdash.

— Media departed, and Persia entered . . .[29]

27 ירמי׳ נא, מו.   28 רש״י דניאל ו, כט.   29 מדרש שוחר טוב עה, ג.

APPENDIX

(תוספת דבר)

Page 102

Rashi in Yeshaya 29:30 and Megilla 31a states that the defeat of Sancheriv took place on the night of Pesach. However, in both Yeshaya 30:31 and 15:2, Rashi comments from Targum Yonassan and the Midrash that it took place on the night of the 16th of Nissan.

Page 103

The day that Achaz died had only 2 daylight hours, so that the people would have no time to eulogize or bury him. Upon Chizkiyahu's recovery Hashem added the missing 10 hours unto that day-time, making it last 22 hours (Sanhedrin 96a and ibid Rashi).

Page 104

To prove how strong the desire for idolatry was in his days, our Sages report (Sanhedrin 102b): Rav Ashi was studying the portion concerning those kings who have no part in Olam Habba. He mentioned three of them, saying: "Tomorrow we will start out with our colleague!" referring to Menashe, King of Yehuda, who had also been a Talmid Chacham but had no part in Olam Habba.

That night Menashe appeared to Rav Ashi in a dream. He said to him: "Since you labeled me your and your father's colleague, perhaps you can tell me on which part of the bread do we make the "Hamotzi." When Rav Ashi answered, "I don't know," Menashe retorted: "Wherefrom they break the bread you don't know, yet you call me a colleague of yours?" Said Rav Ashi: "Teach it to me, and tomorrow I shall expound the matter in your name before the Chachamim!" Said to him Menashe: "Where the crust is well baked." — Asked Rav Ashi: "Now that you are so learned, how come you practiced idolatry?" Replied

353

Menashe: "Had you been there, you would have picked up the edge of your cloak (to speed up the running) and raced after idolatry."

The next day Rav Ashi said to the Chachamim: "Let's start the discussion with our "Master," — and he did not call him anymore "our colleague!"

However, the people of that period were caught in the web of idolatry only (Rashi Chullin 4b). "We see that Achav and his aides practiced idolatry only, but were not corrupted in matters of Neveyla (improperly slaughtered animal). It is proper to say that the evil inclination of idol worship overpowered them."

Page 107

During this period, the Law of keeping the Yovel, which had been abrogated with the exile of the Ten Tribes, went again into effect. For the keeping of the Yovel is obligatory only when *all of her residents* are in Eretz Yisrael, as it is written (Vayikra 25:10): "You shall proclaim freedom in the Land to *all* of her inhabitants" (Erechin 33a).

Page 129

Precisely because of the high Madreyga (spiritual level) of the Jewish people and the ensuing multitude of true prophets in their midst, it was very difficult to identify the false prophets and their false messages. Were the Jewish people to have prophets like Yeshaya, Yirmiyahu and Yechezkel only, there would not have been any possibility for mistaken identity.

However, there was not even one Tribe that did not bring forth prophets (Sukka 27b), and Bnei Yisrael had prophets twice the number of the men who had left Egypt (Megilla 14a), all of them of different levels. In Eliyahu's days there was an outpouring of prophecy (Tossefta Sotta; Russ Rabba 1:2) — six hundred thousand prophets along with prophetesses. Yet, their names were not even recorded nor their prophecies written down, as prophecy relevant only to *all* generations was to be recorded (Shir Hashirim Rabba 4:11). — Thus we find in the days of Ach'av the son of Omri when Queen Izebbel annihilated the prophets of Hashem, only one hundred of them were left, having been rescued by Ovadya, who had hidden them in two caves, — fifty in each — where he supplied them with bread and water (Melachim Alef 18). Add to these the "Bnei Haneviim" (student prophets) (Melachim Beis), who were studying and learning to attain the level of prophecy, their numbers reaching in the thousands and ten thousands, in the different cities. Even in the most corrupt places (Yericho — which Yehoshu'a had cursed, and Beis El — site of the Golden Calf placed there by Yerov'am) we also find the student prophets (Melachim Beis 2 and Shir Hashirim Rabba 4:11). And sometimes there was only a hairsbreath of difference between them and the false prophets whose actions and "prophecies" resembled those of the true prophets. — Indeed a frightening potential for errors. (Consult further Yechezkel (Chapt. 13) and the introduction of the Rambam to his Peirush Hamishna, Order of Zerayim, in which he dwells at length on the matter of the false prophets.)

Page 131

Thus we find four prophets prophesying at the same time: Hoshea, Yeshayahu, Amos and Micha (Pesachim 87a).

Page 135

We find in the Gemara (Neddarim 65a) that Nevuchadnezzar punished Tzidkiyahu not only for breaking his oath of loyalty. Tzidkiyahu had seen Nevuchadnezzar eating a live rabbit. Said to him Nevuchadnezar: "Swear to me that you will not reveal nor publicize the matter." Tzidkiyahu swore to him. Eventually, he asked the Sanhedrin to invalidate his oath, after which he revealed the story. Upon hearing that he was put to shame, Nevuchadnezar had both the Sanhedrin and Tzidkiyahu brought before him and punished brutally.

Page 136

It cannot mean 18 before Nevuchadnezzar laid siege to Yerushalayim, as he became king in 3319 only and the siege began in 3336. Thus we have only 17 years.

Page 144

For 390 years the Bnei Yisrael were angering Hashem — from the time when they entered the Land until the exile of the Ten Tribes. 40 years the Kingdom of Yehuda further angered Him — from the time the Ten Tribes were exiled until Yechezkel's prophecy was revealed to him (Perek 4). Plus 6 more years in which Bnei Yisrael sinned, until Yerushalayim was destroyed — thus we come to 436 years. There are 14 Shemitos and 2 Yovelos in each century, hence 64 Shemitos in 400 years. 5 Shemitos for the 36 years — hence 69. Even for the last Shemito-cycle which barely began (with the 36th year) and was not completed — they were also punished. Hence 70 Shemitos.

Page 154

From Yeshaya (22) it is seen that they did this all *after* the city was breached; when the horsemen turned their faces "to the gates," and "all your commanders together had left," — referring to the flight of Tzidkiyahu and the army commanders.

Page 157

From these figures we can imagine the frightening total of all those who have fallen and were slain in the destruction of the First Beis HaMikdash.

"Two hundred eleven times 10 thousand plus another 90 times 10 thousand" — a total of over 3 million fallen by the sword, and these are only "a third" (Yechezkel 5:12). Add to these another third who died by pestilence and hunger, just in Yerushalayim alone, — thus we have over 6 million. And the last third — "I shall scatter in all directions and I shall empty the sword after them" (ibid). Of these too, many fell and died. — Hence, millions upon millions!

Page 158

As it is written, "Until R'chov, where one comes to Chamas." (Bamidbar 13:21).

Page 158

In "Me'gilas Ta'anis" it says: "on the 6th of Marcheshvan."

356

Page 162

This definitely does not mean that Nevuzaradan *immediately* fled and became a Ger, because only *afterwards* did he cause all this much weeping and mourning in Yehuda, yet before he returned to Bavel. Only *after* Hashem had poured out His anger upon His children through him, Nevuzaradan fled and converted, as mentioned by our Chachamim (Yalkut Shimmoni Yechezkel 24). Thus it says in the Midrash (Eicha Rabbasi 4:17): "The wicked Nevuzaradan *contemplated* doing Teshuva etc." — his first *thought* of Repentance.

Thus we find that "all the harsh and bitter prophecies" of Yirmiyahu came upon them only *after* the Churban of the Beis HaMikdash (Pesichta DeEicha Rabbassi 23).

Page 166

As Moshe had warned the Bnei Yisrael (Devarim 4:25): "When you will father children and grandchildren — Venoshantem — and you will become stale in the Land, and you will make images, etc., I hold forth heaven and earth as witness against you today that you will be completely lost from the Land fast." Moshe thereby indicated to them that they will be exiled from the Land at the end of 852 years, — the numerical total of "Venoshantem." Hashem, however, advanced the Galus by 2 years, exiling them at the end of 850 years (Rashi ibid) so that the subsequent prophecy of being "totally lost" should never be fulfilled. Thus it says (Daniel 9:14): "Hashem was diligent about the evil and He brought it upon us (earlier), for Hashem our God is righteous." He did charity with Yisrael, speeding up the onset of the evil by exiling the Galus of Tzidkiyahu 2 years before its time (Gittin 88a).

Page 168

Although R' Abraham Ibn Ezra and the R'dak explain this as alluding to later times (to the exiles of Titus), yet the plain meaning of the verse is like Rashi and Targum (who explain the P'shat of the Torah), that it concerns the first exile. We find the same in the commentary of Abbarbanel (end of Sefer Me'lachim), who himself was one of the exiles in Spain.

Page 180

Immediately after the destruction of the Mikdash (in Av, the 5th month) Nevuzaradan exiled them. On the 5th of the 10th month (Teves) "came to me the escapee from Yerushalayim saying: 'the city is captured'!" (Yechezkel 33:21) — yet before the exiles had reached Bavel. Hence for 5 months they were ruthlessly marched on the road into Exile.

Neither did Nevuzaradan lead them by the shortest road northward to Bavel. For the exiles passed Kever Rachel, south of Yerushalayim (Bereishis Rabba 82:10). They also came to the Land of the Bnei Yishma'el (Eicha Rabbassi 2:4), east of Eretz Yisrael. They further marched by way of the lands of Ammon and Mo'av (Rashi Tzefanya 2:8) — clearly not the straight road to Bavel.

Page 181

The Bnei Bari received their reward. Hashem showed them special kindliness by making them very beautiful (Yalkut Shimmoni Tehillim 115).

Page 185

"I am the talk of those that sit in the gate, the songs of those that drink beer," (Tehillim 69:13) — was one more verse that came true by the Bnei Yehuda.

The pagans sat in the theatres and circuses, and after they ate and drank and got intoxicated, they would heap complaint, chatter and ridicule upon the Jews saying: From now on we have to be careful about our expenses, otherwise we'll have to eat carob like the Jews. — And one asked the other: How long do you wish to live? The other replied: As long as the Jews' garment which they don from one Sabbath to the other to make it last long. — Then they would bring their camel into the theatre, covered with cloth, and ask one another: Over whom does this one mourn? And they answered: The Jews keep Shemita and they have no vegetables, so they ate up the camel's thorns, and he mourns over them. — They would bring a corpse into the theatre; its head is shaven but it has not been embalmed (for lack of oil). One says to the other: Why is the head of this corpse shaven (but not embalmed?). And he answers: These Jews, they observe the Sabbath; the fruit of their whole week's toil they eat on Shabbos; but they have no wood with which to cook, so they chop up their beds and use them to cook their food, while they themselves sleep on the ground and roll in the dust and smear their bodies with oil — hence oil is expensive (Pessichta DeEicha Rabbassi 17).

Thus the Jews were the topic of their chatter and idle conversation all day long, making them a scorn and derision in the theatres and circuses.

Page 188

The word "Vaydaber" is an expression of talking justice.

Page 196

The Mikdash was burned down on the 10th of the 5th month. Hence 20 days remained for the month of Av, 29 of Ellul, and 3 of Tishri. Hence 52!

Thus we find in the Yalkut Shim'oni (Yechezkel 4) that Gedalyahu was slain on the 3d of Tishrei.

Page 201

Therefore he is mentioned here first in the verse.

Page 217

They came out lauding Nevuchadnezar and said, "The barbarians (the ancient philosophers labeled the Judeans barbarians, meaning uncivilized) ("Shalsheles Hakabbala," "Philosophers of Greece"), a strange nation, you vanquished!" As if their brethren, the Exile of Tzidkiyahu, were indeed strangers to them (Pesichta De'Eicha Rabbasi 23).

Page 220

For there they threw him into the kiln, hence it was called *"Ur Kasdim"* (the fire of Kasdim). Nimrod is also called Amrafel, for having thrown Avram in there. ("Amar — Pull," meaning "he said": 'throw'). Nimrod was king in the land of Shin'or, which is Bavel.

Page 235

As it says (Yechezkel 1:1): "I was in the midst of the exiles by the River K'vor," and the same with Daniel (Daniel 10:4): "and I was near the great river, which is Chidekel."

Page 244

Some (Rashi ibid) say: They ordained it yet in the days of Yechonya's Exile; others however put it at a much later date, — after Rav had descended to Bavel (Babba Kamma 80a).

Page 246

It is hard to say that Rashi referred only to the Mitzva of waiving money-debts, which they observed in Bavel. It is inconceivable that the gentiles' ridicule of Bnei Yisrael: "Now in exile you keep it," referred to observance of Shemitas Kesafim which is concealed from public eye. No one knows whether one waives or collects his debt. The statement of course was made only concerning the Shemita of *the soil* for one full year, which is visible to all.

Page 248

Since in the 4th year of King Darius II (Zecharya 7:5) 70 years were completed in which they had fasted in the 7th month (the Fast of Gedalyahu), it follows that they had began to observe the Fast in the second year of Tzidkiyahu's Exile, having learned already of Gedalyahu's slaying.

Page 249

From the verse in Zecharya (7:5) "These 70 years of Fasts — have you fasted for Me?" it follows that the Fast Days began 2 years after the Churban (3340). For the prophecy of "fasting already 70 years" came in the 4th year of Daryavesh the Second, which was 3410. — Hence 70 years.

Page 253

These are the 8 times; 5 times "Hashem will say." (Yeshayahu 1:11

and 1:18, 33:10, 41:21, 66:9). Add to these "Your God will say" (Yeshaya 40:1). "The Holy One will say" (ibid 40:25). And "the King will say" (ibid 41:21).

Page 255

Rav Sherira Ga'on (in his historical letter) writes that they brought with them stones and sand *from the Beis HaMikdash*. And when they built the Beis-Hakenesses, they laid its foundation with these stones and sand (Sefer "Kaftor Vaferach" 10).

Page 264

He was 15 years old when exiled (Ibn Ezra Daniel 1:4) at the time of King Yehoyakim (3320), hence he was 34 years old in the second year after the Churban (3339).

Page 269

He was very old at the time. For Nevuchadnezar was yet the scribe of Merodach Baladan, shortly before the defeat of Sancheriv (Sanhedrin 96a), in the 14th year of King Chizkiyahu (Melachim Beis 18:13 and 20:1).

Page 270

See Shir Hashirim Rabba (ibid in the commentary "Anaf Yosef" and "Eitz Yosef.") It also appears from Daniel (3:12): "Your idols we will not worship, and to the Statue which you have erected, we will not bow." As the Scriptures differentiate between the Statue and the idols they were worshipping (Avoda Zarra 3a and Tossafos ibid).

Page 281

The decree "They will enslave and torture them 400 years," was to be counted only from the time of Yitzchak's birth, as stated (Bereishis 15:13) "Your *seed* (children) will be alien," — meaning Yitzchak. The Bnei Ephrayim however, miscalculated and counted from the time of the Bris bein Habesarim which preceded Yitzchak's birth by 30 years (Seder Olam). Thus they went out prematurely (Rashi Sanhedrin 92b).

Page 281

From the comments of our Rabbis (Koheles Rabba 4:3) it follows that Hashem commanded him to prophesy to the bones precisely with the words, "Listen to the Word of Hashem!" For only after having listened, and wishing, and desiring to get up yet and live, *only then* will they merit to live.

Yechezkel replied: "Hashem, Elokim, *You* (only) know," and our Chachamim consider this as being remiss (Yechezkel 33). However, it was not, God forbid, lack of belief in the power of the King of kings Who puts to death and brings back life. Yechezkel only questioned the willingness and hearing of the withered bones themselves. Similar to what Moshe Rabbeinu had complained of, "But they will not believe me, etc." (Shemos 4:1) — *Therefore* he was punished.

Page 282

Some say (ibid): immediately after they had risen and said Shira, they died. As if indeed it is only a parable, — to encourage the withered exiles (ibid).

Page 304

According to Rashi (Gittin 6a, Babba Kamma 80a) they were not erudite in the laws of Gittin until Rav descended to Bavel and Yeshivos spread out there.

Page 304

In the Torah we find Aramaic in Breishis 31:47. In the Prophets: Yirmiyahu 10:11. In the Kessuvim: Daniel 2:4.

Page 305

With Hashem's first command to the Bnei Yisrael, "This month be to you the beginning of months," (Shemos 12:3) Hashem made the Bnei Yisrael partners to the "secret of Ibbur" (designating the Leap year) which Avraham Avinu had mastered (Pirkei De R' Eliezer Perek 8). But even though the designation of leap years was handed over to the Beis Din, Hashem, too, would stand with them, approving of their decisions. Said our Chachamim (Shemos Rabba 15:20): "When our Rabbis convened to proclaim a Leap Year, 10 of the elders (erudite in these Halachos) entered the Beis HaMikdash, and the Av-Beis-Din with them. They locked the doors to deliberate over the matter through the night. At midnight they said to the Av Beis Din: 'We wish to proclaim a leap year so that this year will consist of 13 months. Do you concur in our ruling?' And he said to them: 'Whatever your opinion, I am with you!'

Then a light emanated from the Beis Hamidrash, placing itself in front of them. It was then that they knew that Hashem approved of them, as it says (Tehillim 112) "In the darkness a light ("Hashem is my light" ibid 27) shone for the righteous." And whatever they decreed, Hashem agreed with them. As it says (ibid 57): "I call to the Most High God, to the Almighty Who completes it with me."

May Hashem's Name be praised, for His creations decree, and He agrees with them!

Page 317

The year in which Nevuchadnezar died (3364) is also counted as the first year of his son Evvil Merodach, for we have here fragmentary years (Megilla 11a). He ruled an additional 22 years, coming to 3386.

Page 322

Thus it says (Yechezkel 30:18): "In Tachpancheis the day grew dark."

Page 331

The first to establish a kingdom in the world was Nimrod, the grandson of No'ach's son Chom. "The beginning of his kingship was Bavel etc." (Bereishis 10:10). (Already then the Torah calls it Bavel — the name by which it was to be known later — even though it was yet *before* the generation of Haflaga (split) with its ensuing mixing up of languages [Bavel]). From Nimrod to Belshatzar (the last king of Bavel) about 1600 years passed. Bavel had 49 or 51 kings.

Page 337

Even later, in the era of the Ammoraim of Bavel they still used to come to "the Synagogue of Daniel" to pray on Shabbat (a distance of 3 Parsaos) from a place named Barnish (Eiruvim 21a).

Page 344

We find here 3 counts of 70 years: 1. The Kingdom of Bavel: From the beginning of Nevuchadnezar (3319) until the slaying of Belshatzar (3389) — 70 years. 2. From the reign of Yehoyakim (3320) (in the second year of Nevuchadnezar) until Koresh (3390) — 70 years. 3. From the Churban of the First Beis HaMikdash (3338) until the beginning of the construction of the Second Beis HaMikdash (3408) — 70 years.

GLOSSARY

Acharis Hayamim — End of Days
Acharonim — the later Sages
Akeyda — Avraham's Offering (Binding) of Yitzchak
Akeydas Yitzchak — same
Aliyah Le'Regel — going up to Jerusalem for the three Festivals
Am Hasefer — the People of the Book
Am Segula — a treasured nation
Ami — my People
Amora — Sage of the Talmud
Annan — the Divine Cloud
Anshei Kneses Hagdola — Men of the Great Assembly of Ezra
Aron Hakodesh — the Holy Ark
Arye debei Ilohi — The Heavenly Lion
Asseres Yemei Teshuva — 10 days of Repentance
Av — fifth Jewish month
Av Beis-Din — head of the Court
Avinu — our father
Avoda — holy services
Avos — Patriarchs
Azara — courtyard of the Sanctuary

Bamos — altars outside of the Sanctuary or Tabernacle
Bas Kol — a voice from Heaven
B'chora — rights of male firstborn
Beis-Din — Rabbinical Court
Beis HaMikdash — the Sanctuary in Yerushalayim
Ben — son
Bereishis — the beginning of Creation
Bnei Ephraim — Tribe of Ephraim
Bnei Yisrael — the Jewish People
Bnei No'ach — the gentiles

Bnei Neviim — student-prophets
Bracha — blessing, benediction
Bris bein Hab'sarim — Covenant of the Parts
Bris Milah — Covenant of Circumcision
Briyas Haolam — Creation

Chachamim — Sages, wise men
Chadash — the new harvest
Chala — the Kohein's share of the dough
Cheshvan — eighth Jewish month
Chorosh — craftsman
Churban — destruction

David Hamelech — King David

Edom — descendants of Eysav
Elokeinu — our God
Elokim — God
Elul — sixth Jewish month
Emunah — belief, faith
Eys laasos Heyfeyru Torasecha — a time to act: they may circumvent your Torah
Ezras Nashim — women's court in the Mikdash

Galus — exile
Gehinom — Purgatory
Gemarra — Talmud
Geonim — the heads of the Mesivtos in Bavel, after the Savoraim
Gey Chizayon — Valley of Vision
Geyrim — converts to Judaism
Great Sanhedrin — Supreme Court of 71 Sages

365

Haflaga — the generation of the Tower of Bavel

Halacha — Torah-law

Hakadosh Baruch Hu — The Holy One, Blessed Be He

Hamotzi — blessing over bread

Hanhaga — conduct

Har Sinai — Mount Sinai

Hashem — denotes the Almighty

Hashgacha Klallis — Collective Providence

Hashgacha Pratis — Individual Providence

Hazakeyn — the old one

Havdala — benediction recited at end of Shabbos and Festivals

Heichal — vestibule of Sanctuary

Kehuna — priesthood

Kenaan — land of Canaan

Kesuvim — the Scriptures

Kever — grave

Kiddush — benediction sanctifying the beginning of Shabbos and Holidays

Kisey Hakavod — God's Throne of Glory

Kneses Yisrael — the Congregation of Yisrael

Kodesh Hakodoshim — Holy of Holies (in the Mikdash)

Kohanim — (pl. of Kohen) male descendant of Aharon, designated to perform the Holy Services

Kohen Gadol — the Kohen Supreme

Korban Tamid — Daily Offering

Korbanos — holy Offerings

Lehodot — to acknowledge

Luchos — the two stone Tablets

Maamad Har Sinai — the Revelation at Mount Sinai

Maaser — tithe

Maaser Sheyni — the Second Tithe

Mabbul — the Flood

Madreyga — spiritual level

Malachim — angels

Mann — Manna

Mar'eh Mekomos — index of the sources

Masger — locksmith

Mashiach — the anointed

Mattan Torah — giving of the Torah

Megilla — scroll

Melachim — kings

Meraglim — spies

Mesora — Tradition transmitted

Midbar — desert

Minyan Shtaros — special count of years for documents

Mishkan — the Tabernacle

Mishmar — shift (see pl. Mishmaros)

Mishmaros — weekly shifts of Kohanim and Leviim

Mishnayos — the Six Orders of the Oral Torah

Mitzva — a commandment, precept

Mitzvos — pl. of Mitzva

Mitzrayim — Egypt

Modeh — acknowledge

Morey Massnissin — Masters of the Mishna

Moshe Rabbeinu — Moshe, our Teacher

Nissan — first Jewish month

Nassi — head, king

Neviim — prophets, or the Books of the Prophets

Neveyla — not ritually slaughtered

Ninveh — capital of Ashur

Olam Habba — the World to Come

Orla — fruit of trees, forbidden the first three years after planting

Para Aduma — Red Heifer

Passuk — verse

Perek — chapter

Peirush — elaboration, commentary

Pesach — Passover

Petira — demise

Plishtim — Philistines

Pshat — plain meaning

Rishonim — the earlier (medieval) Sages

Rosh Chodesh — beginning of the month

Rosh HaMesivta — Head of Talmudical Academy (called Mesivta)

Rosh Hashana — start of New Year

Ru'ach Hakodesh — the Holy Spirit

Savoraim — the Sages succeeding the Amoraim

Seder night — the first night of Pesach

Sefer — book

Seyir — land of Seyir=Edom

S'farim — books

Shalach — send away

Shalsheles Hakabbala — chain of Oral Torah Transmission

Shannu Rabbanon — the Sages learned

Shas — the Six Orders of Mishna and Torah Transmission

Shechina — Divine Presence

She'ibud — enslavement

Shema — daily prayer of Heavenly subjugation

Shemad — forced conversion

Shemita — the Sabbatical year

Shemitas Kesafim — Sabbatical waiving of money-debts

Shofar — ram's horn

Shoftim — Judges

Sivan — third Jewish month

Small Sanhedrin — Court of 23, dispensing Halachic Law

Sotah — a woman suspected of adultery

Syog — safeguard measure

Tahara — purity

Talmidim — students, disciples

Tammuz — fourth Jewish month

Tanna — they learned

Targum Hashi'vim — Septuagint

Tehillim — Psalms

Teshuva — repentance, return to Hashem

Teves — tenth Jewish month

Teyva — No'ach's Ark

Tish'a Be'av — 9th of Av

Tishri — seventh Jewish month

Tohu — void and emptiness

Torah — God-given laws to Yisrael

Torasecha — Your Torah

Torah Sheb'al Pe — Oral Torah

Torah Shebiksav — Written Torah

Tosefes Davar — appendix

Truma — heave--offering

Tumah — impurity

Tzaddik — righteous man

Tzeddaka — charity

Tzitz — headplate of Kohen Gadol

Tzor — city of Tyre

Tzoraas — leprosy

Ullam — vestibule, hall

Venoshantem — you will become stale (old)

Yatzmiseim — he will cut them off, or he will gather them

Yemos Olam — days (chronicles) of the world; history

Yeriyos — curtains of the Tabernacle

Yerushalayim — Jerusalem

Yetziyas Mitzrayim — Exodus from Egypt

Yovel — the 50th year of the Shemita-cycle

Z'keynim — the Elders

367